# Logic and the Organization of Information

T0214215

Martin Frické

# Logic and the Organization of Information

 Springer

Martin Frické
School of Information Resources
  and Library Science
The University of Arizona
Tucson, AZ
USA

ISBN 978-1-4899-9452-3                    ISBN 978-1-4614-3088-9 (eBook)
DOI 10.1007/978-1-4614-3088-9
Springer New York Heidelberg Dordrecht London

That the study of classification extends into logic ... should not deter the educated librarian, if these matters are treated clearly and not too profoundly. (Bliss 1929) Preface pp. xiv–xv (Broadfield 1946)

**Image 1 Truth rising from her well. Jean-Léon Gérôme 1896**. (Gérôme was a leading French painter in the Academic style. He had views about Truth and Illusion. He painted three paintings of Truth and her well. In two, Truth is hidden, confined, down the well; in the third, this one, Truth emerges. Truth was often depicted as a nude. The face here is that of Bellona, the Goddess of War, and the expression probably derives from ancient theater masks (Des Cars L, de Font-Reaulx D (2010) The Spectacular Art of Jean-Léon Gerome. Skira, Milan, IT). This painting is in the collection of Musée Anne-de-Beaujeu, Moulins.)

# Acknowledgments

Of course, many and various teachers, educators, researchers, students, and colleagues have helped and influenced me extensively. And my hope, in common with all academics, is merely that there is at least something in my work and ideas (personal or recycled) that I can 'pay forward for the next kid who comes along'.

People who helped me specifically for this book include my successive Graduate Assistant Teachers (GATs) Delaina Miller, Judi Alamia, and Diane Daly. I thank them. My friend, and former Director, Jana Bradley offered sage and useful advice. I thank her. My friend, former colleague, and all-round source of wisdom and knowledge, David Ward, provided widespread editorial guidance and insight (and he appeared to confirm that at least some of the philosophical ideas in the book were not totally mangled). David's help, freely and generously given, was truly extensive. I thank him.

My employer, The University of Arizona, granted me a sabbatical leave to write this book. That certainly has been a most useful and welcome accommodation—one that I am very appreciative of. In turn, my sabbatical has necessitated a coverage by my colleagues of my normal work and duties in the SIRLS School and the SBS College. I thank them, the School, the College, and the University.

Two of the images that have been used merit specific attribution. The partial screenshot of the Sabio front end is courtesy of Innovation Interfaces, Inc, and The University of Arizona. And the English version of the Diderot Système is courtesy of Benjamin Heller. Both these images are used with permission. I thank their authors and copyright holders.

# Contents

# Chapter 1
# Overview

## 1.1 Introduction

We are all librarians. We all have email messages, contact lists, friend pages, digital images, bookmarks in our Web Browsers, and documents and files on our computers. Most of us have books, newspapers, journals, and magazines in our homes. Let us call these items 'Information Objects' (IOs). So books, journals, articles, web pages, images, CDs, DVDs, video tapes, letters, podcasts, and perhaps many other kinds of objects, are all 'Information Objects'. The notion of information object is being used very widely here. Novels, fiction, cartoons, and other vehicles of imaginative content, are taken to be information objects even though they probably do not really contain information. And, for better or for worse, we, individually, collectively, and institutionally, organize the information objects (IOs). That activity is librarianship.

The role of IOs is that of being external storage, storage outside what Andy Clark calls the 'skinbag' (Clark 2003). IOs are artifacts of preservation and dissemination. They form *information bridges* from individuals and instants of time to availability between individuals and persistence through time. Our predecessors did us all a great favor when they started to develop the ability to record what they knew or believed or wanted to relate. And our skills at recording continue to improve and to encompass an ever wider range of content.

We organize IOs primarily to enhance what we have and its value to us. We organize to retrieve, and that typically involves knowing what we have, or can obtain, and locating and obtaining the IOs of interest for the occasion or task at hand. We organize to manage; for example, some IOs may need archiving or backing up or updating to the latest formats, other IOs may need special consideration if they are within the purview of information ethics (intellectual property, privacy, integrity, stewardship, etc.). And we can just plain improve or add value to what we have by organizing it. Consider, for example, a critical bibliography that we are maintaining to support a lecture course or a book project; the act of

M. Frické, *Logic and the Organization of Information*,
DOI: 10.1007/978-1-4614-3088-9_1,
© Springer Science+Business Media New York 2012

adding a suitable and relevant IO to that bibliography may well improve both the bibliography and the IO; the bibliography may become more comprehensive, relevant, and accurate, and the IO itself is improved by being explicitly placed among other IOs it relates to, at the forefront of our attention. From one point of view, to organize is to establish filters, and those filters, in conjunction with the source IOs, yield what we need.

## 1.2 The Problem

Right now, there are 1,190,461 files on the Macintosh Mini that is being used to write this document. This is a plain vanilla computer, with a small hard disk. It is being used by one person, a teacher. The computer has on it lecture notes, research papers, and a fair number of computer programming files (plus emails, podcasts, etc.); but it is in no way abnormal.

The story is similar in the world at large. *How much information?* 2003 gives us a ballpark figure of how much information there is (in 2002), and it suggests that the figure is doubling about every three years (Lyman and Varian 2003). So 2009 figures will be around 5 times the 2002 total. In the one year 2002, the various tangible media (print, film, etc.) were used to create 5 exabytes of new information; that is 37,000 times the amount of information in the print volumes of the Library of Congress (and, in turn, in some sense or other the Library of Congress itself has every published book that there is). In 2009, that 'new information figure should be around 200,000 times the Library of Congress. The World Wide Web itself (as of 2002), including the surface and deep Web, contains 676 times the information in those print volumes. The Web 2009 probably will contain something like 3,000 times the information as that is in the print volumes of the Library of Congress. [Note, this is not a measurement of how many IOs there are, it is a measurement of how large those IOs are summed collectively.] And the World Wide Web is only a portion of the Internet (Anderson and Wolff 2010). Roughly speaking, the information out there is hundreds of thousands of times larger than that in all print books.

We are being buried in information.

Digitization, and digital convergence, exacerbate the problem. When, around 1500, Henry VIII first wrote and sang Greensleeves, there was the performance of a song ('Alas, my love, you do me wrong, To cast me off discourteously. For I have loved you well and long, Delighting in your company'). There was no question of storing or organizing or retrieving that performance. To hear the song a second time, listeners would have to witness another performance (the brave, or the foolhardy, might have ventured 'Play it again, Henry'). Fast forward nearly 500 years and Greensleeves was readily available as a recording on vinyl or CD. Those records or CDs are individual physical objects, with particular locations in space and time (be it in a record shop, in a dorm room, or in a school bag). There are some subtleties involving artistic creations (which will be revisited), but basically organizing those records or CDs is more like organizing bottles of pickles and sauces than it is like organizing knowledge. But, coming further forward in time yet again, coming completely up to date, Greensleeves is now available as a digital recording, essentially it is available as digital 0 and 1 s. As 0 and 1 s, it is no different from a web page, from a website; indeed, it is no different to an entry in Wikipedia or Wikipedia itself; it is simply an information object, an IO. Nowadays, organizing musical items like Greensleeves *is* just like organizing knowledge. Digitization, and digital convergence, are irreversible. It is part of the context in which we live, play, work, and organize.

We are in a time of change, due to computers, the digitization of information, and the Internet. There has been disruptive change before, for example when the printing press was invented. But there is change on a grand scale now, and it is a real question as to whether traditional approaches are going to be good enough for the tasks that will arise. What are we to do?

What are we currently trying to do?

## 1.3   Success and Measuring it

It is surprisingly easy to say what we are trying to do. Not only that, it is surprisingly easy to measure success. The difficulty lies in devising systems to excel at these measures.

We organize IOs primarily so that we can retrieve them. Success at retrieval amounts to retrieving *all and only the relevant IOs*. That is the goal. The two properties that indicate the performance of any information retrieval system are those of *precision* and *recall* (Harter and Hert 1997; Salton 1992). Precision is the proportion of retrieved items or IOs that are relevant, and recall is the proportion of relevant IOs that are retrieved from the collection under consideration. (It is assumed here that the IOs are being retrieved from a *collection* of IOs, such as the files on a computer, the documents in a library, the IOs on a website, or even the IOs on the web as a whole.) Either precision or recall can individually be made artificially high—by returning the entire collection to make relevance 100% or by returning almost no IOs to allow precision to approach 100%—but, when both figures are high together, so too is the quality of the system. In the phrase 'all and only relevant IOs', it is recall that provides 'all the relevant IOs' and it is precision that provides 'only relevant IOs'.

Recall is presence of *signal*, precision is absence of *noise*. And what we are looking for is strong signal together with weak noise.

Throughout this book, many and various organizational and retrieval devices, such as Trees of Knowledge and Indexes, will be considered. But always the thought will be there, either explicitly or in the background: *what is the effect of the artifact under discussion on precision and recall?*

### 1.3.1 Relevance

Relevance is usefulness to the User as judged by the User. Relevance is just a user-controlled honorific that connects IOs and utility (on a particular occasion of retrieval). The Patron or User is ultimately the sole arbiter of relevance. It is the User who knows what is relevant on an occasion of use. The User has direct knowledge. And if we wish to know what is relevant we should seek that information from the User.

That said, sometimes Users do not know what they want—that will be discussed shortly in the context of browsing and information seeking. And in settings where Users do not know what they want, ideas of relevance are temporarily set aside until the goals are clear.

Sometimes Users cannot judge relevance. They know what they want, but cannot judge directly whether they have got it. For example, students can require study guides to a topic or discipline, but their very ignorance of the subject area makes them poor judges of what is relevant i.e. what is, or will be, useful to them (given their learning goals). Each such student should have a proxy. What the student needs by way of a reading list, or retrieved IOs, is what an expert, perhaps a teacher, a member of faculty, or a librarian subject specialist, would judge to be useful for a beginner. Proxies may well be operators of the retrieval system, but they do not have to be. There are other types of example of Users not recognizing what they are confronted with. Thus most IOs can have more than one name, and this means that a User can seek an IO under one name, receive it under another, and be unaware that the IO is a, or the, relevant one. A User might wish to have a book written by Samuel Clemens, yet not realize that the wish had been met when given a book authored by Mark Twain (these two are the same person). Ideally, a proxy would be globally omniscient (knowing what is equivalent to what and would indicate as much to the User).

### 1.3.2 Precision

In theory, precision is easy to operationalize and measure. The assessor or experimenter has the retrieved IOs to hand and the measurement is merely a matter of filtering those documents for relevance. Precision is not so easy to measure in practice when the number of retrieved documents is high, as happens occasionally with Internet search engines that can return 200,000 or more 'hits'. In settings like these, with thousands of IOs involved, actual Users would be unable to make good judgments on relevance on all of them. In these cases we assume ideal Users who are always motivated and fresh. And there are experimental and sampling methods to simulate ideal Users.

### *1.3.3  Recall*

Recall is where the problems lie. Recall is extraordinarily difficult to operation-alize and measure (except in the tricked-up case where all the holdings are returned and in some other special cases to be discussed). The problem lies with the need to measure or rationally estimate the relevant documents that have *not* been retrieved: the assessor needs to measure what has not been presented (for traditional techniques on how to do this, see (Tague-Sutcliffe 1992)). In essence, the problem is of the type 'how many needles have you failed to find in the haystack?'.

Oftentimes, recall can be known to be 100% purely on the basis of the returned documents. If the search is for an identified item, or for some definite number of items meeting a description, then often the returned entities can be known to meet the specification and recall defaults to 100%. Cases here, from the library setting, might include finding a book with a particular title or finding three books by a particular author—once you have them, that is an end to it. (This is like finding a labeled or named needle or finding at least three needles in a haystack—when the task is achieved, the unfound needles are just of no significance.) Examples such as these, where recall can be known without considering the unfound items, are certainly useful for measuring recall. Usually, though, the unfound items are the central important factor. And though there are techniques (Fricke 1998), the task is not a simple one.

### *1.3.4  Some Qualifications*

There are other notions or concepts of relevance (Schamber 1994). Indeed Search Engines typically rank the plethora of results they return in order of relevance-relative-to-the-search-query. This kind of relevance admits of degrees, it is not just a yes/no affair—under it, one IO can be *more* relevant than another. And Salton IO similarity fingerprints, which we will meet later, also allows of degrees (Borko 1977; Salton 1975). However, at the heart of it, information retrieval must serve the User, and it is the User's judgment of relevance that matters. Some Users on some occasions might regard one IO as more relevant or less relevant than another, but for our purposes this is just an unnecessary complication. An IO just either is or is not relevant, and it is the User who decides.

Of course, we need to deal with averages. A system would usually be providing a User, or many Users, with IOs on many different occasions, not just on one occasion. And the different retrievals will have different combinations of virtues of precision and recall. Also the relevance of individual IOs is

... time-, order-, and situation-dependent (Harter 1996, p. 39).

A User can cognitively engage items only one at a time, sequentially. So there is an order of access. This order does affect relevance and relevance judgments, e.g. if a later IO entirely encompasses and expands on an earlier one, then both might be judged relevant if the lesser one is presented first, whereas only the fulsome item might be judged relevant if it is presented first. A similar case is where the User seeks an encyclopedia and, say, the library holds five such encyclopedias—any of the encyclopedias individually is relevant but they are not all relevant simultaneously for a recall measurement simply because once the User has one he or she does not want the others. There are problems here for experimenters to address.

Also retrieval often aims at 'satisficing' (producing results that are good enough). Bella Weinberg writes

> Human beings may not require [optimization in classification and indexing]. Pointing the user to a manageable chunk of text or number of documents that can be scanned in a reasonable amount of time for the desired fact or information would constitute satisficing in the field of content analysis.... There is considerable evidence that users don't want ... to retrieve only the single most specific document on a topic. Users want to select from a group of documents and make their own relevance judgments. (Weinberg 1996)

So often the aim can be not just to return the relevant documents but instead to return a collection, perhaps with some noise, that encompasses the relevant documents.

Despite these complications, we will still adopt the trio of User-relevance, precision, and recall as being the core yardstick of evaluation.

## 1.4 Searching, Browsing and Berrypicking

It is convenient to identify three basic, perhaps even truly basic, information retrieval behaviors that should be supported: searching, browsing, and berrypicking. These may be informally and loosely characterized as follows.

Searching is a retrieval process where what is being sought is known by the searcher. So, for example, if you know the author and title of the book you want, and you go into a library to retrieve it—that is a case of searching. Each IO may be assumed to have a unique identifier or 'key'. And, for searching, the task is: given a key or keys find the IOs, the values, with those keys. A searcher might not know explicitly the true keys on every occasion of search, but the searcher will know some suitable surrogates. For example, a key for a book might be an ISBN number (International Standard Book Number); the searcher might not know that number, but the searcher might know the author and title information, which are intimately connected with the ISBN (for most every book has a unique ISBN number). Known item search can be parameterized in various ways. For example, the search may be for *a* novel by Nevil Shute—there is not just one ISBN-identified novel that satisfies this, rather there are about 25 and any one of those 25 will do.

Somewhat similarly, a Google search on a keyword might return hundreds of links, which can be narrowed to something suitable. Search can also be initiated by abstract keys, such as topics or subjects; a search for the subject Zoology is not merely a search for titles or text with the word 'Zoology' in them, it is a search for one or many IOs that address the subject matter Zoology. The Editors of the 15th Edition of the Encyclopaedia described searching as 'hunt-and-find'—they knew that their patrons used Encyclopaedias primarily for hunting and finding. The two features that characterize 'search' are that the goal is known in advance, and that the goal is not changed during the search process.

Browsing, in contrast, is a process where you are trying to learn just what it is that you are looking for, or what it is that might interest or engage you. Having browsed, you might then search for items, or the browsing itself may yield them. So, for example, you go into a library and select a book on your initial topic of interest; you wonder if there might be another book on the same or similar topic, so you browse along the shelf to see if there is anything further to occupy you. There is no known item sought when you start your browsing, but several may emerge. Browsing is considerably looser in concept than searching. It is a process, with a starting point, and there is feedback, which is new data which emerges during the browsing, and the important items encountered are in some sense related to previous items or just plain helpful, useful, or desirable, to the person who is browsing. The goal of 'browsing' is not known in advance, in any definite or specific way, and what goals there are can change during the browsing process.

Berrypicking is more open still. In 1989, Marcia Bates published the important paper 'The Design of Browsing and Berrypicking Techniques for the Online Search Interface' (Bates 1989). The thesis of which is: there is 'berrypicking', in which the original information need itself changes, or can change, through the search process, so there can be evolving search with expansion and side-tracking, and this is in contrast with the traditional search approach, which is successive narrowing to an information need that is unchanged throughout. Bates identifies specific berrypicking techniques (many of which, as she herself stresses, were well known and had been discussed extensively by other authors elsewhere in the literature (and Vannevar Bush, with his memex trails, is an obvious predecessor (Bush 1945))).

Some aspects of berrypicking rely on bibliographical citation networks or webs, so it is useful first to explain those. Many IOs have footnotes, or other references, which they cite ('outcites'); thus a starting or seed IO and other IOs are linked by citation. In turn, these other cited IOs may cite yet further IOs, and so on. Also, in the opposite direction, footnotes in the original IO may have other IOs *which cite them* ('incites'), distinct from IOs *which they cite*. To build a full citation network, both the outcites and incites should be collected for each IO individually.

Bates's berrypicking techniques include:

*Footnote and citation chasing* i.e. exploring the citation network.

*Journal running*. Journals tend to be on the same suite of topics. So, if a relevant article is identified from a particular journal, running through other issues of that same journal may be productive.

*Author searching*. Authors also tend to write on the same suite of topics. So, if a relevant article is identified from an author, running through other works by the same author may be productive.

*Area scanning* This is the plain browsing of physical shelves.

*Subject searches* i.e. using bibliographies and abstracting and indexing (A & I) services.

Berrypicking, as originally sketched, is distinctly an activity of academics (of faculty, researchers, and graduate students). Not many ordinary members of the public go into a library and try to find works that cite the original work they have in mind—not many ordinary folk would even be that clear what a citation is. However, the general point remains—there are ways of pursuing information, semi-rational and directed, which are not fully encompassed by the two notions of searching and browsing.

And the specific berrypicking techniques mentioned as illustrations by Bates are but a small proportion of what is possible and what can actually be used in practice. A range of techniques are employed by Reference Librarians, who are the professionals in this domain. Thomas Mann, general reference librarian to the Main Reading Room of the Library of Congress library, mentions nine methods of subject searches (Mann 1993, 2005)

Controlled vocabulary
Use of subject-classified bookstacks
Keyword searching
Citation searching
Related record searching
Use of published subject bibliographies
Boolean combination searching (with some other computer manipulations)
Using the subject expertise of people sources
Type of literature searching

Quite what these are and how all they are carried out in specific cases need not occupy us. However, there is a point to be made. Almost all of them depend on using bibliographies, indexes, catalogs, subject heading lists, classifications, encyclopedias, and other information retrieval artifacts or tools. In brief, supporting searching, browsing, and berrypicking will often depend on the use of previously created information retrieval tools.

## 1.5 Refining Information Retrieval Tools

Searching, browsing, and berrypicking, certainly describe some information seeking behaviors that should be supported. But, as noted, their effectiveness depends on information retrieval 'tools'.

Librarians have been helping the seekers of information for some two thousand years. And during the course of this, they have devised a suite of information retrieval tools. These tools are to help themselves and their Patrons. Librarians are not the only ones with a long history of use and creation of information retrieval artifacts. Authors, publishers, and various commercial and non-commercial companies, organizations and research groups, have also devised and used information access tools. Merely improving those tools is a valuable goal to have. So what tools are we talking about here? Here are a few.

Abstracts
Bibliographies
Book reviews
Catalogs
Citation Indexes
[Computer Interfaces]
Cumulative Indexes
[Databases]
Dictionaries
Encyclopedias
Finding Aids
Handbooks, manuals, etc.
Indexes
Inventories
[Keyword Searches]
Nomenclature
Outlines, syllabi, etc
Pathfinders
Registers
Reviews
[Search Engines]
Subject Guides
Tables of Contents
Textbooks
[Web Browsers]

(Some are in parentheses to indicate they are of recent origin.)

## 1.6  Functional Bibliography

A sketch of the history of modern library cataloging will also give us insights on what we are trying to achieve. As Richard Smiraglia explains

> Panizzi (1841), Cutter (1876), and Dewey (1876), in the nineteenth century, developed very pragmatic tools (catalogs and classifications), explaining as they did so the principles by which their tools were constructed. Their efforts were influential: The principles they expounded can still be observed in the structure of modern online retrieval systems. (Smiraglia 2002, p. 332)

[See also (Blake 2002; Norris 1969; Denton 2007).]

The work and influence of Sir Anthony Panizzi is a convenient place to start. To some, Panizzi was the 'Prince of Librarians' (Miller 1967); to others, he was a 'fat pedant' (asserted by the famous author, Thomas Carlyle (Espinasse 1893)). In the mid-nineteenth century, Panizzi cataloged the British Museum Library, which was then probably the largest library in the world. Panizzi's catalogs were centrally a *book* catalog of everything that the British Museum held (i.e. one single, relatively fixed and unchanging, book that listed the holdings), supplemented with some other subject and special collections catalogs for scholars and various particular purposes. The main catalog was an alphabetical named catalog (or dictionary catalog)—that is, it was a list of names in alphabetical order. Basically, what the Panizzi main catalog could do is to tell you whether the Library held a particular book. Conceptually, the User supplied as input sufficient detail of the target book (e.g. the author's name and the title), and the catalog would help determine whether the British Museum held that book. So these catalogs supported search, but they were not so strong in their support of browsing and berrypicking. The main catalog was not set up to address such inverse problems as: what does the library hold by author X? what does the library hold with title Y? what does the library hold on topic Z? That information, or much of it, could be extracted from the main catalog; but the catalog did not have the 'entry points' to make this an easy exercise.

The intellectual backdrop to the catalogs was a collection of 91 Rules that Panizzi, and his associates, formulated in 1839 (Carpenter 2002; Lehnus 1974, 1972). The greater part of these rules concerns how to lay out syntactic details of authors' names (for single author, joint author, anonymous author, pseudonymous author, etc., works), how to lay out details of titles (for single works, collections, translations, commentaries, corporate works, untitled works, etc.), and so on. All of this is establishing important and demanding syntactic and conceptual infrastructure, and Panizzi broke the back of the task for the later cataloging tradition to follow.

Panizzi was well aware that many of the items that the Museum Library held were not independent entities all unto themselves. There can be 'bibliographical' relationships between items. As examples, one item might be a translation of another item, or two items might be two different editions of the same work. Recognizing this is also in part recognizing abstraction in the realm of IOs. When two books in the holdings are instances of different editions of the same work, what is this 'work' in common that they are physical examples of? Is it a third physical book on the shelves somewhere? Obviously not, it is an abstraction: the work exists as abstract contents, which find physical expression in the physical books exemplifying copies or instances of the different editions. Panizzi conceptualized libraries as containing three kinds of things: *works*, *publications* (or *editions*), and *copies*. So, for example, there is the work *Hamlet*, which is published in various different editions, and those editions individually consist of a number of copies. Patrons, or scholars, can be interested in any of copies, editions, or works, and so, the Museum, or a library, needs to keep track of information about all three and relations between them.

And the catalog entries themselves also need not be pure isolates. For example, if 'Brontë, Charlotte' is to be the preferred controlled entry for the author Charlotte Brontë, it is important first to use 'Brontë, Charlotte' uniformly throughout the catalog, however it is useful also to help Patrons unaware of this convention by providing cross-references perhaps from 'Brontë, C.' and 'Charlotte Brontë' to 'Brontë, Charlotte'; and it also may help Patrons unaware of other facts to have a cross reference from 'Bell, Currer' to 'Brontë, Charlotte' (after the novel *Jane Eyre* had been rejected for publication by five successive publishers, its author Charlotte Brontë submitted it to the sixth publisher under the pseudonym 'Currer Bell' and representing herself as the agent for the 'real author', Currer Bell).

Of particular interest are Panizzi's Rules 54–69 which concern References and Cross-references. It provides some measure of support for browsing and berry-picking (and, indeed, for search). It creates steps from one item or entry to others. As an example, here is Panizzi's Rule 55

> LV. Cross-references to be divided into three classes, from name to name, from name to work, and from work to work. Those of the first class to contain merely the name, title, or office of the person referred to as entered; those of the second, so much of the title referred to besides, as, together with the size and date, may give the means of at once identifying, under its heading, the book referred to; those of the third class to contain moreover so much of the title referred from, as may be necessary to ascertain the object of the reference. (Lehnus 1972, p. 26)

So, with Panizzi, we really see four features: controlled syntactic infrastructure, abstraction, the three-fold conceptual structure (or 'ontology') of work-publication-copy, and the use of links (cross references) between catalog entries to help Patrons. And the help that the links provide is that they give the Patron the opportunity to increase recall. Cross-referencing is an example of what we would now call 'syndetic' structure—helping us to bound gaps (the term 'syndetic' is from (Cutter 1876, p. 15)).

Cross-referencing can achieve certain ends; but it is limited in others, mainly by its piecemeal nature. If work X and work Y are, in some sense or other, on Topic 1, or of Kind 1, then references between X and Y may capture this fact. But if there are a thousand works on Topic 1, or of Kind 1, then either there would need to be close to two million direct mutual cross-references, or a thousand-link chain of references, to reflect these relationships. Either is awkward. What is better is to construct a 'class' for Topic or Kind 1, on the basis of one or more shared characteristics, and to 'classify' the thousand works by putting them in the class. Putting an item in a class is merely a matter of attaching a label to it, where the labeling process is guided by prior analysis and identification.

There is a historical accident that enters at this point in the narrative. The British Museum library was largely a closed stack model; that is, the books were retrieved for the Users from separate stores which were inaccessible to the public. Librarians were the intermediaries who did this task. But elsewhere, in other libraries, the open stack model was commonplace. In it, the books were on shelves for direct access by Patrons. With open stacks there is the problem of the shelving order of the items, where a core function of the shelving is display.

How do you display the books to help the Patrons? There are two main possibilities: alphabetically (i.e. in the same alphabetical order as that of a Dictionary Catalog), or by similarity (i.e. with books physically close to 'similar' books, i.e. books of similar kinds or forms, or books with similar themes). The word 'themes' being used here is a rough synonym for 'subjects'. And the concept 'form' includes literary form e.g. poetry as contrasted with fiction, and material form e.g. encyclopaedias and magazines as contrasted with ordinary books or volumes. Alphabetical arrangement helps searching but not browsing; but, in contrast, form or thematic arrangement helps browsing but not searching.

Melvil Dewey popularized thematic (and form) classification, with his Dewey Decimal Classification, devised about 1876. The main aim of the Classification was to produce a shelf display suitable both for the readers and the managing librarians. Also, there is an increasing use at this time of *card* catalogs. Gottfried Wilhelm Leibniz two hundred years earlier had used the (fairly obvious) device of writing a library's holdings as entries on individual cards; then the cards could be arranged to provide access by title, by author, or thematically; indeed, if the cards were themselves duplicated, separate stacks of cards could provide all these entry points simultaneously (to produce card catalogs, familiar to those of us of a mature persuasion).

[Dewey made a number of contributions, some of which we will visit later. He was also, to a degree, colorful or even mildly villainous, with eccentricities and peccadilloes. He was in favor of simplified spelling, for a while he called himself 'Dui', and the early Dewey Decimal Classifications had entries for 'Jeolojy' ('Geology') and 'Filosofy' ('Philosophy'). And he was somewhat suspect in his relationship with women librarians

> ...publicly hugging, squeezing, and kissing... [American Library Association] women (Wiegand 1996, p. 301).

It seems that some of the female librarians objected to Dewey's behavior, while others did not. Dewey was forced out of Columbia College (Columbia University), for the gross insubordination of having women in his librarianship classes (and, by modern standards, Dewey's inclusion and education of women presumably was an act of emancipation), and then later, in 1905, he was forced to resign from the American Library Association, and from the New York Library Association, effectively for inappropriate behavior towards women (hugging and kissing the emancipated was a step too far).]

Charles A. Cutter's 1876 *Rules for a Printed Dictionary Catalogue* is particularly important. In 1868, Cutter was the librarian of the Boston Athenaeum (which, at 70,000 volumes, was then the third largest library in the United States). Between 1874 and 1882, Cutter catalogued it (Blake 2002), and he published, in the *Rules*, the theoretical background. These Rules contain the 'OBJECTS' (i.e. objectives) of a catalogue, and the MEANS for obtaining those objects.

OBJECTS

   1. To enable a person to find a book of which either
           a. the author is known
           b. the title is known
           c. the subject is known
   2. To show what the library has
           d. by a given author
           e. on a given subject
           f. in a given kind of literature
   3. To assist in the choice of a book
           g. as to its edition (bibliographically)
           h. as to its character (literary or topical)

MEANS

   1. Author-entry with the necessary references (for A and D).
   2. Title-entry or title-reference (for B).
   3. Subject-entry, cross references, and classed subject table (for C and E).
   4. Form-entry (for F).
   5. Giving edition and imprint, with notes when necessary (for G).
   6. Notes (for H)

(Cutter 1876, p. 10)

And, Cutter both defined classification and made insightful suggestions regarding it.

*Class*, a collection of objects having characteristics in common.

Books are classified by bringing together those which have the same characteristics. Of course any characteristics might be taken, as size, or binding, or publisher. But as nobody wants to know what books there are in the library in folio, or what quartos, or what books bound in russia or calf, or what published by John Smith, or by Brown, Jones, and Robinson, these bases of classification are left to the booksellers and auctioneers and trade sales. [i.e. we readers and scholars generally don't care about such characteristics as the material of a book's cover.] ....

...books are most commonly brought together in catalogues because they have the same authors, or the same subjects, or the same literary form, or are written in the same language, or were given by the same donor, or are designed for the same class of readers....

Classification by subject and classification by form are the most common....
(Cutter 1876, pp. 10–12)

Notice here the emphasis that Cutter puts on *subject*. One of the objectives of a Catalog is to provide the Patron with items by subject; another objective is to allow the institutions to know what they have by subject; and one of the most common, and presumably one of the most important styles of classification, is classification by subject. Unfortunately, the subject, or one of the subjects, of a book may not appear *explicitly* anywhere in the book (in the book's title, in its abstract, in its text). This can make it hard to determine what the subjects of a work are.

For Cutter the main organizational and access device was still the Dictionary Catalog i.e. an alphabetical list of items. However, some of the items represented subjects or classes and there were syndetic cross-references or links, to more comprehensive and less comprehensive subjects (as well as links to related materials). Cutter's work and theories show controlled syntactic infrastructure, abstraction, and the use of (limited) classification for items, and catalog entries, to help individual Patrons and classes of readers.

The adjective 'limited' is being used for a reason. Cutter classifies books by, say, subject, but he does not classify books by cover material, even though both subjects and material-of-cover are characteristics of the books. He does this for two reasons, an internal intellectual reason, or rationale, and an external practical reason. The first he reveals, the second reason he conceals. The intellectual reason he offers is that readers, unlike, say, booksellers, do not care about cover material. But, really, the intellectual reason is an excuse, and it is the practical reason that is driving this. The practical reason, the concealed reason, is that each classification produced in 1876 required its own book, or card catalog, to provide entry for retrieval via that classification. Every characteristic required its own catalog. Cutter's solution to this potential explosion of catalogs is to classify only by those characteristics of interest to his readers (and not, for example, those of interest for booksellers). However, times have changed, not so much, in this context, for the readers, but more for the techniques for producing catalogs. Computers have replaced both book and card catalogs; and, for a computer, once a characteristic is recorded as data for an item, then retrieval, or classification, via that characteristic is usually a trivial and, essentially, a zero cost operation. What this means, for example, is that if the material of the cover of a book is recorded, along with the book's subject or subjects and other data about it, then classification and retrieval via material-of-cover is available free. Of course, decisions still have to be made; in particular, decisions have to be made about what data to record in the first place, on data entry, e.g. whether to record the binding materials of the items. This new technology of cataloging means that the classes of 'readers' that an institution can cater to, can be much wider, much more finely drawn, and more discriminating. If even a single Patron wanders in, on a single occasion, and wants to know, for whatever reason, which volumes of the holdings are bound in calf, in principle the computer based catalog can provide an answer, with no extra effort and cost involved.

What is to be learned at this point from a sketch of the history of modern cataloging? It is wise to be careful with syntax, using controlled names (for Authors, Titles, etc.) and controlled terms or phrases or headings (for Subjects). There is the need for abstraction, and for classification using characteristics. Some of the more important and useful classification characteristics, such as *by subject*, are difficult to implement and apply. Additionally, and entirely distinction from any historical 'objects of the catalog', nowadays we would want to address the more general notion of IOs instead of books, and, for storage, we would invoke information repositories instead of bricks and mortar libraries (where an information repository can be anything from a single directory on a single computer to a 'cloud' of data or information on Internet itself).

One useful way to imagine or visualize functional bibliography is to see the IOs, and their subjects, authors, and the like, as forming a universe of 'bibliographical entities'. Many of these entities are linked one to another in a rich variety of ways to form a complex web or network. The links themselves are 'bibliographical relationships' (essentially a generalization of Panizzi's cross references, and Cutter's classifications). Bibliographical relationships include whether two IOs have the same subject, whether an IO has been written by a specific author, whether two IOs are published in the same journal, and so on (Tillett 1987). Then, what a searcher, browser, or berrypicker, does is to start somewhere in this Universe and then 'navigate' around using the links or bibliographical relations to reach the desired end. So IO retrieval is finding by means of bibliographical relations. And, information organization, which is the prelude to information retrieval, is at its core the identification, establishment, and recording of bibliographical relations. As Robert Maxwell phrases it

> Bibliographic relationships have been at the heart of cataloging theory for more than a century. (Maxwell 2008, p. 71)

## 1.7 Surrogates, Aliases and the Pernicious Effects of Physicality

Computers, and digitization, have brought about many changes, of course. One major one is the removal of physicality from IOs.

Traditionally, to meet the 'objects of the catalog', Users would want, for example, to be able to physically retrieve IOs by author and also by subject (and in many other ways). If a library shelved its books by author, a Patron would be able to retrieve them by author (from a juxtaposition of other books by the same and other authors). If a library located its books by subject on physical shelves, a Patron would be able to retrieve them by subject. But there would be no way the Patron could retrieve them both by author and by subject. A single copy of an Adam Smith book on Economics can be only in one place at a time. It cannot be both on an author shelf and on a separate economics shelf, simultaneously.

The solution to this problem is perfectly obvious, and librarians have been using it for hundreds of years. You use indirection and have a *surrogate*; for example you might have a record card as a surrogate and you write the metadata (i.e. information) about the book on the card. The wonderful thing about surrogates is that the relationship between a surrogate and its original can be *many-one*. That means that a single IO can have many identical surrogates. So, as a simple example, we start with an IO, say Adam Smith's book on economics, and we take *two or more record cards* (*the surrogates or aliases*) and write on each of them all of the metadata, i.e. identical copies on each; then we take one of these surrogates and place it in a 'card catalog' arranged by author, and we take another surrogate and place it in a 'card catalog' arranged by subject. Voila! we can now retrieve perfectly either by author or by subject. Of course, what we retrieve in the first place is the surrogates (i.e. the cards) but then those surrogates will tell us, or need to tell us, where physically the IOs are and then we can retrieve the IOs. With this card-record-surrogate system, we need to make as many surrogates as ways that we intend to retrieve. So, if we also wanted to retrieve by date of publication, we make a third surrogate record and put that in a card catalog arranged by date of publication. And so on.

In the last 25 years, the computer has rendered irrelevant most all of the above practical details. You certainly still want to have surrogates or aliases or references, and they are going to be records, digital 0 and 1 s, in computers. But then you do not need many copies of a particular surrogate, nor a 'card catalog' arranged by author etc. The computer, or the software programs, can do all of the tasks needed 'on the fly', and indefinitely many others! It is trivial for a computer to answer a question/command like 'Find me all the books that Adam Smith wrote on economics that were published in English between 1700 and 1800 and reprinted by University of Chicago Press'.

It is at this point that the biggest continuing mistake in the organization of information occurs: that of seeing the information objects (IOs) as being physical objects. This then makes organizing IOs like organizing physical objects, and, in turn, this has all sorts of pernicious effects. The problem arises because a physical object can be only in one place at a time. So, if several of them are to be organized the question arises as to which places should they be. However, with IOs, IOs, or their surrogates or references, can be in two 'places' at once, and we want them to be in two (or more) places at once.

Two examples. First, consider Classical Librarianship and Call Numbers. The prime purpose of the Classical Librarian organizational scheme is to produce for each IO, qua physical object, a unique number, the Call Number. The Call Number is to allow the IO to be placed at a particular position on a specific shelf (so that it can be 'called'). But many books 'need' to be in two places at once. For example, a book on a composite topic like economic history might need to be on the economics shelf and on the history shelf, or a book on multiple different topics might need to be in multiple places. This cannot happen with a physical book, so wherever it is allocated some injustice is done. However, once there are surrogates for books (e.g. cataloging cards), surrogates can easily be arranged in the desired way. And references, within computer software, are considerably more abstract and general than cataloging cards (after all, cataloging cards themselves are physical objects and each individual one can only be in one place).

The second example is modern computer interfaces. Many Operating Systems proudly present the 'desktop' metaphor with its folders and folders within folders. The User creates 'documents' and the documents, like the physical documents on a real desk, need to go somewhere, and the User figures out a suitable folder structure and places the document in just one folder. The problem is: most documents need to go in two or more places at once. For example, a 1997 holiday

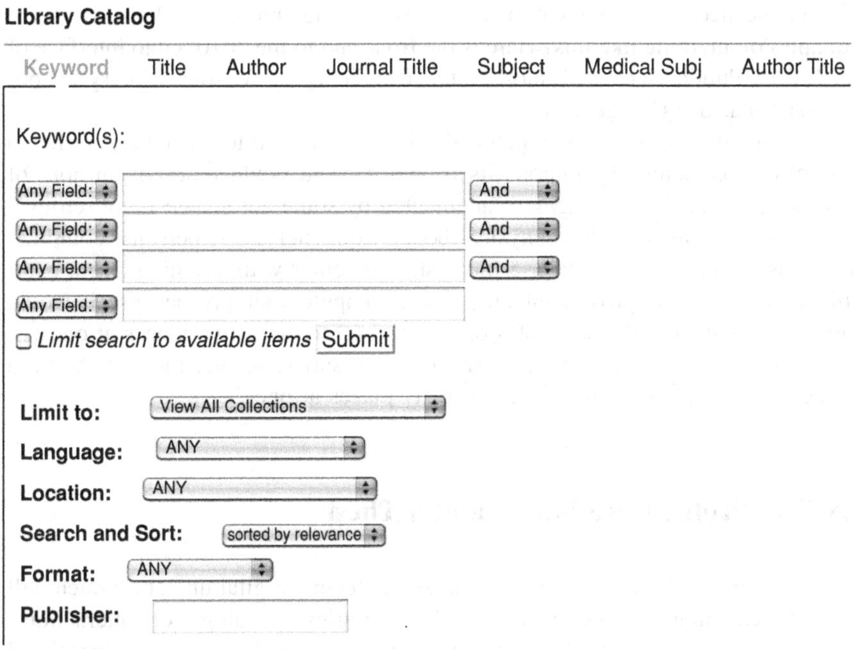

**Library Catalog**

| Keyword | Title | Author | Journal Title | Subject | Medical Subj | Author Title |
|---------|-------|--------|---------------|---------|--------------|--------------|

Keyword(s):

| Any Field: ⬍ | | And ⬍ |
|---|---|---|
| Any Field: ⬍ | | And ⬍ |
| Any Field: ⬍ | | And ⬍ |
| Any Field: ⬍ | | |

☐ *Limit search to available items* Submit

**Limit to:**          View All Collections ⬍

**Language:**      ANY ⬍

**Location:**      ANY ⬍

**Search and Sort:**      sorted by relevance ⬍

**Format:**      ANY ⬍

**Publisher:**      

**Image 1.1:** **The Sabio Online Public Access Catalog** (Software by Innovative Interfaces, Inc. Used with Permission.)

digital snapshot may need to go with the images, may need to go with the holiday documents, and may need to go with the 1997 documents. The snapshot cannot be in all these places at once. So the User is forced to make some artificial decision and then, later, remember that artificial decision when trying find the object for a second time. It is possible, with most Operating Systems, to create a file name alias and to put that alias itself somewhere. But this is awkward for the User and, if followed through, leads to unacceptable complexity and redundancy. File name aliases, the Operating System's closest analog to the catalog card, do not solve the problem. The problem occurs earlier with the idea that the document needs to be put somewhere. Here is a solution. Forget about desktops altogether. Forget about documents. Forget about folders. Forget about folders within folders. Then a User works as follows. She creates or imports or uploads a 'document'; and some metadata, some information, is attached to that document (including that the document is an image, that it concerns 1997, that it concerns holidays, etc.). This metadata is attached part automatically by the computer, part by choice by the User, and part semi-automatically by the computer observing what the User does. Then, as the User moves on to something else, the document is 'released' and disappears off into storage. Later, when the User comes back and wants the 1997 holiday snapshot the system presents a front-end that finds and produces the image without the need for the User to do any burrowing through folders. Are there examples of anything like this? Here is the front-end to the 2010 Sabio interface of the Online Public Access Catalog of the University of Arizona Library (http://sabio.arizona.edu) (Image 1.1).

It is not from a personal computer. But it is a front end to a database, in fact a suite of databases and the Internet itself, and it could produce any of millions of documents. And, if you imagine it augmented by some automated robot retrieval system, it could also produce physical books from shelves. A personal computer could easily consist of a database file system together with a similar 'front-end'. This would be an improvement on present computers simply because it would allow documents (really surrogates of documents) to be in two places at once.

IOs do not have to be physical. Certainly their surrogates need not be. And if a surrogate is not physical it can be 'in many places at once'.

## 1.8  The Problem Re-Stated and a Thesis

The problem is: devise a means to organize the fecund digital universe which will support searching, browsing, berrypicking, retrieval dialogs or interactions, modern versions of the classical information retrieval tools, and functional bibliography.

Of course, this problem, or sub-parts of it, is being tackled tenaciously by any amount of insightful theoreticians, librarians, faculty, researchers, and commercial and academic institutions. And truly impressive progress is being made. However, the problem is not solved. And this book is not going to solve it either. But this book has a suggestion to make, and a thesis to argue. They are:

> Make greater use of Symbolic Logic. It can bring a unification and improvement to organization.

The thesis itself is not entirely novel. Jesse Shera, one of the intellectual giants of librarianship, concurred with it (Shera 1965, p. 105). And so too did others, including Frank Rogers, the inventor of the innovative and powerful MeSH system of medical subject headings (Rogers 1960a, 1960b). The present book is merely the attempt to pick up the ball and to carry it a few steps forward.

## 1.9  How is Information Going to be Organized?

Digitization provides the hint. In so far as organization can be done, it is going to be done by agents working together with computers, computer programs, and computer software. The computers will be intelligent assistants to the agents, and the agents will be intelligent assistants to the computers.

The aforementioned 1,100,000 files on the Macintosh are managed in part by the Operating System of that computer, in particular the File System. That File System can store, manage, and retrieve the files in a variety of semi-intelligent, or useful, or insightful ways. As examples, the File System can retrieve files by name, files by date of creation, files as contents of particular folders or directories, etc. Those abilities are then leveraged by the human agent choosing to give certain files certain names, (names perhaps mnemonically similar to other names on 'similar' files), choosing to place certain files in certain directories, and so forth. Between the computer and the agent, an organizational system emerges.

At the other end of the spectrum, out in the world at large, there are often intermediaries of one kind or another. Information specialists act as intermediaries between the information objects (IOs) and Users or Patrons. To assist with information intermediation, information objects, as collections, must be organized or 'structured'. The processes of creating, devising, designing, developing, modifying and maintaining such structures are a core intellectual concern and activity for some information professionals. One such information professional is the Classical Librarian. Classical Librarians use an elaborate system of organization and retrieval to structure recorded knowledge, recorded information, and other artifacts of record. Librarians have been organizing for thousands of years, and continue to do it today. In the course of these endeavors, they have developed organizational tools or schemes, such as

Classification schemes
Cataloging codes/standards
Controlled vocabularies, structured vocabularies, (thesauri, ontologies, ...)
Authority files (access points—controlling 'form of names'—and access control)

and they have developed retrieval tools, some of which were mentioned earlier.

All of this is wonderful and impressive work, and there is a lot to learn from it. However, there are two points to be made about it in connection with the present and equipping ourselves for the future. As we have explained, the prime purpose of the Classical Librarian organizational scheme is to mark-and-park physical books. This had two aims. It shelves books for calling. And, in intention at least, it supports serendipitous browsing, for books with similar Call Numbers would or should be on similar topics (themes or forms), and they would be next to each other on the shelves (when the books were actually in the library and not out on loan to Patrons). But, thanks to the fact that more than a few books have either composite individual topics or address multiple topics, this mark-and-park by similarity is impossible to do. As Shera writes

Bibliographical classification must be completely *independent* of physical objects (books), for no arrangement of such objects can reveal the complex of relationships that may exist among the many separate thought-units that make up the subject content of these books. (Shera 1965, p. 105)

And he observes

> ...the history of library classification...has been the narrative of a pursuit of impossible
> goals. (Shera 1965, p. 100).

Not only is ideal shelving impossible to do, but there no longer is any need to try
to do it. We do not need Call Numbers anymore for most of what we will face, for
hardly any IOs need to be placed on shelves for calling and browsing. Computers
will do the locating and collocating.

The second point is that the main foundation of librarian schemes is 'cataloging'. A cataloger takes an IO and assigns to it all sorts of information (including
the IO's Call Number). Cataloging is very skilled. A cataloger needs intelligence,
training, experience, and the ability to consult and follow volumes and volumes of
cataloging rules. And the rules themselves have evolved over generations. Crucial,
though, is that the cataloging of an individual IO takes time (and costs money).
Cataloging a book cannot be done in an instant. With the increasing number of
publications, the cohort of actual working catalogers cannot keep up. Certainly,
cataloging as a whole has been made more efficient. Instead of every library doing
their own cataloging, there is central cataloging and the rest 'copy catalog' from
the central source. And computers are helping with cataloging. Modern working
catalogers use computers and software all the time (just as modern authors and
novelists use word processors and, sometimes, software grammar checkers and
indexers). Even so, real cataloging is being left behind. Earlier we estimated that
the Library of Congress held something like one five thousandth of the Web
information out there, but the 2–300 catalogers employed in the Library of Congress cannot keep up even with that 0.02% of the information. The overview of
classical librarianship thus is: we do not need Call Numbers; traditional cataloging
is not going to work; everything else we would like to learn from, adopt or adapt.

The scaffolding for future organization is going to be computers in conjunction
with parts of Classical Librarianship. But we need to have a good idea of the
details and of what computers can and cannot do.

## 1.10  Learning From Failure

One failure that offers a learning opportunity is that of that the Artificial Intelligence fields of Natural Language Processing and Knowledge Representation.

The subject area of computing and information organization has a historical
founder: the seventeenth century librarian, mathematician, philosopher, and dip-
lomat, Gottfried Wilhelm Leibniz. Leibniz co-discovered calculus, with Newton,
contributed to symbolic logic, and offered the theories of possible worlds and of
monads to philosophy. But it is his work on a universal science, composed of the
Universal Characteristic and the Calculus Ratiocinator, that is of interest to us.
Leibniz wished to place all of knowledge into a common language, which showed
its structure, and then, conceptually, into a single Universal Encyclopedia.

One might say that this Universal Characteristic was to be symbolic logic. Then, any request for knowledge, or any dispute, could be settled by calculation; the Calculus Ratiocinator, at work on the Encyclopedia, would provide all the answers. The Calculus Ratiocinator was a computer, a symbolic logic computer. In the modern terms of Artificial Intelligence, it would be said that Leibniz suggested knowledge representation by symbolic logic, and access to, or calculation on, that represented knowledge also by symbolic logic. So logic was to be both the program and the data. [One of the smaller steps that Leibniz made along the way was to write the title information of all the books in one of the libraries he was managing on to sheets of paper, thirty titles at a time, then to cut each of these sheets up into thirty fragments, one fragment per title. Finally, he sorted the fragments by author name, etc. In brief, he invented the card catalog.]

Sadly, Leibniz's dream was never realized, and probably never will be. The reason is: computers can only do so much. In particular, right now they cannot understand natural language, and they cannot represent grand-scale information. A central issue in the everyday conveying of information is the distinction between implicit and explicit and just how little is explicit. Spoken or written natural language is the tip of the iceberg. It leverages off a vast amount of hidden implicit knowledge that we humans have. There can be an awful lot in the context of utterance. The physical setting, separately from the verbal context, is often used for disambiguation—the word 'bank' said by fly fishermen standing by a cash supplying ATM (Automatic Teller Machine), in the dawn hours departing on their day's outing, will likely mean something different to the word 'bank' said by the very same fishermen, just a few hours later, standing in their waders in the middle of a river. And context can be widened to include social context: a piece of paper can be just a piece of paper, but it can also be a contract, a poem, a check, part of a ticker tape celebration. And the meaning of what we have to say about that piece of paper may be fleshed out by the setting. Our languages do not stand on their own. For computers to be able to understand, and converse appropriately in, natural language they would need to appreciate both the context and this 'outside' knowledge. And giving them the outside knowledge is not easy: there is the quantity of it, and then questions of organization and processing. As Gobinda Chowdhury phrases it

> ... we do not know how to compute the meaning of a sentence based on the meanings of its words and its context. (Chowdhury 2003, p. 79)

Computer understanding of natural language may never happen; it certainly is not going to happen anytime soon.

Computers struggle to represent knowledge for much the same reasons as they struggle to understand natural language: there is that hidden part of the iceberg. There is the vast amount of implicit or tacit knowledge that we use in conjunction with the explicit, but, for a computer, everything has to be explicit or explicitly represented. It is certainly true that some knowledge can be represented in computers; apparently databases contain an unnerving amount of knowledge about us and many other things. But caution is needed over what is being asserted here.

Take, for example, a database for a train timetable. Such a repository can answer sophisticated questions about what is in that repository (such as, how many trains are scheduled to leave from a particular platform during a particular period). In addition to this contingent information the database can contain necessary information, or constraints, such as no train instance can be in two different places at once. Even so, what is known here is very limited. What the computer knows about is its representation or model, it does not know so much about the world. Were inclement weather to close one of the railway tracks, the computer would have no idea what the train timetable might be. Certainly some of that outside information can be added in (for example, that if track 7 is closed, specific changes in schedule will occur). But there is still a huge and indefinite amount of external knowledge that is not in the representation. In Artificial Intelligence, there is the *symbol system*, or *formal system*, *hypothesis* to the effect that manipulating symbols will be sufficient for intelligent reasoning and knowledge representation. Progress with establishing this hypothesis has been fitful, pretty well precisely for the reasons given here.

The argument establishing the limits of computer representation is not an in principle argument, it is not an irrefutable theoretical result. Rather it is to the effect that where we are today, with what our computers can do and what we know about getting them to do things, means that true knowledge representation at best lies some time in the future. Computers are not going to solve our information retrieval problems anytime soon. We also know that the sheer bulk of existing and new information is just too much for us to manage by ourselves. So right now, we need to be thinking of different approaches.

The appropriate line, or perhaps even the lifeline, here is the intelligent assistant model. In so far as organization can be done, it is going to be done by agents working together with computers, computer programs, and computer software. The computers will be intelligent assistants to the agents, and the agents will be intelligent assistants to the computers. We have to work symbiotically with computers, using them as assistants.

# References

Anderson C, Wolff M (2010) The web is dead. Long live the internet. Wired 18(9):118–127
Bates MJ (1989) The design of browsing and berrypicking techniques for the online search interface. Online Rev 13:407–424
Blake VLP (2002) Forging the anglo-american cataloging alliance: descriptive cataloging, 1830–1908. Cataloging Classification Q 35(1):3–22
Borko H (1977) Toward a theory of indexing. Inf Process Manage 13(6):355–365
Bush V (1945) As we may think. Atl Monthly 176(1):101–108
Carpenter M (2002) The original 73 rules of the British museum: a preliminary analysis. Cataloging Classification Q 35(1):23–36
Chowdhury GG (2003) Natural language processing. Ann Rev Inf Sci Technol 37(1):51–89. doi:10.1002/aris.1440370103

Clark A (2003) Natural-born Cyborgs: minds, technologies, and the future of human intelligence. Oxford University Press, Oxford

Cutter CA (1876) Rules for a printed dictionary catalogue. Government Printing Office, Washington

Denton W (2007) FRBR and the history of cataloging. In: Taylor AG (ed) Understanding FRBR: what it is and how it will affect our retrieval. Westport, Connecticut

Espinasse F (1893) Literary recollections and sketches. Hodder and Stoughton, London

Frické M (1998) Measuring recall. J Inf Sci 24(6):409–417

Harter SP (1996) Variations in relevance assessments and the measurement of retrieval effectiveness. J Am Soc Inf Sci 47(1):37–49

Harter SP, Hert CA (1997) Evaluation of information retrieval systems: approaches, issues and methods. In: Williams ME (ed) Annual review of information science and technology, vol 32, Information Today Inc, Medford, NJ, pp 3–94

Lehnus DJ (1972) A comparison of Panizzi's 91 rules and the AACR of 1967. Univ Illinois Graduate School Library Sci Occasional Pap 105:1–40

Lehnus DJ (1974) Milestones in cataloging. Libraries Unlimited, Inc., Littleton

Lyman P, Varian HR (2003) How Much Information? 2003. http://www2.sims.berkeley.edu/research/projects/how-much-info-2003/. Accessed November 20 2008

Mann T (1993) Library research models. Oxford University Press, New York

Mann T (2005) The oxford guide to library research, 3rd edn. Oxford University Press, New York

Maxwell RL (2008) FRBR: A guide for the perplexed. American Library Association, Chicago

Miller E (1967) Prince of librarians: the life and times of Antonio Panizzi of the British museum. The Ohio University Press, Athens

Norris DM (1969) A history of cataloguing and cataloguing methods. Gale Research Company, Detroit

Rogers FB (1960a) Medical subject headings. Preface and introduction. In. U.S. Department of Health, Education, and Welfare, Washington D.C., pp i–xix

Rogers FB (1960b) Review of Taube, Mortimer. Studies in coordinate indexing. Bull Med Libr Assoc 42:380–384 (July 1954)

Salton G (1975) A theory of indexing. Regional conference series in applied mathematics, society for industrial and applied mathematics. Philadelphia, PA

Salton G (1992) The state of retrieval system evaluation. Inf Process Manage 28(4):441–449

Schamber L (1994) Relevance and information behavior. In: Williams ME (ed) Annual review of information science and technology, vol 29. Learned Information Inc, Medford, pp 3–48

Shera JH (1965) Classification: current functions and applications to the subject analysis of library materials. In: Libraries and the organization of knowledge. Archon, Hamden, CT, pp 97–111

Smiraglia RP (2002) The progress of theory in knowledge. Library Trends 50(1):330–349

Tague-Sutcliffe J (1992) The pragmatics of information retrieval experiments, revisited. Inf Process Manage 28(4):467–490

Tillett BB (1987) Bibliographic relationships: toward a conceptual structure of bibliographic information used in cataloging. University of California, Los Angeles

Weinberg BH (1996) Compexity in indexing systems—Abandonment and failure: implications for organizing the internet. http://www.asis.org/annual-96/ElectronicProceedings/weinberg.html. Accessed 12 Oct 2010

Wiegand W (1996) Dewey declassified: a revelatory look at the "irrepressible reformer". Am Libraries 27(1):54–60

# Chapter 2
# Some Useful Ideas and Background Theories

## 2.1 Reid on Abstraction and Classification

There are some valuable arguments in Thomas Reid's 1785 essay 'Abstraction' (Reid 1785). [Reid was a nineteenth century Scottish 'common sense' philosopher and the essay is from his *Essays on the Intellectual Powers of Man*. Interestingly enough the librarian pioneer, Charles Cutter, was influenced by exactly this essay (Miksa 1983). Indeed, Reid himself had worked as a librarian. (Fraser 1898 p. 27).]

Once a child understands plurals, that, for example, he or she has *two* brothers or *two* sisters or *several* toys, he or she understands that there are *attributes* such that the same attribute can be possessed by different things. There is the one item, one of the toys, that has perhaps several different *attributes*, such as being red, chewed, being in the play pen, and being a toy, and another item, which also has several attributes, such as being blue, being in a person's hand, being desired, and also being a toy. And at least one of these attributes, 'being a toy', is possessed by two different things. Thus, the child sees, touches, and interacts with things individually, and understands that there are attributes which are possessed by, or are instantiated by, different individual things. There are two processes here: the distilling out of one property of interest (being a toy) from the many other properties that the each item individually possesses (being chewed, being blue), and the recognition that the property is common to more than one different subject.

This is the basis of classification, as Reid puts it

> Our ability to distinguish and give names to the different attributes belonging to a single thing goes along with an ability to observe that many things have certain attributes in common while they differ in others. This enables us to put the countless hordes of individuals into a limited number of classes, which are called 'kinds' and 'sorts'—and in the scholastic language are called 'genera' and 'species'. (Reid 1785, p. 191)

M. Frické, *Logic and the Organization of Information*,
DOI: 10.1007/978-1-4614-3088-9_2,
© Springer Science+Business Media New York 2012

[Notice that Reid, uses the words 'kinds' or 'sorts' as synonyms for 'classes'. This usage is common, both then and now, and we will adopt it. The word 'sort' is particularly useful in classification in as much it is not overused and, unlike, for example, 'class' or 'type', does not carry the baggage of many other meanings.]

Attributes allow us to form classes, and these classes are often related one to another other as subclasses or superclasses; for example, the class of humans is a subclass of the class of animals. One of Reid's examples is the class hierarchy

Animal
Man
Frenchman
Parisian

The animal class can be identified by the possession of the being-an-animal attribute. The 'genus' of animal can then be subdivided as a class by the application of further attributes to produce the 'species' of man. Then man, considered itself as a genus, can then be further divided in a similar way to produce the species of Frenchman. And so on. Items belonging to classes lower down the hierarchy inherit all the attributes from the superclasses (so, for example, a Parisian inherits the attributes of Frenchman, and if one of those attributes is 'living in France' then a Parisian lives in France).

So, classification results in a compression and codification of knowledge and meaning

> It is by means of such extensive and comprehensive propositions that human knowledge is condensed, as it were, to a size suitable for the capacity of the human mind, adding greatly to its beauty without making it any less clear or any harder to absorb (Reid 1785, p. 193).

The classes, or the general words or labels for them, can be used either as subjects in sentences or propositions, or as predicates or straight attributes. So, for example, in 'A Parisian lives at the center of the cultural world' or 'A Parisian is French' the general word or general conception 'Parisian' is the subject of the sentences and the assertions are in terms of classes (or genus and species), and in 'Suzette is a Parisian' the 'is a Parisian' is a predicate being attributed to the individual person Suzette (who is an instance of the class or sort). So there is a kind of duality between the sort Parisian and the attribute 'is a Parisian' which generates it.

And, as Reid tells us, this ability to classify is possessed by almost everyone in every culture.

> Such divisions and subdivisions of things into genera and species, with general names, are not confined to learned and polished languages; they are found in the languages of the most primitive human tribes. This tells us that the invention and the use of general words, to signify both the attributes that things have and the genera and species that they fall into, is not a subtle invention of philosophers but rather an operation that all men perform by the light of common sense. (Reid 1785, p. 192)

## 2.2 Ontologies, Gerrymanders, Natural Kinds and Taxonomies

These relations between classes, mentioned by Reid, result usually either from the way our world is, or from decisions we make and formulate in language. This is addressed by *ontology* and related topics.

The word 'ontology' is used in traditional philosophy and it means 'what there is or what exists'. There is a modern use of 'ontology', within Computer Science and Artificial Intelligence, where it has a slightly different meaning and that is 'conceptual scheme' or 'conceptualization'. 'Ontology' also gets used in database design where it amounts to 'a description of the types or kinds of entities, and the properties or attributes, that are assumed to exist for the purposes of the database'.

These various uses of the word are not that different one from another and here it will be most useful to adopt a fairly modern style under which ontologies are generally small, local, and confined to particular areas or domains. So, as examples, if the focus of interest is with military personnel and armies, a suitable ontology might contain soldiers, ranks, squads, companies, brigades, divisions, weapons, and so forth; if the focus of interest is with cooking, an ontology might contain recipes, ingredients, proteins, flavoring, condiments, carbohydrates, fats, and so on.

There is an important distinction that can be made between ontologies that depend on us, depend on us humans, and those that do not. An ontology for the military of soldiers, ranks, squads, companies, etc. is a human creation. It is just conjured up to suit a purpose. It depends on us. It is *gerrymandered*. But not all ontologies are like this. There is a world we live in external to us, and there are things in that world, and things happening in that world. As examples, there are species of animals, such as tigers and lions and lizards, and there are chemical elements and compounds, such as hydrogen and oxygen and iron and rust. That there is a kind of animal that is a tiger does not depend on us, it has to do with the way the world is. Similarly, that there is the kind of substance iron, and a type of process in which some iron turns to rust over time, is a feature of the world. There is an evocative metaphorical phrase that comes into play here, and that is 'carving nature at its joints' (Hempel 1965). Nature is not a blooming buzzing confusion, on which we impose order; rather it consists of perfectly good things existing on their own, and going about their own business, without help from us. And if an ontology carves nature (or some of it) at its joints, the ontology fits what is there. An ontology that does this is an ontology of *natural kinds* for it deals with the kinds that are in nature (Reid calls these 'natural substances'). Rust is a natural kind, whereas a company of soldiers is not.

Natural kinds feature in the causal structure of the world. And gerrymandered kinds do not. Here is what John Stuart Mill had to say in 1843 about the gerrymandered kind of white objects, as contrasted with some of the natural kinds of biology and chemistry

> White things are not distinguished by any common properties, except whiteness; or if they are, it is only by such as are in some way connected with whiteness. But a hundred

generations have not exhausted the common properties of animals, of plants, of sulphur or
phosphorus; nor do we suppose them to be exhaustible, but proceed to new observations and
experiments, in the full confidence of discovering new properties, which were by no means
implied by those we previously knew (Mill 1843) quoted from (Koslicki 2008, p. 791)

These additional common properties come from the causal structure of the
world.

Of course, we do not have a direct infallible insight as to what it is in the world,
as to what the natural kind ontologies are. We have to do science, to conjecture,
and to propose theories to find out [see also (Haack 1999)]. For example, Mendeleev's 1869 familiar periodic table of chemical elements was a classification of
chemical elements; it was an elaborate catalog. Mendeleev suggested on the basis
of it that there were three missing elements that were yet to be discovered; and,
indeed, the elements gallium, scandium, and germanium were later discovered.
That this happened resulted from the fact that Mendeleev's classification in some
sense locked on to what is actually there in the world. And, to contrast with our
successes, there are plenty of examples where we have been mistaken. Prior to
Lavoisier, about 1770, *phlogiston* was supposed to be a chemical element; so early
eighteenth century chemical ontologies would have included phlogiston as a
natural kind; but Lavoisier showed that there was no such element as phlogiston,
hence the natural kind chemical ontology of the time needed revision. As Brian
Ellis phrases it

Every distinct kind of chemical substance would appear to be an example of a natural
kind, since the known kinds of chemical substances all exist independently of human
knowledge and understanding, and the distinctions between them are all real and absolute.
Of course, we could not have discovered the differences between the kinds of chemical
substances without a lot of scientific investigation. But these differences were not invented
by us, or chosen pragmatically to impose order on an otherwise amorphous mass of data.
There is not continuous spectrum of chemical variety that we had somehow to categorize.
The chemical world is just not like that. On the contrary, it gives every appearance of
being a world made up of substances of chemically discrete kinds, each with its own
distinctive chemical properties. To suppose otherwise is to make nonsense of the whole
history of chemistry since Lavoisier. (Ellis 2008, p. 140)

[See also (Smith 2004).]

Another label for a natural kind hierarchical ontology is a 'taxonomy' (clas-
sically, 'taxonomy' means 'arrangement by law', the ancient Greek 'taxis' is
'arrangement' and 'nomos' is 'law'). The notion of natural kinds, or natural kind
ontologies, can be extended from the empirical world to mathematics and logic.
Mathematical entities typically have many properties that are not of our creation.

In a sense there is a third possibility between natural kinds and gerrymanders,
and that is *conventional* or *constructed* ontologies. And these are *structured gerrymanders*. For example, in knowledge representation—a discipline of interest to
Artificial Intelligence, to Database design and to Information Retrieval—the use of
ontologies, especially taxonomies is widespread. A typical problem here might be
how to model or represent Human or Employee Resources for a large company,
and data of interest might include who the employees are, their salaries, their

qualifications, whether they are full or part-time, what their benefits are, and so on. And a suitable representational scheme might use a hierarchical taxonomy where every item is an employee, but then a subtype of these are full-time, another subtype part-time, and so on. Such a taxonomy is not a natural kind ontology—it is not a feature of the world we live in that part-time employees work less than, say, 25 h a week. The Database designers, with input from the company, simply decided that. The ontology is a human construction. It is a gerrymander. However, there is a lot more to it than there is to Mill's collection of white things. It has structure, and although it is a creation of humans, humans might not be immediately aware of all the properties and features is has. And it can be used for inference. For example, learning that John Smith is a full-time employee may well permit an inference to what his benefits are. And it could be that no one knows what John Smith's benefits are prior to this inference being made—knowledge is acquired from the ontology in conjunction with facts about the world.

When representing knowledge or information, a distinction might be made between items of knowledge that are specific or particular and items which are generalizations or are conventional or natural laws. So, that John Smith is a full-time employee is an item of information that is specific, that all full-time employees receive benefits is an item of information that is a generalization of convention. One system of organization puts the items of information that are specific into a database or similar structure, and the items of information that are general into an ontology or classification scheme. Then the classification scheme can be used with the facts to make further inferences. This approach can be used either with natural kind ontologies or with structured gerrymandered ontologies.

Reid alerted us to the advantage of using classification to compress human knowledge (that it allows us to absorb and retain that knowledge). But for this to happen the classifications need to be correct, or true, or realistic. The classifications must constitute knowledge. This is exactly the advantage and importance of natural kind ontologies. They are realistic, and they do embody knowledge about the world we live in.

## 2.3 Concrete Objects and Abstractions

There is a important distinction to be made between 'concrete' and 'abstract'. Many things are physical and concrete, that is, they are located in space and time. Consider diamonds, those forever gemstones. The Hope Diamond is a physical thing, and, at any particular time, it is in a particular place (usually the Smithsonian Museum in Washington). But things can also be abstract. Jane Austen's novel *Pride and Prejudice* certainly exists embodied in many concrete physical forms (as the actual manuscript she wrote, as the physical book in the local public library, etc.). But when a high school class reads *Pride and Prejudice*, as part of their syllabus and studies, they all read the same novel or book, namely *Pride and Prejudice*, but they very likely will be physically reading different physical concrete copies, because each pupil will have his or her own copy. The 'same' book that they read is an abstraction.

It will be useful for us to spend a moment or two on the nature of concrete objects and abstractions and the distinction between the two.

The ancient Greeks drew a different twofold distinction among existing entities viz., a distinction between physical entities and mental entities. So papyrus copies of *Goatherd and the Palace Guards* were physical, but the novel itself, as discussed at dinner parties in ancient Greece, was, or would have been considered to be, mental or a mental idea (i.e. existing among the contents of someone's consciousness or mind or, perhaps, in many peoples' minds).

That, more or less, would have been the received philosophical view for 2000 years until the work of the late nineteenth century German philosopher, Gottlob Frege. Frege was not content with the twofold distinction between the physical and the mental, because, in this context, the 'mental' simply would not do the work it was supposed to. When, at that ancient Greek dinner, Aesop and Agatha were discussing *Goatherd and the Palace Guards*, they certainly would have thought that they were discussing the *same* thing. But if that thing was a mental idea, or just a mental idea, whose idea was it? Were they discussing Aesop's mental consciousness? Or were they discussing Agatha's mental consciousness? Or what? Clearly, what they were discussing was indeed the same thing, but it was not either of their individual mental consciousnesses; rather it was something that was common to those consciousnesses, it was what those consciousnesses were *of* or *about* (i.e. in this case, *Goatherd and the Palace Guards*), it was the content of those consciousnesses. Just as separate papyri can be instances relating *Goatherd and the Palace Guards* so too can separate psychological states share the commonality of referring to or depicting, in part, *Goatherd and the Palace Guards*. Frege invoked a 'third realm'. And that third realm consisted of abstractions (which were not mental or psychological ideas). Frege's view was later taken up by others; for example, the twentieth century philosopher Karl Popper distinguished between three worlds: the physical world, the mental world, and the world of abstract contents (Popper 1972). We also will use this same threefold distinction, but our focus will be with the abstract and the concrete (the notion of mental or psychological phenomena is worthy of considerable study and research, but it is not one of the topics of this book).

How is the concrete to be distinguished from the abstract? The concrete is located in space and in time; at a particular time, concrete items are in particular locations (as we noted earlier, on April 17, 2010, the Hope Diamond is some definite place, perhaps in the Smithsonian Museum). Concrete items are also causally efficacious; that is: they can be the causes of effects on other items, and other items can be the causes of effects on them; a 'concrete' physical copy of *Pride and Prejudice* can be dropped and it can knock over a cup of tea, and, in turn, the spilled tea can stain the pages of the copy of the book. In contrast, the abstract work *Pride and Prejudice* (which the High School class read) has no definite physical location, it is nowhere in particular, and it is not causally efficacious, it cannot knock over cups of tea nor can its pages be stained. In most of the cases we will be interested in, abstractions can be exemplified in concrete objects. The abstract *Pride and Prejudice* has many concrete books and volumes that exemplify, or instantiate, it.

Returning for one moment to Reid, the child and toys. The individual toys are concrete and physical; but the attribute 'being a toy' is not concrete and physical, it—the attribute that is—is an abstraction. The attribute 'being a toy' does not exist in space and time and it cannot be causally efficacious. Reid counsels us that there is nothing mysterious here: the abstraction 'being a toy' exists in the sense that it is capable of being instantiated by the individual toys.

> When we ascribe existence to [abstractions], it is not existence *in time or place* but existence *in some individual subject*; and all that *this* existence means is that they are truly attributes of such a subject. Their existence is merely predicability, i.e. the capacity to be attributed to a subject. The name 'predicables' that was given them in ancient philosophy is the one that best expresses their nature. (Reid 1785, p. 210)

Abstractions exist as possibilities (the possibility of being instantiated).

## 2.4 Entities, Properties and Statements

As language users, we have a way of viewing the world that is going to pervade the present work, it is going to reveal itself in how we think, in how we talk, in how we classify, in how we analyze logically, and in other places besides. Let us be explicit about it.

In broad terms, we see, and talk about, the world as though it consists of two kinds of items. There are *entities* (which are things, or objects, or individuals, or events, or processes), thus in the world, there are trees, tables, cars, people, clouds, rugby games, etc. We certainly can talk about these in language, and when we do so we use *nouns* or *noun phrases* to do so. And the second kind of item is true or false *statements* or *propositions*. One way statements arise is when we ascribe properties to the things. We might say, or think, or envisage, or know, or believe, that a particular tree is green or that people are kind or that the rugby final was exciting. Our ascriptions of properties to things constitute, or result in, statements or propositions. And when we talk about true or false statements or propositions in language, we use *sentences* to do so.

As hinted above, there is some 'mortar' or 'construction material' that allows entities to take part in statements: we described it as being 'the ascription of properties to the things'. So, for example, we start with the rugby final and apply the 'was exciting' paste or paint to it and get an ascription or statement (that the rugby final was exciting). This glue transformation step is paralleled in language. There are nouns or noun phrases, and we apply to these the glue of verbs, or the copula 'is', often mediated by adverbs or adjectives, or other complexities, and sentences are result.

Michel Foucault (1970) used to talk about 'the theory of the verb', and of noun and verb. Primitives can utter sounds, 'cat', 'tree', 'man' and mean thereby some of the entities immediately to hand ('mean' in the sense of 'designate' or 'refer to' or 'draw attention to'). These noise nouns give us some of the things in the present.

But once verbs are added, for example, the verb 'springs' to form 'the cat springs', affirmation is possible, and statements and propositions result. Adding the copula 'is', tenses, adjectives, adverbs, determiners, nouns, etc. to the verbs allows the propositions to be richer. But the overall conceptualization is still: things and property, or function, 'mortar', yield statements.

The Greek philosophers discussed substances (the things) and properties that the substances might have, and the resulting combinations, in thought or expression, of substances with properties, or subjects with predicates, were the statements or assertions or propositions. This basic distinction, and combination of the distinct kinds, is seen nowadays in many theories. Categorical and Generative Grammars of natural languages use it (Heim and Kratzer 1998; Partee et al. 1990). And in First Order Symbolic logic, to be visited later, there are just two kinds of basic expressions: 'terms', which name things, and 'formulas or well-formed-formulas', which are the logical representation, or names, of statements.

George Bealer describes this

> What function does the subject/predicate distinction have? First, in speech the distinction shows up as follows. A subject expression is the kind of expression that functions to identify a thing about which something is to be said. A predicate expression, by contrast, functions to say something about things so identified. ...subjects fix the subject matter, and predicates (verbs) do the saying. Secondly, the subject/predicate distinction plays a role in syntax.... The definition of [an atomic] sentence is roughly this: subjects combine with predicates to form sentences.... Thirdly, the subject/predicate distinction plays the role in the construction of a natural economical semantics that tallies with the intuitive concept of meaning. (Bealer 1982, p. 86)

As we have just seen in the previous section, entities might be concrete or abstract. Within this classification, statements themselves are abstract, they do not have location. When a gardener asserts that the tree in the garden is green, he may say or write sentences to that effect on many different occasions—all of those sentences or utterances are concrete. But what he asserts—that the tree is green—is abstract. Of course, we can treat the assertions or statements as things, then they would be abstract things, and we can make further statements about them. We regularly do that. Imagine a court of law. When the accused protests that the insinuations of a witness are false, the accused is treating statements as things and then making further statements about those statements.

The distinction between entity and statement has immediate application in librarianship as it underpins the distinction between the retrieval of documents and the retrieval of information. A document is an entity, (usually a concrete entity); information is, or consists of, one or more statements (and they are abstract).

## 2.5  The Triangle of Meaning

Another distinction that will be useful is that arising from the 'Triangle of Meaning' (Fig. 2.1). The 'Triangle of Meaning' is a phrase originating with Ogden and Richards *The Meaning of Meaning* in the 1920s (Ogden and Richards 1972).

**Fig. 2.1** The triangle of meaning

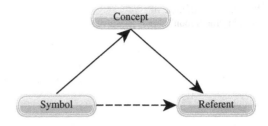

Shiyali Ranganathan (1937, p. 327), the pre-eminent modern theorist of librarianship, also used the distinction in 1937; he called the Symbol Vertex the 'verbal plane' and the Concept Vertex the 'idea plane'. Actually, the distinction goes back at least to Aristotle (*De Interpretatione*) and it was discussed by the aforementioned early twentieth century German philosopher Frege (Tichy 1988).

Consider written or spoken words; for example, the word 'moon'. What does 'moon' mean? The word 'moon' does not and cannot mean that actual physical object in the night sky, for the following reason. Suppose the moon disappeared or was destroyed (perhaps one of those NASA water seeking rockets blows it up). If the word 'moon' meant that physical object, then, when the physical object disappeared, the meaning of 'moon' would disappear as well; the word 'moon' would not have a meaning. That is obviously wrong. The word 'moon' would still have a meaning; it is just that the word would not refer to anything if there were no moon. We see much the same with words like 'unicorn'; 'unicorn' is a perfectly good word, and it has a perfectly good meaning; even though no unicorns exist.

To understand what 'moon' means, we need the notion of a concept (Fig. 2.2). The Triangle of Meaning makes distinctions, first between a concept and an expression or symbol or sign that names or identifies the concept, and then between the concept and the things it applies to or refers to. So, there might be the word 'horse', the concept of horse, and those particular delightful creatures which fall under that concept, for example, Secretariat, Sea Biscuit, Little Sorel, Trigger, Silver, Black Beauty, etc. The terminology commonly used here is: a property, like being a horse, is an *intension* or *connotation*, and those things in the world which satisfy a property, the horses, say, form the *extension* or *denotation* of that property.

So, what is a concept? In this context, the word 'concept' gets used in pretty well the same way as in ordinary speech and life, and that amounts roughly to 'general notion' or 'general idea' or even 'meaning'. Many describe concepts as being mental or mental constructions; however, we regard them as abstractions or abstract objects (in the standard Fregean third realm).

A concept can have, and, in fact, usually does have, more than one word or phrase that names it. That occurs in the case of *synonyms*. The words 'butterfly' and 'rhopalocera' are synonyms, they have the same meaning—they are different words but they identify the same underlying concept. It also occurs with translations across languages; the French 'papillon', Japanese 'choo choo', German 'schmetterling', Welsh 'pili pala' are also all words or phrases that identify the butterfly-concept.

**Fig. 2.2** The triangle of
meaning for 'moon'

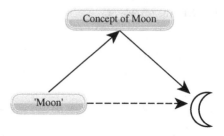

Also, and also unfortunately, some words for concepts are *homographs*. An
individual homograph, on its own, is ambiguous in that it can name different
concepts. Consider the word 'bank'. It is a homograph. There is

'bank', the noun, meaning 'the place that looks after money'
'bank', the noun, meaning 'the place at the side of a river'
'bank', the verb, meaning 'to lean over'
'bank', the verb, meaning 'to rely upon'
etc.

So, there are banks to rivers, banks with cash in them, and banks that airplane
aerobatics teams do. The one label 'bank' is being used to label three or more
entirely different concepts.

Two different concepts, two different intensions, can have the same extension
(when this occurs, that they have the same extension does not mean that they are
the same concept). Imagine this. Say everything in our world that was red was also
round, and also that everything that was round was red. So there are two concepts
here 'red' and 'round', and the red things are {a, b, c, etc. say} and the round
things are also {a, b, c, etc. say}. But red is a color, and round is a shape, and it just
so happens that in our world their extensions are the same.

How do we apply an intension to get the extension? How do we determine just
what a particular intension is? These are not easy questions to answer. It is not
even easy to understand quite what is being sought. Are we doing logic here? Or
psychology? Or methodology? Certainly, even young children can apply simple
and basic concepts pretty well. Then the interest becomes how is a person to
manage with learning and applying a new and unfamiliar concept, say the concept
of a rose. There are theories [including Rosch's Prototype Theory and the Classical
Theory of Categories (Rosch 1973, 1975, 1978; Rosch and Mervis 1975; Rosch
et al. 1976; Jacob 2004; Taylor 2004)]. We will just take it as an unanalyzed datum
that we can work with concepts and their intensions and extensions.

A point to be aware of is that the Symbol Vertex is relatively accessible to
computers, and that is where the strengths of computers lie. In contrast, the
Concept Vertex plays to the abilities and strengths of human beings. So, for
example, if we are analyzing a book, questions like, how many words are there in
the book?, how many occurrence are there of the word 'dog'?, and how many
concordances are there of the words 'dog' and 'owner' in the same paragraphs? are

all Symbol Vertex questions and are trivial for computers to answer. In contrast, a question like 'Is the book about betrayal and unrequited love?' is a Concept Vertex question (in particular, it is certainly *not* asking whether the words 'betrayal', 'unrequited', and 'love' occur in the book). Humans can answer it, but here computers are in the realm of guesswork.

What we will find is that the important questions of information organization and retrieval involve the Concept Vertex. They need humans if they are to be answered. But the volume of information is such that humans cannot keep up with organizational questions and tasks. Thus the global task for organization of information is to try to get computers to do a task which they are not well suited for doing.

## 2.6  Identifier Mappings

We have an interest in the relationship between names, labels, or identifiers and those items that the identifiers identify. We saw with the Triangle of Meaning the issue of synonyms and homographs. With synonyms, several different labels pick out the same concept, so the relationship between synonyms and their concepts is many-to-one. With homographs, the same label names several different concepts, so the relationship between the name and the items named is one-to-many. And, for the third category, there are nouns which are neither synonyms nor homographs, and the relation between them and the concepts they name is one-to-one.

The many-to-one mapping kind is common in information retrieval. We see it with aliases, pen-names, and the like. The author Samuel Clemens wrote under the pen-name of Mark Twain; so the names Samuel Clemens and Mark Twain each named exactly one person, indeed the same person, but the person that they named had, so-to-speak, two, or maybe more, names. There are also what might be characterized as spelling variations of the same name. Works in the Library of Congress have about 50 versions of the name for the 2011 President of Libya, including

Qaddafi, Muammar
Gadhafi, Mo ammar
Kaddafi, Muammar
Qadhafi, Muammar
El Kadhafi, Moammar

[See (Mann 1993, p. 26).] The familiar URLs (Uniform Resource Locators) on the Web, for example,

http://www.msn.com

are a many-to-one scheme. It could be, and often is, the case that two different URLs name the same page. Moreover, it is often desirable to do exactly that. 'www.msn.com' is the address for the home page of MSN (News). But MSN will have bought a number of similar names, including perhaps 'www.msn.org' and use all of them as names of that same home page. The reason is that Users might not know the exact address and so MSN wants to help them with close variants. (There are also other good reasons for allowing many-to-one naming. For example, different contexts, that is different audiences, experts as contrasted with children, or different languages, French or English, may invite the use of different names for the same page or resource such as a list of addresses and phone numbers.)

We are going to assume the every Information Object (IO) has, or can be given, at least one name or identifier that uniquely identifies it. So, conceptually, there is IO #1, IO #2, IO # 3 etc. This assumption lets us know which IO we are talking about. We know this assumption can be met. There is a generalization of the URL naming system and that is the URI (Uniform Resource Identifier) naming system— the generalization is that URIs are suitable for naming anything, any 'resource' (and anything includes web pages). There are enough URIs for all resources. URI naming is many-to-one. (There is a subtlety that should be mentioned. An URL names a web page or file, and web pages can change. For example, the URL http://www.msn.com is a news page and likely yesterday's news is different from today's. So URLs are naming 'containers' yet we may have reason to name 'content' so that yesterday's news is a different IO to the IO which is today's news. There are complementary naming schemes to the URI system, such as Digital Object Identifiers (DOIs) and the Handle System, which can do exactly this. So all IOs, containers and content, can have their own names, as assumed.)

At a theoretical level, one-to-one schemes seem the cleanest and most incisive. But, actually, for the purpose of naming IOs, many-to-one schemes seem more useful and more in tune with practical reality.

With IOs, there is always the question of granularity or what constitutes a 'documentary unit' (Anderson 1997). For some purposes, a book as a whole might be an IO, for other purposes, Chapters, Sections, Pages, Paragraphs, and even Sentences, in that very same book might all be IOs. However, whatever the IOs are, we are going to assume we have names for them, that we can identify them.

(Even one-to-many schemes can have their uses, though perhaps not in information retrieval. There is the apocryphal senior academic who was proud of the fact that he knew and remembered the names of all the students that he had taught during his long career of 40 years or more—all the male students were 'Mate' and the females 'Honey'.)

## 2.7 Graph Theory

Graph theory will be useful both for discussing the links and structure that underlie the World Wide Web (and citation webs) and for providing the theoretical basis for trees and hierarchies which are the foundations of classification systems. They also can be used, in a tricked out way, via Resource Description Framework (RDF), for representing statements in logic, and then using those statements in the Web, particularly the Semantic Web.

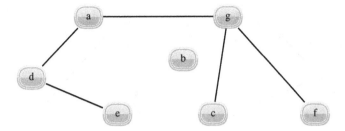

**Fig. 2.3**  An example of a graph

**Fig. 2.4**  Two visually
different presentations of the
same underlying graph

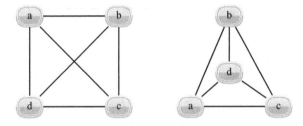

Graphs consist of two things: nodes (other words for these: 'vertices', 'points')
and links (other words for these: 'edges', 'lines', 'ties'). In applications, nodes
typically model individual people, countries, businesses, web pages, genes, amino
acids, etc. Links typically model friendships, web hyperlinks, telephone lines,
communications, etc. A node can be thought of as being a dot or a point, and a link
as being a line or an edge which runs from a node to a node. So here is a graph
(Fig. 2.3).

The *size* of a graph is the number of nodes in it. This graph is of size 7. Graphs can
have the same size but different link structure. The graphs of interest to us will all be
*finite* graphs; at most they will have finitely many nodes in them. The *degree* of a
node is the number of links that connect to it. So, in the example, three of the nodes
have degree 1, but nodes a and d have degree 2, g has degree 3, and b degree 0.

How the links are drawn is irrelevant (they can be drawn as curves or straight
lines, and the links can cross each other without that meaning anything), and where
the nodes are located is also irrelevant—all that matters is which nodes are connected by which links. These two graphs are actually the same graph (Fig. 2.4).

A *walk* is an alternating sequence of nodes and links, which starts and ends with
a node. So, in first example graph, a->e->b is a walk. A *path* is a walk with no
repeated nodes. The *length* of a walk is the number of links included in it. Two
nodes are *adjacent* if there is a link between them. A graph has a *cycle*, or is *cyclic*,
if there is a walk of non-zero length that starts and ends on the same node
(otherwise the graph is said to be *acyclic*). A graph is *connected* if there is a path
between every two nodes in it. The example graph is connected.

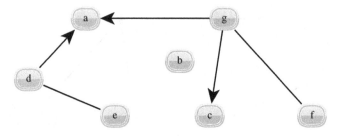

**Fig. 2.5** An example graph with some directed links and some links which are not directed

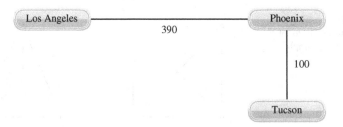

**Fig. 2.6** A schematic road map shown as a fragment of a labeled graph

**Fig. 2.7** An example graph
which is labeled and directed

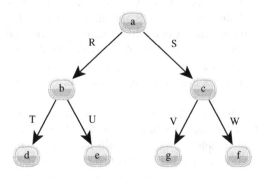

Links can be *directed*. The following graph has some directed links (from d to a, from g to a, and from g to c—shown by arrows) and some links which are not directed (Fig. 2.5). Having directed links invites an update of some of the notions. *Indegree* is the number of links coming into a node and *outdegree* is the number of links going out. And the notions of path and walk can also be revised depending on whether the traveling is required to follow the direction of the links. Then, for example, a graph would have a *directed cycle* if there is a walk of non-zero length that starts and ends on the same node and which follows the direction of the links.

Links can also be *labeled*. This just means that the links have labels on them. This is useful, for example, with schematic road maps. The labels could represent the distances between the places that are the nodes on the graph (Fig. 2.6).

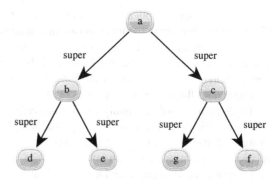

**Fig. 2.8** A labeled directed graph depicting a organization chart

## 2.7.1 Triple Stores

Of particular interest to us will be graphs that are both directed and labeled. Here is a generic diagram (Fig. 2.7). This might be a fragment of an 'org chart (organization chart)' in an institution. In which case, the labels might all be the same, and they might represent the 'supervises' relation. Thus (Fig. 2.8). There is flexibility here over what a labeled directed graph can do (pretty well everything!).

There are many ways of encoding graphs into computers—the use of matrices is common and widespread. But of particular interest to us are *triple stores*. One way of representing two nodes and a labeled directed link between them, is just to write it as an ordered triple;

&lt;firstnode, label, secondnode&gt;

so &lt;a, super, b&gt; represents the top left supervision labeled link. Then the entire of the above org chart is

&lt;a, super, b&gt;,
&lt;b, super, d&gt;,
&lt;b, super, e&gt;,
&lt;a, super, c&gt;,
&lt;c, super, f&gt;,
&lt;f, super, g&gt;

This is a *triple store*. Its contents are triples, and they represent an ordered labeled graph. The order of items within a triple matters, &lt;a, super, b&gt; is different from &lt;b, super, a&gt;. But the order of the triples themselves within the store does not matter, it is irrelevant. For example,

&lt;c, super, f&gt;,
&lt;b, super, d&gt;,
&lt;b, super, e&gt;,
&lt;a, super, b&gt;,
&lt;a, super, c&gt;,
&lt;f, super, g&gt;

is the same graph. Duplicate triples are also irrelevant and extra ones should be discarded (within graph theory, you can have a labeled link between nodes, but not a second identical labeled link between the same two nodes). In the general case, a graph can have nodes that have no links to or from them (this is not common in our applications). A triple store would need to make an ad hoc convention to accommodate these (say <a, noLinks, a>).

Triple stores would probably not ordinarily be used if the label or relation was absolutely identical throughout the graph, simply because pairs could be used instead of triples. Usually a triple store, and its graph, would have a mix of relations. For example, with an investigation of communication channels within an organization there might be an interest both in who supervised whom and who was friends with whom (Fig. 2.9).

And that would be

<c, super, f>,
<b, super, d>,
<b, super, e>,
<a, super, b>,
<a, super, c>,
<f, super, g>,
<a, friend, d>,
<b, friend, c>,
<d, friend, e>,
<e, friend, d>

For every labeled directed graph there is a triple store that captures it entirely. But also this can be used the other way around. If there is some data from elsewhere that is in the form of a triple store [and all data can be cast that way] that triple store can be regarded as a generator of a directed labeled graph.

A number of large triple stores have been implemented (W3C 2010); for example, *Open Link Virtuoso*, 2010, a single triple store, contains more than 15 billion triples.

## 2.8 Elementary Data Structures and Their Algorithms

One field of study in Computer Science is Data Structures, or Abstract Data Structures. In this, certain mathematical structures (lists, stacks, arrays, queues, deques, trees, and others) are defined in terms of objects and operations on those objects. The operations typically include inserting, deleting, updating or retrieving the objects to and from the relevant data structures. Then the computer science discussion moves to algorithms, and languages, to support the structures and operations. This has proved to be a particularly fruitful style of analysis. The abstract data structures are set at a level above the implementing algorithms and computer programming languages. They are a commonality that ranges across many working implementations and programs.

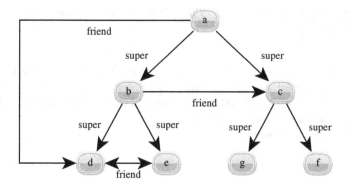

**Fig. 2.9** A labeled directed graph depicting both supervision and friendship relations

Something similar will prove useful here. We too are interested in certain Abstract Data Structures. But for us the operations to focus on generally are not those of inserting, deleting and updating objects, rather they are often to do with accessing the objects in the data structures. Now, 'accessing' an object may simply be looking at it, so that presupposes a displayed instantiation or implementation of the abstract data structure. 'Accessing' may be a little more complicated than plain looking, it may require a fancy front-end or a retrieval tool or the right moves on the part of a human agent. Access is partly to do with the structures, partly to do with algorithms and partly to do with human cognitive abilities.

## 2.8.1 Lists and Strings

We are all familiar with lists (shopping lists, bullet point lists, numbered item lists in html and web pages etc.). Considered in the abstract, a list is a sequence, or total order, of items, where the items have a position (first item, second item, and so on; and each item, except the first and last, has a previous or predecessor item and a next or successor item).

There are differences in the convenience of manipulations between human produced lists, say a written list on a sheet of paper, and lists within computers. With a human list, it is easy to grow it by writing items on the end; it is not so easy to shrink it by taking items out (but that can be done by erasing items or striking through them); it is especially difficult to insert into the middle of a list, for that requires either squeezing items in or leaving gaps in the initial list to take the few new items (and that needs guesses as to where the gaps should be). With lists within a computer, growing, shrinking, and insertion anywhere are readily available.

As a special example of a list: lists—or sequences—of characters are known as 'strings' of characters so ordinary words like 'Hello' and 'today' are regarded as strings, as are nonsense strings like 'bod!12H'.

## 2.8.2 The Alphabetical List: The 'Wheel' of Information Retrieval

A list of words or strings, ordered, or sorted, alphabetically (i.e. in so-called 'filing order') has wonderful properties. What can be done with alphabetical lists by humans is truly astonishing [And all of us would be indeed be astonished, but for the fact that we are so familiar with it.]

Say we have list of words,

Banana,
Cabbage,
Apple,
Cauliflower,
Date,
…

And we are interested in whether a supplied word, or key, say 'Plum' is in the list. There are really only two ways to find out; to start at the beginning and look through the list forward, or to start at the end and look through the list backward. How well we will do with this will depend on how large the list is, and where 'Plum' is (if, indeed, it is there at all). The list certainly has an order, 'Banana' is first, 'Cabbage' second, and so on; but the order it has is independent of the values or the words taking those positions (i.e. 'Plum') could be anywhere.

Consider now the same words, but in an alphabetical list.

Apple,
Banana,
Cabbage,
Cauliflower,
Date, …

and the same problem of finding 'Plum'. This time, we do not have to start at the beginning or end and do a total comprehensive search. Instead we can jump in the middle somewhere and, with a quick scan back and forth, find 'Plum' if it is there. The list has an order, 'Apple' is first, 'Banana' second, and so on; and the *absolute* position an item has is still independent of the values of the words taking those positions (i.e. 'Plum') could be anywhere. But the *relative* positions of entries *does* depend on the values of the items 'Plum' is always going to appear later than 'Cabbage' and earlier than 'Quince', if all those words are there. And that relative position feature makes all the difference.

For retrieval, an alphabetical list of words is something special. Imagine paper copy volumes of a New York telephone book of 7 million entries. If the names in the book are in alphabetical order, even a child can do name retrieval in moments. If the names in it are there in random order, basically they are not findable by ordinary human search.

Alphabetical order is magic, as Sherman Kuhn phrases it,

ALPHABETIZATION seems as indispensable to twentieth century life as the wheel; and, like the wheel, it was invented by some unknown genius of remote antiquity, who probably never realized the importance of his gift to mankind. Today, libraries, telephone communications, much of commerce and industry, even the lower levels of government, would be paralyzed if the art of alphabetization, and the tools which it has produced, were suddenly lost. (Kuhn 1972, p. 300)

Historically, lists of words in alphabetical order were slow to appear. There are three reasons for this: it was unclear what alphabetical order itself actually was; second, until the advent of association lists, there was no imperative to produce alphabetical lists; and, finally, it is hard to produce such lists by hand, without physical paper, or something similar, being readily available. Alphabets themselves, and alphabetical order on words were often ill-defined. In many of the alphabets of history, new letters appeared, old letters disappeared, and the order was sometimes changed (although change of order was not common). Then, even if alphabetical order by the first letters of words was understood, that this needed to be used in conjunction with alphabetical order on the second, third, and further letters of the words (to produce a total order in the list itself) was just beyond comprehension. Also, the need for alphabetical lists was unclear. What really shows the advantages of alphabetical lists are 'association lists' (to be discussed shortly) and historically these are tied to indexes, which are also relatively recent. Indexes themselves are connected with pagination of printed books, and printed books are the outcome of the Gutenberg's printing press, circa 1450CE. Finally, actually producing an alphabetical list is difficult. Say you were given a random list of a 100 words, written on a page, and asked to produce a list of the same words that was in alphabetical order. How would you do it? You could scan through, find what you thought was the first alphabetical entry, write that down in a new list, cross it out of the old list, and repeat another 99 times. That technique would be error prone. It might work for a hundred words, but it would be under stress for a 1000 words. The right way to do this by hand is to write each of the words on its own separate piece of paper or card, and then sort those cards by your favorite sorting method [quicksort, bubble sort etc. (Sedgewick 1988)] then write the result of the sorted cards back to another sheet of paper. But paper itself (i.e. cheap and plentiful material to write on) was not produced mechanically until about 1200 (and not that many people could write). So, the technique of writing onto cards and sorting those cards was not really even a possibility until the fourteenth century or so. [By 1545, Conrad Gessner was able to describe a cut-and-paste technique in his *Bibliotheca Universalis* (Wellisch 1981; Blair 2003).] It would have been easy to produce short alphabetical lists, say with 5 or 10 entries, but short alphabetical lists do not really have any advantages over short random lists, for they are both easily scanned and accessed by eye. Shermann Kuhn describes early efforts

There is no steady advance from no alphabetization to first letter to second and on to full alphabetization. Glossaries organized by categories appear side by side in time with glossaries in some type of alphabetic order, and chronological ledgers and records side by side with ones which are in alphabetic order or no order at all. Full alphabetization is discovered, then abandoned for simpler systems, recovered or rediscovered, abandoned again, recovered again (Kuhn 1972, p. 302).

In sum, it took until about 1300CE before people were aware of what it was to put a list of words into alphabetical order (Daly 1967), and it is not until 17-1800CE that such lists are common.

### 2.8.3 Association Lists

An association list contains pairs of items, not single items. It consists of a list of key-value pairs, so, for example, it might consist of

Smith 471,
Jones 134,
Mercy 32,
etc.

The 'Smith', 'Jones', 'Mercy', are the *keys*, and '471', '134', '32', the *values*. And, conceptually and algorithmically, the list is required to have the ability to return the value of a key-value pair when it is supplied with the key. So, asking the question '(value of) Jones?' should result in '134'. To do this, each of the keys needs to be unique (i.e. 'Jones' cannot be there more than once because then the relevant value for the key 'Jones' might be ambiguous). (Well, there is a slight qualification to this. Most implementations of association lists do permit duplicate entries. However, the retrieval algorithm is designed to scan the list in order from the beginning and to return the *first* value encountered for any particular input key. And 'first' is unique. Essentially the duplicate entries are junk on the end.) That the keys need to be unique means that any homographs should be disambiguated if there is any plan to use them as keys; so, instead of having two keys with the value 'bank', there should be one key perhaps with the value 'bank (money)' and another with the value 'bank (river)'.

An association list can be thought of as a table with two columns (provided it is remembered that the keys in the key column have to be different one from another so that they can act as unique identifiers).

Within the theory of Data Structures, association lists are not usually deemed to have any order—particular key-value pairs can be anywhere in the list. But, for us, it is valuable to think of a certain class of association lists as being *sorted association lists*. Of particular significance are ordered association lists where the list is sorted alphabetically by key, thus

Jones 134,
Mercy 32,
Smith 471.

And this give us the familiar book indexes. So, for example, the index fragment

absurdity, rule of 137
accessibility relation 166

adequate: for truth-functional logic 44;
       sets of connectives vii, 44ff
algorithm 17
alpha ($\alpha$) sentence 49
alternative denial 44
ancestral trees vii, 6, 33ff.

is just a sorted association list. Another point worth remarking on is that the values in a book index are really pointers or references or directions to what is wanted. For example, in the above index fragment 'algorithm' has the value 17, but it is not really the number 17 that you are after, rather it is a particular page in the book, page 17 in fact, and the 17 is just a stepping stone to get there. The alphabetical Index is a microscope into the text itself. Other alphabetical association lists include telephone directories, library catalogs, the standard bureaucratic 'papered' office with its filing cabinets, and so forth. It is hard to over emphasize the importance of the alphabetical list and the alphabetical association list.

Alphabetical, or filing, order is certainly not the only useful order that can be used with ordered association lists. There are other possibilities. For example, a 'To do' list might usefully be produced with the entries in the order that the tasks have to be done, similarly for Schedules and Agendas. Day Planners would be in the order of the days; TV Guides would be in temporal order (although a second index of programs, inverted, and in alphabetical order, would help in finding, say, when Bonanza was on without having to search the time slots). Lists of finishers in Olympic events, or Marathons, would often need to be in the order the participants finish, not in alphabetical order (although to find where a particular competitor finished among the 35,000 participants in the Chicago Marathon a supplementary alphabetical index would be a distinct help). Often computers return lists in order of relevance or importance—that ordering can be valuable too.

### 2.8.4 Filing Order and Key Syntax

Alphabetical order is often known as 'filing order' (for obvious reasons). Actually defining a filing order requires some decisions, discipline and conventions. With a computer, there will an order defined on each character in the available character set in the programming language; so, for example, 'a' will come before 'b'; and this total order applies to every character including all the punctuation and special characters. Unicode ('... the most widely adopted software standard in the world...') has a representation for 107,000 characters, which basically amounts to most every character in most every language, and it defines a total order for those characters (Unicode 1991–2010). This means that 'alphabetical order' is immediately available for all strings i.e. for all words (for example, place all strings of length one before all strings of length two etc. then order strings of the same length by character comparison of characters in the same position in the different strings). So, this is trivial and uninteresting intellectually.

Outside a computer, the task is more challenging. The reason is: the order needs to meet the expectations of the human Users. For example, the computer order of the last paragraph could produce an ordered list like

A,
B,
Ab.

And nobody would expect that as an alphabetical order (for example, in a phone book). They would be expecting all the A strings together, all the B strings together and so on. Thus

A,
Ab,
B.

Of course, computers do not have to produce the original computer 'internal' order that was described. But the programmers writing the software need to know what is wanted.

So, what do, or should, users expect? Actually, there are different schemes and different books of rules for those schemes. Here are some of the choices.

The main decision is: word-by-word or letter-by-letter. What turns on this is, for example, whether 'New York' files before 'Newark' or after it. Word-by-word is the more common and that would place 'New York' before 'Newark'. Letter-by-letter places 'New York' after 'Newark'. Here is some explanation. The blank character or space ' ' is a character like any other. So the string 'New York' is actually the string 'New' followed by the blank character, followed by the string 'York'. In word-by-word order, the blank character is left in, and the blank character is considered to come early in the alphabet, in fact, before any of the other real writable or printable letters. So, when 'New York' is compared with 'Newark' letter-by-letter left to right, they are the same for 'N', 'e', 'w' but then blank is compared with 'a' and blank comes earlier, so 'New York' files before 'Newark'. Letter-by-letter is different. For the purposes of this comparison, the blanks or spaces are discarded completely, so what gets compared is 'NewYork' (note, no space) and 'Newark' and this time the fourth letter 'Y' comes after 'a' and so the order is 'Newark' before 'New York'. Similar considerations occur for hyphens and some other punctuation (e.g. how to fit 'New-York' in). Generally word-by-word order is the conventionally preferred form. There is an argument in favor of letter-by-letter order. Compound nouns from double stems can often be written as one word, as two words, or as a hyphenated word ('particle board', 'particle-board', and 'particleboard'). If all three forms ended up in the same index, dictionary, or file, then letter-by-letter order would put them next to each other (which is what you would want), word-by-word order would scatter them (which is what you do not want).

Word-by-word has one terrific advantage—if employed intelligently it can be used to give fine structure to the alphabetical lists or alphabetical association lists, that is: it can help determine where the key, or key-value pairs occur, and what is proximate to what. If an alphabetical list has just single word keys, then it is just an alphabetical list. If it has two word keys, it is not 'just' an alphabetical list, it is in effect embedded alphabetical lists nested to a depth of two. If there are three word keys, there can be nesting to depth three, and so on. For example, say there are, perhaps as subjects for study, small, medium, and large animals which are fish, mammals, and crustaceans; if two word keys are used for these then placing the sizes first in the syntax of the keys gives, using word-by-word filing

large crustaceans
large fish
large mammals
medium crustaceans
medium fish
medium mammals
small crustaceans
small fish
small mammals

or, to use a better visual display,

large

  crustaceans
  fish
  mammals

medium

  crustaceans
  fish
  mammals

small

  crustaceans
  fish
  mammals

but placing the animal type before the size, in the key, gives

crustaceans

  large
  medium
  small

fish

  large
  medium
  small

mammals

  large
  medium
  small

so, there is grouping or fine structure here that can be designed and controlled. The 'trick' is to use multiple word keys. This technique could be used, for example, with a book, calling the keys 'Chapter1 Section1' etc., and then an alphabetical list ordered word-by-word would produce a structure similar to a Table of Contents. This fine structure is a matter of *key syntax* (coupled with word-by-word filing order).

There are other decisions. Typically, with most systems, numbers precede letters and English language precedes other languages. From then on it can get pretty complicated, with strings consisting of a mix of languages, with other punctuation (quotes, apostrophes, and dashes etc.) and hyphenated words. There also can be such subtleties as 'nonfiling characters'. The librarian data carrier, the MARC record, has a field to set the 'nonfiling characters', and this is the number of leading characters from a string to ignore when filing; it typically has the value 2, 3, or 4; what this is able to do, for example, is to remove the leading 'A's, 'An's, and 'The's from titles when considering filing order; so a title like 'The Pilgrim's Progress', with 'nonfiling characters' set to 4, is filed with other titles beginning with 'P' (from 'Pilgrim') and not with titles beginning with 'T' (from 'The'). And plurals can be a problem: without special consideration, 'mate' likely will not file next to 'mates', they could have 'maternity' in between them. Folk that produce artifacts that depend on filing order, for example, phone books, spend some considerable time and effort specifying their rules. Unfortunately, there is no universal filing order used by everybody everywhere. As Jessica Milstead writes

Nearly all library catalogues and telephone books, and most book indexes, use word-by-word arrangement. Encyclopedia indexes are frequently arranged word-by-word but the text is usually arranged letter-by-letter. Dictionaries are nearly universally arranged letter-by-letter. Abstracting and indexing services vary, with firm exponents of both means of arrangement being easy to find. Thesauri, and the services which use them, are frequently arranged letter-by-letter (Milstead 1984, p. 48).

There is an entirely separate, and slightly subtle, issue about alphabetical lists. An alphabetical association list associates strings with values. But much of the time, in practice, that association is used merely as a component in a wider association between something else, perhaps a person, a thing, or a concept, and a value. Think again about phone books. They associate strings with numbers, phone numbers. But the User is not trying to find the phone number of a *string*. The User is trying to find the phone number of a person or business. There is a gap here. There are persons, institutions, businesses, etc., and these have names or labels, which are transformed into string keys, which represent or identify them. But there needs to be a controlled conventionality at the point of insertion of those strings into the list or else the User will not know what string represents the item sought. Say there is the person John Jones and another person Jane Smith; if the string key for one of them is the form <last name>, <first name> i.e. 'Jones, John' and the other in the form <first name> <last name> i.e. 'Jane Smith', we start to be in trouble. If there is not suitable discipline here, the alphabetical list, while perfect on filing order string retrieval, will not work as a retrieval device for what we want.

### 2.8.5  *Precoordination and Postcoordination*

There is the consideration of *coordination* or *coordinate indexing*, in particular *precoordination* versus *postcoordination*. These ideas really come from Mortimer Taube, in the 1950s (Taube and Thompson 1951; Taube 1961, 1953, 1951), and they appear in a number of different settings in librarianship and with association lists. [Dagobert Soergel (1974) suggests the alternative terminology of 'precombination' for 'precoordination' and 'postcombination' for 'postcoordination' because those labels are more accurate to, and evocative of, the underlying operations. He is exactly right. Unfortunately the field of information science has ignored this excellent suggestion.]

An example from the standard use of Web Search Engines, especially Boolean search, can illustrate precoordination and postcoordination. The keys here are the text that is typed into the Search box, and the values are the lists of pages that are returned. Say our interest is in the astronomy and cosmology of stars; and, in reality, stars include 'white dwarfs', 'red dwarfs', 'yellow dwarfs', 'brown dwarfs', 'red giants', 'blue giants' and a variety of others. Initially, we might type in a series of one word keys such as

dwarf
giant

and the Search Engine will produce lists of web pages as results. What is going on behind the scenes here is that the Search Engine will have indexed in advance as much of the Web as it can. And it will do so for keys that people are likely to ask for (and that certainly would include 'dwarf' and 'giant'). It will look up the relevant pages in its indexes and return them. However, in these queries, likely there will be a problem with homographs. Dwarf stars are not the only kind of dwarves there are, there are also dwarf dwarves (like the ones that accompany Snow White). And giant stars are not the only kind of giants there are; there is Goliath, a baseball team, and a film with Elizabeth Taylor as an acting lead. So the pages returned to us may contain irrelevant material. No doubt we could tidy up our request by moving to two words, and by asking about

dwarf star
giant star

What the Search Engine does behind the scenes will be similar to the first time around but it may or may not be exactly the same. In its own internal indexes, the Engine may have indexed in advance at least some two word keys, including perhaps 'dwarf star' and 'giant star'. If so, it would just look up the relevant values and return them. This technique is that of *precoordination* or *precombination* (so-called because the words in the composite key are put together into the complex prior to the indexing and the determination of values for that key). However, it could be that the Engine works in a different way. It might *not* have internal indexes for two word keys, or it might *not* have values for the keys 'dwarf star' and 'giant star', in which case, it would proceed using what it does have which, we may suppose, includes entries for the single word keys 'dwarf' and, separately, 'star'; it would find all the values for 'dwarf', say {a, b, c, d, e} and all the values for 'star', say {d, e, f, g} and form the set theoretical intersection of the two sets of values to get {d, e} as the sought for result. This is to perform Boolean, or set theoretic, operations on the results of index retrieval after the fact. This is to *postcoordinate* the keys and values (Taube and Thompson 1951). There is no indexed entry for 'dwarf star' until the query is made, the two component words are post combined into the composite key. With real search engines, likely strings such as 'dwarf star' and 'giant star' would be precoordinated. However, we could ask about three word strings such as

white dwarf star
red giant star

and so on. There are so many possibilities as the strings get longer that eventually any engine would be swamped (if there are 40,000 indexed word, i.e. strings of length 1, there will be approximately (40,000 × 40,000) strings of length 2, and approximately (40,000 × 40,000 × 40,000) strings of length 3, and so on). Eventually there has to be some postcoordination (or plain abandonment of the task). [Postcoordination, with search engines, is exactly the same as Boolean AND searches i.e. a postcoordinate search for 'dwarf star' effectively is a Boolean search for (dwarf AND star).]

Precoordination will always give better precision and recall, because it pays attention to the order of words in composite strings. For example, precoordination can separate index values for 'Venetian blind' from those for 'blind Venetian' whereas postcoordination on 'Venetian' and 'blind' will not do that. However, longer composite key strings face two problems. As shown above, the combinatory explosion means that eventually there are just too many keys. And, secondly, it can be difficult for the User to find the composite keys in an index, especially if the index is on paper. Imagine the engineers to the Three Mile Island nuclear accident wondering whether the proper string index entry to the manual was 'significance of alarms to incipient uncontrolled thermonuclear runaway', or 'alarms, significance to incipient uncontrolled thermonuclear runaway', or 'incipient uncontrolled thermonuclear runaway, significance of alarms', or what. This issue of controlled conventionality with the form of the string keys can be considered as another concern with key syntax.

There is, or was, an area of research, *string indexing*, given to the question of how to present multiword keys like 'significance of alarms to incipient uncontrolled thermonuclear runaway' so that they can be found (Craven 1986; Svenonius 1978). Basically, before the computer, there were three ways. The key could be put in the index just once. Then there would be so-called 'citation order' questions as to what the order of those multiword keys should be (e.g. natural word order, nouns then verbs or qualifiers, concrete to abstract, etc.). Second, variants of the key could be put in to the index as additional entries. So, for example, all of 'significance of alarms to incipient uncontrolled thermonuclear runaway', 'alarms, significance to incipient uncontrolled thermonuclear runaway', and 'incipient uncontrolled thermonuclear runaway, significance of alarms', and many others, might be there. This makes the index much larger and creates noise. For example, Timothy Craven reports that one of the authority lists of the PRECIS system has a 100 entries starting with the word 'acquisition' (Craven 1986, p. 101). Such an index is not easy to use. Third, parts of the key could be put in to the index as additional entries. So, for example, not only would there be 'significance of alarms to incipient uncontrolled thermonuclear runaway' as an entire key but also there might be entries for fragments of it such as 'uncontrolled thermonuclear runaway', 'alarms', etc. This also makes the index much larger and creates noise.

This kind of string indexing research, and its resultant proposals and technologies, does not have the urgency it once had. It used to be that published indexes were to be on paper. But nowadays the indexes are electronic, or available in electronic or digital formats. And string-in-string search is available for the keywords or phrases within the actual keys of any indexes. So, for example, if 'significance of alarms to incipient uncontrolled thermonuclear runaway' was an index entry, there would be no need whatsoever to have any parts of it as additional entries in the index simply because the User could do a search for, say, 'uncontrolled thermonuclear runaway' and the software (string-in-string search) would find all the keys containing that phrase.

The Library of Congress Subject Headings (LCSH) are an interesting example. To most intents and purposes, there are 320,000 of these 'headings' (or keys) and they are precoordinated. Effectively, these headings can be used as keys in subject indexes and a recent Library of Congress Review concludes about the precoordination of their headings

> ... pre-coordinated strings provide context, which is needed for "disambiguation, suggestibility, and precision" and browsability. Pre-coordinated strings have a sophisticated syntax that can express concepts better than single words, yet also can be faceted by systems to group topics into categories for post-coordinated displays when desirable. Post-coordinated terms have serious limitations for recall, precision, understanding, and relevance ranking. (Cataloging 2007, p. 1)

All of which is correct, but it does not tell the whole story. We would expect that ordinary people would not be that accomplished at finding the headings suited to their needs among the 320,000. And, indeed, a few years ago, when the lists of LCSH entries used to be principally on paper, the headings were not that useful to Users. However, the LCSH list is now available electronically. But, as Lois Mai Chan points out in the same report, Users usually do not search LCSH lists using the actual LCSH string headings. Instead, Users often will keyword search, and that search will search among the headings. So, for example, 'Tea making paraphernalia in art' is an actual LCSH precoordinated heading i.e. a potential index key. This heading, and its associated heading-values indexes, certainly facilitates precision and recall for those searching for IOs on tea making paraphernalia in art. However, without the use of computers, many Users would not be able to find the *actual heading* because likely they would not know whether the heading string was 'Tea making paraphernalia in art' or 'Art, tea making paraphernalia in' or 'Tea pots depicted in art' or what. With computers, many Users would be able to reach the heading string. But they would not do so by searching for 'Tea making paraphernalia in art', because of the reasons given above i.e. they do not know the requisite heading string, instead they would search for keyword combinations like ''tea' AND 'art'' among the headings. And the keyword search would narrow to the sought for heading. So the process really would be a postcoordinated search among precoordinated headings. The precoordination takes place behind the scenes, largely hidden from the User.

When Taube first devised postcoordination, he envisaged a uniterm system where the keys were single words (i.e. strings of word length one) and the postcoordination was carried out on those single words. That kind of system will suffer from precision and recall problems. It will be improved by having some precoordinated keys which consisted of two or three word strings (i.e. strings of word length two or three, for example, 'school library', 'library school', 'birth control', etc.). However, longer and longer multi-word keys introduce problems of their own.

In sum, usually some precoordination will be good, but it should be limited and possibly supplemented with some postcoordination.

### 2.8.6  Hashing and Key Jumping

'Hashing' is an algorithmic technique devised in the 1950s, to help with, and speed up, the finding of items in a data structure. It is an intelligent generalization of alphabetical lists or ordinary everyday office filing. Say we have a school, with children who bring their lunches, and a rack of 26 pigeonholes or cubbies that are going to hold those lunches. We could let the children put their lunches anywhere, in which case the lunchroom helper might need to look through all 26 cubbies to find a particular lunch, say Charley's lunch. Alternatively, we could label the cubbies alphabetically 'A'–'Z' and use a system where the children put their lunches in the appropriate cubby suggested by their name. With this, a lunchroom helper can find Charley's lunch without having to look through all the cubbies— the helper can jump to the right place merely by doing a calculation on the key 'Charley' and using that to get the correct cubby. Full blown hashing is a little more elaborate than this, but the basic idea is the same; namely, a calculation can be done on what you are looking for, its key or entry or string value, and that will tell you where it is likely to be and where you are likely to find it.

Hashing may not sound terribly important with lunches and cubbies. But if we scale up the problem to, say, a few 100 million people and their social security records keyed by social security number, hashing can make the difference between data processing being viable or not.

In traditional data structure terms, hashing is slightly different to retrieving from an alphabetically ordered association list. A list can be of any size, and it can grow and shrink; a particular item can have any absolute position; there is no interest in determining absolute position, and alphabetical retrieval uses the key in conjunction, with other keys and the relative values of the keys themselves. Hashing is normally done in the context of arrays, which are fixed size data structures (cubbies of fixed number), and a calculation on the key is used to determine the absolute position in the array. So, there are differences, but both use information available from the key itself to suggest where to find it.

There are sufficient similarities to accessing an alphabetical list and using hashing that it would be convenient to have a label to cover both. Let us coin and use the term 'key jumping' to cover the use of features of a key as a heuristic to discover where it is in a data structure.

### 2.8.7 Metadata

Returning for one moment to IOs, in addition to one of more identifiers (i.e. names or labels), each IO will have many properties of interest for information retrieval. Almost all of these properties can be conceived of as *metadata* about the IO or IOs. Say we have a copy of the book *Geography for Younger Readers* by 'Jane Smith'. This book is an Information Object; and, indeed, it contains information or data; for example, data about the longest rivers, the highest mountains, etc. In addition to the data that the book contains or conveys, there is other data, which is data about the book itself—this is the metadata. For example, the author's name, the publisher's name, the publication date, the edition, the subject matter, and the like—all of these items are metadata.

Conceptually, metadata is merely an association list of key-value (or field-value) pairs for each individual IO. So, for example, metadata for a particular IO, say IO with ID# = 97, might be

| Field (Key) | Value |
| --- | --- |
| Author | Smith, Jane |
| Title | Geography for Younger Readers |
| Date | 2011 |
| Subject | Geography |

Metadata is infrastructure for the organization of IOs. How do you arrange or organize IOs? You give those information objects metadata, preferably using metadata fields whose values can be determined easily (i.e. by viable algorithm on the information objects).

There is the question of whether the number of metadata fields that there are within a particular conventional system is fixed or whether the number of fields is arbitrarily extensible. Providing for, and accommodating, arbitrary extensions to

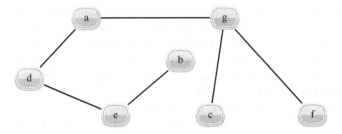

**Fig. 2.10** A free tree

metadata, sometimes called 'extended attributes', is a desirable end in itself (Siracusa 2001, 2005). Usually with a pure association list, the actual number of entries, the number of key-value pairs is not limited (just as an ordinary shopping list can have as many entries as needed to suit the task at hand). But in practice many metadata standards or schemas have a fixed number of fields. For example, the ordinary original Dublin Core metadata standard had 13 fields in it. It is better if the number of metadata fields is *not* fixed i.e. that we can add more fields if we wish to. The reason for this is that the metadata fields are used to organize the IOs, but we cannot envisage now all the different ways that folk will want to organize their IOs, so we cannot know now, once and for all, just what fields to have. A metadata scheme should allow augmentation. A single item of metadata, or a metadata field, is an annotation. And a new grouping amounts to a new annotation. There is no reason to limit annotations.

### 2.8.8 Trees, Hierarchies, Forests and DAGs

We will have a special interest in what is known as *rooted directed trees* and *directed acyclic graphs*. We will often call the former just *trees* and the latter *DAGs*. [For the connection between trees and information retrieval see, for example, (Salton 1962).]

A *free tree* is a connected graph, which has only one path between every two nodes (i.e. there are no 'cycles'). For example, (Fig. 2.10) is a free tree (you can walk from node to node (so it is connected) but you cannot walk around in a circle (so there are no cycles)). A free tree can be converted into a *rooted tree*, by choosing one of the tree's nodes as being the 'root'. Then it is common to draw it with the root at the top, and the other nodes appearing below. So if the node d were to be chosen as the root of a rooted tree from the first diagram, the tree might be re-drawn (Fig. 2.11). With a rooted tree, there are nodes which do not have other nodes below them. These are *leaves*. So, in the above tree, 'a' is the root, and d, f and g are leaves. With any leaf, there is exactly one path from the root to it, such a path is a *branch* (Fig. 2.12).

The emphasized lines indicate a branch in the above tree, i.e. d-a-g-f, (and the tree has two other branches).

**Fig. 2.11** A rooted tree

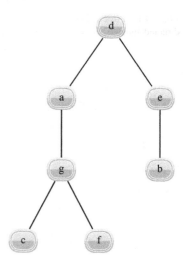

**Fig. 2.12** A branch

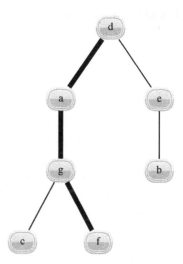

Trees can be characterized, and drawn, as having directed links (and that will be the preferred form for us). Thus (Fig. 2.13).

The root has in degree 0, no links come into the root. All other nodes have in degree 1 (the incoming link picks a node's 'parent'). The leaves have out degree 0, no links go out from a leaf. All other nodes have an out degree that is not 0. (The outlinks identify a node's children.) All the links point away from the root. Sometimes these rooted trees with directed links are called *rooted directed trees* or *arborescences*. We will tend to abbreviate this and just call them *trees*.

The number of children that a node has is a matter for the tree and its intended use. There are *binary* trees in which every non-leaf node has exactly two children. But there are also many other types of tree. Sometimes the words 'branching

**Fig. 2.13** A tree using directed links

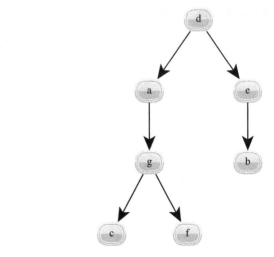

**Fig. 2.14** A tree showing levels

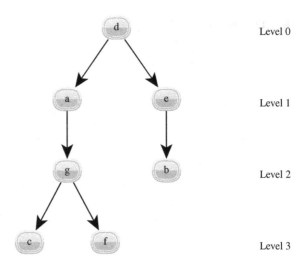

factor' are used to indicate the relative number of children, so a tree with a high branching factor would tend to be a fat or wide tree.

*Rank* or *level* can also be given to the nodes in accordance with a node's distance from the root. So, in the following diagram, the root (i.e. a) itself is level 0, the nodes a and e are of level 1, b and g level 2 and c and f level 3 (Fig. 2.14).

The notion of 'hierarchy' often appears in this setting. A hierarchy is a structure of entities where there is a ranking by status or importance or authority. Many hierarchies can be depicted as trees. Then the most important item becomes the root, the second most important items are shown as the children of the root i.e. they are of distance 1 from the root and so on. Hierarchies can depict governments, committee structures, military ranks, etc.

**Fig. 2.15** A tree drawn
horizontally

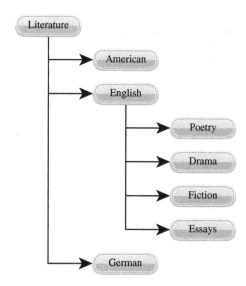

Common examples of trees are organizational ('org') charts, genealogical trees, and the display of any hierarchy (such as genus-species in biology, classification schedules and subject schedules in librarianship).

The last displayed tree could be a genealogical tree where the links are showing the 'mother of' relation (with a = Alice, b = Betty, c = Chloe etc.). Notice that each of the individual nodes (the root, the leaves, and the internal nodes) depict someone (i.e. the 'data' is everywhere), and the relation connecting two nodes ('mother of') is the same throughout. Each person is somewhere, at a node, and there are exactly the same number of nodes as people. And the levels can be used to pick out grandmothers, great grandmothers, etc.

[An oddity, that is occasionally remarked on, is that, strictly speaking, family trees are not trees. In a family tree, a child has two parents, in a graph theoretic tree a child has one parent. The work-around we used above was to use just a partial family tree, linking nodes using only the 'mother of' relation.]

One familiar use of trees is to depict directory or folder structure on a computer. For that use, a tree will typically be drawn horizontally, thus (Fig. 2.15).

With standard trees, there is no notion of an order to the children (which is the first child, which is the second...)—all that matters is what is connected to what. So, for example, the following two trees are the same tree, or copies of each other (Fig. 2.16).

For certain purposes, for example for representing books, it is convenient to have an order on the children so that, for example, b is the first child of a, in the above graph, and c the second child, etc. These types of trees are *ordered* trees. Order can be depicted just by labeling or tagging the nodes, thus (Fig. 2.17).

Here the numbers are showing which is the first child, which the second, etc. Often, for casual work, we can just let the left to right order on the page represent the order of the children.

**Fig. 2.16** Two different
depictions of the same tree
illustrating indifference to the
order of children

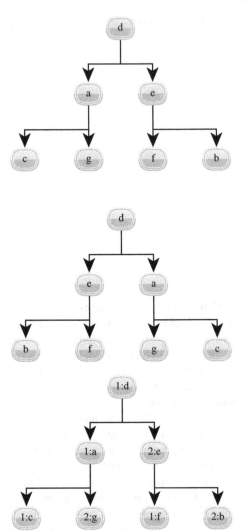

**Fig. 2.17** An example tree
with ordered children

There is often the need to locate, or provide a reference to a node in a tree. As
examples, in a genealogical tree there may be an interest in where Mary Queen of
Scots occurs. And in a classification tree, such as the Dewey Decimal Classification (DDC), there may be an interest as to where the topic 'Physics' occurs.

One easy way to do this is to provide a *notation* that identifies the individual nodes
via parents and children (a combination of levels in the tree and order among the
children). So, for example, the numeral 1 could label the root; 11, 12, 13 etc. label the
first, second, third, etc. child of the node 1; 111, 112, 113, etc. label the first, second,
third, etc. child of the node 11; and so on. There are indefinitely many such notational schemes. One attractive feature that many notations can have is that of being
*expressive* and that means that the notation indicates the hierarchy and the nodes'

individual lineages. For example, if we choose the label of a node from the sample scheme, say 1,221, that node is a child of the node 122, it is a grandchild of the node 12, and it is a great-grandchild of the node 1. The node's lineage is available directly from the notation for it; and that is true for all nodes labeled using the sample scheme; the sample scheme is expressive. [If a tree is depicting a classification, the notation can tell of class numbers or classification numbers.]

Alternatively, with a tree, there is a unique path from the root to each individual node which can generate a description. That is the technique used on personal (and other) computers. You might see a 'path' from the document root of the computer down to the file of interest

/Users/Documents/Synch/Readings/Pliny.pdf

and that locates the document 'Pliny.pdf'. And the User follows this path by finding the correct child (folder, directory) of the root (Users), then the right child of that child (Documents), and so on. How difficult this would be, depends on how many children there are, at each stage, and whether the children themselves have some arrangement. When the tree is an ordered tree, the children will be in alphabetical (or hopefully some other useful) order. In which case, following the path just involves a sequence of jumped key entries.

One can go further by providing an association list, preferably an ordered association list, with the node names (or file names) as keys and the notation for the nodes (paths of the files) as values. That, to take one example, could be an alphabetically sorted association list which amounted to an index from ordered topics ('Chemistry', 'Mathematics', 'Physics') to their positions in a scheme such as DDC; indeed, that is what the Dewey Relative Index is.

Sometimes a graph amounts to several different independent trees. These graphs are *forests*. A tree is acyclic (it has no cycles) and it is connected. Since the trees in a forest are not connected to each other, effectively a forest is a collection of nodes which are acyclic. A forest as a whole does not have to be connected, but the parts of it that are connected form the individual trees. When talking about cycles in connection with trees and forests, no attention is paid to the direction of the links. However, we favor directed links for illustrating trees. And that leads to the notion of a *directed cycle* (having the ability to follow the links in the right direction and get back to where you started).

Graphs that do not have directed cycles are, surprise, *directed acyclic graphs* (or DAGs). Roughly, a DAG is like a forest but requiring the absence of directed cycles instead of the absence of plain cycles. Any tree is a DAG, any forest is a DAG also. But there are DAGs which are neither trees nor forests, this occurs when they contain cycles but not directed cycles. They contain one or more (larger or smaller) 'diamonds'; a simple example is (Fig. 2.18).

What a DAG amounts to for us is this: any node might have several children and thus many descendants down different paths; *any node might also have several parents* and thus many ancestors up different paths; also different descendants might have a child in common, or different ancestors might themselves have a parent in common (i.e. there might be cycles); however, no node can be a descendant or an ancestor of itself. This is a generalization of tree or forest.

**Fig. 2.18** A graph fragment
with nodes connected in a
'diamond'

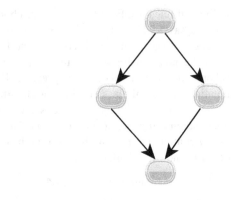

**Fig. 2.19** A tree that will be
traversed

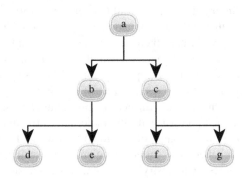

With DAGs, the notion of branch does not fit too well, but the idea of path can
pretty well serve as a replacement. Starting at any node, it may have children, and
they may have children, and so on; but following the links downward must
eventually come to a stop (because, with the graphs of interest to us, the graph is
finite.). This means that effectively each node sits as the source of paths of
descendants going down. Similarly that node may have parents and they may have
parents, and so on. Now, a link goes from a parent to a child so to travel from a
child to a parent is traveling against the direction of the link; so, following the
links upwards, against the direction of the links, produces paths of ancestors going
up. The paths going through a node are the combinations of these downward paths
to the descendants and upward paths to ancestors.

### 2.8.9  Converting an Ordered Tree to a List

There are various ways of 'traversing' an ordered tree. The task of traversing is
that of visiting all the nodes in a tree (just once) i.e. the root, the interior nodes, and
the leaves. The output from a traversal is a list; it is a list of all the nodes visited,
and it needs to contain all nodes in the ordered tree. So, with the tree (Fig. 2.19).

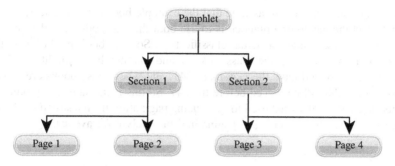

**Fig. 2.20** A tree depicting the structure of a pamphlet

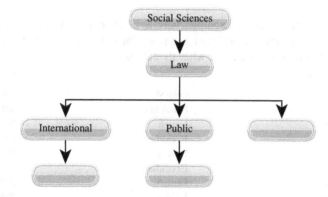

**Fig. 2.21** A fragment of universal decimal classification (UDC)

The list a, b, c, d, e, f, g is a traversal, so too is a, b, d, e, c, f, g. The latter style of traversal is of particular interest to us. There are two reasons.

Any book, or magazine, or pamphlet, of Chapters, Sections, Sub-sections, Pages, etc. can be thought of as a structured object, in fact all of them are ordered trees. The book itself it the root, the Chapters come at level 1, the Sections at level 2, and so on. Thus (Fig. 2.20). And the described traversal is how the document would be printed and bound (or presented).

The second reason is that librarians use subject classification to produce classmarks and, in turn, the classmarks are used to place physical IOs in order on shelves. The end result is IOs collocated by subject. The subject classification is often a hierarchical tree, and the shelving order is a list. So the process is that of converting an ordered tree to a list. For example, here are a couple of fragment branches from the Universal Decimal Classification (UDC) (Fig. 2.21).

| | |
|---|---|
| 3 | Social Sciences |
| 34 | Law |
| 341 | International Law |
| 342 | Public Law |

For simplification we will assume that the example books are assigned just one subject. And the cataloging practice is to use both the leaf nodes and the internal nodes from the schedule for actual classification. So, one book might be on the subject of Law and have the classmark 34 and another book might be about International Law and have the classmark 341; and when those books are placed on shelves the 34 will be placed before the 341. So this is the same list producing ordered tree traversal as that used for producing pagination from a structured book.

We will label this traversal, a 'paginating' or 'shelving' traversal.

## 2.8.10 Tables, Citation Order, Filing Order

Tables are very familiar; for example, here is a schematic from an Email application showing each individual email as a row. The columns identify the sender of the email, what its subject is, and what its date is

| Name | Subject | Date |
|---|---|---|
| Ann | Breakfast | 2010 |
| Ann | Lunch | 2008 |
| Beryl | Breakfast | 2009 |
| Beryl | Lunch | 2008 |
| Charley | Breakfast | 2009 |
| Charley | Dinner | 2008 |
| Charley | Lunch | 2010 |

So each row here is an ordered triple, for example the first row is

<Ann, Breakfast, 2010>

where each of the components of the triple are the particular column values for that row e.g. 2010 is the date of that first email. And an individual row represents information about one item or token. So, typically, there are rows and columns, and often row headers and column headers (which identify the rows and columns). Each row contains data pertaining to one item or object (the above table has seven rows, so it has data about seven items, seven emails). Each column contains values for each of the properties that each item might have [so, for example, the Date property has a value of '2008' for three of the emails (i.e. three emails have 2008 as their date)].

With headers in place, in one sense the table and its layout are flexible. The following table is identical to the last one in as much as it contains the same information.

| Subject | Name | Date |
|---|---|---|
| **Breakfast** | **Ann** | **2010** |
| **Lunch** | **Ann** | **2008** |
| **Breakfast** | **Beryl** | **2009** |
| **Lunch** | **Beryl** | **2008** |
| **Breakfast** | **Charley** | **2009** |
| **Dinner** | **Charley** | **2008** |
| **Lunch** | **Charley** | **2010** |

And tables in general can contain many columns, certainly more than three, in which case, for an n-column table the row entry would be not an ordered triple, it would be an ordered *n-tuple*, and these row values are often called just *tuples*.

In the setting of information resources, it is convenient to call the column order the *citation order*. So the citation order of the first table is Name-Subject-Date, and the citation order of the second table is Subject-Name-Date. The order of the columns, the citations order, is a matter of indifference as far as the total information in the table is concerned. The order of the rows is also a matter of indifference as far as the total information in the table is concerned. However, having the rows sorted is of definite value for the purposes of looking up or finding a row, and of having related rows contiguous with each other. The actual sorting can be done alphabetically, or inverse alphabetically, for names, by currency for dates, or any number of other ways. The result of sorting the first table, by sorting the columns by subject, then ties by name, and finally the ties of those by date (i.e. in citation order) is

| Subject | Name | Date |
|---|---|---|
| **Breakfast** | **Ann** | **2010** |
| **Breakfast** | **Beryl** | **2008** |
| **Breakfast** | **Charley** | **2008** |
| **Dinner** | **Charley** | **2008** |
| **Lunch** | **Ann** | **2008** |
| **Lunch** | **Beryl** | **2008** |
| **Lunch** | **Charley** | **2010** |

To actually produce that result the columns of the table are sorted successively from right to left (somewhat counter-intuitively). Sorting one column, after sorting another, may to a degree overwrite, or unravel, the first one—so the last column sorted becomes, so-to-speak, the master sort. So sorting by Date, then by Name, then, last, by Subject will give the desired citation order sort. And if we change the citation order to Date-Name-Subject, and do a table sort on that, the result is

| Date | Name | Subject |
|------|------|---------|
| **2008** | **Ann** | **Lunch** |
| **2008** | **Beryl** | **Lunch** |
| **2008** | **Charley** | **Dinner** |
| **2009** | **Beryl** | **Breakfast** |
| **2009** | **Charley** | **Breakfast** |
| **2010** | **Ann** | **Breakfast** |
| **2010** | **Charley** | **Lunch** |

Notice here that the sorting and the citation order combine in the following way: rows are contiguous with other rows having similar values for the first column of the citation order, but they are scattered with respect to values for other columns in the citation order. So, for example, you can have all of Ann's and Beryl's and Charley's emails together, or you can have all the 2008, 2009, and 2010 emails together, but you cannot have both of these associations at the same time. In classification theory, this is known as *the problem of distributed relatives* (Savage 1946).

There is an analogy here with the word-by-word filing order sorting of alphabetical lists. Each column entry needs to be a separate word in the key string, and the citation order is the order of those words in the keys. Then, if the columns can be sorted alphabetically (so, for example, no column consists of numbers sorted by size), a plain alphabetical list and the row order in the table are much the same.

The contents of a table can be linearized, or provided as output in a list form, merely by listing the rows in order. That linearization, its order and what it makes contiguous and what scattered, will depend on the citation order and the ordering or sorting operations that are done on the columns.

Using once again terminology common in the setting of information resources, that (output) list of rows from a table is known as the *filing order* for the rows.

More can be said about the sorting using the columns. Mention has been made of alphabetical sorting, and sorting by date, but, actually any operation will do that produces an order. Consider, for example, our sort on the subjects. There were the subjects 'Breakfast', 'Dinner', and 'Lunch', which were sorted alphabetically. But there are indefinitely many other sorting operations that could have been used. These subjects might gain an order by being just three subjects chosen from a ordered list of 100 possible subjects, or controlled annotations. This larger list, a controlled vocabulary of subjects, could be ordered from general to specific, from most urgent to least urgent, from most interesting to least interesting, from most relevant to financial taxes to least relevant, and in other ways. The sorting on a column groups certain rows and separates them from other rows or groups of rows; for example, an alphabetical sort puts the entries starting with 'C' closer to each other than to entries starting with 'Z'. This means that rows can be grouped or scattered just by virtue of a single column sort.

So, filing order depends both on citation order and on the individual sorting operations on the individual columns. And filing order is an expression of what is collocated and what is scattered. There is much flexibility.

## 2.9  Roget's Thesaurus

*Roget's Thesaurus*, written by Dr Peter Mark Roget in 1805, is, inadvertently and unintentionally, the single most important work in the theory of information retrieval.

Roget sought to remedy his 'own deficiencies' in finding the appropriate word or words to use when composing and writing ((Roget 1852) Introduction). And to do this he produced a 'system of verbal classification' which was a 'classed catalogue' ((Roget 1852) Introduction). In it, words were partitioned into clusters of synonyms, or near-synonyms, and then these synonym clusters were classified as leaves in a tree. In turn, the non-leaf interior nodes in the tree represented organizing principles, such as

Abstract Relations
Space
Matter
Intellect
Volition
Sentient and Moral Powers

These organizational nodes went from the more general to the more specific as the leaves are approached. Typically sibling leaves, being under the same organizational parent, would be related in some way, though not as synonyms; for example, the 'life' leaf and the 'death' leaf are sibling leaves. Roget then combined this classification of synonym clusters with an alphabetical index. And the result, *Roget's Thesaurus*, has been invaluable to writers and scholars ever since.

In the setting of information retrieval, there is no special interest in using apposite or elegant words when writing. So, what *Roget's Thesaurus* was designed for, and what it is popular for nowadays, is tangential to the present enterprise.

However, Roget's techniques, what he did and the way that he did it, are vital for information retrieval. Roget combined (part of) Reid's classifications, the Triangle of Meaning, the problem of synonyms and homographs, and alphabetical indexing in such a way that all obvious problems are solved. There has been no improvement in Roget's approach in the last 200 years, and it looks doubtful that there could be any major improvement.

So, what did Roget do? He produced a Reid-style classification of some concepts. In fact, this amounted to a tree with about 1,000 leaves. The tree was about of depth 3, so it was shallow and broad (There were Classes, Sections, Subsections, and Leaves.). He labeled each of the nodes, so, schematically, there was

Class #1, Section #1, Subsection #1, Leaf #1,... Leaf #1,000. His choice of concepts for the tree was inspired by the works of Leibniz and Aristotle. What Roget's concepts actually were is unimportant to us. Roget was choosing concepts to be helpful for writers. In information retrieval or librarianship, we might choose concepts for other reasons (for example, to depict topics or subjects or area of knowledge). Each of the leaves in the tree was to be a near-synonym cluster. Each cluster had a 'headword', which, in effect, was a label for its cluster. So, for example, the word

life

is a headword, and it is a label for the cluster

life, vitality, viability; animation; vital spark, vital flame, soul, spirit. [and more].

Roget was not trying to produce true synonyms—he would not have thought for one moment that 'life' and 'vitality' were synonyms. He was trying to help himself and other writers searching for the right word, the right nuance, and so he clustered near-synonyms. The 'life' cluster is a node in the tree and as such it has a node number and, in fact, that number is Leaf 359. So, thus far there is the example data

359: life, vitality, viability; animation; vital spark, vital flame, soul, spirit.

and this data is a leaf in a classification tree. So, if a User has found Leaf 359 in the tree, the User can read off near-synonyms of 'life'; the User can also go up a link to the Organizational Subsection 'Vitality in general' and, if desired, come down to Leaf 360 with headword 'death' and read off near-antonyms of 'life'. What about the problem of finding the 'life' Leaf in the first place? If the User fully understands the organizational principles, and where the concept of 'life' would be classified, that User would be able to find Leaf 359 and thus access the sought for synonyms. However, there are 1,000 leaves in the tree, and what fits where is always a bit of an open question for a User. What would make the system better is jumped key entry from the headwords to their nodes, from, for example, 'life' to Leaf 359. And Roget provided exactly this by including a supplementary alphabetical index from the headwords to their nodes. So, for example, here is a schematic of that alphabetical index for a fragment around 'life':

| | |
|---|---|
| ... | |
| lieu | 182 |
| lieutenant | 745 |
| life | 359 |
| lifeblood | 5 |
| lifeboat | 273 |
| ... | |

[The numbers are the numbers of the respective leaf nodes. The leaf nodes are themselves presented in order, in the appropriate section of the entire Thesaurus, so finding one from its number is trivial.]

Roget met the problem of homographs by refusing to use them as headwords (so each actual headword names only one concept). He disambiguated any potential headword homographs, and then used the disambiguations both as headwords and in the alphabetical index. A more complete version of the above index fragment is

| lieu | 182 |
|------|-----|
| lieutenant | |
|    officer | 745 |
|    deputy | 759 |
| life | 359 |
| lifeblood | 5 |
| lifeboat | 273 |
| ... | |

and this recognizes the plain 'lieutenant' as being a homograph and disambiguates it to 'lieutenant (officer)' and 'lieutenant (deputy)', and those latter two are headwords (or head strings or head phrases).

From our point of view, the only thing that Roget did not do was to use the depth of the classification and make proper use of the interior nodes. To explain:- One of Reid's examples is the class hierarchy

Animal
Man
Frenchman
Parisian.

All of these are perfectly good concepts (or words for concepts). So, 'Animal', 'Man', 'Frenchman', 'Parisian' could all be headwords and have their associated clusters. However, when these clusters are put in a classification tree, they do not all want to be leaves simply because some are subclasses of others (Parisian is a subclass of Frenchman, which is a subclass of Man, etc.). So, the superclasses all need to be interior nodes, and it is only the terminal subclasses, Parisian in this case, that should be leaves.

We definitely want this modification, because we want well-behaved names (headwords) for all the classificatory concepts including the interior nodes. And, actually, the modification even makes for a better Thesaurus for the purposes of writing. The directed links in the tree would now depict whether one cluster was more specific than another. By this means, a writer could find a hypernym (a word more general than the one in hand) or a hyponym (a word more specific than the initial one). So, if the writer wanted a word more general than 'Parisian', the Thesaurus could suggest 'Frenchman' as a possibility.

There are some minor details. There is the question of which words to index. In the original Thesaurus there were 1,000 headwords and 15,000 words in total. The headwords have to be in the alphabetical index. Should the other words be indexed? If they are, there would be an index of 15,000 entries (or 325,000 entries nowadays, for Roget's Thesaurus has grown with the passage of time), which is large for an alphabetical index (but not large compared with the New York Telephone Book, which is also an alphabetical index). If the other words are not indexed, then there is a problem with finding synonyms etc. of non-headwords. For example, take the word 'viability' (actually from the life cluster 359): it may be difficult for a User to find synonyms for it, without knowing where it is in the classification. Nowadays, with computers, there would be no reason not to index everything, either by way of an alphabetical index or by keyword entry and search. Additionally, Roget himself enhanced the basic structure by adding many cross references and heuristic guides, both to the clusters in the classification and to the index. These are valuable.

For our purposes, it will be useful to mention some alternative terminology. We do not have much use for the actual word 'headword', though its role and what it signifies are vital. We will tend to use 'preferred term', or 'name of the concept' or 'canonical name of the concept' or 'canonical name', all as synonyms for 'headword'. [The reason is 'headword' alludes to the first word in a list of words, but our interest is in well-behaved one-to-one names of concepts.]

One major way that we are going to want to adapt Roget's original work is that in the setting of information retrieval it needs to be generalized from atomic or elemental concepts to compound concepts. In Roget, the concepts in the tree are atoms and, for the most part, the headwords and quasi-synonyms are single words. But, with IO retrieval, a greater proportion of the interest is with compound concepts not atomic ones. Searchers are not just interested in 'life', they are interested in 'moral life', 'life in nineteenth century France', 'the good life', 'right to life', 'healthy life', 'extending life', 'the life of Nelson', and indefinitely more compound concepts. The compound concepts will likely need some special treatment to produce 'headwords' which, actually, would likely be 'headphrases'; and, similarly, the phrase near-synonyms, and alphabetical indexing will raise demanding questions.

## 2.10  The Dewey Relativ Index

It was Dewey who devised or re-invented the use of a combination of classing with an A/Z alphabetical index. He wanted classes to relate books one to another and to shelve books. But that on its own does not help the User either to find which class a book belongs to or to find where the classes are on the shelves. The solution to these problems is first to label each of the classes, with its Dewey Decimal Number, and to put the classes on the shelves in order of their numbers, and second to provide an alphabetical index from class name to class number, the 'Relativ' index. Here is Dewey, writing in the language of full Dui

The plan of this Clasification and Index was developt erly in 1873 ….

Only a fraction of the servis posibl cud be got from [libraries] without clasification, catalogs, indexes and other aids, to tel librarians and readers what they containd on any givn subject….

It was chiefly necesary to find a method that wud clas, arranje and index books and pamflets on shelvs, cards of a catalog, clippings and notes in scrapbooks and index rerums, references to all these items, and indeed any literary material in any form, as redily as an ordinary index gyds to proper paje of a bound book. This difficult problem was solvd by uzing no reference marks except the simplest simbols known to the human mind, arabic numerals with their uzual arithmetic values, and by aiding their unequald simplicity by many practical nemonic devices.

Tho the importance of clasification was recognized, the filosofic sistems proposed wer so difficult fully to understand or apply that not 1 person in 1000 cud uze them practicaly. Decimal Clasification simplicity and even more its Relativ Index hav made this work 10-fold eazier. In recent years, use of the sistem has spred rapidly in all civilized cuntries, meeting success in thousands of different applications. In its simpl form a skoolboy can quikly master it and keep for instant reference not only his books but every note, clipping or pamflet. Almost every profession and occupation has lernd its wonderful laborsaving powers. It is in daily use by miriads of business and professional men who wud never even attempt to understand or uze the old sistems.

By mere adition of figures, without chanjing this shorter form, this very simpl sistem is redily made to record the utmost refinements of specialists, and the Relativ Index, as simpl as a, b, c, sends the novis to the exact place where the expert has clasifyd the matter sought (Dewey 1926) Introduction.

And, to an extent, Dewey constructed his keystrings for the Relativ Index in such a way that problems of vocabulary control (synonyms and homographs) were addressed. The keys also often showed the subclassing.

Although the setting, context and interpretation, of the two contributions are very different, what is going on here is very similar structurally to the construction of Roget's Thesaurus (with Dewey's decimal numbers substituted for the Roget's leaf numbers).

[The reason that the Dewey 'Relativ' index is called a Relative Index is that it collects together relatives. As we noted, classification typically collocates some items and distributes others (the so-called 'distributed relatives'). So, for example, in the Dewey Decimal System, items of Poetry are distributed (because they appear separately under English Literature, American Literature, etc.); the Relative Index, among other virtues, tells where these are. The Dewey Relative A/Z Index fulfils two functions: it helps to find classes, and it helps to find relatives.]

## 2.11  Tables of Contents and Back-of-the-Book Indexes

Any book, or series of volumes, might be accompanied by a Table of Contents, and an Index. These are access or retrieval tools. Pliny's *Natural History* of 77CE had Tables of Contents and rudimentary lists of author references (by way of source acknowledgment and citation). A Table of Contents will be similar structurally to the actual contents—it will show the Chapters and Sections in the same order as they are in the book itself. So, really, looking though a Table of Contents is just an abbreviated and quicker version of looking through the book. Tables of Contents usually list Chapters, and Sections, but not pages themselves (except

**Table 2.1** Table of contents for Pliny's Natural History

| | |
|---|---|
| 1. Of land creatures: the commendation of elephants: their understanding. | 15. Of the animals of scythia, and of the north countries. |
| 2. When elephants were first yoked. | 16. Of lions. |
| 3. The docility of elephants. | 17. Of panthers. |
| 4. The clemency of elephants: that they know their own dangers; also of the ferocity of the tiger. | 18. The nature of the tiger: of camels, and the camelopard: when it was first seen at Rome. |
| 5. The understanding and memory of elephants. | 19. Of the stag-wolf named Chaus: and the Cephus. |
| 6. When elephants were first seen in Italy. | 20. Of the rhinoceros. |
| 7. Combats by elephants. | 21. Of lynxes, sphinges, crocutes, marmosets, of Indian oxen, of leucrocutes, of eale, of the Ethiopian bulls, of the Man- tichora, the unicorn, of the catoblepa, and the basilisk. |
| 8. The manner of taking elephants. | 22. Of wolves. |
| 9. The manner how elephants are tamed. | 23. Of serpents. |
| 10. How long an elephant goeth with young, and of their nature. | 24. Of the ichneumon. |
| 11. The countries where elephants breed: the discord between elephants and dragons. | 25. Of the crocodile and the hippopotamus. |
| 12. The industry and wit of dragons and elephants. | 26. Who shewed first at Rome the hippopotamus and crocodiles. Medicines discovered by animals. |
| 13. Of dragons. | 27. Of animals which have shewn certain herbs; the red deer, lizards, swallows, tortoises, the weasel, the stork, the boar, the snake, panther, elephant, bears, stock-doves, house-doves, cranes, and ravens. |
| 14. Serpents of prodigious magnitude: of serpents named Boae. | |

perhaps as references identifying the locations of the Chapters and Sections). For example, here is a Table of Contents from Pliny (Pliny 78)

IN THE EIGHTH BOOK IS CONTAINED THE NATURE OF LAND ANIMALS THAT GO ON FOOT (Table 2.1).

A Table of Contents supports browsing and searching, but it is better for browsing than it is for searching. To search, you have to find what you interested in within the Table of Contents itself. For example, say you are interested in 'Stock-Doves', such a topic, or part heading, may or may not be in the Table of Contents, it may or may not be there under that exact name (it could be there under 'Doves-Stock'), and there is no key jumping from 'Stock-Doves' to its location in the Table of Contents, so, in the worst case you might just have to start at the beginning of the Table of Contents and look through sequentially until you either did or did not find 'Stock-Doves' (or some title that you recognized as being related). However, even with all those difficulties, looking for your topic in the Table of Contents is easier and quicker than looking for it in the book itself. Because of the isomorphism between contents and Tables of Contents, no special decisions have to be made by the author or publisher about making or constructing a Table of Contents. If a book is in the form of Chapters and Sections, the structure of a Table of Contents is a trivial distillation or abstraction of that structure. There is a qualification here. Getting the structure of the Table of Contents from the book itself is trivial. But which actual labels to use is an important and non-trivial consideration. Of course, typically the labels will come from the author (or authors). But all that means is that it is the author that has to do the intelligent thinking. The author will have given the Chapters, Sections, etc. titles or labels. And suitable choices are important. Pliny calls one of his sections 'When Elephants were first seen in Italy' and another 'Of wolves'—there are different levels of guidance and help that are being offered here.

Back-of-the-book Indexes are quite different to Tables of Contents. Indexes were slow to emerge (Witty 1973), and there are reasons why. Many books from around the period of Pliny's *Natural History* were in the form of scrolls, so there was only one 'page' (although, of course, any particular book might consist of several scrolls) and usually there were no line numbers. The text was hand written, so what was on a particular line in one version might not be on that line in another. If a Table of Contents already informed as to sequential order within a scroll, what problem would invite an index as its solution? It is hard to identify one. Presumably any desired access to a scroll, via rolling and unrolling, could be guided and accomplished by a suitable Table of Contents. In the first three centuries AD, *codexes* (i.e. books with pages) start to have a real impact, but these also were hand written. There could be multiple copies of a work, sometimes hundreds, but these copies were often not the same as each other in physical form. It is only with the advent of the printing press, around 1450, that there starts to be large numbers of copies of works with the individual copies having the same pagination. From about 1500, indexes start to appear, but it is probably as late as 1700 before alphabetical indexes are common (Wellisch 1983, 1986, 1991; Witty 1973). As we have already noted, the notion of an alphabetical list itself was slow to be recognized and appreciated. Recognizable modern style alphabetical indexes are relatively recent. As Witty tells us

> Index entries were not always alphabetized by considering every letter in a word from beginning to end, as people are wont to do today. Most early indexes were arranged only by the first letter of the first word, the rest being left in no particular order at all. Gradually, alphabetization advanced to an arrangement by the first syllable, that is, the first two or three letters, the rest of an entry still being left unordered. Only very few indexes compiled in the 16th and early 17th centuries had fully alphabetized entries, but by the 18th century full alphabetization became the rule... (Witty 1973, p. 136)

Indexes are usually not ordered in the same way as contents of the book. Contiguous index entries do not have to refer to contiguous passages or sections. An index is an association list of labels (or keys) and references. The labels are the names of the entries, and the references are the Chapters or Sections (or page or line numbers) that those names individually refer to. An index has to have some order, presumably a principled order. As we have noted, an alphabetical index has jumped key entry, which is a pleasant property. But an index does not have to be alphabetical. There may be reasons to encourage sequential access to the index itself. For example, it might be better to learn or study a particular subject matter in a certain order, and the index could support this. Or, certain tasks might need to be done in a certain order and indexes can support this, so, for instances, an index to Aircraft Flight Manual might amount to a checklist for pilots (for pre-flight checks and similar).

Nowadays we would reason that there are two complementary accessing tasks of interest and value to the reader: browsing and searching. A Table of Contents supports primarily browsing, and an Index supports primarily searching. The reader needs to be able to do both tasks well; therefore many books need both a Table of Contents and a separate, and differently structured, Index. But it requires insight to realize this. It is easy to be tempted by the following line of thought. Suppose you do feel you would like an Index. Why not just structure the text itself in exactly the same way as the structure of the Index you favor? So, if you would like an alphabetical Index, just make the text itself ordered alphabetically by section entry (as is done in a Dictionary). The moment the text has the same structure as the Index, the Table of Contents and the Index both would have the same structure—they are the same, and so one is redundant. This makes an Index unnecessary. We do not have indexes into Dictionaries, there is no need (Dictionaries also do not have Tables of Contents; that is because there is no need for them to support browsing; the individual entries are essentially independent.).

## 2.12 More on Back-of-the-Book Indexes

Here, for example, is an index fragment from Colin Howson's *Logic with trees*

absurdity, rule of 137
accessibility relation 166
adequate: for truth-functional logic 44;
    sets of connectives vii, 44ff

algorithm 17
alpha (α) sentence 49
alternative denial 44
ancestral trees vii, 6, 33ff.

and the parts of the OED dictionary definition of 'index' of interest to us read

**1.** The fore-finger: so-called because used in pointing.
**5. a.** A table of contents prefixed to a book, a brief list or summary of the matters treated in it, an argument; also, a preface, prologue. *Obs.* **b.** An alphabetical list, placed (usually) at

the end of a book, of the names, subjects, etc. occurring in it, with indication of the places in which they occur. One work may have several indexes, e.g. an index of names of persons and places, of subjects, of words, etc. For these the Latin phrases *index nominum, locorum, rerum, verborum* are often employed as headings. **c.** A reference list. *Obs.* **d.** *Computers.* A set of items each of which specifies one of the records of a file and contains information about its address.

So there is here the notion of pointing or direction and an index is a collection or list of those items that do the pointing and those items that are pointed to. The purpose of an index is to help with finding or retrieving.

Often, but not always, the items pointed to can be accessed themselves, one after another, in an enumeration or a sequential scan. In which case, a direct search through the items pointed to could amount to, in the worst case, a possibly laborious, and potentially complete, sequential scan. An indirect search, via a search of the items doing the pointing, is intended to make this more efficient; it is intended to offer access to short cuts. It is certainly possible for a search through the items doing the pointing also to be a somewhat laborious, exhaustive, and entire sequential scan; however, the pointing items themselves are usually smaller in number than the items pointed to and also they have an arrangement, for example, alphabetical order, that allows searches of them to be guided, efficient, and direct. So, for example, if you were interested in the concept of 'algorithm', or the word 'algorithm', in Howson's *Logic with trees*, looking directly through the 190 odd pages of the book would take some time; so, you look through the index (partially extracted above) for the term 'algorithm'; this task also might take you some time if the list of indexed terms themselves had no structure and if the term 'algorithm' may or may not be among the list; but, the index terms are presented in alphabetical order, you can avail yourself of jumped key entry and find thereby the important page 17, the single and only page in the book that discusses or mentions algorithms.

Conceptually an index is an association list of key-value pairs. The keys are usually strings; they are headings or index entry names or terms. The values are lists of strings or lists of numbers, they are lists of items or descriptions of items (such as page numbers or web page URLs). So, in the above example, 'algorithm' is a key, and {17} is the value associated with it.

Index entries, or the keys, are often structured. So, for example, Howson has

adequate: for truth-functional logic 44;
        sets of connectives vii, 44ff

this is showing that there are two subtopics, or sub-keys, for 'adequate', one concerning 'truth-functional logic' and the other 'sets of connectives'. [We saw the idea of this earlier in Sect. 2.8.4 on word-by-word filing order.]

The structuring here is a clue to an important underlying feature. With Roget's Thesaurus we saw the use of structured keys to disambiguate homographs, to separate, for example, 'lieutenant (officer)' and 'lieutenant (deputy)'. But the

Howson index word 'adequate' is not a homograph. The word 'adequate' labels just one concept and that is an end to the matter. But in the index, it is not 'adequate' *itself* that is being indexed, rather it is 'adequate for truth-functional logic' and 'adequate sets of connectives'. These are labels for compound concepts, not elemental or atomic concepts. Roughly speaking, the original historical Roget Thesaurus used mostly atomic concepts and vocabularies for them, but we are going to want to generalize this to compound concepts.

The entry terms themselves, the keys or keywords, have to be found in the index and such devices as alphabetical lists help with this. This is worth mentioning because finding the entry names does not have to be easy. A medical text might have an index with key entries associated together by human body structure or function; in which case, finding the entry for, say, 'thyroid', might be a challenge for some Users. An approach here would be to use a second index, possibly an alphabetical index, to show where entries (like 'thyroid') appeared in the first index. So the second index gives locations in the first index, and the first index gives the pages in the book (This is somewhat similar to the two-step entry used with indexes in Thesauri.). In short, finding key entry terms, in the general case, is anything but trivial, with considerations of jumped key entry, key syntax, and indirect or stepping stone indexing.

## 2.13  Themes, Aboutness, Subjects and Polytopicality

There have been Tables of Contents pretty well since there have been written forms. What does a Table of Contents do? It tells you the contents and structure (especially if the IO is something like a linearized ordered tree of chapters, sections etc.). There is a coarseness to a Table of Contents. An IO itself, or a part of an IO, may have many words, sentences, and statements. A Table of Contents for that IO will have a lesser number of words. It is a distillation, an abstracting, a pilot text, as to the true full actual contents. One atom in a Table of Contents may point to an entire chapter in the text. It achieves this distillation by labeling what sections of the content are *about,* its *subjects* or *topics.*

Cutter described the notion of *subject* as being

> ... the matter on which the author is seeking to give or the reader to obtain information;
> (Cutter 1876, p. 12)

It is one of the most important notions in information retrieval. In this book, we use 'subject' and 'topic' interchangeably, and both of them in a very casual and open fashion. Anything can be a subject. Or, to qualify this slightly, any entity can be a subject; that is, anything that can be denoted grammatically by noun or a noun phrase, can be a subject; any grammatical subject can be an information retrieval subject (or information retrieval topic).

To return to Pliny. Here again is one section heading from Pliny's *The Natural History*

21. Of Lynxes, Sphinges, Crocutes, Marmosets, of Indian Oxen, of Leucrocutes, of Eale, of the Ethiopian Bulls, of the Mantichora, the Unicorn, of the Catoblepa, and the Basilisk.

This section, Sect. 21, is about Lynxes. But, obviously, it is also about Sphinges (and about Crocutes, Marmosets, etc.). It follows that a section, book, chapter, etc. can be *about more than one subject or topic*. The same is a possibility for any IO. When this occurs, the IO can be described as being 'polytopical'.

Any section, chapter, book etc. can be about more than one subject. But also, different sections, chapters, books etc. can be about the same subject or overlapping subjects. For example, the first 12 chapters of Pliny's *The Natural History* Book 8 (Table of Contents above) are all about elephants, perhaps among other things.

So, there can be an association list between IOs and subjects (that is the one between sections etc. and subjects). And this can be 'inverted' to produce an association list between subjects and IOs [The process of inversion is that of taking the keys in the first list to be the values in the second and the values in the first list to be the keys in the second. So

Chap1 elephants,
Chap2 elephants,
Chap3 elephants,
…
Chap 21 {Lynxes, Sphinges, Crocutes, Marmosets, …}
Etc.

gets inverted to

crocutes    Chap 21
elephants   {Chap1,Chap2,Chap3, etc.},
lynxes      Chap 21
Etc.

].
And the result is a *subject index*. And, in principle, there could be a subject index that ranges over every IO (or, at least, a very large number of them in a particular collection or union of collections). And, indeed, ordinary indexes do not have to be confined to single books or related IOs—they too can range over many IOs.

An ordinary index and a subject index usually would not be the same, but they are not a lot different either. On various occasions, and for various reasons, there may be the need to index peoples' names, or names of places, or names of battles, or historical periods, or topics, or themes, or subjects, etc. Of course, the categories of the items being indexed is different or can be different and the means for creating the indexes can be different (for example, with some being more amenable, and some less amenable, to automation). But the end result is much the same. A name index, for example, might be presented separately from a general index; and the main purpose of doing so would be just to make access and jumped key entry more effective.

## 2.14 Tag, Concept and Topic Annotation Languages

Let us rework the last section in a slightly different direction.

An ordinary back-of-the-book index is an association list between keys and values

> absurdity, rule of 137
> accessibility relation 166
> adequate: for truth-functional logic 44;
>                   sets of connectives vii, 44ff
> algorithm 17
> alpha ($\alpha$) sentence 49
> alternative denial 44
> ancestral trees vii, 6, 33ff.

To see how this was produced, consider the first entry 'absurdity, rule of' and imagine how it was arrived at. An indexer, or some algorithms, looked through the book and when they hit page 137 they decided that it should be labeled, or tagged, or annotated with the key 'absurdity, rule of'.

Let us for the moment adopt the word 'tags' instead of 'keys', so back-of-the-book indexing is just tagging the pages—so too for subject indexing: it also is tagging. We know that the index keys can be structured, so, in the general case, the tags also can be structured. And in a standard index, a particular key might have several pages as its values (in the example fragment, 'ancestral trees' has the three values vii, 6, 33ff.), and any particular page might be among the values for several different keys (e.g. page 44).

That gives us the following tag structure and use. We can imagine a tag vocabulary or language, which consists of words or terms or phrases. There can be a hierarchy or tree of tags, with parent tags, child tags, leaf tags and a root tag. [In fact, more generally, these tags may be a directed acyclic graph, a DAG, not just a tree, and so some tags might have multiple parents.] Let us call this graph of tags the *schedule*. We can use our tag vocabulary and schedule to label, or annotate, or 'tag' anything we wish (book pages, the items in our rumpus room, bottles of pickles and sauces, or IOs). Any tag can be used on more than one item, and any item might have more than one tag.

A *tag language* is just the language of the actual and potential keys. Alternatively, and perhaps more commonly, it can be called an *index language*. It is an *annotation language*.

Now let us start with a particular leaf tag in a schedule and work our way up a branch. A leaf tag produces for us, or can be used to produce, a collection or class of those items which are tagged with it. So, the 'hockey stick' tag might pick out three hockey sticks in our rumpus room. The next tag up the tree might be 'recreational equipment'. We understand this to denote anything it itself is tagged to, together with all those items tagged by its descendant tags. So this is going to identify a collection including the hockey sticks perhaps with a few tennis rackets and some golf clubs, and so on. The root tag 'rumpus room' might not itself directly tag anything however, its descendant tags may tag most things in the room (It depends how assiduous we have been with our labeling.). If we repeated this for a different leaf, say that for 'vacation items' we would get a similar outcome. The end result effectively is a structure gerrymander for the whole rumpus room. This structured gerrymander is not the best for physically organizing the room simply because there might be overlap between leaves, a hockey stick might be tagged both 'hockey stick' and 'vacation item' i.e. two tags which are tags from different branches and which might require those items to be in two places at once—the old problem of physicality. However, the system does help search. We can start with any tag (or combination of tags) and use those tags to retrieve what we wish, and, if we also use the schedule to gain information on parents and children, we can broaden or narrow our search to suit our purposes.

The tagging helps the process of search. In a way, it does not really matter what the tags mean, or indeed if they have meaning in any ordinary sense of meaning. They can be just labels. What matters is that they have some significance for the searcher and there is an appreciation of how the search will work (i.e. with what it retrieves and what broadening and narrowing amount to).

In the setting of information resources and the retrieval of IOs, tags are often used to signify *topics* or *subjects*. So, for example, an IO may be tagged with the string '1915 San Francisco World's Fair' and that tag would be used to indicate one of the topics or subjects of the IO. In turn, this means that apparently a language of subject headings, used for discussing topics or subjects, can also be seen as being a tag language or an index language or an annotation language.

At this point we can use the Triangle of Meaning to make a large step forward for IO tagging and indexing. Tags, and tag and index languages, if understood in terms of strings, all belong to the Symbol Vertex of the Triangle of Meaning. But we can move to the Concept Vertex of the Triangle of Meaning and tag and index IOs using concepts and a *concept language*.

This can have two great advantages. It steps around problems of synonyms and homographs. And, largely by itself, it can tell of parents and children. With a tag language, there is the need to determine, or decide on, a tree of tags (or a directed acyclic graph of tags), for this informs us which tags are parents of which children. But, with concepts, that may come free, or with little cost. Concepts are related to other concepts; for example, one concept can be a sub-concept (i.e. child) of another concept. Reid has given an example of this with his Parisian-Frenchman-Man-Animal hierarchy.

Concept languages are an attractive destination. And the suggestion of the present text is that symbolic logic that can provide the concept languages. For our purposes, the concepts are going to represent subjects or *topics*. So really the target is topic languages.

[The view that back-of-the-book indexing and subject tagging or annotation are essentially the same was certainly recognized by such pioneers as Rogers, who devised MeSH, the medical subject headings list, and Mortimer Taube, who suggested coordination and postcoordination (Rogers 1960a, b). Rogers and Taube were also both in favor of coordination.

... define coordinate indexing as a system of subject cataloging which capitalizes on the concept of the logical conjunction of ideas (the phrase comes from symbolic logic).... Taube is simply stressing the fact that complex ideas are often best expressed, or even solely expressed, by the intersection of two or more widely separated ideas, and by the intersection, or conjunction, of their separate word symbols when an attempt is made to catalog those ideas. (Rogers 1960b, p. 381)

And they were possibly also both in favor of the use of symbolic logic ['the logical conjunction of ideas (the phrase comes from symbolic logic)'] and of the use of the Concept Vertex as opposed to the Symbol Vertex.

I cannot believe that the system can ever demonstrate its full potentialities so long as what is being coordinated are just words (Rogers 1960b, p. 383).
]

## 2.14.1 Free and Controlled Vocabularies

There is an issue in information retrieval that arises in many different places (as examples, with keys in indexes, with the insertion of keywords, with subject classification, with metadata, and with tagging) and that concerns *vocabularies*, in particular whether they are *free* or *controlled*.

This issue can be explained in the setting of keywords. Keywords are words that authors and editors attach usually to academic papers to assist with retrieval. In fact, the attaching of keywords is the forming of a kind of index, or the forming of the inverse of an index. If, for example, IO#1 has keywords {Art, Paris}, and IO#2 has keyword {London, Museum, Paris} that generates an association list of IOs and their keywords, with fragment

```
IO#1    {Art, Paris}
IO#2    {London, Museum, Paris}
```

And an inversion of that is

```
Art        {IO#1}
London     {IO#2}
Museum     {IO#2}
Paris      {IO#1, IO#2}
```

which is a recognizable index.

Words, or collections of words, that get used in these contexts are vocabularies. (Really they are languages, but 'vocabulary' is the word most commonly used here.) So, for instance, the collection of words that is used as keys or keywords in a particular journal of academic papers is a vocabulary. There is a choice concerning such vocabularies. Either the authors, editors, and publishers can use whatever words they wish as keywords, in which case the vocabulary is a *free vocabulary*, or there is a fixed list of proscribed and permitted words that can be used as keywords and the authors etc. have to choose from among them, in which case the vocabulary is a *controlled vocabulary*.

The advantages and disadvantages of controlled vocabularies are easy to summarize. No one knows better than the author of an article what that article is about, so the author is the best person to attach keywords and further the author is best placed to judge exactly what word or words should be the keywords. Score one for free vocabularies. However, this leads to two problems, the patron problem and the several authors problem. The reason there are keywords, indexes, subject classifications etc. is to allow patrons to browse, find, and retrieve IOs. So the keywords, for example, need to be words that patrons or users are familiar with and would use for retrieval. Users are important in the choice of keywords. Seemingly, no one knows better what a searcher are looking for than the actual searcher. Second, if there are two authors each writing a paper on the same topic, and one of them uses one keyword or set of keywords, and the other uses different synonym keywords, then the patron will not be able to retrieve both papers using either authors keywords individually. Here is an example of both these problems. Take the words 'butterflies' and 'rhopalocera'. (As noted, these mean more-or-less the same thing, one is a common everyday word, the other a mildly technical term from biology.) If author one uses the keyword 'rhopalocera', and the patron searches for 'butterflies', the patron will not find the paper (by string match). Recall will be lower than it might have been had the author and the patron been in tune with each other. If author one uses the keyword 'rhopalocera' and author two uses the keyword 'butterflies', then a patron will not find both papers by searching either for 'butterflies' or 'rhopalocera'. Again, recall will be lower than it might have been (and precision might also be adversely affected). The solution to these problems is to use a controlled vocabulary. Such a vocabulary might have the word 'butterflies' in it as a preferred term, but *not* 'rhopalocera'; then all authors writing on this topic *must* use the keyword 'butterflies', and all patrons searching for this topic *must* also use the search term 'butterflies'. Score two for controlled vocabularies. Controlled vocabularies will not usually contain synonyms. For each 'synset' (set or class of synonyms), a choice will be made as to a single *preferred* term or canonical representative for it; and there may be links or references from the other *lead in* terms to the preferred term.

Controlled vocabularies are typically used in conjunction with thesauri (which inform of synonyms, preferred terms etc.). So, for example, if a controlled vocabulary had the term 'butterflies', its associated thesaurus might have an entry

  rhopalocera, use butterflies.

Ordinary indexes sometimes mesh together a controlled vocabulary and a thesaurus. For example, a key entry, or fake key, might be 'rhopalocera, see butterflies' (such a key is 'fake' because it is not really part of the association list, rather it is a helpful directive on how to use the association list).

The fact is: controlled vocabularies increase precision and recall. It would take a book-length monograph to argue that point, to cover the different cases and logical and experimental results. But, at the end of the day, almost always controlled vocabularies are better. As Elaine Svenonius writes

> Perhaps as near as one can come to generalization about the value of a CV [Controlled Vocabulary] is simply to say where precision and recall are important retrieval objectives, then a CV of some kind is mandated. (Svenonius 2003, p. 837)

We will take that as a given.

## 2.14.2  Information Retrieval Thesauri

Modern information retrieval thesauri date from about the 1960s (Dahlberg 1993; Gilchrist 2003; Evens 2002). In their simplest examples, such thesauri are just lists of preferred terms and their synonyms for use with a controlled vocabulary. However, especially with hierarchical vocabularies, it is possible to pack more information into a thesaurus. There can be information not merely about synonyms, but there can be information about antonyms (love/hate), broader terms (BT), narrower terms (NT), and related terms (RT). So, an entry for 'butterfly' might note 'used for (UF) 'rhopalocera' and 'lepidoptera' as a broader term (BT) (for lepidoptera include moths as well as butterflies); an entry for 'yellow' might note 'colored' as a broader term, 'mustard yellow' as a narrower term, and 'jaundiced' as a related term. There can also be Scope Notes, which are explanations of the usages [See, for example, Lexical FreeNet (Datamuse 2003).]. As Jean Aitchison, Alan Gilchrist, and David Bawden write

> [a thesaurus is a] vocabulary of a controlled indexing language, formally organized so that
> *a priori* relationships between concepts are made explicit (Aitchison et al. 2000, p. 1)

Aitchison, Gilchrist, and Bawden are very much experts in this area, and the phrasing they use here in this quotation is interesting. The important relationships are those between concepts (and concepts occupy the Concept Vertex of the Triangle of Meaning). But the vocabulary (words, phrases, and the like) belong to the Symbol Vertex. So what a thesaurus is doing is giving explicit Symbol Vertex representation to important abstract Concept Vertex relationships.

The plainest thesauri deal for the most part with *single* words or terms, not multi-word phrases or expressions (International Standard ISO 2788). In this, they are like Dictionaries. Occasionally Dictionaries have entries consisting of a couple words or a phrase (e.g. 'birth control'), and so too do plain Thesauri. But phrases are not the standard form for entry key strings for either Dictionaries or plain Thesauri. Single words are the standard form. The reason for this is that, in their basic core, thesauri are to address the problem of synonyms, and synonyms are largely single words.

In the modern era, thesauri are often just seen as indexing languages. And indexing languages often do need compound terms and sometimes even compound terms of some length. Anthony Foskett mentions a real example, from the *British Technology Index*, the manufacture of multi-wall kraft paper sacks for the packaging of cement (Foskett 1996, p. 97)

A string like 'the manufacture of multi-wall kraft paper sacks for the packaging of cement' can be a subject heading, and so it can be part of a subject indexing language; it thus can also be part of a index-thesaurus; however, it will have no synonyms and no obvious broader or narrower terms so it does not really have any of the special qualities of typical thesaurus entries.

Our sympathies are very much with Aitchison, Gilchrist, and Bawden, but we would give pride of place to conceptual structure. There are concepts, and, for any particular concept in a conceptual scheme, there might be one or more Broader Concepts (BCs), and there might be one or more Narrower Concepts (NCs). Broader concepts and narrower concepts are just inverses of each other. Quite what establishes this broader to narrower link will be discussed in detail later in the book (There might also be Equivalent Concepts (ECs), but they are not so much of interest.). Each concept is an entity unto itself, however, it may be atomic or elemental or it may be complex or compound. Thus the conceptual scheme consists of a Directed Acyclic Graph (DAG) of concepts.

This DAG of concepts can be talked about using such node labels as terms, words, phrases, or symbols. Any concept, atomic or compound, may have a single word term that names it, or short phrases, or long phrases (and there may also be clusters of synonym terms or 'synonym phrases' for the node). If the nodes do have terms or short phrases as labels we are in the territory of the classical information retrieval thesaurus. However, even if the labels are long there is still the idea of Broader Phrase (BP) and Narrower Phrase (NP) and these just mean phrases for a broader (narrower) concept.

In sum, the DAG of concepts lurks in the background, and the classical indexing thesaurus has cashed out only some of the value in it.

## 2.14.3 Tidying up the Nomenclature of Tags and Topics

The word 'tag' is in widespread use nowadays, denoting a core element or feature of many popular websites (such as Flickr, for photographs or image, Digg, for endorsement of web-based information items, for Del.icio.us, for ranking items, etc.) (Heymann and Garcia-Molina, 2008, 2009; Heymann et al. 2010). And the word 'tag' means a certain sort of thing: essentially a free vocabulary string. The Users are at liberty to make up and use as a tag any word, phrase, or even nonsense string they wish. That the vocabulary or vocabularies are free tends to mean that they are independent of any hierarchical structure or hierarchical thesauri. The tags in common use are annotations using strings from a free vocabulary that does not have a hierarchy.

Topics are also going to be used for annotation. Topics, for us, are concepts. These are going to be described by symbolic logic, and they will have a controlled form and inter-related structure. Topics can also be described by more ordinary strings. If so, the strings would often be called topic or subject *headings*; and those subject headings would amount to a controlled vocabulary, usually with structure and thesauri-like graph-theoretical hierarchical or other relations among them.

In large part, then, we will used 'tagging' to mean free string annotation, and 'assigning a topic' ('topic-ing'?) to mean annotation with controlled concepts, topics, or, perhaps, subject headings.

## 2.15  The Lesson of the Museum and its Written Guides

There is a central device or distinction within information resources that it is easy to get confused over.

It can be brought to life with the example of museums and literature written about the contents of those museums. Museums classify, catalog and inventory what they have. So, for example, a museum might have sarcophagi—including Egyptian sarcophagi—and coins, including Roman coins. Typically a museum would use a fairly elaborate classification scheme which would include concepts related to other concepts in hierarchies or other graph-theoretical structures. The curators of the museum have an interest in concepts but their principal interest is: which artifacts fall under the denotation of which concepts, for example, in determining which of their items are Egyptian sarcophagi. In imagination, we could certainly suppose that they used their scheme to produce very small labels that they attached or associated with their artifacts; so, for example, an Egyptian sarcophagus might have an 'Egyptian sarcophagus' label on it.

In addition to its actual contents, a museum will likely have an Information Desk, Bookstore, or Gift Shop containing written guides about what the museum has. Some of these guides could be more comprehensive than others. Some could be about all the holdings, some could be about coins, some could be about just Roman coins. The visitors have an interest in what the topics or subject matters of those guides are. The museum could certainly indicate topics by sticking exactly the same labels on the pamphlets as they do on the items that are actually in the display halls. So, a guide may have an 'Egyptian sarcophagi' label on it. Of course, this does not mean that the guide is an Egyptian sarcophagus, it means that the guide addresses the topic of 'Egyptian sarcophagi'. The authors of the guides also have an interest in much the same concepts as the museum curators; but they are not interested in those concepts to classify actual relics, they are interested in them as labels of topics. So, now the classificatory concepts, and their labels, are playing double duty. They are identifying things and they are identifying topics. Not only that, the relations between topics is parasitic upon, or symbiotic with, the classification scheme. A reader would generally expect that the topic 'Roman coins' would be a sub-topic of the topic 'Coins' and this is because Roman Coins are a subclass of Coins.

We are going to have an interest in the various styles of classification of 'things' simply because those classifications and classification styles are the inspirations for the topic hierarchies.

But there is a further point of potential confusion. Classical libraries certainly have some commonalities with museums. And librarians have also classified what they have. Most actual existing IO classification schemes use what an IO is *about*, its subject or topic, to classify what the item *is*. In the Dewey Decimal Classification, for example, a book on physics is classified differently to a book on chemistry, and the basis of this difference is that the books are about different subjects.

Books can have many properties. A book might be an encyclopaedia, a dictionary, a monograph, a research study, a conference proceedings, a report, and so on. But in addition to what a book *presents as* there seems to be the question of what a book *is about*. There can be research studies on physics, research studies on juvenile anti-social behavior, and so on. All these IOs are research studies but they are about different subjects. Often the subjects lead. Certainly, there is a lot going on.

The way to be clear here is to rely on Reid. All classification is the possession of attributes (or properties). Attributes of interest within information retrieval include

...is an encyclopaedia
...is a research study
...addresses the subject 'physics'
...addresses the subject 'chemistry'
...

and so on. And individual IOs possess a selection of these.

# References

Aitchison J, Gilchrist A, Bawden D (2000) Thesaurus construction and use: a practical manual, 4th edn. Fitzroy Dearborn, Chicago

Anderson JD (1997) Organization of knowledge. In: Feather J, Sturges P (eds) International dictionary of library and information science. Routledge, London, pp 336–353

Bealer G (1982) Quality and concept. Oxford University Press, Oxford

Blair A (2003) Coping with information overload in early modern Europe

Cataloging PaSO (2007) Library of congress subject headings: pre- vs. post-coordination and related issues. http://www.loc.gov/catdir/cpso/pre_vs_post.pdf.

Craven TC (1986) String indexing. Academic, Orlando

Cutter CA (1876) Rules for a printed dictionary catalogue. Government Printing Office, Washington

Dahlberg I (1993) Current trends in knowledge organization. Paper presented at the first conference on knowledge organization and documentary systems, Madrid

Daly LW (1967) Contributions to a history of alphabetization in antiquity and the middle ages. Latomus, Brussels

Datamuse (2003) Lexical FreeNet. http://www.lexfn.com/. Accessed 12 Oct 2010

Dewey M (1926) Dewey decimal classification and relativ index for libraries, 12 edn. Library Bureau, Boston

Ellis B (2008) Essentialism and natural kinds. In: Psillos S, Curd M (eds) The routledge companion to philosophy of science. Routledge, London, pp 139–148

Evens M (2002) Thesaural relations in information retrieval. In: Green R, Bean CA, Myaeng SH (eds) The semantics of relationships: an interdisciplinary perspective. Kluwer Academic Publishers, Dordrecht, pp 143–160

Foskett AC (1996) Subject approach to information, 5th edn. Facet Publishing, London

Foucault M (1970) The order of things. Random House, New York

Fraser AC (1898) Thomas Reid. Oliphant, Anderson & Ferrier, Edinburgh

Gilchrist A (2003) Thesauri, taxonomies and ontologies—an etymological note. J. Documentation 59(1):7–18

Haack S (1999) A fallibilist among the cynics. Skeptical Inquirer 23(1):47–50

Heim I, Kratzer A (1998) Semantics in generative grammar. Blackwell, Oxford

Hempel CG (1965) Fundamentals of taxonomy. In: Hempel CG (ed) Aspects of scientific explanation and other essays in the philosophy of science. The Free Press, New York, pp 137–154

Heymann P, Garcia-Molina H (2008) Can tagging organize human knowledge? Technical report. Stanford University, Palo Alto

Heymann P, Garcia-Molina H (2009) Contrasting controlled vocabulary and tagging: Do experts choose the right names to label the wrong things? WSDM '09, Barcelona, Spain

Heymann P, Paepcke A, Garcia-Molina H (2010) Tagging human knowledge. In: Third ACM international conference on web search and data mining. New York City, New York

Jacob EK (2004) Classification and categorization: a difference that makes a difference. Library Trends 52(3):515–540

Koslicki K (2008) Natural kinds and natural kind terms. Philos Compass 3(4):789–802

Kuhn SM (1972) Review of contributions to a history of alphabetization in antiquity and the middle ages by Lloyd W. Daly. Speculum 47(2):300–303

Mann T (1993) Library research models. Oxford University Press, New York

Miksa F (1983) The subject in the dictionary catalog from cutter to the present. American Library Association, Chicago

Mill JS (1843) A system of logic: ratiocinative and inductive; being a connected view of the principles and evidence and the methods of scientific investigation. Reprinted in collected works. University of Toronto Press, Toronto, p 1963

Milstead JL (1984) Subject access systems: alternatives in design. Academic, Orlando

Ogden CK, Richards IA (1972) The meaning of meaning: a study of the influence of language upon thought and of the science of symbolism. Harcourt & Brace, New York

Partee BH, Ter Meulen A, Wall RE (1990) Mathematical methods in linguistics. Kluwer Academic Publishers, Dordrecht

Pliny the Elder (78) The natural history. http://www.perseus.tufts.edu/hopper/text?doc=Perseus:text:1999.02.0137. Accessed Dec 21 2011

Popper KR (1972) Objective knowledge; an evolutionary approach. Clarendon Press, Oxford

Ranganathan SR (1937) Prolegomena to library classification, 3rd edn 1967; 1st edn 1937. The Madras library association, Madras

Reid T (1785) Abstraction. In: Bennett JF (ed) Essays on the intellectual powers of man (redacted text)

Rogers FB (1960a) Medical subject headings. Preface and introduction. U.S. Department of Health, Education and Welfare, Washington, pp i–xix

Rogers FB (1960b) Review of taube, mortimer. Studies in coordinate indexing. Bull Med Libr Assoc 42 (July 1954): 380–384

Roget PM (1852) Roget's thesaurus. Longman Group Limited, Burnt Mill, Harlow, Essex

Rosch E (1973) Natural categories. Cogn Psychol 4(3):328–350

Rosch E (1975) Cognitive representations of semantic categories. J Exp Psychol Gen 104: 192–233

Rosch E (1978) Principles of categorization. In: Rosch E, Lloyd B (eds) Cognition and categorization. Lawrence Erlbaum, Hillsdale, pp 27–48

Rosch E, Mervis CB (1975) Family resemblances: studies in the internal structure of categories. Cogn Psychol 7(4):573–605

Rosch E, Mervis CB, Gray W, Johnson D, Boyes-Braem P (1976) Basic objects in natural categories. Cogn Psychol 8(4):382–439

Salton G (1962) Manipulation of trees in information retrieval. Commun ACM 5(2):103–114

Savage E (1946) Manual of book classification and display. Allen & Unwin, London

Sedgewick R (1988) Algorithms, 2nd edn. Addison-Wesley, Reading

Siracusa J (2001) Metadata, the mac, and you. http://arstechnica.com/apple/reviews/2001/08/metadata.ars. Accessed 10 Oct 2010

Siracusa J (2005) Mac OS X 10.4 tiger. http://arstechnica.com/apple/reviews/2005/04/macosx-10-4.ars. Accessed 10 Oct 2010

Smith B (2004) Beyond concepts: ontology as reality representation. In: Varzi A, Vieu L (eds) Proceedings of FOIS 2004. International conference on formal ontology and information systems, IOS Press, Turin, pp 73–84

Soergel D (1974) Indexing languages and thesauri: construction and maintenance. Melville, Los angeles

Svenonius E (ed) (1978) String indexing. School of Library and Information Science, The University of Western Ontario, London

Svenonius E (2003) Design of controlled vocabularies. In: Encyclopedia of library and information science. Marcel Dekker, New York, pp 822–838

Taube M (1951) Functional approach to bibliographic organization: a critique and a proposal. In: Shera JH, Egan M (eds) Bibliographic organization: fifteenth annual conference of the graduate library school. University of Chicago Press, Chicago, 24–29 July 1950, pp 57–71

Taube M (1953) Studies in coordinate indexing. Documentation Incorporated, Washington

Taube M (1961) On the use of roles and links in co-ordinate indexing. Am Documentation 12:98–100

Taube M, Thompson AF (1951) The Coordinate indexing of scientific fields. Unpublished paper read before the symposium on mechanical aids to chemical documentation of the division of chemical literature of the American chemical society, 4 Sept 1951

Taylor AG (2004) The organization of information, 2nd edn. Libraries Unlimited, Westport

Tichy P (1988) The foundations of Frege's logic. de Gruyter, Berlin

Unicode I (1991–2010) The unicode consortium. http://unicode.org/. Accessed 10 Oct 2010

W3C (2010) Large triple stores. http://esw.w3.org/LargeTripleStores. Accessed 10 Oct 2010

Wellisch HH (1981) How to make an index—16th century style: Conrad Gessner on indexes and catalogs. Int Classif 8(1):10–15

Wellisch HH (1983) 'Index' - the word, its history, meanings and usages. The Indexer 13(3):147–151

Wellisch HH (1986) The oldest printed indexes. The Indexer 15(2):73–82

Wellisch HH (1991) Indexing from A to Z. H.W.Wilson Co, New York

Witty FJ (1973) The beginnings of indexing and abstracting: some notes towards a history of indexing and abstracting in antiquity and the middle ages. The Indexer 8(4):193–198

# Chapter 3
# Catalogs, Inventories and Propaedias

## 3.1 Introduction

At one level, we are very clear on what Catalogs and Inventories are. Many of us receive Catalogs unsolicited through the mail. A typical one of these, say from the retailer Crate and Barrel, will list the kinds of things that Crate and Barrel currently offer for sale. Then, having used the Catalog to make our choice to purchase, say, a *Henley Floor Cushion (Peacock),* our interest moves to a different question, does our local branch of Crate and Barrel have any of these cushions in stock? And that is a question of the branch's Inventory. Usually Catalogs are more than mere lists; they are often structured classifications or *classification schemes* or *schedules.* Crate and Barrel Catalogs organize: they divide up what they hold into *outdoor; kitchen; home; entertaining; bed* and *bath;* etc., and then divide those categories up further—*Henley Floor Cushion (Peacock)* will appear at suitable locations in this classificatory structure. So, a Catalog is a classification of kinds of things, and an Inventory is a list, or association list, of the actual things of those kinds.

This distinction is central to librarianship. A library holds titles, and it identifies these by ISBN numbers, and it holds items with those titles, which it identifies with Bar Codes or RFID (Radio Frequency Identification) codes. The titles and ISBN numbers are central to the library's Catalog; the individual books, and the Bar Codes, are central to the library's circulation records, collection, and inventory. Care needs to be taken here: we might, for other purposes, need to compare libraries by 'size of collection'; however if one library counts titles and another library counts volumes, the two libraries would be counting different things.

A first sight this distinction seems easy enough. The items, the *Henley Floor Cushions (Peacock)* and, similarly, for example, the particular volumes of the novel *Pride and Prejudice* are all physical objects with locations in space and time. They are 'concrete'. Then these items have kinds; the items are each instances or exemplifications of particular kinds. The individual *Henley Floor Cushions*

M. Frické, *Logic and the Organization of Information,*
DOI: 10.1007/978-1-4614-3088-9_3,
© Springer Science+Business Media New York 2012

*(Peacock)* items are all similar to each other. [This does not mean that they are identical, one might be more faded than another, but it does mean that, in terms of the way we approach the world and classify the things we encounter, they are sufficiently similar to be considered the same are far as being examples or instances of that kind of cushion.] Similarly, the individual item volumes of *Pride and Prejudice* are all copies of that book; they all exemplify the requisite kind. The kinds themselves are not located in space or time; they are abstract. So, one characteristic that seems to be present is that Inventories list the concrete and Catalogs list the abstract.

Unfortunately it is not that simple. We can catalog and inventory the abstract. As an example, consider the notion of a species of bird or animal, such as, Kiwi, Moa, Tiger, etc. Species are abstract. The *species* Kiwi (the flightless bird, national bird of New Zealand) is not concrete and located in space and time (although, of course, instances or examples of Kiwis are concrete and have location). In addition, species themselves can have properties or be of certain kinds, for example, a species can be extinct or non-extinct. A species is extinct if there are no concrete living examples of it. The species Moa (another flightless New Zealand bird) is extinct—there are no living Moas (there are Moa skeletons, Moa feathers, Moa footprints, and Moa bones, but no actual living Moas). Then there can be catalogs and inventories of extinct species; for instance, Ross Piper's *Extinct Animals: An Encyclopaedia of Species that Have Disappeared during Human History* (Piper 2009) which inventories under kinds: those species extinct for less than a hundred years, those species extinct for more than one hundred but less than two hundred years, and so on.

We need to get clear on catalogs, inventories, and related distinctions. They are widespread in the theory and practice of information management. These distinctions are central to librarianship, as explained above. They are central to the Functional Requirements for Bibliographical Records (FRBR) (Taylor 2007). They are central to Basic Formal Ontology (BFO), to Descriptive Ontology for Linguistic and Cognitive Engineering (DOLCE), to Suggested Upper Merged Ontology (SUMO), to CYC, and to similar efforts (Lenat 1996; Masolo et al. 2001). BFO and DOLCE themselves are vital for the management of information about, for example, high throughput experimentation, medical records, biodiversity etc. This contention is evident when Luc Schneider writes about *Aristotle's Ontological Square*, to be discussed later in this chapter,

> [it] arguably embodies common-sense intuitions as to how things are to be classified, underpins not only conceptual modelling in relational database design and object-oriented programming, but also foundational ontologies like DOLCE or BFO. It is not yet another top-level ontology, but a formal paradigm that pervades a wide range of theoretical frameworks used in conceptual modelling and in knowledge representation (Schneider 2009 p. 26).

It would have been pleasant to find a milieu in which everyone was using the same terminology, with the same meaning, i.e. uniform standards, and then for the terminology to be transparently clear. Sad to say, the different intellectual ventures use different terminologies. Libraries talk of 'titles' and 'volumes' or 'copies'.

FRBR talks of 'manifestations' and 'items'. BFO talks of 'universals' and 'instances', etc.

So now our task is to produce some general scheme that can make sense of it all and provide translations—cross walks if you will—of the terminologies when need be. To that end we need to look at some similar, but slightly different, approaches to this area. Then we will conclude by seeing if they can be drawn together to provide a schema which will serve to correlate the various views in an enlightening manner.

## 3.2 (Peirce)Types vs. Tokens

The early twentieth century American philosopher Charles Sanders Peirce highlighted the distinction between type and token. It is a distinction that is vital in this setting. It can be explained by means of an example. [We are going to follow (Wetzel 2006) here.]

When Edgar Allan Poe wrote

Of the bells, bells, bells, bells,
Bells, bells, bells
In the clamor and the clangor of the bells!

How many words did he write? 'Eighteen' is one reasonable answer, so too is 'seven'. The answer 'seven' counts the word 'bells' as a *type* (and similarly for 'the' and 'of'); the answer 'eighteen' refers to the *tokens* of the words. (Of course, the Word Count function available in typical software word processors counts the tokens.)

Here is a relevant passage from Peirce.

A common mode of estimating the amount of matter in a MS. or printed book is to count the number of words. There will ordinarily be about twenty *the's* on a page, and of course they count as twenty words. In another sense of the word "word," however, there is but one word "the" in the English language; and it is impossible that this word should lie visibly on a page or be heard in any voice, for the reason that it is not a Single thing or Single event. It does not exist; it only determines things that do exist. Such a definitely significant Form, I propose to term a *Type*. A Single event which happens once and whose identity is limited to that one happening or a Single object or thing which is in some single place at any one instant of time, such event or thing being significant only as occurring just when and where it does, such as this or that word on a single line of a single page of a single copy of a book, I will venture to call a *Token*.... In order that a Type may be used, it has to be embodied in a Token which shall be a sign of the Type, and thereby of the object the Type signifies. I propose to call such a Token of a Type an *Instance* of the Type. ('Prolegomena to an Apology for Pragmaticism', CP 4.537, 1906) (Peirce 1906)

Tokens are concrete objects. They are particular individuals, usually identified grammatically by singular nouns, which are also specific. Cynthia's personal copy of Henry Gray's *Anatomy of the Human Body* is an example of a token book and of a concrete object.

Types are a good deal more elusive than items. Types are also identified grammatically by singular nouns (we say, for example, that the second word of the exclamation 'hells bells!' is *the word* 'bells' (note, the grammatical determiner noun combination 'the word' is singular)); in fact, types are singular nouns, but they refer generally not to a specific item. That types are identified by singular nouns makes types objects or quasi-objects. However, types are not concrete objects. Consider the book type 'personal copy of Henry Gray's *Anatomy of the Human Body*'. This is a completely non-mysterious type. Every reader of this passage knows exactly what it is. Cynthia's own personal copy, a concrete item, is an instance or exemplification or token of this type. Maybe Cynthia's father also has his own personal copy; if so, that would be a second concrete item of the type. And, in all likelihood, there are hundreds of other concrete object items that fall under this type. All these individual items or tokens are in space and time—they have location. But what about the type itself, where is it? Where is the type 'personal copy of Henry Gray's *Anatomy of the Human Body*'? Where was this type on January 15th? Clearly, the type is not a concrete object. It is abstract. The concrete can, of course, be related to the abstract; the concrete personal items are exemplifications of the abstract type.

Counting, or the process of counting, is often revealing when trying to distinguish tokens and types. With any particular type, there can be only *one* of them. So with the word type 'bells', there is only one of it, and there cannot be other numerically distinct word types that are the same word type as the word type 'bells'. But, with any particular token, there can be *many* of them. With the word token 'bells', there can be many of them—indeed, there were eight in the Poe passage reproduced earlier.

Types and tokens arise at the foundation level with bibliographic records. Cynthia may want to convey how extensive her personal library is. To do this, even in a most cursory fashion, she needs notions of books and volumes, of titles, of two titles being different, of two titles/books/volumes being different or being merely copies of each other. Cynthia might have two books by Jane Austen, meaning two different books (one token each of two different types) or two copies of the same book (two tokens of the same type). The same point is emphasized when a wider range of creative items is brought into the domain. A work of art may consist of a single token (Mona Lisa), a definite artistically identified number of items (numbered prints, numbered sculptures, numbered reproductions), arbitrarily many item performances (of a symphony or play), then copies of all these, etc.

Reid's essay on abstraction, discussed earlier, is largely about 'general words' i.e. types—types as they appear, or are described, in language.

## 3.3 Plato on Universals vs. Particulars

The discussion of Peirce-style types and tokens, in the last section, concerns things or entities; in a way, it concerns specific things and general things. Now we want to look at ascribing properties to those things. Recall, in Sect. 2.1 there was discussion of Reid's views about ascribing attributes to things; and, in Sect. 2.3, there was mention of humanity's world view that the world consists of entities possessing properties. This section is about the properties and attributes.

Here is an argument from Plato, from two thousand years before Peirce (Plato 360 BCE-a, b, c; 370 BCE; Russell 1912). Consider justice and just acts. Plato reasoned that particular just acts must have some common nature that they share by virtue of which they are just acts. There must be a common nature that they have which makes them just acts. This common nature, *justice*, is not itself a 'particular'. Rather it is a 'universal'; indeed it is a universal that is abstract and does not exist at a specific place and time. Just acts are not the only things with common natures. Another example is white things (or particulars), they all share in, or participate in, or exemplify, or instantiate, the universal *whiteness*. Indeed, our whole world consists of things with common natures.

Thus, the metaphysical or ontological picture is that there are concrete particulars (things, objects) and abstract universals (concepts, properties, attributes). And the universals can be instantiated or exemplified by numerically distinct particulars.

Plato gives an underpinning to our ordinary everyday talk. We typically talk about things (or entities) and about properties (attributes) that those things have. The things are the particulars and the properties are the universals.

Universals can be related to the earlier type-token distinction. A token of the word 'bells' and another token of the word 'bells' share a common essence by virtue of which they are both tokens of 'bells'; so there is a universal that they share; that universal may be regarded as the type 'bells' or, rather, the type 'bells' is a universal which is instantiated or exemplified in the particular token 'bells'.

It seems that we might be able to explicate the type-token distinction as just that of a special case of the relation between a universal and a particular. There was mention of the universal *whiteness*. Let us develop a different example using whiteness. There is a type 'golf ball' which has millions of tokens which instantiate it, most of those tokens share the common nature of being white and thus are particulars instantiating the universal white. And maybe the golf ball of a specific golfer, Old Tom, is white, thus where the arrows, or directed links, are showing the instantiation from a universal to a particular. However, when you think about it, the type (white) golf ball can also *itself* be, or be asserted to be, white. Some golf balls are orange or pink, but golf balls are mostly white and certainly white golf balls are white. Old Tom, who happens to be a cantankerous traditional golfer, might remark 'those orange and pink golf balls are an abomination, in my foursome the golf ball is white'. The 'the golf ball' that is being spoken of is not a token golf ball in someone's golf bag, it is the type golf ball. So there needs to be a directed link from the Attribute to the Type. Thus (Figs. 3.1, 3.2). This third arrow might not mean exactly the same as the other two arrows, but the arrow is similar and it is hard to deny the motivation behind it. Tokens are objects and their corresponding individual types or kinds are quasi-objects. And, as a result of this, tokens and their corresponding individual types often share properties. The token word 'bells' has five letters in it, and the type word 'bells' also seems to have five

**Fig. 3.1** Instantiations from universal to particular

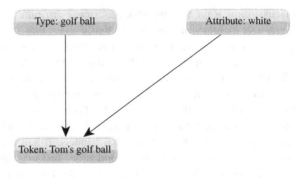

**Fig. 3.2** Instantiations with attributes applying to types

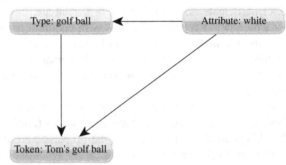

letters in it in exactly the same or a very similar way. Linda Wetzel gives a good example of this: Beethoven's Symphony No. 9 (i.e. the type) is in the same key, has the same number of measures, same number of notes, etc. as a great many of its tokens (i.e. of its performances) (Wetzel 2006).

This diagram certainly seems short in at least one respect. When the golfer Old Tom finds his ball in the rough due to the sunlight shining off the white color of the ball, it is the whiteness in the particular ball that causes his eye to see the ball and his attention to be drawn to it. But the universal/attribute white, or whiteness, is abstract and cannot cause anything. One response here is to invoke particular 'pieces' of whiteness, and to suggest that they exist in the tokens. These pieces are often called *modes*, and introducing them brings with it the notion of a four-category ontology. Thus (Fig. 3.3).

## 3.4  Aristotle

Thus far in this chapter we have been addressing one part of general *ontology*—what things there are—and we have advocated an enhanced mixture of the views of Peirce and Plato. This has given us a four-category ontology: Tokens, Types, Attributes, and Modes.

Aristotle's theories need discussion. Aristotle is the most important and influential figure in the history of classification (and he certainly anticipated Peirce on

**Fig. 3.3** A four category
ontology

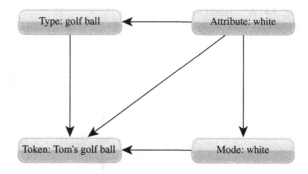

Types and Tokens). With Aristotle, there is a qualification. Aristotle's texts are
hard to understand and interpret, especially his writings in *The Categories* and
*Topics,* which are treatises from the *Organon* that are of special interest to us.
Sometimes Aristotle seems to be talking about language, sometimes he seems to
be talking about the world. In addition the Greek language itself allows for the
word 'the' to be placed in front of both nouns and adjectives (to form nouns from
adjectives, for example, 'the red', or 'the tall') and thus it does not make the kinds
of distinctions we are used to between nouns and adjectives. Also Aristotle's
actual texts seem poorly organized and possibly even inconsistent. In sum, even
experts (Bäck 2000; Studtmann 2008) have difficulties. So, let us offer apologies in
advance to Aristotle's legacy and to genuine Aristotle scholars.

### 3.4.1 Predicables and Definition

Aristotle offered a theory of definition in *Topics* and this later became part of the
theory of 'predicables' (Berg 1982; Smith 2009).

Predicables are close enough to being constructions on Reid attributes. And
there are five kinds of predicables

Definition
Genus
Differentiae (or Difference)
Common Properties
Accidents

To explain these, it is convenient to have an example classification hierarchy, for
Aristotle's theory of definition rests on his ideas of classification (Fig. 3.4). Each
of the parent kinds or classes in this diagram is a *genus*. So, 'living being' is a
genus, and so too is 'animal'.

It is the child classes or child sorts that get *defined*, and they are defined by
identifying their parent i.e. their genus and putting that together with the *differentiae* which is the difference which separates or distinguishes them from their

**Fig. 3.4** A fragment of a
classification hierarchy

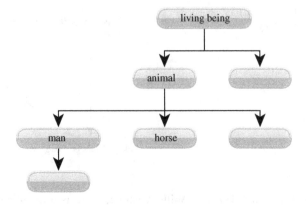

siblings. So, for example, the sort 'man' can be defined, and it has 'animal' as its
genus; and Aristotle thought that what picked the kind 'man' out was the property
of 'having the capacity to reason' (the above diagram itself does not show this). So
the definition is

man = $_{df.}$ animal having the capacity to reason

Centuries after Aristotle, with porphyry and Boethius, the defined class became
called the *species*. So all definitions had the form

<species> = $_{df.}$ < genus> < difference>

When a class or species is defined this way, the defining properties on the right
hand side of the definition are *essential* properties that all instances of the species
must have. Definition—this kind of definition—is the definition of a species by
means of its genus and difference (Berg 1982; Smith 2004b).

There are other properties, *common properties*, that all instances of a species also
have but which are not part of the essential definition of that species. For example,
humans or 'man' all have the capacity to laugh (so we might assume), but that
common property is not used as part of the genus-difference definition of man.

Finally, there are *accidental properties*, which individual instances of a species
may or may not have. So, for example, being tall or short or fat or thin are all
accidental properties. Individual humans may or may not have some or several of
them.

### 3.4.2  The Ontological Square

Aristotle, some two thousand years ago, in *The Categories* discussed ontology and
proposed pretty well the same answer as the mixture favored here, with one
qualification. The qualification concerns universals and Plato's unrestricted use of

universals; Aristotle did not subscribe to this. So, really he had tokens, individual types or kinds, some categories of universals, and modes. One point that Aristotle insisted on was that universals had to be instantiated; that is, there only could be a type man if there also was (had been/will be) at least one token man (Berg 1982). Uninstantiated universals or types simply did not exist. Aristotle's metaphysics was grounded in a way that Plato's was not.

Aristotle also offered a theory of what it is to ascribe a property to an individual thing or to make a predication of an individual thing. He anticipates or uses the familiar subject-predicate, or entity-attribute, form. He makes a further distinction between 'predicable of' and 'present in'. This is related to the kind or kinds of thing that an entity is, and to the other properties that a thing has. Consider

    ... is a man
    ... is white.

The noun or subject or entity 'man' can stand alone, we can talk of 'a man' or 'the man', so when we say 'Socrates is a man' we are predicating 'is a man' of Socrates. 'is a man' is predicable of Socrates. In modern terms, 'man' is a sort (it is a kind of thing). In contrast, the noun or subject or entity 'white' *cannot* stand alone, we *cannot* talk of 'a white' or 'the white', white always has to be present in something, so when we say 'Snow is white' we are saying that whiteness is present in snow. 'Man' is a sort, whereas 'white' is not a sort. So there are two forms of predication

    ... is a—
    ... is—.

The first says *what* something is (that is, what kind or sort it is or belongs to) and the second says *how* it is (that is, what properties or attributes or features it has). So, 'Socrates is a man' tells *what* he is, and 'Socrates is wise' tells, in part, *how* he is.

This notion of 'present in' also suggests modes. Universals, or attributes, like 'is white' are present in the appropriate tokens, but the universals are abstract and not in space and time. How exactly are they present in the individual tokens, which are in space and time? The universals are particularized as modes, and it is the modes that are present in the tokens. Thus (Fig. 3.5). And this four category ontology is known as *Aristotle's Ontological Square* [see, for example, (Lowe 2006; Smith 2005)]. [Notice we have omitted Plato's diagonal arrow from Attribute(Universals) to Tokens(Particulars)]. The arrows have slightly different meanings one to another, it is sufficient for our purposes to say that the vertical arrows are going from the general to the specific, and that the horizontal arrows are showing what is possessed by what.

It is then possible to write data out in a table. Aristotle often called what something was its 'substance' or 'essence'. So here is a table for a token man with a beard and he is, of course, an instance of the type man with a beard (Table 3.1).

**Fig. 3.5** Aristotle's
ontological square

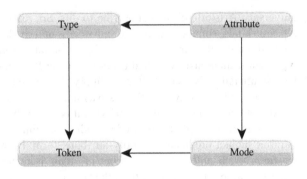

**Table 3.1** Example of type,
token, attribute, mode

|          | Substance/Essence | Accident         |
|----------|-------------------|------------------|
| **General**  | Man [type]        | Beard [attribute] |
| **Specific** | This man [token]  | Beard [mode]      |

**Table 3.2** Example of
essential and accidental
properties

|                     | Substance | Essential       | Accidental        |
|---------------------|-----------|-----------------|-------------------|
| **Individual type** | Man       | Rational animal | Beard [attribute] |

For the purposes of diagramming essential properties in a table, we can drop the
bottom row of tokens and add an extra column for the essential properties. Many
of these essential properties could be expanded as 'essential definitions', that is,
explicated in terms of other conditions or predicates. In the case of 'man',
Aristotle thought that what was essential was being a 'rational animal'. Thus
(Table 3.2). Usually essential properties were connected with sorts. The essence
is what makes a substrate the sort that it is. It is reasonable to read this distinction
as one concerning natural kinds. Man, to use an example, is a natural kind, and as
such it might have essential properties which identify it, in this case the properties of being a rational animal identify or define it.

But it is also possible to use essential properties in connection with tokens, or
individuals, or particulars. Socrates was a particular; indeed, as it happened,
Socrates instantiated a sort, he was a man; *one could certainly take the view that is
was of the essence of Socrates that he be a man (in other words that he could not
have been a chicken or a table)*; in which case, Socrates had the essential properties of being a man (and being an animal, and being rational) and he may or may
not have had the accidental properties of having a beard and having brown hair.
That man in front of us, Socrates say, has to be a man: being a man is an essential
property. If Socrates was not a man, he, or it, simply would not be Socrates. In
contrast, Socrates may or may not have a beard, may or may not have brown hair,
may or may not be smart. Thus having a beard, having brown hair, being smart, are
all accidental properties.

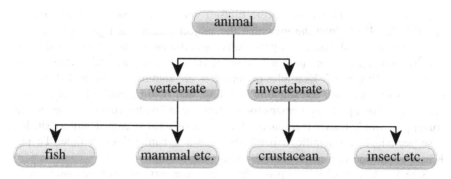

**Fig. 3.6**  A fragment of a genus-species classification

### 3.4.3  Classification

Essential properties, expanded essential properties, give rise to extended classification in hierarchies, to natural kind hierarchies in taxonomies: for example, if man is a rational animal, man is an animal; so if animal is itself an Individual Type, then man-type is a subtype of animal-type.

Aristotle, in his work *History of Animals*, also sought to classify living things by the way that they reproduced. He classified into 'animals with blood' (i.e. vertebrates) and 'animals without blood' (invertebrates), and then to sub-divide these categories into mammals, fish, and so on. Aristotle himself did not portray classification hierarchies in diagrams. But Porphyry, some six hundred years later, did so in *On Aristotle's Categories*. And thus, from about the third century CE it was possible to see Aristotelian genus-species classification diagrams similar to (Fig. 3.6). Interestingly enough, Aristotle also classified living things in a different way, in accordance with a *Scala Naturae* (a Ladder of Life). The idea here was that there was a Great Chain of Being from the simplest of plants climbing a hierarchy of complexity and perfection to end with humans at the pinnacle (all very flattering to us).

Aristotle also had an interest in change and processes, largely because his main scientific focus was the natural world and biology. And he addressed the intellectual problem of how living things grow and die. And his framework allowed him to address this: basically, the essences endure and persist through time while the accidental properties can change over time.

This finds its modern expression with 'continuants' and 'occurrents'.

## 3.5  Continuants and Occurrents

One way of introducing the next topic or distinction is by means of the work of the early twentieth century theorist (and practitioner) of librarianship, Julius O. Kaiser (Kaiser 1911). Kaiser worked mainly in industrial or commercial libraries, so, for example, he did not have to concern himself with fiction, poetry, encyclopedias, and the like. He formed the view that the subject matters, or topics, of the documents he dealt with concerned principally two different kinds of things, and often usually also, interactions between items of those two kinds. There were 'Concretes' and 'Processes'. Examples of concretes are aluminum, iron, and steel; and examples of processes are smelting, welding, and rusting. And, of course, concretes can play a part in processes (or processes can involve concretes); as in, the 'rusting of iron'. Kaiser recognized that much of what occupied writers (in his case, technical or scientific writers) involved a dynamic through time. To put Kaiser's intuition in a more general ontological setting...

Suppose doctors identify a particular tumor in a particular patient—so there is a token tumor (and also a type tumor); often they will track that tumor, perhaps it starts small, grows somewhat larger, then diminishes in size and disappears. What they are tracking and what they are talking about with the words 'the tumor' or 'it' is one thing that endures through time or through a period of time. Now, the tumor itself gains new cells as it grows, loses cells as it diminishes, and also there is the general turnover of cells as cells themselves are created and destroyed. We can imagine that the tumor at the end has absolutely no cells in common with the tumor at the beginning. This plays havoc with a 'snapshot' using Aristotle's Square or Table, as we have laid it out thus far—for the tumor both has some particular cells and does not have those very same cells. There is a similar consideration with Socrates. As a young man maybe he did not have a beard, as a mature adult maybe he had a beard; well, does he have a beard or doesn't he?

Obviously time needs to be taken into account. Socrates had a beard at one time and did not have a beard at another. What is going on needs to be indexed to time. There are processes, taking place in time, and within those processes there may be change to items that endure through those processes. Generally speaking, philosophers have not given a lot of attention to these areas historically, and what theories there are can be tricky and difficult. Fortunately, one of the modern schools of ontology, that from IFOMIS, and one of their creations Basic Formal Ontology (BFO) is both crystal clear and on a sound philosophical and evidential basis (Ifomis 2009). We will just subscribe to what they say in matters of this kind.

There is a metaphor that helps enormously in these areas. It is that of the photograph, or a still image, as contrasted with the film, a continuous sequence of still images. So we want to be thinking here, snapshot versus movie (or, using their labels, SNAP versus SPAN (Grenon and Smith 2004; Grenon 2003)). Now consider, as an example, the 2010 Super Bowl. That is a 'movie', a SPAN. There is a special word for this in ontology, that is *occurrent*. So the Super Bowl 2010 is an occurrent. Occurrents themselves do not change. There might be earlier or later parts of an occurrent. But there can be no change at all to an occurrent *itself*.

Occurrents are unchanging in their parts or phases. Within occurrents various things happen. In the Super Bowl, the teams came on and played, the rock band The Who came on at half time and performed, and so on. The entities that are doing this, the teams, the players, the Who, the cheer-leaders, the spectators, and many more are *continuants*. The continuants exist, and can change, within an occurrent. If we take a snapshot, or a single frame from the movie, we may capture the state of the continuants at a particular time; two or more such snapshots can show change. And an enduring continuant can be very different later in an occurrent to earlier in the occurrent (a player can become bloody and bruised). Continuants continue, and occurrents occur. A continuant can be available as a whole at a single time, and occurrent cannot (though phases of it can).

When continuants change, what they are doing is to gain or lose or change accidental properties. When the player runs out, he, or his uniform, is un-muddied; sometime later he is a mess; his uniform, which had the accidental property of being clean, later has the accidental property of being dirty.

Continuants and occurrents are everywhere. When Crate and Barrel address inventory, they are actually usually also interested in supply chain. The local branch may have 3 *Henley Floor Cushions (Peacock)* in stock today, and they may have 3 *Henley Floor Cushions (Peacock)* in stock tomorrow, but there may be different token cushions tomorrow because some will have sold and then been re-placed by re-stocking. The ability to do this is a matter of supply chain. So when Crate and Barrel think about inventory, they will be thinking video as well as snapshot. The same is true in libraries, for libraries issue and circulate books.

## 3.6 Higher Order Properties or 'Metaproperties'

The basic Plato account leaves it open as to whether there are 'higher-order' universals, that is: universals which apply to other universals. But his argument used earlier to establish plain universals can be used to establish higher-order universals. Consider the properties of being white and being red. Both these properties participate in a common essence, namely the essence of being color properties. In which case there is, or can be, the higher order universal 'being a color property', which is instantiated or exemplified not now by concrete partic-ulars but rather by lower order universals, types and attributes, including the universals being white and being red. If that example seems a little high-flown, there are any number of everyday examples that may have application in librari-anship. Consider military battles and the properties 'in the seventeenth century', 'in the eighteenth century', 'in the nineteenth century', 'in Belgium', 'in England', 'in France'; these properties are different in kind, the first three are Period properties, they themselves individually each have the property of being a Period property, the second three are Place properties. The Battle of Waterloo was fought in the nineteenth century in Belgium, but in itself, the battle, does not have the Period property nor the Place property, what it has is the property of being fought in the nineteenth century and it is *that* property that has the property of being a Period property. Periods and Places, as above, are higher-order properties, they are properties of properties.

Reid also mentions higher order properties in his Essay

> As well as attributes belonging to individual things there are attributes of *attributes*, which we could call 'secondary attributes'. Most attributes are capable of different degrees and different modifications, which must be expressed by general words. Thus, being-in-motion is an attribute of many bodies, but motion has many modifications, for example it can be in countless different directions, can be quick or slow, in a straight line or on a curve, uniform or accelerating or decelerating. (Reid 1785 p. 191)

So, the example that Reid offers is that of 'modifiers' which modify existing attributes.

There is a relatively recent terminological innovation that is often seen at this point, and that is the use of the word 'metaproperties' to signify second-order properties. Elsewhere there has been much use in recent years of the word 'metadata'. There is data, central to database design and construction, and to librarianship as widely understood, and there is data about this data (for example, about its format or owner or author etc.); and this data about data is almost universally called 'metadata'. On an analogy with this, on those relatively rare occasions when information scientists and web-site designers want to discuss properties of—or about—properties, they will call these 'metaproperties'. So there are properties and metaproperties. Typically philosophers and logicians would not talk in this way, although they would have no trouble understanding what was being said when others did so. On the other hand, a label like 'second-order properties' would be completely mystifying to many information scientists. This is a reason to use 'metaproperties', especially in contexts outside pure philosophy and we will do that.

If there are metaproperties, then those items which instantiate them are particulars. However, those particulars are themselves abstract and not concrete, which means that they are not tokens. Some (Plato) particulars are tokens, some are not.

## 3.7 Francis Bacon and Trees of Knowledge

Francis Bacon (1561–1626) changed the Aristotelian approach in two separate ways (Bacon 1605, 1620) (and what is usually considered to be the minor one is the one of importance to us).

The major change is that Bacon laid an emphasis on observation—and even on experiment—as the means of acquiring knowledge about the world. Aristotle had basically thought that the source of knowledge lay within ourselves, and that reason was the source of all knowledge. Aristotle was a naturalist in that he felt that the basis of our knowledge lay in our ordinary everyday of experience. However, he spent more effort on thinking about that everyday experience than he did on actually observing nature closely or deliberately experimenting on it. Bertrand Russell has a remark about this. Aristotle had proclaimed that women had fewer teeth than men (in *History of Animals* 2.3), a view that he had arrived at by reason enlightened by experience. Russell dryly observed

> Aristotle could have avoided the mistake of thinking that women have fewer teeth than men, by the simple device of asking Mrs. Aristotle to keep her mouth open while he counted. (Russell 1943 p. 22)

Bacon anticipated Russell by 300 years by suggesting that if you wanted to know what the world was like, you should look at it and see.

One of Aristotle's famous works was the *Organon* (*The Categories*, mentioned earlier, was one of the components of the *Organon*). Aristotle did have ideas on how education or learning or knowledge should be organized and—to an extent—the *Organon* embodied this: first you learn language and reasoning (i.e. grammar and logic), and then you go on to the specific sciences. Bacon's response was the *Novum Organum* (i.e. the *New Organon*). This contained his account of learning and discovery, which amounted to observation, induction, and, the beginnings of empirical science as we know it. Bacon's project was the *Great Instauration* (Bacon 1620).

The Frontispiece image of *Great Instauration* shows Bacon (he was the Baron of Verulam), and others, setting out on a voyage of discovery, sailing through the pillars of Hercules, which hitherto had marked the limits of human learning.

**Image 3.1 Frontispiece to Francis Bacon's *Great Instauration***

The minor part of the Baconian revolution, but the important part for us, is something else; namely, Bacon sought to classify knowledge. What Aristotle was doing with his taxonomic classification systems was classifying *things*, natural kinds, the things of the world (plants, animals, and the like). Aristotle was doing ontology or taxonomy. But Bacon wanted to classify *knowledge*. He set out in the *Great Instauration* on a 130 part study, which was divided in a hierarchy of types of knowledge, subtypes and further subtypes until all of knowledge was covered.

There is a categorization of Bacon's Tree of Knowledge itself that we need to be aware of. Bacon was influenced by how learning is taught in colleges and Universities, and his Tree of Knowledge divides knowledge by *discipline* (or area of study or learning), such as chemistry and physics. This is not the only way the division might have been carried out. An alternative is to reason that what we know about is 'things' or phenomena, and so a Tree of Knowledge could, or should, be divided by *phenomena* (or *objects of knowledge* or *objects of study*), such as water and air. Historically and traditionally, the Trees of Knowledge used in organization of knowledge for librarianship typically divide by discipline. However, there certainly is an active modern school that wishes to organize by phenomena (Gnoli 2008; Gnoli et al. 2007, 2008; Szostak et al. 2007). [The main complaint, or criticism, of discipline-based organization is that so much of modern knowledge is interdisciplinary or multidisciplinary and so a cogent discipline-based division cannot be made. That is an option; but it flies in the face of the fact that high schools and universities are organized by discipline to allow students to study Biology, Sociology, Philosophy, History, Anthropology, and the like. Of course, nowadays, in the digital environment, we can choose to use *both* discipline-based and phenomena-based Trees of Knowledge as complements to each other (cf. (Hjørland 2008)).

## 3.8 The Organization of Encyclopaedias

If there could be such a thing as an organized totality of knowledge, there could also presumably be the organized totality of knowledge in a book or in multiple volumes of a book. And the result, of course, is the Encyclopaedia. Needless to say, there were 'Encyclopaedias' before Bacon. Pliny the Elder had written *The Natural History* about 77CE, some 1500 years earlier. But it is with Bacon that we really start to see the organization of the knowledge in Encyclopaedias.

Encyclopaedias contain the knowledge, but our focus is not with the contents of Encyclopaedias as such, not with the knowledge itself, but rather with the way the knowledge is organized, arranged, and accessed i.e. with the classifications of knowledge. An Encyclopaedia is an entire non-fiction library in a single book: what is good for accessing Encyclopaedias may well be a guide to what is good for accessing the contents of libraries or, indeed, the Internet.

What are the problems here? An Encyclopaedia is a work, perhaps consisting of many volumes or 'books', and it will usually have chapters, sections and so forth. These have sequential order: one item is first, another is second, and so on. Structurally, an Encyclopaedia is a list. The problem is to linearize knowledge. The knowledge in an Encyclopaedia has to be set out in some sequential fashion. [Typically, modern Encyclopaedias will be paginated also, with pages that have page numbers; however, particular page numbers for topics and entries may vary according to print runs, page size, and how many words a printer can fit on a page, so page numbers are of lesser importance as far as structure is concerned.] There has to be an order and contiguity to the depicted knowledge. So, a question is: what should that order be?

An Encyclopaedia need not have either a Table of Contents or an Index. And often they do not; in fact, most do not, even today. Instead of having an alphabetical index to sections, the sections themselves could be arranged alphabetically. That approach, which results in a Dictionary of Knowledge or Dictionary-Encyclopaedia builds the index into the text itself; it makes a real Index redundant, and it also makes a Table of Contents redundant. Searching is supported by direct jumped key entry into the text. An entry on 'Stock-Doves', if there is one, appears late in the S entries (after the R entries and before the T entries). However, this approach tends to destroy meaningful browsing, simply because alphabetically contiguous entries usually will *not* signify related subjects, or will do so only by accident.

Another historical thinker on organizational principles that should be mentioned, is the Frenchman Peter Ramus (Pierre de la Ramée). Ramus was a Huguenot convert, born 1515 and stabbed to death during the St. Bartholomew's Day massacre in August 1572. Ramus's biographer, Fregius, tells us that Ramus's academic career began with a public disputation in which he defended the thesis *Everything that Aristotle said is false*. [This story may be apocryphal.] The modern authority on Ramus, Father Ong, adds to this report two observations: first, it was standard in this intellectual setting to make extreme claims against Aristotle, it was a way of attracting attention, and second, Ramus's real complaint was not that Aristotle was false, but rather that Aristotle's works were poorly organized (Ong 1958). Ramus sought to reform the educational curriculum, and existing learning or knowledge was not organized in a suitable form. Ramus's solution on organization was to invoke the device of division by Chapters, Sections, Headings, etc. and to use these to add structure. So, basically, what he advocated was the use of ordered trees, often ordered binary trees, (on the pattern of genealogical trees) as a means of division and access. This gave rise to 'Ramism', which itself relied on the use of binary trees to organize. Between 1550 and 1650 there were about 1,100 separate printings of different individual works by Ramus, so Ramus was certainly very well known and influential (Ong 1958). The authors we are looking at, including Bacon, Chambers, Diderot, and d'Alembert, would have been very familiar with Ramus's ideas on organization of educational materials.

A (binary) tree can accelerate search, by successive narrowing, and it can support browsing in as much as sibling children can and should be related to each other. The tree, or a tree, can simply be the structure of the book as a whole; in which case, the book itself is just a sequential 'paginating' traversal of the tree, and the tree and the Table of Contents are really just one and the same. But it is also possible, as we will see, for a tree to be a third access device, a Tree of Knowledge (or Contents, or Themes) additional to a Table of Contents and an Index.

Consider how a reader might approach a search of a Table of Contents, for example, to find 'Stock-Doves' in Pliny's *The Natural History*. The reader can scan through the Table of Contents sequentially; that would be one way, perhaps the standard way. But the reader might alternatively look through the Chapter headings *only* and, if knowledgeable enough about the various fields, then make a choice as to the appropriate Chapter. Then the reader might scan the Sections of that Chapter and make an appropriate choice and so on. This would be quicker and easier than a sequential search (given a suitable reader and a suitable Table of Contents). What this second search technique is doing, algorithmically, is identifying that the structure of the book is that of a Ramist tree, and then it is descending the levels the tree, narrowing and narrowing, following one branch Chapter-> Section-> Topic to the desired topic. The Table of Contents data structure supports both styles of search.

The two problems of interest right now are: how are we going to organize the Encyclopaedias, and what access tools are we going to provide.

As mentioned, there were 'Encyclopaedias' going back some considerable time, perhaps a couple of thousand years to the Romans and the Greeks. And there were Natural Histories, some perhaps amounting to alphabetical encyclopaedias (in France, in 1674, there was L Moréri's, *Grand Dictionnaire Historique*). But Bacon marks a real turning point. In 1624, without insight or intellectual guidance from Bacon, Thomas Heywood published a proto-encyclopaedia, the *Gunaikeion*; or, *Nine Bookes of Various History Concerninge Women*, which was a somewhat scattered collection of works about women. In 1704, there was John Harris's *Lexicon Technicum* ('An Universal English Dictionary of Arts and Sciences: Explaining not only the Terms of Art, but the Arts Themselves.') Then, a hundred years later after Heywood, in 1728, Ephraim Chambers (1680–1740) published the Chamber's *Cyclopaedia* or a *Universal Dictionary of Arts and Sciences* (which Chambers described as 'The Best Book in the Universe', for 'it effectively reduced the body of learning to manageable proportions' (Yeo 1996) [*Editor's note*: it has been recently superseded in its best book role by the present work] see also (Bradshaw 1981). As the title suggests, this was more of a Dictionary than an Encyclopaedia. Chambers did have a tree diagram 'View of Knowledge' in the Preface. But, really, the organizational approach was to extract suitable terms for the branches of knowledge, and then to use an alphabetical index to arrange these and to access the Cyclopaedia (Yeo 1996)

Some French scholars set out in 1745 to translate and publish Chambers's work. But the attempt was never followed through to completion. Instead a group of intellectuals, led by Denis Diderot, produced their own Encyclopedia. (Jean le Rond d'Alembert is often mentioned in connection with the project—he wrote the mathematical sections and parts of the introduction.) As Wright informs us

History's greatest encyclopedist was Denis Diderot, a Frenchman who adopted Bacon's classification as the foundation for his monumental *Encyclopédie*, published in a succession of volumes from 1751 to 1772. A massive collection of 72,000 articles written by 160 eminent contributors (including notables like Voltaire, Rousseau, and Buffon), Diderot created a compendium of knowledge unrivaled in any previously published work. (Wright 2007 p. 148)

The *Encyclopédie* was monumental in conception and monumental in effect. Here is Charles-Nicolas Cochin (the Younger)'s frontispiece illustration to the 1772 edition, Diderot, adopting the mantle of art critic, tells us what this depicts

**Image 3.2 Frontispiece to Diderot's *Encyclopédie***

On voit en haut la Vérité entre la Raison et l'Imagination: la Raison qui cherche à lui arracher son voile, l'Imagination qui se prépare à l'embellir. Au-dessous de ce groupe, une foule de philosophes spéculatifs; plus bas la troupe des artistes. Les philosophes ont les yeux attachés sur la Vérité; la Métaphysique orgueilleuse chercher moins à la voir qu' à la deviner; la Théologie lui tourne le dos et attend sa lumière d'en haut. Il y a certainement dans cette composition une grande variété de caractères et d'expressions.... (Diderot 1765 p. 397)

There are here Memory, Imagination, and Reason, the search for Truth, and the concept of Education. The lady top center is Truth, and the gentlemen ripping her clothes off are Reason and Philosophy. The central light is Knowledge, or Insight, or Understanding. The folk bottom left are holding up a tray to catch any fragments of truth ('pearls of wisdom') that might come off with her diaphanous garments. Steamy! This was marketing!

Diderot's *Encyclopédie* was truly liberating. Prior to Bacon, and the astronomers and cosmologists Copernicus, Kepler and Galileo, the source of knowledge was widely believed to lie with authorities—with Aristotle, with the Church, and with Royalty. The Copernican revolution in cosmology, around 1,600, which made the Sun, not the Earth, the center of the universe, changed this (Koestler 1959)—so too did Bacon. And Diderot's *Encyclopédie*, in France, placed knowledge directly in the hands of ordinary people, no authorities required. [Diderot was imprisoned a couple of times for doing this.]

Diderot chose to include considerable information about trades (carpentry, stone masonry, etc.) and how trades people worked. This practical knowledge again took the contents of the *Encyclopédie* away from the bailiwick of traditional authorities. However, it also meant that the Industrial Revolution of the seventeenth and eighteenth centuries, which mechanized trades, rendered a large component of the *Encyclopédie* obsolete, irrelevant or of historical interest only.

D'Alembert discussed the organization of knowledge, and tells us that the choice of organization scheme is 'arbitrary'.

One could construct the tree of our knowledge by dividing it into natural and revealed knowledge, or useful and pleasing knowledge, or speculative and practical knowledge, or evident, certain, probable, and sensitive knowledge, or knowledge of things and knowledge of signs, and so on into infinity. We have chosen a division which has appeared to us most nearly satisfactory for the encyclopedic arrangement of our knowledge and, at the same time, for its genealogical arrangement. We owe this division to a celebrated author [Bacon] .... we are too aware of the arbitrariness which will always prevail in such a division to believe that our system is the only one or the best. (d'Alembert 1751) [No pagination in source.]

Elsewhere, Ranganathan talks about a knowledge classification system setting out to be 'helpful'. And, of course, what is helpful may change from context to context. D'Alembert's and Ranganathan's insight seems exactly right. There is no one single best knowledge organizational scheme.

Diderot and d'Alembert set out to

exhibit as far as is possible the order and concatenation of human learning [by examining] their genealogy and their filiation, the causes that must have given rise to them and the characteristics that distinguish them (d'Alembert 1751)

And that certainly sounds pretty reasonable. And this is the result, in French,

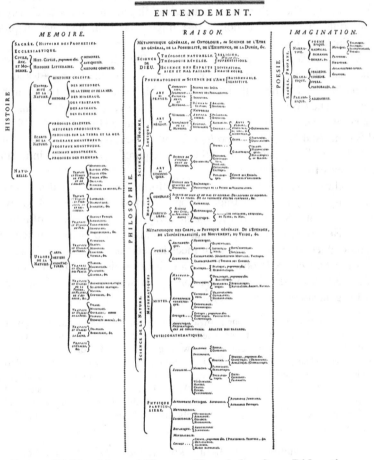

**Image 3.3 The Map of Human Knowledge from Diderot's** *Encyclopédie*, **in French**

or, in English

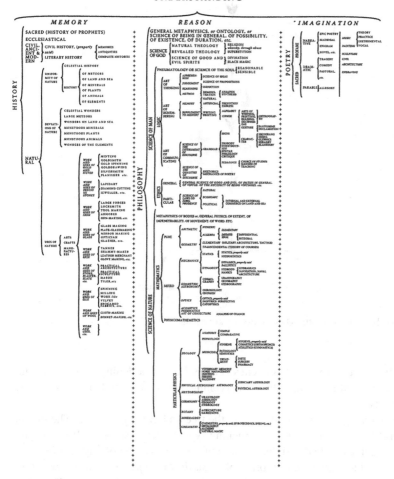

**Image 3.4 The Map of Human Knowledge from Diderot's** *Encyclopédie*, **in English**

[see http://quod.lib.umich.edu/d/did/tree.html, used with permission from Benjamin Heller]

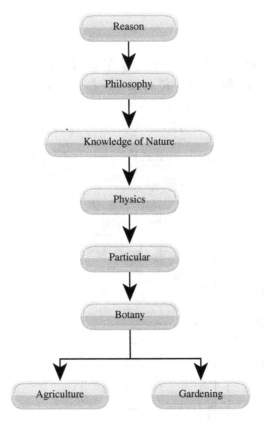

**Fig. 3.7** Two branches from the Diderot tree of knowledge

And, here are two example branches (Fig. 3.7). So Gardening is a leaf of the Reason branch, with several other intervening areas of knowledge, as nodes, between the two.

What exactly is being asserted here, in the tree and in the branches? The tree is not a natural kind hierarchy, with Gardening type objects also being Reason type objects. Nor is it a simple classification structured gerrymander of physical objects. Rather it is a principled, or partly principled, *subject* or *topic* or *area* or *discipline* or *chunk of knowledge topic hierarchy*. Gardening, as described in an Encyclopaedia, is a body of knowledge: it is a collection of statements about the theories, practices, history, examples, etc. of gardening. The Gardening entry or chapter or IO has gardening as its *single, most specific*, subject matter. Generally, as we have noted with Pliny (and Sphinges and Crocutes), an IO will have multiple non-overlapping subjects, IOs tend to be *polytopical*. However, in the writing of an Encyclopaedia the subject or topic comes first, and the author or authors are supposed to be writing on it. The authors of the Gardening entry undertook to write on gardening, that is what they were supposed to do. Similarly the Botany entry has botany as its sole subject matter. Then, as d'Alembert tells us, one might choose to relate subject matters by order, concatenation, learning, genealogy, filiation, causes that gave rise to them, and characteristics. And, in those terms, Gardening is a child of Botany, and similar relations hold for the subjects in the rest of the branch and, indeed, for the subjects in the whole tree. That Gardening is a child of Botany means that the subject Gardening is a sub-subject, or sub-topic, or sub-area of knowledge, of the subject Botany, and it is also a sub-subject, or sub-topic, of the subject Physics (Natural Philosophy) etc. That means that the Gardening entry actually has seven subjects, however these seven overlap and are nested from the most specific to the most general. Thus, if one were berrypicking from Gardening, up the branch to Botany and on, might be a good route to go, and so too, would be the horizontal steps to Gardening's brothers and sisters, such as to Agriculture. Of course, there is not a 1-1 correspondence between the article entries and the tree nodes. There were about 72,000 articles and nowhere near that number of nodes in the Tree of Knowledge. But, in concept at least, a fleshed out tree would cover the articles.

The initial division of the Bacon-Diderot-d'Alembert overall scheme is to Memory, Reason, and Imagination. And d'Alembert invites us to smile by observing, in a side note, that this tree of knowledge also divides the literary world into Scholars (memory), Philosophers (reason), and Poets (imagination), and that none of these have particularly high opinions of the others

> Scholars, Philosophers, and beaux esprits… men of letters ordinarily have nothing in common, except the lack of esteem in which they hold one another. The poet and the philosopher treat each other as madmen who feed on fancies. Both regard the scholar as a sort of miser who thinks only of amassing without enjoying and who indiscriminately heaps up the basest metals along with the most precious. And the scholar, who considers everything which is not fact to be idle words, holds the poet and the philosopher in contempt as being men who think they are rich because their expenses exceed their resources. (d'Alembert 1751)

Then there is the question of how the Encyclopedia is to be accessed. And the answer is, at root, *by alphabetical index*. The Encyclopedié offered three organizational and navigational components: (a) alphabetically indexed entries built straight into the text by virtue of alphabetical topic structure, (b) a tree of knowledge that shows how topics are related to one another (although you had to find the particular topic of interest within the tree), and (c) cross references from article to article. d'Alembert writes

> Thus, three things make up the encyclopedic arrangement: the name of the science to which the article belongs, the position of that science in the tree, and the connection of the article with others in the same science or in a different science. This connection is indicated by the references to other articles or is easy to understand by means of the technical terms explained in their alphabetical place. (d'Alembert 1751)

D'Alembert then offered an argument for preferring alphabetical arrangement over thematic topical arrangement: the convenience of the reader

... if we had treated each science in a separate and continuing discourse which conformed to the order of ideas and not of words, the form of this work would have been still less convenient for most of our readers. They would not have been able to find anything without difficulty. (d'Alembert 1751)

And he concludes

...we wanted to use it [Chamber's English Encyclopaedia] because of its reputation and the promises of the old Prospectus [1745], which was approved by the public and to which we wished to conform. The entire translation of that encyclopedia has been placed in our hands by the publishers who undertook to publish it. We have distributed it among our colleagues, who have preferred to undertake to revise, correct, and augment it, rather than to commit themselves to the task of compiling articles without having any preparatory materials .... some of these scholars... were already well into their work following the original alphabetical project; consequently, it would have been impossible for us to change this project.... Finally... there had been no criticism of the alphabetical arrangement to which our model, the English author, had compiled. (d'Alembert 1751)

That is, the Diderot ensemble of scholars were using Chambers's *Cyclopaedia* as a foundation or template, and Chambers's work had an alphabetical arrangement. Some of the ensemble had already invested considerable time and effort into this venture. And no one had criticized Chambers's alphabetical arrangement. So there was a happy melding of what legacy material committed them to, practically, and what, in fact, they believed to be best.

In sum, the central intellectual concern was that had the Encyclopaedia been arranged by topic, the reader would not be able to find anything.

Of course, it seems ridiculous to organize knowledge alphabetically. Why? Well, the names topics have, in particular the first letters of those names, which is the basis of the organization, are presumably arbitrary—or close to it. Yet knowledge is not arbitrary. 'Geophysics' is presumably related to 'physics', but the letter 'g' is not a close alphabetical relation to the letter 'p'. Cutter had made exactly this point in 1900, when writing about the (alphabetical) Dictionary Catalog

The dictionary catalog .... Its subject-entries, individual, general, limited, extensive, thrown together without any logical arrangement, in most absurd proximity—*Abscess* followed by *Absenteeism* and that by *Absolution*, *Club-foot* next to *Club*s, and *Communion* to *Communism*, while *Bibliography* and *Literary history*, *Christianity* and *Theology*, are separated by half the length of the catalogue—are a mass of utterly disconnected particles without any relation to one another, each useful in itself but only by itself. (Cutter 1904 p. 79) cited in (Olson 2004)

Richard Yeo phrases this blemish on encyclopedias thus

For at least the last thousand years encyclopedias-arguably the most striking publishing enterprise of Western Culture- have had to confront an apparent absurdity: the combination of universal knowledge and alphabetical order (Yeo 1991 p. 24)

But, actually, it is not so much of an absurdity. Alphabetical order supports jumped key searching or retrieval, which is very effective. It does not help with browsing; for that, you need cross-references, Tables of Contents, Trees of Knowledge, and the like. Simply, it is hard to get searching and browsing support into the same device. It is also not so much of an absurdity for another reason. As we noted in connection with word-by-word filing order (Sect. 2.7.8), it is perfectly possible to do a great deal of 'thematic' organization using just alphabetical order merely by making some topics sub-topics of others. So, for example, if geology is related to physics, you do not file them both alphabetically at the top level; instead you give geology the title 'physics: geology' and alphabetical order will make geology a child of physics. Talking in terms of trees, what alphabetical order does is to arrange siblings; but the sibling relationship is not as important, thematically speaking, as the parent–child relationship and alphabetical order does not interfere with that.

This is not the end of the story though. There were attempts to access Encyclopaedias by means of a schematic of knowledge. The famous poet Samuel Taylor Coleridge devised a plan for the 1827 *Encyclopaedia Metropolitana* which was based on the 'twofold advantage of a philosophical and an alphabetical arrangement' (Coleridge 1827). This encyclopaedia did not become a popular success. Probably the most heroic attempt to combine themes with encyclopaedias is the 1974 *Propaedia* (Outline of knowledge) to the fifteenth edition of the *Encyclopedia Britannica*.

## 3.9 Mortimer Adler and Propaedias

Adler was the editor and inspirational force of the 1974 *Propaedia*. Adler had dropped out of school at the age of 14, and he died at 98. He spent most of his life, in between, studying the great thinkers and their ideas, and in puzzling about how these should be presented to the world at large (to what he called the 'Joe Doakes' of the world). Adler certainly had worked in Universities, in Columbia and the University of Chicago, but more than a few University academics had misgivings about the quality of his work so Adler was something of an outsider as an academic. For a long while he was employed by the publishers of the *Encyclopaedia Brittanica*. (Some of Adler's ideas are reviewed in (Selinger 1976); see also (Weinberger 2007).)

The opening four chapter section of his *A Guidebook to Learning: For the Lifelong Pursuit of Wisdom* (Adler 1986) is an extended critique of 'Alphabetiasis' which, as you would expect, is a mauling of the refusal to go beyond the alphabetical index.

In the case of Encyclopedias, alphabetical arrangement, were it to be the only guide, was a refusal to acknowledge that Encyclopedias should be like Universities,

> A great general encyclopedia is not just a reference book. It is also an instrument of learning in the same way that a great university is an institute of learning. Inherent in the things to be learned we should be able to find inner connections that might enable us to discover a significant pattern of their relationships to one another. (Adler 1986 p. 10)

Adler knew full well the value of alphabetical indexes, he just wanted to go further and to supplement those indexes with thematic guides to learning or similar.

> [supplementing] does not necessitate abandoning an alphabetical ordering of the same materials for look-it-up or reference purposes. I would certainly not advocate a totally nonalphabetical encyclopedia, devoid of any use as a reference book... (Adler 1986 p. 11)

The 1974 fifteenth edition of the *Encyclopaedia Britannica* consisted of three parts a *Propaedia* (an Outline of knowledge), a *Micropaedia* (which was a collection of short articles, arranged in alphabetical order) and a *Macropaedia* (which was a 29 volume collection of longer articles, arranged part thematically and part in alphabetical order). And there were alphabetical indexes, cross-references, and the like.

Then the question arises: why not have a thematic guide only, and do entirely without an alphabetical index? Adler gave two reasons for not doing so. The first was the standard observation that alphabetical indexes were invaluable for reference work. The second is slightly odd and points to a stress in his work. It was that to provide a study guide at all was to suggest that there was only one study guide, the, so-to-speak, 'true study guide' and this is in tension with cultural pluralism which Adler wanted to promote. As McArthur phrases it

> A purely topical (thematic) organization 'cannot avoid the appearance of a certain tendentiousness or arbitrariness in the editorial commitment to one rather than another organizing schema or set of principles', provoking thereby awkward questions about whether the adopted schema is the One True Presentation. (McArthur 1986 p. 159)

This reason also motivated Adler to present knowledge as a circle of knowledge rather than a hierarchy

> We live in an age and in a society that is dominated by cultural pluralism and intellectual heterodoxy. Unacceptable, therefore, would be any ordering of the departments of knowledge or the fields of learning that is hierarchical or that is ascending or descending in a scale of values involving judgments about what is more or less fundamental, important, or significant, or about what should be studied from first to last for logical or pedagogical reasons. Such an ordering would be regarded as culturally monolithic instead of pluralistic, and as the expression of an orthodoxy that was purely subjective instead of accommodating the intellectual heterodoxy. (Adler 1986 pp. 90–1)

What is odd here is that Adler wants to give us 'inner connections' but yet seems to want to combine that with the view that everyone, or every culture, might have their own equally good inner connections. Yet one would think that whether, for example, geophysics has an inner connection to physics is a matter of the nature of those subject areas or disciplines, not of cultures.

Adler thought that knowledge was a unity: in fact that knowledge was a circle of learning or circle of knowledge rather than a hierarchy of knowledge. (The word 'Encyclopaedia' means, the 'world of knowledge'.) And, as noted, Adler was opposed to value judgments or foundational judgments as to what was more important or basic, and this opposition rules out a hierarchical scheme (where the root and close levels are in some sense more important than the leaf levels). Yeo writes

The Propaedia acknowledges the extreme specialization of disciplines and discusses whether the knowledge they produce can be seen as complementary, as constitute parts of an integrated whole. Thus the editor of the Propaedia, Mortimer Adler, asks: 'Do the various disciplines adhere together harmoniously?' Adler suggests that today there may indeed be a 'circle of learning instead of a hierarchy of the branches of knowledge' found in traditional schemes of classification and he proposes the conception of the encyclopedia as a totality, exemplifying the conviction that 'the whole world of knowledge is a single universe of discourse' (Yeo 1991 pp. 24–5)

Essentially the Propaedia was a 'pie' of knowledge divided into ten major segments or slices or helpings:

matter and energy,
the earth,
life on earth,
human life,
human society,
art,
technology,
religion,
the history of mankind,
the branches of knowledge.

The ten segments themselves were divided into 42 divisions, 189 sections and 15,000 separate subjects. Thus, the reader accessing via the *Propaedia* would explore the circle of knowledge until they found the topic or subject or title they wanted; then that topic would provide a reference to the proper relevant full article in the *Macropaedia* or *Macropaedia*.

What was this *Propaedia* trying to do? In its essence, it was a study guide to learning subjects or disciplines. A student could start at a particular place, and then by reading 'around' the topic they could become acquainted with the appropriate relevant materials.

This set of themes and sub-themes makes up the bulk of the one-volume *Propaedia* that the users may consult or ignore, but which offers a rational reading plan for any range of subjects in the in-depth *Macropaedia* volumes. (McArthur 1986 p. 157)

This can be contrasted with a hierarchical arrangement. With a hierarchy, there is a 'narrowing' as a branch is followed. At each level there is a division. So, as the leaves are approached, there is less material, but that material is condensed and more focused. So a hierarchy is more the tool of a researcher, than it is of a student or learner.

Libraries—ordinary present day libraries—organized on principles from the early twentieth century, do not use alphabetical arrangement; they use thematic arrangement. Books are placed on shelves not alphabetically by title or author; they are placed on shelves by subject or by classification. In fact, the origin of their central thematic arrangement, Jefferson's library, which was the seed for the dominant Library of Congress classification, uses Bacon's threefold division of memory, reason, and imagination. And, separately, Dewey, influenced by Harris, used an 'inverted' Baconian classification for the Dewey Decimal Classification.

So, as we have observed, encyclopedias and libraries are counterparts in providing the whole world of knowledge. Historically they both have used Bacon's Tree of Knowledge. But, from 1700, encyclopaedias drifted to alphabetical arrangement, whereas, around 1860, libraries forked from this to a thematic Tree of Knowledge. It was Adler that realized that a mistake had been made and tried to re-unite the fork in 1971 by once again providing a thematic access to encyclopaedias. In fact, the *Propaedia* failed, it was criticized and revised by the *Encyclopaedia Brittanica* and re-released as a second version in 1985. [The tri-partite style is still available as the *New Encyclopaedia Brittanica*]. At least some of the main critics of the *Propaedia* were librarians (Auchter 1999). And, in fact, the librarians had a genuine intellectual complaint. The *Propaedia* itself was supplied without an index. That was a blunder. Whenever there is a classed or graph-structured arrangement, there needs to be an index to locate the nodes (as we saw with the Roget Thesaurus and the Dewey Relativ Index). [Not to worry, a publisher reassured the librarian critics, you librarians pay me in advance for an index, and I will produce one for you. They did, he did not, and he was convicted of mail fraud (Whitely 1992).]

Also, as a side remark, one of the two thematic tasks that librarians were attempting to do was much more difficult than giving a thematic arrangement to an encyclopaedia. With encyclopaedia articles, each individual article will have its single primary subject, they are written that way, and thus each will have a single proper place for itself in a Tree of Knowledge. But with arbitrary books, arbitrary IOs, the IO might have multiple non-overlapping subjects (remember, Sphinges and Crocutes): an IO might easily have 10 different subjects in which case it might have 10 different candidate slots in any Tree of Knowledge. This is not of any great consequence for 'subject classification': an IO can have many subjects. But Jefferson, Dewey, and the organizers of the early Library of Congress were trying to do another additional, different task with a Tree of Knowledge. They were trying to place or locate each book at a single node in the Tree of Knowledge so that they could shelve the books. And, this meant that they had to force each book rationally into one slot; they had to winnow the perhaps 10 candidate subject slots down to one kind slot; and that is a demanding task.

## 3.10 Catalogs vs. Propaedias

Aristotle cataloged and classified mostly tokens, individual types, kinds, entities, or things, whereas Baconian Trees of Knowledge, and later propaedias, 'organized' mostly knowledge. What are the differences here?

There are some differences between catalogs and propaedias (to be sketched shortly). But, for our purposes, propaedias are being used as vehicles to establish classifications of IOs. Furthermore a propaedia is the basis of a tag or topic language, which can be used to annotate the IOs. (In this use, the differences between catalogs and propaedias-for-IO-classification are not so great.)

We follow Reid in thinking that classification is just applying an attribute. With a catalog, there are attributes or concepts or types, and particulars having those attributes or falling under or instantiating those types. So, to use the Reid example hierarchy:

Animal
Man
Frenchman
Parisian

Parisian, Frenchman, Man, and Animal are all types. And Henri de Toulouse-Lautrec was a particular who instantiated the type Parisian (and also the types Frenchman, Man, and Animal). This structure can be the basis of an extensive catalog (likely then, in a more extensive classification tree, the Reid hierarchy would be just one branch).

What about propaedias? Propaedias are *not* themselves classification type-hierarchies. They amount to structures for topic languages, or structures for what librarians would call subject headings. One of the leaves in the d'Alembert Tree of Knowledge is *Gardening*. Now, gardening is an area of knowledge or learning and it is *not* itself a type. It is a particular, not a universal. (We are not, in this context, talking of gardening, that pleasant Sunday afternoon *activity* beloved by many.) There are no instances or particulars of the knowledge area gardening. Rather it is just an area of knowledge. And as such, it is a somewhat poorly delineated abstraction. In the d'Alembert tree, gardening has *botany* as its parent. Botany is also not a type, it also is an area of study, learning, or knowledge. And so too for all the nodes in a Tree of Knowledge. The nodes in the tree are not related to other nodes by being subtypes of each other. Nor are they instances of each other. None of them have instances. Gardening is not an instance of Botany. So, what is the linking relation between a node and its parent, between, for example, Gardening and Botany? D'Alembert tells us. A tree of knowledge shows thematic relations, and d'Alembert's choice was that it should

> exhibit as far as is possible the order and concatenation of human learning [by examining] their genealogy and their filiation, the causes that must have given rise to them and the characteristics that distinguish them (d'Alembert 1751)

Gardening and Botany are examples of human learning, and there is a genealogical relation between them covering their origins and characteristics.

At this point, catalogs of types and propaedias of knowledge seem to be very different. One can be used to classify and the other cannot. But then the important step is made: IOs can be *about* topics or subjects or areas of knowledge. And that can be used in conjunction with a propaedia to create attributes, for example, that an IO addresses the subject matter Gardening, that an IO addresses the subject matter of Botany, so on, i.e

... addresses the topic Gardening
... addresses the topic Botany

In turn, these attributes create types and a type hierarchy for example, the type of IOs addressing the topic of Gardening, the type of IOs addressing the topic Botany, and the propaedia tells that gardening is a sub-topic of Botany. So these attributes, together with the relations between topics, form a type hierarchy, just like the more familiar ones of Reid and Aristotle. A book on gardening is (to a somewhat lesser extent) a book on botany (well, according to d'Alembert it is). And the nodes of this newly created or generated type hierarchy do have instances. For example, consider the type *being an IO with topic Botany*; Linnaeus's historically famous book or text *Species Plantarum* instantiates that type. In sum, a propaedia is not itself a standalone classification hierarchy, but it can be used to produce a classification hierarchy of IOs.

From the point of view of librarianship, a propaedia is a labeling, tagging, or annotation system, which supports labeling by subjects or topics. And this allows the specification and retrieval of IOs having those labels i.e. IOs on those subjects. And if the propaedia is in the form of a hierarchy or tree, which it usually is, the labeling system allows the specification and retrieval of IOs on topics related to those of a given label such as topics more general, topics more specific, and 'sibling' topics.

An important point to note of contrast between plain classifications and propaedia-generated classifications arises from polytopicality. IOs can be on several different topics—the same IO can even be on different topics that 'contradict' each other. To express this somewhat enigmatically: Nothing can be a man and a horse, at the same time, yet a book certainly can address the subject 'man' and address the subject 'horse' at the same time.

# References

Adler MJ (1986) A guidebook to learning: for a lifelong pursuit of wisdom. Macmillan, New York

Auchter D (1999) The evolution of the encyclopaedia britannica: from the macropaedia to britannica online. Ref Serv Rev 27(3):291–299

Bäck AT (2000) Aristotle's theory of predication. Brill Academic Publishers, Leiden

Bacon F (1605) The advancement of learning. http://www.gutenberg.org/ebooks/5500. Accessed 10 Oct 2010

Bacon F (1620) The great instauration. http://www.constitution.org/bacon/instauration.htm. Accessed 10 Oct 2010

Berg J (1982) Aristotle's theory of definition. ATTI del Convegno Internazionale di Storia della Logica, San Gimignano, 4–8 Dec 1982, CLUEB, Bologna, 1983, pp 19–30

Bradshaw LE (1981) Ephraim chambers' cyclopedia. In: Kafker F (ed) Notable encyclopedias of the seventeenth and eighteenth centuries: nine predecessors of the Encyclopédie. The voltaire foundation, Oxford, pp 123–137

Coleridge ST (1827) General introduction or preliminary treatise on method. In: Smedley E, Rose HJ, Henry R (eds) Encyclopaedia metropolitana; or, universal dictionary of knowledge, on an original plan: comprising the twofold advantage of a philosophical and an alphabetical arrangement., 26 vols. Fellowes B, Rivington J et al. 1827-45, vol 1, pp 1–43

Cutter CA (1904) Rules for a dictionary catalog, 4th edn. U.S. Government Printing Office, Washington

d'Alembert JLR (1751) Preliminary discourse. Scholarly publishing office of the university of michigan library, 2009. Web Transactions of discourse préliminaire, Encyclopédie ou Dictionnaire raisonné des sciences, des arts et des métiers, vol 1. Paris. http://quod.lib.umich.edu/d/did/. Accessed 2 Feb 2010

Diderot D (1765) Salon de . Essai sur la peinture. http://books.google.com/books?id=qJVAAAAAYAAJ. Accessed 10 Oct 2010

Gnoli C, Bosch M, Mazzocchi F (2007) A new relationship for multidisciplinary knowledge organization systems: dependence. In: Alvite-Díez M-L, Rodríguez-Bravo B (eds) Interdisciplinarity and transdisciplinarity in the organization of scientific knowledge. Universidad de León, Secretariado de Publicaciones, León, Spain, proceedings of the Eighth ISKO-Spain Conference 18-20 April 2007, pp 399–409. http://hdl.handle.net/10760/9558

Gnoli C (2008a) Categories and facets in integrative levels. Axiomathes 18(2):177–192

Gnoli C, Merli G, Pavan G, Bernuzzi E, Priano M (2008) Freely faceted classification for a web-based bibliographic archive. Paper presented at the repositories of knowledge in digital spaces: accessibility, sustainability, semantic interoperability: 11th German ISKO conference, Konstanz, 20–22 Feb 2008

Grenon P (2003) BFO in a nutshell: a bi-categorial axiomatization for BFO and comparison with DOLCE. IFOMIS report 06 Dec 2003

Grenon P, Smith B (2004) SNAP and SPAN: towards dynamic spatial ontology. Spatial Cognition Comput 4(1):69–104

Hjørland B (2008a) Core classification theory: a reply to Szostak. J Doc 64(3):333–342

Ifomis (2009) Basic formal ontology (BFO). http://www.ifomis.org/bfo. Accessed 10 Oct 2010

Kaiser JO (1911) Systematic indexing. Pitman, London

Koestler A (1959) The sleepwalkers. Penguin, London

Lenat DB (1996) From 2001 to 2001: common sense and the mind of HAL

Lowe EJ (2006) The four category ontology. a metaphysical foundation for natural science. Oxford University Press, Oxford

Masolo C, Borgo S, Gangemi A, Guarino N, Oltramari A (2001) Wonderweb deliverable D18. http://wonderweb.semanticweb.org/deliverables/documents/D18.pdf.

McArthur T (1986) Worlds of reference: lexicography, learning and language from the clay tablet to the computer. Cambridge University Press, New York

Olson HA (2004) The ubiquitous hierarchy: an army to overcome the threat of a mob. Library Trends 52(3):604–616

Ong WJ (1958) Ramus, method, and the decay of dialogue: from the art of discourse to the art of reason. Harvard University Press, Cambridge

Peirce CS (1906) Prolegomena to an apology for pragmaticism. In: Hartshorne C, Weiss P (eds) Collected Papers of Charles Sanders Peirce, vol 4. Harvard University Press, Cambridge, pp 530–572

Piper R (2009) Extinct animals: an encyclopaedia of species that have disappeared during human history. Greenwood Press, Westport. doi:10.1336/0313349878

Plato (360 BCE-a) (2010) Phaedo. http://classics.mit.edu/Plato/phaedo.html. Accessed 10 Oct 2010

Plato (360 BCE-b) (2010) The republic. http://classics.mit.edu/Plato/republic.html. Accessed 10 Oct 2010

Plato (360 BCE-c) (2010) Sophist. http://classics.mit.edu/Plato/sophist.html. Accessed 10 Oct 2010

Plato (370 BCE) (2010) Parminides. http://classics.mit.edu/Plato/parmenides.html. Accessed 10 Oct 2010

Reid T (1785) abstraction. In: Bennett JF (ed) Essays on the intellectual powers of man (redacted text)

Russell B (1912) The problems of philosophy. Home University Library

Russell B (1943) An outline of intellectual rubbish: a hilarious catalogue of organized and individual stupidity. Haldeman-Julius, London

Schneider L (2009) The logic of the ontological square. Stud Logica 91(1):25–51. doi:10.1007/s11225-009-9165-6

Selinger S (1976) Review: encyclopedic guides to the study of ideas: a review article. Library Q 46(4):440–447

Smith B (2004) The logic of biological classification and the foundations of biomedical ontology. In: Westerståhl D (ed) Invited papers from the 10th international conference in logic methodology and philosophy of science. Elsevier North Holland, Oviedo 2003

Smith B (2005) Against fantology. In: Reicher ME, Marek JC (eds) Experience and analysis. HPT and OBV, Wien, pp 153–170

Smith R (2009) Aristotle's logic. http://plato.stanford.edu/archives/spr2009/entries/aristotle-logic/%3E. Accessed 10 Oct 2010

Studtmann P (2008) Aristotle's categories. http://plato.stanford.edu/archives/fall2008/entries/aristotle-categories. Accessed 10 Oct 2010

Szostak R et al. (2007) The León manifesto. http://www.iskoi.org/ilc/leon.htm. Accessed 21 May 2011

Taylor AG (2007) An introduction to functional requirements for bibliographic records. In: Taylor AG (ed) FRBR: what it is and how it will affect our retrieval tools. Libraries Unlimited

Weinberger D (2007) Everything is miscellaneous. Times Books, New York

Wetzel L (2006) Types and tokens. http://plato.stanford.edu/entries/types-tokens/. Accessed 10 Oct 2010

Whitely S (1992) The circle of learning: encyclopaedia brittanica. In: Rettig J (ed) Distinguished classics of reference publishing. The Oryx Press, Phoenix, pp 77–88

Wright A (2007) Glut: mastering information throughout the ages. Joseph Henry Press, Washington

Yeo RR (1991) Reading encyclopedias: science and the organization of knowledge in british dictionaries of arts and sciences, 1730-1850. ISIS 82(1):24–49

Yeo RR (1996) Ephraim chambers's cyclopaedia (1728) and the tradition of commonplaces. J Hist Idea 57(1):157–175

# Chapter 4
# A Logic for Organizing Information

## 4.1 First Order Logic

A greatly underappreciated and unused theoretical background to the organization of information is that of symbolic logic. (The monumental and authoritative *Encyclopedia of Library and Information Sciences*, Third Edition, 2009, does not have an entry for logic in its 6,856 pages (Bates and Maack 2009).)

What is the role for logic? And why is it important? There are a number of reasons. We would like to engage with our information problems in natural language. We talk and understand natural language, and natural language has sufficient richness to address reference, self-reference and layers of meta-languages (all of which are necessary for organizing information). However, for reasons developed in Sect. 1.10.1, computers are not going to understand natural language anytime soon, if ever. A fruitful line in response to this obstacle is to use something approximating natural language when interacting with computers. This is what is done, for example, with the ubiquitous database access language SQL (Structured Query Language). It is done with Prolog for Logic Programming and, to a lesser extent, with Functional Programming and Rewrite Systems like Mathematica. It is similar in a large portion of the Artificial Intelligence field of Knowledge Representation. The common theme here is the use of logic. SQL is logic, Prolog is logic, etc. As Sowa writes

> Natural languages display the widest range of knowledge that can be expressed, and logic enables the precisely formulated subset to be expressed in a computable form. Perhaps there are some kinds of knowledge that cannot be expressed in logic. But if such knowledge exists, it cannot be represented or manipulated on any digital computer in any other notation. The expressive power of logic includes every kind of information that can be stored or programmed on any digital computer (Sowa 2000, p. 12).

An independent argument for the desirability of logic is the following. As mentioned, traditional librarianship, has, over the last 5,000 years, evolved data structures, such as the 'organization of knowledge', to assist with the task at hand.

M. Frické, *Logic and the Organization of Information*,
DOI: 10.1007/978-1-4614-3088-9_4,
© Springer Science+Business Media New York 2012

The systems typically use trees, hierarchies, lattices, sets, subsets, types, parts, mereology, etc. The properties of the classification systems are more subtle than they seem and, in fact, the systems are more subtle than traditional cataloging seems to be aware of. A simple example: a scheme might contain the information that Ford is a make of car, and that a Ford car is an American car. Putting this together with the fact that my car is a Ford, it can be inferred that my car is an American car but *not* that my car is a make of car. How is this? It arises because almost all realistic classification schemes contain different orders, sorts, and types, and the built-in knowledge of their interrelations. Logic is the discipline to be used to clarify this. Logic has not been in widespread use here, but it should be.

Also, databases are central. Many, or even most, information repositories and web sites have computer databases, sometimes distributed databases, as their foundations. In turn, logic is the natural design or specification language for databases. It is common, in information science or computer science circles, to use Entity-Relationship (E-R) modeling to design databases (this will be seen later with Functional Requirements for Bibliographical Records (FRBR)). But E-R modeling, while perhaps a valuable heuristic visual aid, is known to be incomplete and inadequate when it comes to database specification (Thalheim 2000). What is needed is logic. Then, most databases are manipulated using SQL-like programming languages; and SQL is just logic in simplified natural language. Thus, learning logic assists with understanding, designing, and using databases.

What are we going to do with logic, and what kind of logic do we need? Logic, for us, will be used primarily to specify aspects of the various structures of interest. Plain English is not good enough for this purpose, if the aim is to be concise, clear, accurate, and friendly to algorithms. The main role of logic elsewhere is to assess reasoning, to assess whether arguments are valid. We are not doing that here as the main task. Instead we are using logic as an artificial language of specification. It will turn out, though, that the various information structures often support reasoning—and, indeed, reasoning is often used, as, for example, in 'smart data'. Logic will clarify this for us

The logic we need is First Order Predicate Calculus. Peter Norvig writes

> Philosophers and psychologists will argue the question of how appropriate predicate calculus is as a model of human thought, but one point stands clear: predicate calculus is sufficient to represent anything that can be represented in a digital computer. (Norvig 1992, p. 463)

And Sowa makes the case that First Order Predicate Calculus is the main, or the one true, logic. Sowa writes:

> Among all the varieties of logic, classical first-order logic has a privileged status. It has enough expressive power to define all of mathematics, every digital computer that has ever been built, and the semantics of every version of logic including itself. Fuzzy logic, modal logic, neural networks, and even higher-order logic can be defined in [first-order logic].... Besides expressive power, first-order logic has the best-defined, least problematic model theory and proof theory, and it can be defined in terms of a bare minimum of primitives.... Since first-order logic has such great power, many philosophers and logicians such as Quine have argued strongly that classical [first-order logic] is in some sense the "one true logic" and that the other versions are redundant, unnecessary, or ill-conceived. (Sowa 2000, p. 41)

Sowa's statement is probably a mild exaggeration. The point is often made that mathematicians have an essential need for Second Order Logic (i.e. for 'meta-properties'). However, where this occurs probably the relevant subject matter is mathematics itself or in the border between mathematics and logic, and not pure logic. Furthermore, if the interest is with computers and computation, it is First Order Logic that is required. The richer expressiveness of Second Order Logic—in areas beyond First Order Logic—just make it unsuitable as a general vehicle for algorithms and computer programming. Second Order Logic is more problematical on a number of fronts, most particularly by being infused with the set theory of infinite sets (Enderton 2009). It would be better to avoid it if possible. However, classification requires higher order properties (Genus and Species are higher order properties). But classification seems not require quantification over properties in full generality. It should be possible to give an adequate account of classification using only First Order Logic. That is the plan for the present work.

Introductions to First Order Logic are readily available, one is provided in Appendix A (see also (Fricke 2005)). We will take acquaintance with that material as a given in what follows.

## 4.2 Symbolizing Attributes, Concepts or Types

Types, concepts, or attributes are going to be symbolized by *abstractions* or *intensional* abstractions.

This can be done using the abstraction or comprehension notation

$\{x:\Phi(x)\}$

(which is sometimes written with a vertical bar like this $\{x|\Phi(x)\}$). This notation is used in naïve set theory (where it is sometimes called 'set builder notation'). It is also common in all of mathematics, and in many computer programming languages, such as Haskell or Python.

In an *intensional abstraction* $\{x:\Phi(x)\}$, the $\Phi(x)$ itself denotes an 'open sentence' (a formula of the predicate calculus, usually with a free occurrence of x.) So the three formulas

$\{x:Friend(x)\&Male(x)\}$
$\{y:Book(y)\&LeatherBound(y)\}$
$\{x:F(x)\}$

are examples of abstractions. In the logic, abstractions are terms, i.e. they amount to names or nouns.

Keep in mind, the $\Phi(x)$ has to be an open sentence, and not itself a term. So

$\{x:F(x)\}$

is a perfectly good abstraction, but

{x:x} or
{x:f(x)}

are not (because neither x nor f(x) are open sentences).

Not all predicates are monadic or one-place predicates, some are polyadic or n-place relations. For example, while the predicate '…is red' in 'The fire engine is red' is monadic, the predicate '… is taller than …' in 'Henry is taller than Jim' is polyadic, it involves two items, it is a 2-place relation. Thus far, the formal schemas for abstractions have all been created using a single variable i.e. they are set up for monadic predicates or open sentences with only one variable of interest. It is possible to generalize this to the several variable case. This might give abstractions of the form

{x,y: Taller(x,y)}, where x,y is an ordered list of different variables

For much of the work here, the single variable case is all that is needed, though, it is worth knowing that the approach can be generalized if that is required.

Abstractions are understood as properties or attributes. So {x:Friend(x)& Male(x)} is understood as the property 'male friend'. There is an approach to First Order Logic proposed by George Bealer (1982, 1998) which uses 'intensional abstractions' to capture properties (and propositions, and relations). We are adopting a simplified version of Bealer's logic. The word 'property' is being used in a semi-technical sense here: it is roughly synonymous with 'concept' or 'type' or 'notion'.

The intensional abstraction notation can be used with zero, one, or many binding variables. So, all of the following are well formed terms

{: T(x)&F(y)}
{x : T(x)&F(y)}
{x,y : T(x)&F(y)}
{x,y,z : T(x)&F(y)}

One classical distinction that gets lost in modern predicate calculus is that between substance and accident. In Aristotle, the two sentences

Socrates is a man.
Socrates is wise.

are distinctly different. The first identifies a sort for Socrates, and the second ascribes a property to him. But in modern logic, both these sentences would be symbolized by simple predicates

Man(socrates)
Wise(socrates)

So they look very similar from a logical point of view. And the associated types or concepts would be

{x : Man(x)}
{x : Wise(x)}

But, although these two concepts appear similar in their logical form, the first represents a classic sort or natural kind whereas the second is a gerrymander. And it is the natural kinds that are of most use for classification.


### 4.2.1  Symbolizing Aspects (and More)

Classifying information is different to classifying things. Here is one way of explaining the central difference. When classifying a thing, the interest is with what *kind* that thing is, that is, with whether it is a rabbit, a piece of aluminum, a cloud, and so forth. But information ranges more widely than this. For example, with rabbits, there is knowledge of their food, their coats, their habitat, their life stages, and so on. One way to characterize this is to say that this information is about *aspects* of rabbits. Brian Vickery writes

> Taxonomy is basically concerned with classifying 'natural kinds'—of organisms, of soils, of substances. Documentation has to classify what is written about these objects, and must take into account not only the natural kinds but also their properties, behaviour, interactions, and operations on them. (Vickery 1975, p. 9)

[Explanations of 'aspects' can be found in (Broughton 2004; Broughton et al. 2005; Hjørland 2006; Mills and Broughton 1977).]

How is the logical symbolism to be used with aspects? For example,

$\{x:Rabbit(x)\}$

identifies the type 'rabbit', what is needed as a symbolization for the type 'habitat of rabbits'?

The 'habitat of rabbits' is a habitat, so if a Habitat(?x) predicate is used, likely that will be a component of the symbolization

$\{x:Habitat(x)....\}$ (**a start**)

On the other hand, the 'habitat of rabbits' is definitely not a rabbit, so any symbolization involving a direct application of the Rabbit(?x) predicate is going to be wrong

$\{x:Rabbit(x)....\}$ (**wrong**)

What is needed now is a means to connect the habitat with rabbits. If a two-place relation is used

IsHabitatOf(?x,?y)

with the meaning that the entity ?x is the habitat of the type ?y then

$\{x:Habitat(x)\&IsHabitatOf(x,rabbit)\}$

would be an acceptable symbolization (the term 'rabbit', of course, picks out the rabbit-type). Types like the habitat-of-rabbits can be constructed using relations (these can be called *relation* types).

If the relation of symbolization

IsHabitatOf(?x,?y)

is really understood semantically to have the fact that ?x is a habitat built into it, then

{x: IsHabitatOf(x,rabbit)}

would be an acceptable shorter version. (Usually it is better to be more explicit rather than less explicit. Eventually we are going to want to consider how different types relate one to another, and explicit formalizations help with that judgment.)

There are occasions when functions can be used as an alternative to relations (usually that can be done when one of the components of the relation is single valued or unique). In the case of habitats, one could certainly take the view that each animal type has its own (single) habitat so there is the habitat of rabbits, the habitat of deer, the habitat of lions, and so on. That invites the use of a function, say

habitatOf(?x)

which picks out the actual habitat of the animal of type ?x. And then the 'habitat of rabbits' could be symbolized

{x: (x=habitatOf(rabbit))}

This time the type has been constructed using a function (and it can be called a *function* type).

This is a technique for dealing with aspects. It is important to draw attention to it because in information retrieval logical operations are usually limited to Boolean operations (i.e. doing ANDs, ORs, and NOTs with the formulas). But Boolean operations are not strong enough logically for aspects. You cannot start with 'rabbits' and 'habitat' and get to 'the habitat of rabbits' by Boolean operations. What is needed are relations and functions.

Actually even 'aspects' are nowhere near strong enough for a full range of topics for IOs. Here is Brian Vickery again, now writing in 2008,

Books may be written about single-termed subjects such as War, Primates, Tulips, Railways, or Cookery, but many of the documents with which we must deal have compound subjects: the causes of war, the evolution of primates, the propagation of tulips, the financing of railways, vegetable cookery. Many subjects are even more complex, for example:

Ecological study of the skin colour of desert animals
Streptomycin therapy for osteomyelitis of femur
Effect of humus on crumb formation in loamy sand
Radiographic diagnosis of bone cancer
Grey wool ankle socks for hiking
Damages for personal injury in English law
Plating the spokes of bicycle wheels
Prevention of mould spoilage of parboiled rice in storage in silo
Wind tunnel measurement of Reynolds number for boundary layer transition in model aircraft

(Vickery 2008, pp. 147, 148)

It is a bit of a stretch to regard the subject

Ecological study of the skin colour of desert animals

as being an *aspect* of anything. It is, however, a compound or complex concept, which can be captured in symbolic logic. (This will be revisited later under Compound Types and Ranganathan's Heritage.)

## 4.2.2  Symbolizing 'Subjects': Nouns and Modifiers

With subject annotation and indexing, the notion of a subject-as-topic will be important. Grammatically speaking, it turns out that topics, and index entry terms, are *nouns* or *noun phrases*. For example, Cutter in his rules for compound subject names identifies six kinds of compounds

The name of a subject may be—
(a) A single word, as **Botany**, **Economics**, **Ethics**,
Or several words taken together, either—
(b) A noun preceded by an adjective, as **Ancient history**, **Capital punishment**, **Moral philosophy**, **Political economy**.
(c) A noun preceded by another noun used like an adjective, as **Death penalty**, **Flower fertilization**.
(d) A noun connected with another by a preposition, as **Penalty of death**, **Fertilization of flowers**.
(e) A noun connected with another by "and", as **Ancients and moderns**.
(f) A phrase or sentence, as in the titles **"Sur la regle Paterna paternis maternal maternis"**... where the whole phrase would be the subject of the dissertation. (Cutter 1904, p. 174)

[The single-word cases are nouns, the extended phrases are noun phrases, and the sentences are nominalized sentences.]

Consequently it is worthwhile to given some attention to the symbolization of nouns and noun phrases. Logical relations between different subject headings, or the components of such headings, will establish some important so-called 'syndetic' relations, i.e. links or cross references from one place to another.

Standard grammar tells us that substantives, or nominals, might be proper names, pronouns, simple nouns (which can be common nouns or proper nouns), compound nouns, noun phrases, or nominal clauses.

The most important two umbrella cases for classification are those of common nouns and of the way those nouns work with adjectives and other 'modifiers'.

The sentence

Jane Austen is an author.

could be symbolized

Author(austen)

That is, the type or sort 'author' is

{x:Author(x)}

So, common nouns, such as 'author' would ordinarily be read as a sort and each such noun-sort could be produced by using a predicate, say $\lambda x(\text{Author}(x))$, to form the intensional abstraction

{x:Author(x)}

So, a starting point is to regard common nouns as unanalysable wholes and to assign simple predicates to them.

There is a complexity here that is worth noting: many simple common nouns are constructed from affixes and other simple nouns (for example, 'friend', 'friendship', 'ex-friend'). So simple nouns need not be independent of each other—in effect some can consist of common stems coupled with prefixes, suffixes, and even infixes to make other simple nouns related to the stems.

We have a choice here: a new predicate could be used for each new simple noun (in which case the stemming information would be lost) or, where suitable, a more complete symbolization could be used to retain the information (for example, a symbolization of 'ex-friend' would need to reflect that the entity concerned used to be a friend).

The last concern with complexity of symbolization is an instance of something general that occurs when symbolizing parts of a language. Decisions have to be made on detail. Consider the statement 'Brer is a rascally rabbit'. One could let 'being a rascally rabbit' be a single predicate in the symbolization and end up with a formula like 'R(b)'. But then, the information that Brer was a rabbit would be lost, and so the symbolization would not be able to show that the conclusion Brer is a rabbit follows from the premise that Brer is a rascally rabbit. We have no direct interest in inference here. But we are interested in subtypes and supertypes for they are among the stepping stones of classification and search. With simple nouns, affixes are used to make plurals out of singulars, among other things, so the word 'affix' itself is affixed to 'affixes', 'boy' to 'boys', 'mouse' to 'mice' and so on. We need to retain stem information, so the appropriate choice for symbolizing affixed simple nouns is to attempt to represent and symbolize the stem.

Moving on from simple nouns, adjectives can be conjoined with nouns to produce noun phrases such as 'an English author', 'a woman author, 'an English woman author'. The predicates for these are often symbolized by conjoining predicates for the adjectives to the predicates for the noun. So

Author(austen)
English(austen)&Author(austen)
Woman(austen)&Author(austen)
English(austen)&Woman(austen)&Author(austen)

are some sample sentences and the sorts would be

{x:Author(x)} becomes

{x:(English(x)&Author(x))} or, further,
{x:(English(x)&Woman(x)&Author(x))}

Adjectives are a type of *modifier*. The noun, or sort, is modified by the adjective.

Modifiers are important but care is needed with compounding adjectives or compounding modifiers. A 'red star' is both red and a star, so the adjective gets ANDED to the noun. And a 'large ant' is an ant but it is not so clear that it is large. And, even worse, a 'former student' is presumably neither a student nor former or a former (what is that? what is a 'former'?).

Linguists often distinguish intersective, subsective, and non-predicating adjectives (Chierchia and McConnell-Ginet 1990). With 'an English author', anything that is an English author is English (so the English-author-type is a subtype of the English type)—also anything that is an English author is an author (so the English-author-type is a subtype of the author type). So the English-author-type lies at the intersection of the English-type and the Author-type. And a symbolization like

{x:(English(x)&Author(x))}

is entirely acceptable.

With a 'large ant', anything that is a large ant is an ant (so the large-ant-type is a subtype of the ant-type). The problems arise with the adjective and modifier 'large' because a large ant is not large (certainly not large in the way that a large elephant is large). So it would be a mistake to consider that large ants are a subtype of the large-item-type, i.e. this symbolization is wrong

{x:(Large(x)&Ant(x))} **is wrong**

There are different ways to deal with this (Parsons 1970). One way is to say that what is needed is a large-for-an-ant predicate which divides ants up into the large-for-an-ant ones and the others. Thus

{x:(LargeForAnAnt(x)&Ant(x))}

and similarly for elephants

{x:(LargeForAnElephant(x)&Elephant(x))}

and for anything else that we wish to qualify as being large. This symbolization loses something. When we describe two items before us as being a large ant and a large elephant, we actually are saying something similar about the two of them. And the above symbolization omits that. What we are saying similar about the two things is not that they are both large; what we are saying is something like 'of all those things which are ants, this one is one of the larger ones and of all those things which are elephants, this one is one of the larger ones'. So the commonality is something like 'larger one of these kinds of things'. We could build this in if we wished to. It may need lambda abstractions and quantifiers to do it. The important point is that modified nouns like 'large ants' are subtypes but not intersective subtypes.

With a 'former student', anything that is a former student is not a student (so the former-student-type is not a subtype of the student-type). And quite what a former-item-type might be, if anything, is very unclear. What seems to be happening here is that the application of the adjective 'former' to the noun 'student' seems to produce an entirely new noun on its own, in which case the symbolization should be something like

{x:FormerStudent(x)}

Again this symbolization loses something. Former students, former beauty queens, and former Catholics do have something in common. We could spell this out. It would probably take notions of time or occurrents, and the saying that this person used to be one of these (e.g. a student) but is not one of these (a student) now. These complexities may not be needed often. The important point is there are non-predicating uses of modifiers which do not produce either intersective subtypes or pure subtypes; they do not directly produce subtypes at all.

Adjectives are not the only modifiers. Consider the type 'man who shot Liberty Valance': it is a noun phrase consisting of a noun 'man' and a relative clause 'who shot Liberty Valance'. Relative clauses, usually introduced by 'who', 'which', 'that', etc.), are also modifiers. A relative clause is effectively an adjective and can be analyzed as above. Prepositional phrases (usually started with such prepositions as 'at', 'in', 'from', 'under', 'of', 'with', 'by', 'through'), for example, 'the man at the Inauguration' can also be treated essentially as adjectives or modifiers. Symbolizations of prepositional phrases can sometimes be more transparent if two-place relations are used. For example, the prepositional part of the phrases 'a man in Paris' and 'a man in London' could be represented by plain predicates like 'InParis(?x)' and 'InLondon(?x)'; but, for some uses, it would be better to use a relation, say, 'In(?x,?y)' and then represent the prepositional parts with 'In(?x, paris)' and 'In(?x, london)' where 'paris' and 'london' are the symbolization terms or names for the proper names Paris and London. Once again, this is a level of detail consideration. (It allows for symbolizations of phrases like 'a man in a French city', which could be something like 'Man(x) & In(x,y) & FrenchCity(y)'.)

Now we have the idea of adjectives and modifiers we should at least mention compound nouns, which are a case of ordinary common nouns. Compound nouns are those with the appearance of two or more nouns jammed into one, such as 'darkroom', 'redhead', and 'washer-dryer'. These will be discussed in detail in the setting of classification for it is classification that is the motivating factor for us. For the moment, it can the observed that a darkroom is a room which is dark, so that case is just going to be the familiar adjectival modification. Other compound nouns are more of a challenge.

In sum, nouns, noun phrases, and clauses, etc. can usually symbolized by predicates, and other predicates ('modifiers'), supplemented by lambdas and sometimes quantifiers; usually those modifiers, and supplementary subformulas, are modifying 'what the noun applies to', but occasionally they can be modifying the noun or combinations of other modifiers which are modifying the noun. Attention needs to be paid to whether modification results in intersective types (i.e. the conjunctive composition of types), non-intersective subtypes, or new types.

### 4.2.3 Symbolizing Annotated Types

We noted in connection with propaedias that there can be an interest in those IOs which are on a particular subject. Such IOs address a topic, or, more generally, have a subject, a subject heading, a concept, or a tag attached to them. Notice here that there is—so-to-speak—a two-step process going on. There is the subject or topic (which itself is a concept) but the IOs of interest do not themselves instantiate that concept: instead they have that concept as a topic and this creates the further concept or type of IOs with that topic.

To capture these, we need a two-place relation, or relational attribute, such as

AddressesSubject(?x,?y) or
IsAbout(?x,?y) or
HasTopic(?x,?y) or
HasTag(?x,?y)

which says that the first item, the IO, has the second item, the subject, as its subject, topic, or tag.

Suppose there was an interest in horses. We could start with a predicate

Horses(?y)

to mean '?y is a horse' then

{y:Horses(y)}

would be the type horses (with an extension that includes Secretariat, Trigger etc.). And this could be named using the identity

horses = {y:Horses(y)}

Then annotated types for IOs about horses would be symbolized

{x: AddressesSubject(x,horses)} or
{x: IsAbout(x,horses)} or
{x: HasTopic(x,horses)} or
{x: HasTag(x,horses)}

or, in longer form

{x: AddressesSubject(x, {y:Horses(y)})} or
{x: IsAbout(x, {y:Horses(y)})} or
{x: HasTopic(x, {y:Horses(y)})} or
{x: HasTag(x, {y:Horses(y)})}

and any of these would be suitable to represent the type IOs-on-horses (with an extension that includes books on Secretariat, films about Trigger etc.).

## 4.3 A Logic for Classification

Considerable progress can be made with classification using just the notions of particular (or item or instance or token), property (or attribute or universal or concept or type), and the relations 'is a subtype of' and 'is an instance of'. We will usually center on the relation 'is an instance of'. Existing approaches make extensive use of this relation. But typically they do so only for the case where it is particulars or items or tokens that are instances of the types. This amounts to applying a property (the type) to an item. As such, this is a case of *first order instantiation* or the application of *first order properties*. But this is not the only kind of instantiation there is: first order types themselves can have properties applied to them; when they do, these are cases of *second order instantiation* or the application of *second order properties,* for example, the property tiger itself has the property of being a species, so tiger is an instance of the second order type species (notice the syntax here, 'tiger is an instance of species' not *'a* tiger is an instance of species'.). (There can be yet higher order properties but they are not of immediate interest.) As noted, sometimes the word 'metaproperties' is used to signify second-order properties.

Classification requires higher order properties or second order concepts or metaproperties (Sowa 2000). Why? Consider three examples. Genus and Species, the foundations of Aristotelian and Linnaean classification, are higher order properties, period. Second, within librarianship, such entry points as 'Search by Literary Form' use second order properties. Finally there is the rising star of classification, namely faceted classification (both seen in the traditional library classifications and central also to the pure faceted classifications now dominating the Web). With faceted classification, it is usual to categorize concepts or types to obtain the facets—and categorization of concepts uses second order properties. When Ranganathan had the insight that there were kinds of concepts, that insight was the insight that we should address second order instantiation (Ranganathan 1937, 1951). In addition, within any facet, there is the notion of an enumeration of foci, required to construct indexes (enumerations which, essentially, are either linear or a hierarchical ordered tree traversals) and the notion of a sequence or enumeration of foci or concepts is second order. Thus when Users employ faceted schemes in their searches, the navigation and search process relies on and should rely on, second order properties: entry via facet is entry via a second order property.

Somewhat surprisingly, ordinary first order logic is adequate to discuss the second order properties that are required for classification. Technically, this can be done first via the 'intensional abstraction' of George Bealer (1982) which allows properties and relations to be terms and thus have further properties applied to them and, second, via order sorted first order logic, restricted quantifiers, and general models (Blasius et al. 1989; Kriesel and Krivine 1971; Manzano 1996; Oberschelp 1990; Wang 1952; Manzano 1993) and these can provide clarity to the semantics.

Our intention is to use two different devices. First to understand some of the terms of the logic as denoting types (or concepts or 'sorts') and to permit both statements about those types and the formation of further types from existing types. So, for example, s and t might be understood as types, F(t) and s<t might be statements about types, and (s+t), (s.t), (s-t) might identify further types.

Second, to use the abstraction or comprehension notation {x:Φ(x)} to identify types. So, for example, the abstraction {x:F(x)} is a term—i.e. a substantive or a noun—and it picks out a type; and, since an abstraction is a term, G({x:F(x)}), for example, is a well formed formula (it applies the monadic predicate G(x) to the abstraction).

The upshot is that we can take a predicate like Tiger(x), or T(x), and use that to signify 'x is a Tiger'. Then use the familiar abstraction or comprehension or 'set builder' notation

{x: Φ(x)} (or {x| Φ(x)})

to construct an intensional abstraction or type.

What exactly is an abstraction, say {x:Friend(x)&Male(x)}? Syntactically it is a term (i.e. a name). Semantically, it is a property or notion, or concept, or type, in this case 'male friend'. Readers with a knowledge of set theory might read {x:Friend(x)&Male(x)} as being the set or collection of male friends. But, set theory should not be used here. In set theory, if two sets have the same extension—i.e. if they have the same members—they are identical, they are the same set. This means that concepts cannot be sets, because concepts can have the same extensions without being the same concept. (We saw that earlier, in connection with the Triangle of Meaning, where it was shown that the different concepts red and round might nevertheless have the same extension.) So {x:Friend(x)&Male(x)} is understood as the property or concept or type or intension 'male friend' and not the set of the male friends.

The abstraction

{x: Tiger(x)} (or, more briefly, {x: T(x)}

can be read 'the property Tiger' or 'the type Tiger'.

These abstractions are intended to be terms or names, so—formally—predicates can be applied to them, and statements of identity can be formed between them and other terms. So

S({x: T(x)}) or Species({x: T(x)})

applies the 'species' predicate to the abstraction. And

t={x: Tiger(x)}

states an identity between the term 't' (i.e. the type 't') and the abstraction. Then

S(t) or Species(t)

is a second order application of the property or predicate 'is a Species' to the type tiger. So there could be formal sentences

T(s)& S({x:Tx}) or
T(s)& (t= {x:Tx}) & S(t)
to symbolize
'Shere Khan is a tiger and tiger is a species of animal'.

In sum, the proposal here is standard first order logic augmented with a certain semantic understanding of the formulas and some syntactic devices to help with notation. The proposal has as its intellectual heritage, sorted logic or order-sorted logic (Blasius et al. 1989; Kriesel and Krivine 1971; Manzano 1996; Oberschelp 1990; Wang 1952; Manzano 1993).

The wider intellectual setting is that of Description Logics (themselves a precursor of OWL, the ontology language for the web) (Baader et al. 2007, 2003). However, there are two differences in emphasis between the content here and mainstream Description Logics. Typically, Description Logics have a classification scheme (Terminological Box or TBox, and TBox reasoning) and extra-classification knowledge or assertions (Assertional or ABox and ABox reasoning) and meld the two together to produce knowledge representation and reasoning; for example, a classification scheme may contain the knowledge that fish are vertebrates, the asserted knowledge might contain the facts that vertebrates have backbones and that Livingston is a fish, and from the composite it may be inferred that Livingston has a backbone. The present work addresses primarily classification, it concerns search and information retrieval, not knowledge and knowledge representation, so it has an interest only in 'TBox'. Also, it is rare for Description Logics to use second order concepts or second order properties; however, with classification for the purposes of the search for information objects, second order concepts are vital. One example is that it is second order concepts that give such entry points as 'Search by literary form'. A second core example, is that it is usual to categorize concepts to obtain the facets (now ubiquitous in both ordinary Bliss, Universal Decimal Classification (UDC), Dewey Decimal Classification (DDC), Library of Congress Classification (LCC), and Library of Congress Subject Headings (LCSH) classifications and in the pure faceted classifications dominating the Web) and categorization of concepts uses second order concepts. [The wider literature includes other research that approaches these problems in similar or different ways, for example that by Smith or by Welty and Guarino (Guarino and Welty 2002; Smith 2004; Welty and Guarino 2001).]

Here is an example of the formal machinery. Consider a fragment of Dewey Decimal Classification, around 820 (Fig. 4.1).

There are the properties/concepts/meanings

Lit(?x) 'x is literature'
AmerLit(?x) 'x is American (Literature)'
EngLit(?x) 'x is English (Literature)'
GermLit(?x) 'x is German (Literature)'
Poetry(?x) 'x is Poetry (English Literature)'
Etc

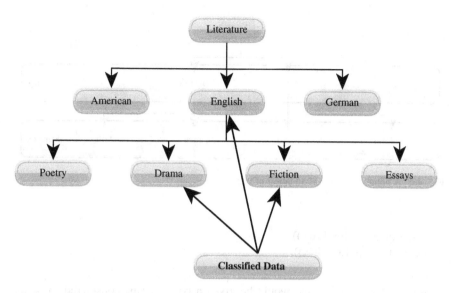

**Fig. 4.1** Fragment of the dewey decimal classification around 820

There are the types

l={x:Lit(x)},
a={x:AmerLit(x)},
e={x:EngLit(x)},
g={x:GermLit(x)},
p={x:Drama(x)},
p={x:Poetry(x)},
Etc.

and the types l, a, e, g, p are subject to the type relations

a<l,
e<l,
g<l,
d<e,
p<e,
etc.

The tree itself can be described by the type relations (indeed, one way is by considering as a directed tree and using a triple store of a<l, e<l, g<l, d<e, p<e, etc. to do it).

The tree can also be described by logical formulas that parallel the type relations (one formula for each directed link)

∀x(AmerLit(x)→Lit(x)),
∀x(EngLit(x)→Lit(x)),
∀x(GerLit(x)→Lit(x)),

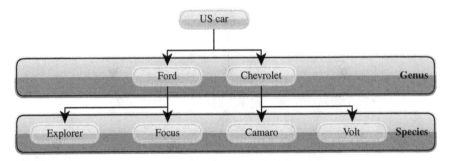

**Fig. 4.2** A genus-species classification of cars

$\forall x(Drama(x) \rightarrow EngLit(x))$,
$\forall x(Poetry(x) \rightarrow EngLit(x))$,
etc.

Any data to be classified would be given a type, that is, considered to be an instance of a (narrow) type. If a standard Aristotelian-Linnaean Genus-Species hierarchical classification were in use, those narrowest types for actual data classification would come from the leaf or terminal nodes only. The Dewey Classification is a little odd in this regard in that some internal nodes are used as terminal nodes for classification also (as illustrated by the heading English itself). Types across a horizontal level typically form higher order types, essentially, the Genus, Species, etc. Thus, for example, the types Poetry, Drama, Fiction, Essays are of (higher-order) type 'Literary Form'. So, as an illustration, a book might be Fiction and Fiction (not the book) might be a Literary Form. Formally this could be represented as

L(f) (i.e. fiction is a literary form)

A different example might clarify this (Fig. 4.2) or, more usually, (Fig. 4.3). So, an Explorer is a Ford and a Ford is a US Car, but Ford (notice 'Ford' not 'a Ford') is a make of car.

Having the higher order types as horizontal layers is important because it permits alternative access and navigation. Let us remember what classification of information objects is for: we are trying to help Users or Patrons find whatever they wish to and they may be able to do that directly or they may resort to doing it by broadening or narrowing or stepping from other items and the positions of those items in the classification (and hence the standard 'BT (Broader Term)', 'NT (Narrower Term)', 'See also' notations in thesauri and similar).

Types themselves can be structured. Structured types are evident in the Dewey 800 classification—one of the leaves is the structured type Literature-English-Poetry. The abstraction or comprehension operator can provide transparency on structure. In more detail, abstraction uses any formula $\Phi(x)$ in which there is at least one free occurrence of the variable x ('open sentences'). Then the notation is

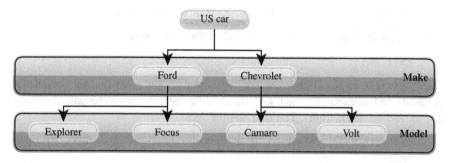

**Fig. 4.3**  A make-model classification of cars

{x: Φ(x)}

So

{x: (English(x)&Poetry(x))}

could abstract to 'English-Poetry' (i.e. English and poetry) and a parallel notation can be used for types, using '. + -' for 'and or not' e.g.

e.p

The extension of this, as a sketch, is

e={x: English(x)}
p={x: Poetry(x)}

then

e.p={x: English(x)&Poetry(x)}
e+p={x: English(x)vPoetry(x)}
-e={x: ~English(x)}

As previously stated, the Φ(x) can be an arbitrary formula (with free x), for example the concept 'English Poetry written by a man' might have the abstraction

{x: English(x)&Poetry(x)&∃y(Man(y)&Wrote(y,x))}i.e. 'English and poetry and there is a man who wrote it'

Since Φ(x) can actually be most any formula in predicate logic (with free x), most any type or sort can be built. The theoretical framework is very rich.

Often there might not be a convenient type notation for a complicated sort or type. However, definitions can be used to reduce complexity in notation. For example the Φ(x) above, used for 'English Poetry written by a man', above can be abbreviated by a definition, a definition by equivalence, using some convenient monadic or one-place predicate say

$$\forall x(N(x) \equiv English(x)\&Poetry(x)\&\exists y(Man(y)\&Wrote(y,x)))$$

and the new defining predicate $N(x)$ used to produce a type

$$n=\{x: N(x)\}$$

There are two means of introducing 'definitions': via equivalences between a predicate and an expanded form and via identities between terms (usually between a term and an abstraction). The first has the form

$\forall x(A(x) \equiv \Phi(x))$ (where A is a monadic predicate and $\Phi(x)$ an open sentence)

The second has the form

a=b or
a= $\{x:\Phi(x)\}$

Note: the type ordering relations themselves are established by the inference relations among the open sentences in the intensional abstractions so, for example, if we have types for English and for English Poetry

e=$\{x: English(x)\}$
pEnglish=$\{x: English(x)\&Poetry(x)\}$

the open sentences are

$English(x)$

and

$English(x)\&Poetry(x)$

and the first one follows from, or can be inferred validly from, the second. More formally

$$\forall x((English(x)\&Poetry(x))\rightarrow English(x))$$

and this is used to establish

pEnglish<e

i.e. that the English-poetry-type is a subtype of the English-type

[Care needs to be taken with definitions so as not, for example, to use the same abbreviation for two different expansions or to define around in a circle of definitions.]

Those familiar with set theory might be tempted to remark 'Isn't this all just set theory, or a bit like set theory?' Well, it is and it is not. It is true that subtypes, intersections and unions of types, etc. are a little bit like subsets, intersections and unions of sets. But there are some crucial differences. In particular, set theory has some properties that make it unsuitable for classification work. Here are two: the empty set, or an empty set, is a subset of all sets. That means that the set of unicorns (which is empty) is a subset of all sets. In turn, that means the set of unicorns is a subset of animals, of vertebrates, of invertebrates, of fish, of clams, of US cars, of Fords, of Explorers. So unicorns would be, or could be, noise permeating any classification scheme we cared to devise (and so too for countless other empty sets (e.g. the Nobel prize winners with IQs under 10)). The second is: sets are identified, mathematically, by their members, so if membership changes the set itself changes; for example, were there to be a classification with the present set of English Poetry as a classified item, the mere publication of one further work of English Poetry would render the classification obsolete (the new set of poetry items would not be in the old classification). We need to use types, not sets; for types themselves do not change when their denotations changes. As stated earlier, concepts are not sets, and it is concepts that we need to work with.

In ordinary First Order Logic, predicates get applied to individuals, they do not get applied to other predicates. This is immediately at odds with what we do all the time in natural language. Being a tiger is a property, so '... is a tiger' is a predicate and the statement 'Shere Khan is a tiger' applies a predicate to an individual. But tiger is a species of animal, so asserting that fact, i.e. saying 'Tiger is a species', seems to apply one predicate '... is a species' to another '...is a tiger' or 'being a tiger'. The use of types accommodates this. We allow 't' to be a type (say t={x: x is a tiger}) then the ordinary first order logic formula S(t) says that t is a species of animal. In use here are higher order predicates or higher order types. The predicate S(x), 'x is a species', does not get applied to individuals; the sentence 'Shere Khan is a species' is nonsense or false; the predicate gets applied to first order types S(t) ('tiger is a species'), S(l) ('lion is a species'). etc. This difference in use can be marked by a small notational change, if this is considered desirable; the predicate symbol 'S' can be given a subscript one, thus '$S_1$' to show that it applies to first order types not individuals. And this technique and notation can be generalized to higher order types, with subscript twos etc. So there could be sentences

$$T(s) \& S_1(\{x:T(x)\}) \text{ or } T(s) \& (t= \{x:T(x)\}) \& S_1(t)$$

to symbolize

'Shere Khan is a tiger and tiger is a species of animal'.

## 4.4 More on the Features of Conditions for Classification

### 4.4.1 Necessary and Sufficient Conditions

In the context of classification, there are the notions of *necessary* and *sufficient* in connection with properties or collections of properties—in particular their role in determining whether a particular is an instance of a type. To use an example: within an Aristotelian classification of living beings, a *human* is a type (or species). And to be a human an entity has to be an *animal*. Being an animal is a *necessary* condition (or necessary property) for being a human i.e

$\forall x(\text{Human}(x) \rightarrow \text{Animal}(x))$

Being a rational being is also a necessary condition for being a human i.e

$\forall x(\text{Human}(x) \rightarrow \text{Rational}(x))$

In turn, in this case, if an entity is both an animal and rational that is *sufficient* for the entity to be human i.e

$\forall x((\text{Rational}(x) \& \text{Animal}(x)) \rightarrow \text{Human}(x))$

Necessary conditions and sufficient conditions can be rolled into one to form *necessary and sufficient conditions*. Thus, being a rational animal is necessary and sufficient for being a human i.e

$\forall x((\text{Rational}(x) \& \text{Animal}(x)) \equiv \text{Human}(x))$

## 4.4.2 Essential Properties and Natural Kinds

Necessary and sufficient conditions are often spoken of in the context of essential properties and natural kinds. So, for example, within the Aristotelian world view, man is a natural kind, and being a rational animal are both necessary and sufficient conditions for being a man and essential properties of the kind man. It is possible for a type to have necessary and sufficient conditions—and maybe even essential properties—without the type being a natural kind. Consider the type *bachelor*, necessary and sufficient conditions for being a bachelor are those of being an unmarried man—but the type or kind 'bachelor' is not a natural kind.

## 4.4.3 Determinate and Indeterminate Properties

Entirely separately from this, some properties are *determinate* and others are not. Consider the property of having 3 sides as a property of geometrical figures. Whether a given figure has that property or not is an entirely *determinate* matter; triangles have the property, squares do not. There is a definite fact of the matter. Contrast this with the property of being bald; some men are definitely bald, some men are definitely not bald, but there is also a third category of men, perhaps 'balding'—these are not quite bald and maybe not quite not bald either. So, in some cases, there is not a definite fact of the matter in regard to a particular man's being bald. Having 3 sides is a determinate property, whereas being bald is an indeterminate property.

This matters for classification in the following way. Roughly characterized there are two tasks to classification: establishing the classification scheme, or schedule, then assigning the entities to their proper places (to their slots or buckets) in the scheme. Using indeterminate properties is entirely unproblematical with regard to

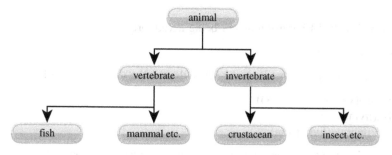

**Fig. 4.4**  A miniature taxonomy

the first task of creating the classification scheme: a bald man type in a scheme is fine. Indeterminate properties cause difficulties with the second task (does Joe Smith, with his comb-over hair belong in the bald man bucket or not?). For classification, at a practical level, it is probably better to avoid indeterminate properties, if possible.

### 4.4.4 Fallibility, Labeling Specimens, Violating Taxonomic Constraints

As already noted, there is fallibility in the *construction of natural kind schedules*. It is for science to tell us what these ontologies should be, and there is no absolute certainty in science. In contrast, gerrymandered schedules would usually be infallible in the types they invoke and the relations between the types—it is within the power of the designer to make decisions as appropriate.

There is also the fallibility of *the cataloging or labeling process*. Consider the determinate property of having 993 sides, as a property of geometrical figures. Given a geometrical figure, there is a definite fact of the matter as to whether that figure has 993 sides. The property is a determinate property. However, actually ascertaining whether a given figure does have 993 sides is not the easiest of tasks. We may set about counting the sides, but we could certainly miscount. So, even with determinate properties, actually ascribing those properties to items (and making classifications on that basis) can have its difficulties.

There can also be 'specimen violation of taxonomic constraints', where there is conflict between the schedule or taxonomy and the classified or cataloged data. Consider, for example, the miniature taxonomy (Fig. 4.4). Among other things, this asserts that All fish are vertebrates

$\forall x(Fish(x) \rightarrow Vertebrate(x))$

Suppose that a Marine Museum holds specimens, including Livingston, and that the curator has classified Livingston as being a fish

Fish(livingston)

and also classified Livingston as *not* being a vertebrate

$\sim$ Vertebrate(livingston)

There is a conflict here between the schedule and the classified data for

$\forall$x(Fish(x)$\rightarrow$Vertebrate(x))
Fish(livingston)
$\sim$ Vertebrate(livingston)

are inconsistent. Quite where the mistake has been made—i.e. with the scientists' conjecture of the taxonomy or with the curator's labeling of the data—is a open question, but definitely a mistake has been made. In a general sense, fallibility opens the way to mistakes like these. Resolving such inconsistencies will need to be done on a case by case basis.

### 4.4.5 Exclusive and Exhaustive Properties (JEPD)

Often in classification, we will have a number of 'buckets' or 'slots' or 'positions' and, for each of the items that we are going to classify, there is exactly one bucket that it belongs in, and the buckets are adequate for the task. So the buckets collectively exhaust all the items, and the buckets are exclusive in that if an item is in one bucket that very item cannot also be in another bucket. To give a simple example: we may have a billiards table with red and white billiard balls on it, and we are going to classify each ball individually according to whether the ball is white or whether it is red. Every ball is either white or it is red, and no ball is both white and red. So, for billiard balls, and for the properties Red(x) and White(x), everything is red or white

$\forall$x(Red(x) v White(x)) [*Exhaustive*]

and nothing is both red and white

$\sim$$\exists$x(Red(x) & White(x)) [*Exclusive*]

These definitions, or explanations, can then generalized to collections of properties.

There can be some alternative nomenclature here: 'cover' or 'coverage' for 'exhaustive', and 'disjoint' for 'exclusive'. So sometimes, with trees, there is an interest in sibling coverage and sibling disjointedness. The first is whether all of the instances of the children of a parent are also instances of that parent,

$\forall$x(Parent(x)$\rightarrow$(Child$_1$(x) v Child$_2$(x) ....)) [for each of the parents and their children]

and the second whether anything is an instance of two siblings at the same time.

~∃x(Child$_1$(x) & Child$_2$(x)) [for each of pairs of children of the particular parents]

The exclusivity and exhaustivity of collections of predicates is also sometimes called the **JEPD** (Jointly Exhaustive Pairwise Disjoint) property.

There are important metaphysical and epistemological issues that arise practically in connection with exclusive and exhaustive properties. The first is whether the properties are JEPD just as a matter of logic (and of the meaning of the properties concerned), or whether the properties are JEPD is a matter of logic together with the causal structure of the world we live in. So there is *logical* JEPD and *empirical* JEPD. (Any collection of properties that logically is JEPD automatically is empirically JEPD.) The second issue concerns whether we know whether properties are JEPD—in either of the senses of JEPD.

For example, if we are classifying animals into vertebrates and invertebrates and we choose to use the property of having a backbone as being the defining characteristic of being a vertebrate, then the property being used is Backbone(x), and, for invertebrate, the 'negative property' ~Backbone(x), then, trivially,

∀x(Backbone(x) ∨ ~Backbone(x)) [*Exhaustive*]
~∃x(Backbone(x) & ~Backbone(x)) [*Exclusive*]

The JEPD here holds as a matter of logic, and also, in this case, it is easy for us to know it.

By contrast, say we were classifying carnivores as part of a biological investigation of the world we live in, and we had come across wolves in the wild, say Wolf(x), and coyotes, say Coyote(x), we would know that wolves and coyotes were exclusive—no carnivore was both—but we might not know whether the two of them jointly exhausted the possibilities, i.e.

∀x(Wolf(x) ∨ Coyote(x)) [*Exhaustive????*]
~∃x(Wolf(x) & Coyote(x)) [*Exclusive*]

And, indeed, later in our investigation, we might discover dingoes (Dingo(x)) and other carnivores.

The practical repercussions of this are: we might not know, or know for certain, that a schedule or classification scheme that we use does have the JEPD property (in either sense of JEPD property) especially schemes that were natural kind schemes arrived at by scientific research.

## 4.4.6 Some Common Conditions in the Context of IOs

Almost all IO organization and retrieval operations and techniques have classification and annotation at their foundation, and, in turn, that classification or annotation often appeals to a relatively small core of conditions. These include classifying

By author
By title
By publication date
By keyword
By subject or topic
...

(a more complete list can be obtained by combining the suggestions of the Dublin Core and those of the Functional Requirements for Bibliographical Records (FRBR)—both of these will be studied later).

Many of these conditions for classification are both relatively determinate and relatively easy to apply—'having the author' property is one such example. Others, especially the more abstract ones, such as 'addressing the subject', can be both relatively indeterminate and hard to assess correctly. Unfortunately, it is often the latter which are the most valuable.

## 4.5  Classification of Things and Topic Classification of IOs

We have already indicated how we are going to approach this. There are 'things' and this notion is understood very widely so as to include concrete things, abstract things, processes, occurrents, events, and so forth. These are all to be classified into kinds via attributes and types. So this style of classification will have many logical items with the form

$\{x: \Phi(x)\}$

But we also have a particular interest to classify IOs by their topics or subject matters or by what they are about. And to do this a special relational attribute is used

IsAbout(?x,?y)

which means that the IO ?x is about the subject ?y. ['AddressesSubject(?x,?y)' or 'HasTopic(?x,?y)' might alternatively have been used here but 'IsAbout(?x,?y)' is a convenient and brief notation.] For the variable ?y, any term or logical name can be inserted. While, in a sense, all terms are the same, what they signify can be different. In particular, some terms are, in effect, proper names of particulars; for example,

'austen' might be the term for Jane Austen

in which case

$\{x:IsAbout(x,austen)\}$

are the IOs about Jane Austen. Other terms name concepts, types, or universals. So, for example, the type 'man' can be defined as

$\{x:IsAbout(x,man)\}$

Usually when we are classifying things, there is an interest in the things there actually are or might be. We classify coyotes, wolves, dingoes and the like. But not many useful real world classifications have a whole lot of types like unicorns, centaurs, and winged horses (or the need for such types). This real world aim tends to impose certain logical and pragmatic features on the classifications. With topics of IOs, though, almost anything goes. There are, as topics, all the things in the world, aspects of those things, combinations and comparisons of the things, of the topics, and so on. This is not all. Think of topics in fiction: there can be 'fictional topics' and all sorts of esoterica. Thus Sherlock Holmes, Pegasus, or the Ring of Gyges can certainly be topics. And there can even be impossible things as topics. A stock philosophical example of an impossible thing is the 'round square'—there are no round squares and there can be no round squares. However, a philosopher could certainly write a journal article with the title 'Round squares revisited' and if we asked 'what is the topic of that article?' or 'what is the subject matter of that article?' the best answer would seem to be 'round squares'. The obvious way to approach this is just to use the logical machinery we already have, so the topic, or concept, round squares is

$$\text{roundSquares} = \{x: (Round(x)\&Square(x))\}$$

And for a topic like 'Energon Cubes', we just introduce a term for that fictional entity—say 'energonCubes'—and annotate the IOs in just the same way as we annotate books about Jane Austen.

Topics are annotations, part of an annotation language or languages. There is the need to identify them, i.e. the subject matter or topic, and the need to identify the parent–child relationships between the annotations. The first can be done by properties or by name. So, as examples, there are the topics austen, man, roundSquares, and energonCubes. The parent–child relationships among the annotations are more problematical. The parent–child links come from outside. They can come from the types used, by means of logical inference relations among the open sentences. They can come from logic in conjunction with real world ontologies; they can come from real world partitive hierarchies (as we will see shortly); they can come from schedules, hierarchies, or Tree of Knowledge. And with fiction, or fantasy, presumably it is for the fiction to say. Thus, the links and link-types can be many and varied.

IO might be included under more than one topic. The aforementioned *Species Plantarum* could be considered as having more than one subject matter—it could be Botany and, separately, Nomenclature; it could fall under *more than one different topic*. That is just to say, IOs can be polytopical. But can the same topic appear more than once in the schedule of topics? The subject matter Botany appears in many topic classification schedules (along with other subjects) but 'apparently' it could appear *more than once*—Botany could be a child subject of Natural Philosophy and, also, a child subject of Biological Classification.

## 4.5.1 To Clone Topic Annotations or Not?

This latter point needs some clarification and explanation. Dewey had this to say about water as a subject matter

> a work on water may be classed with many disciplines, such as metaphysics, religion, economics, commerce, physics, chemistry, geology, oceanography, meteorology, and history. *No other feature of the DDC is more basic than this: that it scatters subjects by discipline* (M. Dewey, 1979, p. xxxi; emphasis added. Quoted from (Hjørland 2008) article on 'Aspect Classification').

That is, water, the subject, is scattered in different places in the Dewey Decimal Classification (DDC) system. Dewey is not being overly careful here. The fact that water-in-economics appears in a different place in the schedule to water-in-chemistry does not have to mean that the same subject, water, appears in different places, for water-in-economics is, or might be, a different subject to water-in-chemistry. Think for one moment about an ordinary genealogical family tree: it might have 'Henrys' all over the place but it does not have the same Henry all over the place: it has Henry Jones in one place, Henry Smith in another, and so on. 'Water-in-economics' could be a compound or complex subject, and one of its components, namely water, appears elsewhere in other compound subjects, for example, in water-in-chemistry. Many subjects are compounds. Foskett mentions our favorite

> the manufacture of multi-wall kraft paper sacks for the packaging of cement (Foskett 1977).

And, of course, many of the components of this compound, e.g. manufacture, kraft, paper, sacks, cement, etc., may appear elsewhere as components of other compound subjects. But it is an open question as to whether the exact same atomic or compound subject should appear in several places.

There is a distinction to be made between distributed relatives and distributed clones. We know that, for example, if four compound concepts, say, 'American Fiction', 'American Poetry', 'English Fiction', 'English Poetry' are inserted into a standard hierarchy, we can collocate some concepts at the expense of scattering others. Thus 'Poetry' might be a scattered subject; that is, 'American Poetry' might not have 'English Poetry' as a sibling, rather it would be a (possibly distant) distributed relative. But this possibility is very different to taking, say, 'American Poetry' on its own (no more no less) and then cloning it to make a second identical 'American Poetry' and then inserting the clone elsewhere in the classification schedule to produce distributed clones.

An example, as a candidate for cloning and multiple location, is a compound subject like economic history, which might, in some subject schedules, appear to belong as a child of economics, and, as exactly the same subject, as a child of history (see also (Salton 1962, p. 106)).

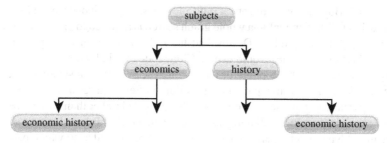

**Fig. 4.5**  A tree with cloned nodes

**Fig. 4.6**  A graph with a
child node that has two
parents

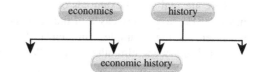

**Fig. 4.7**  A DAG with a child
node that has two parents

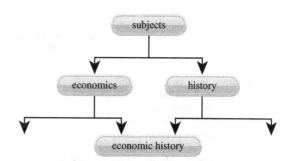

The view here is that this, or something akin to it, is entirely acceptable. However, there is a choice in how to depict the configuration graph theoretically: a tree can be used with the same label being used on different nodes, i.e. clones, or nodes can have multiple parents and then the structure would not be a tree, it would be a directed acyclic graph (DAG). So, if economic history is a label for a node, then two or more nodes could be clones and have the same label, thus (Fig. 4.5). Or there can be just one labeled node for economic history and then it needs to be shown as being the child of two parents, namely of Economics and of History, perhaps either (Fig. 4.6) or (Fig. 4.7). Neither of these graphs are (rooted directed) trees. The first seems to have two 'roots' and the second has a cycle (but not a directed cycle). Both are types of directed acyclic graphs (DAGs).

We tend to prefer the latter multiple parent, DAG, representations, rather than clones. It is clearer and easier to have just one of each topic, say 'economic history', and to have each topic in just one place in the topic graph. Here is a specific reason. If a topic appears at most once in a graph, if it is found, by User or computer, then it is found period. But if a topic can appear multiple times, finding it once, even finding it multiple times, is not enough—a whole graph search is required to ensure it does not appear yet again. Remember, Dewey had his Relativ Index in large part to find distributed relatives; clones would need a Clone index to find them.

Topics are used for broadening or narrowing a search. With a standard tree, the narrowing of a search from a parent to its children often requires a choice, because often the parent will have several children. Using a DAG rather than a tree, does not add any special difficulties. All it means is that when the User is broadening a search, a node might have several parents and a choice will be needed as to which parent to broaden the search to. In the above diagram, if the User has IOs on economic history and would like something less specific, the User will have to make a choice between pursuing the (parent) topic of economics or the (parent) topic of history.

There are real world examples of apparent clones: the Medical Subject Headings (MeSH) have many cases of the same heading appearing twice or more in a tree. Here is the example, 'Influenza, Human' identified by MeSH's online browser (http://www.nlm.nih.gov/mesh/MBrowser.html)

```
[First Branch]
Virus Diseases [C02]
        RNA Virus Infections [C02.782]
            Orthomyxoviridae Infections [C02.782.620]
                    ->Influenza, Human [C02.782.620.365]<-
                    Influenza in Birds [C02.782.620.375]

[Second Branch]
Respiratory Tract Diseases [C08]
    Respiratory Tract Infections [C08.730]
            Bovine Respiratory Disease Complex [C08.730.085]
            Bronchitis [C08.730.099]
            Common Cold [C08.730.162]
            Empyema, Pleural [C08.730.265]
            ->Influenza, Human [C08.730.310]<-
            Laryngitis [C08.730.368]
```

So, 'Influenza, Human' is a great-grandchild of 'Virus Diseases' in the first branch, and a grandchild of 'Respiratory Tract Diseases in the second branch; and both these branches are in the 'C. Diseases' tree. However, this is not quite what it seems to be at first glance. These branches establish context (or aspect): the first gives 'Human-Influenza-as-a-Virus-Disease', the second gives 'Human-Influenza-as-a-Respiratory-Tract-Disease'. The two nodes are not clones; they have different identifiers C02.782.620.365 and C08.730.310 (and different heading identifiers, so-called Descriptor IDs). And when the human catalogers actually annotate the IOs with these headings they will make the appropriate choice between the two headings—the catalogers will not be indifferent to their use (NLM 2009, 2011). This is not an example of distributed clones, it is a (standard) example of distributed relatives; that is, compound concepts (which in this case have human influenza as a component concept) which are scattered.

# 4.6   Structured Types for Topics: Ranganathan's Heritage

Any concept or type can be a topic—which is to say there can be an indefinite number of topics of indefinite variety. However, when an index is created for IOs, or when IOs are given subject topics only a small number of these possibilities are brought into use—and also the variety is relatively small. What is to be expected?

Ranganathan sketched the territory here: he had views on how types were to be composed to form possibly ever more complex structured types suitable for the subject classification or annotation of IOs (he was, after all, a mathematician). [Some of the intellectual seeds for material developed in the first part of what follows have their origins in Brian Buchanan's book (Buchanan 1979).]

For a toy example, suppose we have the predicates (or conditions)

Forest(x) ('x is the habitat forest')
Tropical(x) ('x is the tropical region')
Temperate(x) ('x is the temperate region')

Then there are the (simple *elemental* or *atomic*) classes formed from one condition only i.e

(x:Forest(x)} (i.e. forests)
{x:Tropical(x)} (i.e. tropical regions)
{x:Temperate(x)} (i.e. temperate regions)

There is an extension to this terminology that can be introduced here. The class

(x:Forest(x)}

is a class of forests; that is to say, instances of it are forests. And the class has been described as an *elemental* or *atomic class*, and that means that those forest instances are being picked out by one condition only. But our interest is not with forests, it is directed towards IOs that have the topic 'forests' and those IOs are being picked out by the expression or type

(x:Forest(x)}

being used as a topic. So it is natural to say that such a topic is an *elemental* or *atomic topic*. In sum, there can and will be a certain casualness between talk of classes and talk of topics, but our focus is with topics.

In addition there are the (simple *superimposed* (Ranganathan 1960)) classes (or topics) formed from two or more conditions conjoined together i.e

(x:Tropical(x) & Forest(x)} (i.e. tropical forests)

A useful heuristic here for recognizing superimposed classes is the 'which is also' test. A tropical forest is a forest *which is also* tropical (or a tropical region *which is also* a forest).

Superimposed classes are what we have called earlier—in connection with nouns and modifiers—*intersective* types or *conjunctive* types.

But there are non-elemental classes which are *not* superimposed classes. Consider

The fur of animals,
Statistics for biologists,
History of philosophy

The fur of animals is fur, it is a subtype of the fur-type, so that encourages us to start a symbolization

{x:Fur(x)&....}

However, it is *not* the superimposed type

{x:Fur(x)&Animal(x)}

for that would be 'furry animals' (which is not 'fur of animals'). It is not a fur *which is also* an animal. What we need here is to say here is that the fur belongs to animals, so we need a symbolization akin to

{x:Fur(x)&BelongsTo(x,animals)}

and that is a *relation* type. Notice here that with superimposed types we were using two or more monadic or one-place predicates or attributes and ANDing them together; but now we are using some monadic predicate and some dyadic or two-place relations and ANDing all of those. As usual, with symbolizations, there is a choice of how explicit to be. The choice above is fairly explicit, for it allows other types such as

{x:Bones(x)&BelongsTo(x,animals)}
{x:Skin(x)&BelongsTo(x,animals)}

'bones of animals' and 'skin of animals' to be constructed using the same 'BelongsTo(?x,?y)' relation. A less explicit choice would have been to build the fur into the relation, thus

{x:FurBelongingTo(x,animals)}

Also, as usual, we prefer functions to relations and so would like to work either with a function

furOf(?x)

which carries ?x to its fur, giving

{y:y=furOf(animals)}

or with the function

belongsTo(?x)

which carries ?x to those items that belong to it, giving

{y: Fur(y)&y=belongsTo(animals)}

[There are some complexities here that are omitted; they concern single and multiple valued functions.]

The upshot is: a type like 'the fur of animals' should be construed as a *function* or a *relation* type i.e. a type that contains functions or relations in its symbolization. Such types are not superimposed types.

Functions are exactly what is required in this setting. Conceptually, we start with animals, and then we think of their food, their habitat, their fur, etc. We take the animals and then transform that starting point into something else and that is exactly what functions do.

Subjects like 'Statistics for biologists' are an interesting example of what Ranganathan called 'bias'. The subject matter 'statistics' has certain subtopics or subfields to it for example, 'Parametric statistics' and 'Non-parametric statistics'. And what that means is that a fragment of a subject hierarchy or propaedia for mathematics or statistics should have parametric and non-parametric statistics as children, or descendants, of statistics. But 'Statistics for biologists' is *not* one of those subfields. A statistics student attempting to master statistics does not study parametric statistics, non-parametric statistics, and then, also, statistics-for-biologists. Nor is 'Statistics for biologists' a sub-topic of biology. This means that 'Statistics for biologists' is not a superimposed topic of the topics statistics and biology. Statistics for biologists includes so-to-speak all of statistics, but all of statistics filtered ('biased') in a certain way (perhaps to omit certain technical proofs and subfields, and to add certain relevant biological examples). Since 'filtering' is just applying a function, so what is needed is

{x: x=forBiologists(statistics)}

Similarly History of philosophy is

{x: x=historyOf(philosophy)}

There are also *relation* classes which are more naturally left as relation classes. Consider the subject matter

Comparisons of Temperate Forests with Tropical Forests.

It has components—namely Temperate and Tropical Forests—but it is not really about them and it is certainly not a superimposed class of them: instead it is about comparisons of them. It is a relation composite. One way of forming this class is to define the types

tropForest={x:Tropical(x) & Forest(x)}
tempForest={x:Tropical(x) & Temperate(x)}

then what we need is

{x:Comparison(x,tropForest, tempForest)}

Ranganathan called these 'loose assemblages', which consisted of 'phase relations' between 'phases'. There are several other obvious loose assemblage constructors; for example,

Compare(x,y,z) ('x is a comparison of y to z')
Influence(x,y) ('x influences y')
ExampleOf(x,y) ('x is an example of y')

These constructors can then be combined together—recursively synthesized—to arbitrary complexity. In fact, *Comparisons of Temperate Forests with Tropical Forests*, which is a relation class, has components which are themselves superimposed classes.

It is even possible to go further with the analysis of atomic or elemental classes. One way of thinking about this—and related material—is to approach it from the grammar of natural languages. Words labeling concepts for classification are going to be nouns, grammatically speaking (Foskett 1977; Cutter 1904). That is not to say that all nouns might be used for classification, but we need to be awake to the possibility that all *kinds* of nouns might be used for classification (and we already know how to symbolize most nouns, noun phrases, etc.). However, we did not really discuss nouns which themselves are compound nouns such as 'darkroom', 'redhead', or 'washer-dryer'.

Compound nouns are often classified—using themes from the Sanskrit language (which Ranganathan would have known)—as endocentric, exocentric, copulative, or appositional. (The explanation here follows Bloomfield (1935)). Endocentric is where one of the nouns is used to form a subtype of the other e.g. 'darkroom' is a subtype of 'room'. The form is that of a *head* (in this case 'room') and a *modifier* ('dark').

Somewhat similarly to the case of simple nouns, a single predicate, say E(x), could be used for 'x is a darkroom'. But the subtyping in the noun invites subtyping in symbolization, thus

{x:Room(x) & Dark(x)} i.e. the x such that x is a room and x is dark

The head-modifier form, although compressed into one word, hints at following the common head-modifier form of a noun modified by a separate adjective i.e. using conjunction of separate predicates to achieve the symbolization. Roughly, predicates are ANDED to get endocentric compounds. So endocentric compounds generate superimposed classes. Exocentric compound nouns are compounds where the stem is missing completely e.g. a 'redhead' is neither red, nor a head, rather he or she is a person—in fact, a person with red hair. For these the missing stem should be added

{x:Person(x) & RedHair(x)} i.e. the x such that x is a person and x has red hair

It is hard, even for experts, to be clear on the copulative and appositional cases. To simplify, we will consider these together as being an 'as well as' construction. The 'as well as' construction appears in such compounds as washer-dryer (a washer as well as a dryer), sleepwalk (sleeping as well as walking), Czechoslovakia (the region that was the Czech Republic as well as the region that was Slovakia). These compounds are tricky and might have to be dealt with on a case-by-case basis. A washer-dryer is a subtype of washer, it is also a subtype of dryer (and similarly, at a stretch, for sleepwalking being a subtype of sleeping and of walking). That suggests AND-ING the components {x:Washer(x) & Dryer(x)} i.e. the x such that x is a washer and x is a dryer

but Czechoslovakia is (or was) that region that was the Czech Republic or was Slovakia, and that suggests OR-ING the components.

{x:Czech(x) v Slovakia(x)}

All nouns, noun phrases, and clauses can be symbolized using the techniques from here and the last chapter. Were we to have the need to classify 'the friends of Usain Bolt that run with him occasionally and casually' there is an open sentence to do it.

What is important with the symbolization is the ability to support a suitably rich search, based on logical relations between the types.

[Charles Dickens's *Pickwick Papers* provides an illustration of why we need more than logical AND-ING of concepts. The example subject is Chinese Metaphysics

"An abstruse subject, I should conceive," said Mr. Pickwick.

"Very, sir," responded Pott, looking intensely sage. "He crammed for it, to use a technical but expressive term; he read up for the subject, at my desire, in the Encyclopedia Britannica."

"Indeed!" said Mr. Pickwick; "I was not aware that that valuable work contained any information respecting Chinese metaphysics."

"He read, sir," rejoined Pott, laying his hand on Mr. Pickwick's knee, and looking around with a smile of intellectual superiority, "he read for metaphysics under the letter M, and for China under the letter C, and combined his information, sir." (Dickens 1836, p. 769). (Rogers 1960)
]

# 4.7 Splitting or Clumping: Parts and Wholes: Mereology: Structure

While 'instance of' and 'subtype of' are certainly two important relations in classification, there is another relation, 'part of', which also has special significance. The partitive relation ('part of', or 'part-whole' relation) has two different roles in the classification of IOs. It is important concerning the items actually being classified, since some IOs are, in fact, parts of other IOs (the individual collected papers from a conference might be part of a single conference proceedings). And it is important concerning relations among the concepts or tags of classification, since a User interested in IOs with information about components of a composite structure (for example, a carburetor in gas engine) will likely also have an interest in IOs about other parts of the same composite (spark plugs) or indeed the composite as a whole (the gas engine itself).

Consider an edited collection of scholarly papers: each individual paper may be an IO (maybe with its own names, metadata, etc.) and the edited collection as a whole may also be an IO (with its own names, metadata, etc.). There is a relationship between the papers (the chapters) and the book: the papers are 'parts' of the book. There can be a part-whole relationship between IOs. This leads to the notion of a structured IO which is a compound IO consisting of component IOs put together in a certain way. Think of a book, for example: a book typically consists of chapters, which follow one another: with sections, and pages which follow one another; the pages may have paragraphs; and the book may start with a preface and end with an index. A book is a structured IO.

Here is Barbara Tillett, Chief of the Library of Congress Policy and Support Office, writing in the voice of a professional cataloger

> When a cataloger begins the work of describing a resource, the first decision is "what am I cataloging?" is it a single logical unit, an aggregate, or a component? (Tillett 2009)

In the analysis of a structured IO there is no 'natural' granularity. The granularity is conventional (and is adopted to suit a purpose, usually the purpose of retrieval). So, for example, we can treat a single book as a single IO without components (i.e. it is a black box); on the other hand, we could move to a finer level of granularity and treat the same single book as a composite IO with chapters which are themselves IOs and we might, in turn, leave the chapters as IOs without components (the chapters are black boxes); on the other hand,…. Clearly, what we do is up to us. Typically, to date, as an example, the practice has been to treat ordinary books, for example, as single IOs and books which are edited collections as composite IOs. The theory of parts and wholes is 'mereology'.

Items are concrete objects. Sometimes a single item can be more than one physical object. This is analogous to the mereological notion of parts and wholes. Say there is a race car which has a wheel that flies off into the crowd. Where is that race car? It is somewhat spread. Part of it is in the crowd, the other parts of it are on the track. Similarly, one item may consist of one volume (one part) in one library, and another volume (another part) *perhaps in a completely different library*.

It follows that, entirely independent of the question of composite IOs, the partitive relation should play a role in subject annotation. Often enough, when searching, we resort to conceptualizations via the 'part of' relation. A patron might arrive at 'kidney' via a search for 'urinary system' or search for 'carburetor' via a search for 'gas engine'. And this style is recognized by thesauri standards, for example Z39.19 (ANSI/NISO 2005).

'Part of' is a new kind of relation in the this presentation. A carburetor is not a subtype of engine, nor is it an instance of an engine, nor is engine either a genus or species (in this context). The 'part of' relation is sufficiently important to be included in the discussion of hierarchies, especially annotation hierarchies. Mereology, a rich and active research area, provides the background to the philosophy and logic of parts (Hovda 2009; Varzi 2009; Pribbenow 2002; Simons 1987). Fortunately, there are a couple of simplifications that we can make. Usually the 'part of' relation allows for the case that anything is a part of itself but, for our use, we do not need this case (because we are not, for example, going to advise anyone who is struggling to find works on the concept carburetor that they might want to try, as an alternative strategy, searching for the concept carburetor). We can also ignore the especially demanding philosophical question of 'fusions', which involve putting parts together in ordinary and not so ordinary ways. We simply do not need these difficult cases of fusions.

That leaves us with a 'proper part of' relation, and this is a strict partial ordering. That is, it is irreflexive (nothing is a (proper) part of itself), asymmetric (if a is a part of b, then b is not a part of a), and transitive (if a is a part of b, and b a part of c, then a is a part of c). The transitivity is the important relation. Here is an illustration. If a section is a part of a chapter, and the chapter is a part of the book, then that section is part of the book. For the present, we have no need of any further concepts or axioms from mereology.

We can symbolize the '(proper) part of relation' either by a binary predicate, say PartOf(x,y) which is to mean 'x is a part of y'. Or, perhaps more perspicuously, by means of an infix binary symbol '$x \subset y$', which also reads 'x is a part of y'. And we will incorporate transitivity into the semantics and to the reasoning about parts and part hierarchies i.e. there is the axiom$\forall x \forall y \forall z((x \subset y \& y \subset z) \rightarrow (x \subset z))$

## 4.8 DAGs of Topics

The topics are relatively easy to come by. They are just concepts or types, i.e. simple or complex intensional abstractions as we have defined and explained them. Of course, which topics are needed in particular cases (from the indefinitely many that are available) is a matter for empirical investigation on the Users, or User communities, and what their interests and searching practices are. And it is going to differ between, say, an audience of school children and an audience of nuclear physicists. Nevertheless, topics are easily dealt with.

What poses the intellectual challenge is to determine the *links* that there should be between the topics.

There is a parallel, or analogue, which it is useful to draw attention to. Modern information retrieval thesauri usually lay out a hierarchy of terms (or synsets of terms) and the various international standards for thesauri permit three kinds of linking relationships: subtype, instance, and part (Zeng 2005; NISO 2005). So, in a thesaurus tree, a child node might be a subtype, an instance or a part of its parent node. Our approach is similar, but with four substantial differences. First, the thesauri nodes are strings and that is to work at the Symbol Vertex level; our nodes are concepts, and they locate with the Concept Vertex. Second, thesauri nodes are typically atomic (or single or elemental terms), ours can be composite with arbitrary complexity. Third, the thesaurus graph structure is a hierarchy or tree (with nodes having only single parent); our topic graphs are Directed Acyclic Graphs (DAGs) with at least some nodes typically having multiple parents. And, finally, thesauri permit subtype, instance, and partitive links *only*; we allow those kinds of links, and more besides (for example, there might be a propaedia style link between 'gardening' and 'botany' but 'gardening' is not a subtype, nor an instance, nor a part of 'botany').

There are several possible means of generating the links: one is central, the others more peripheral. The central one is type hierarchies.

## 4.8.1  Links from Taxonomies and Quasi-Taxonomies

One assumption or piece of reasoning that we make is that the structures of classifications of things carries over directly to a desired structure, or part of a desired structure, for topic annotations for IOs about those things. So, for example, in the real world, there might be the classification

    Animal
    Man
    Frenchman
    Parisian

And this motivates the adoption of the topic annotations

    Animal-topic
    Man-topic
    Frenchman-topic
    Parisian-topic

which can be used to annotate IOs. Not only this, but also the topic annotations as topics are related in the same way as the types are related in the taxonomy; thus the Parisian-topic is, or should be, a sub-topic of the Frenchman-topic. This is a very reasonable move to make. Parisians are Frenchman, and as such they possess all the properties or attributes of Frenchmen. This means that a book about Frenchmen carries or may carry, to a degree, knowledge, information, gossip, or anecdotes about Parisians—not information specific to Parisians *only*, but nonetheless content about Parisians. As Reid tells us, we classify to compress our knowledge, and part of the knowledge about Parisians is located with knowledge about Frenchmen.

So kind-classification—taxonomies or quasi-taxonomies—can guide us with regard to topic annotations. Expertise as to kind-classification is individually limited and distributed. With natural kinds, the expertise is with scientists. With gerrymanders and structured gerrymanders, the expertise is with the creators, users, or adopters. True librarians have to be skilled at this point. They may not, themselves, know directly much about needlepoint, quarks, or croquet. But they need to become subject specialists before they can design a good annotation system which will be of benefit to the Users.

This parallel between kind classification and desired subject annotations and links can act as a heuristic to suggest what categories of annotations might be encountered or be useful. We could even call this the

**Reid Principle**: classification is a heuristic for DAGs of topics.

## 4.8.2 Links from Logic

Logical inference will generate automatically many of the topic links by the mechanism that subclasses need to be subtopics. So, if for example, as with superimposed topics,

{x:Tropical(x) & Forest(x)} (i.e. tropical forests)
{x:Forest(x)} (i.e. forests)
{x:Tropical(x)} (i.e. tropical regions)

tropical forests are a subclass of both forests and—separately—tropical regions, so the topics forest-topic and the tropical-region-topic need both to have the tropical-forest-topic as a subtopic.

In principle, generating these links is not too difficult, and most of it can be done by computer. There is a language of topics (potential topics). When any of those topics is actually used to annotate an IO, logic alone can produce many of the desired links to other topics that are already in use. There is a directed acyclic graph of topics, a DAG, and the use of a new topic adds a topic, then logic can shortly thereafter add the desired links to extend the DAG.

Logical inference would be able to work immediately with any information that was explicit in the topics but it could also generate links from type hierarchies. If an automatic reasoner is given merely the topics

{x:Frenchman(x)}
{x:Parisian(x)}

it would not be able on that basis alone to put a link between the topics. However, if information about the type hierarchy is added

parisian<frenchman or
$\forall x(Parisian(x) \rightarrow Frenchman(x))$

then the requisite inferences can go through.

## 4.8.3 Parameterized Topics and Links

As mentioned, much of the knowledge about taxonomies, and even about desirable topic annotations and links, is distributed. To take an example, in chemistry, chemists and research chemists have identified and can thus study some 20 million elements and compounds. The chemists themselves have ontologies, classifications and identification schemes to label and pick out any of these 20 million. And when research papers are written their topics can be identified with absolute accuracy and precision (thus, a paper might have the title 'A study on $H_2O$'). Chemists know that if they put one or more of their chemical identifiers in the title of their papers, or among keywords or annotations, the papers will be easily found. Should the chemical classification and topic scheme be part of general IO classification? The answer is Yes and No. It is needed to help chemists, or those interested in chemistry, to find what they want. But the actual chemical organizational schema does not have wider application in IO classification. So, there is the idea of the chemical ontology being outside the main IO topic languages but being imported for indirect use. In a sense, the main direct classifications are *parameterized*, occasionally with values coming from elsewhere. Hierarchies of natural kinds, and other desirable topics, are for (all of) science to determine. Librarians, or organizers of general systems, do not create these classifications. However, librarians, and Patrons, will want to use the classifications.

This phenomenon is commonplace. Church buildings might include Abbey Churches, Basilica and Cathedrals. Some of these might be Early English or Roman or Gothic, and the buildings might have as parts Naves or Atria. When historians of church architecture use this terminology—their own terminology—to identify such interesting sites as 'The atrium of the Basilica di San Clemente, Rome', they are using their own classification system to classify buildings, locations, and things. They are not classifying IOs. However, once books, articles, and IOs start to be written about Church buildings and their architecture—and those IOs need classifying as to topic—it is very natural and sensible to import some or all of the classification scheme that is used in the field (for, front and center among the Users will be those same historians of church architecture). And thus there may well be IOs about Gothic Cathedrals and these should bear a subtopical relationship to IOs about Cathedrals.

A note of caution here: the outside field might not itself be settled in its terminology, concepts, and classifications. For example, in 1953 Alex Ladenson reported on the great difficulty in subject cataloging (i.e. topic annotation) in the Social Sciences due to the fact that the Social Sciences themselves were new disciplines—rapidly growing—and that they lacked a uniform standardized terminology (Ladenson 1953). There is not a whole lot that can be done about this. There are, though, certain pieces of evidence or resources—such as the existence of discipline encyclopaedias—that can become available; for example, when there arose an Encyclopaedia of Social Science, that both was evidence of some stability and a resource as to what topic DAGs might be.

### 4.8.4 Links from Outside Propaedias

There are also propaedias. There are many bodies of knowledge; for example, about the law, about scuba diving, and about carpentry. Often students, practitioners, and researchers working in these areas of knowledge have their own topic structures through which to organize their disciplines: they have propaedias. We certainly can offer advice on desirable features of propaedias. And we can also just import propaedias to assist with link structures among the topics.

As d'Alembert has told us, there no one single Tree of Knowledge. There are indefinitely many of them. Similarly, no matter what the general discipline or topic area, there are indefinitely many good propaedias. What matters is that the propaedia be 'helpful'. And 'helpful' here has a definite meaning: it should allow the User to broaden a topic, to narrow a topic, and to step to related topics. But what actually is helpful on a particular occasion may well depend on the User, or User group, and the occasion or occasions.

A good system may well be able to change propaedia, or topic DAG, depending on the setting, for example, depending on whether the User is a student or a researcher. Classical librarians provide such a facility with their *pathfinders* or *subject guides*. Standard classification schemes—such as the Dewey Decimal Scheme—relate topics, but then a pathfinder can tell a student how to navigate through this in a way conducive to his or her ends—and that path could be slightly novel or unorthodox.

### 4.8.5  Mereological and Other Links

There also, on occasions, can be value in having links between topics which represent whole entities to other topics which represent parts of those entities (for example, from 'engines' to 'spark plugs').

## 4.9  Polytopicality and Subject Vectors

As we have noted, many IOs address more than one topic: our example has been an IO which tells of sphinges and crocutes.

Polytopicality raises an issue for classical librarianship. Traditional cataloging of an ordinary book encompasses two separate acts of classification: (shelving) classification and subject classification (topic annotation). Subject classification typically permits a book to have up to ten subjects, so our sample IO could have the subjects or topics 'sphinges' and 'crocutes'. It would be polytopical with two subjects. (Shelving) classification must produce a unique call number and any IO can have only one place in the schedule (and thus on the shelves). It is here that the problem arises: the (shelving) schedule is by theme or topic. Sphinges might have a place—and so too might the separate crocutes—but it is unlikely that 'sphinges and crocutes' has an entry, so our sample IO just has to be forced in somewhere— perhaps into a location where it does not really belong.

A solution to this is to rule out polytopicality by combining the polytopics into a single topic. Ranganathan, for one, was certainly in favor of polytopic reduction. He had the notion of the *Specific subject of a book*, and each book had exactly one of these (see, for example, (Ranganathan 1962, p. 12)). Once a book, or IO, has a single topic (which is perhaps a polytopic) siting it in a suitable (shelving) classification is relatively easy. So, instead of saying that an IO has the two topics *sphinges* and, separately, *crocutes*, you say that it has the one topic *sphinges and crocutes*.

There is a different approach to polytopicality that is sometimes seen in the field of automatic document retrieval. It emanates principally from the work of Gerard Salton and his colleagues (Borko 1977; Salton 1968, 1975). Suppose, indeed, that an IO is on sphinges and crocutes: thus far we have suggested that you could choose to say either that it has two topics {sphinges, crocutes} or that it has one topic {sphinges and crocutes}. Those approaches use atomic concepts and logic for combination of those topics. Salton also used atomic concepts but instead used mathematics, principally vectors, to do the combining. Imagine that the topics of sphinges and crocutes could admit of *degrees* in a document, so that a work could be equally about sphinges and about crocutes, or mostly about sphinges and only partially about crocutes, and so on, and that these individual degrees could be represented by a number, a *weight*. The full representation for a document could then be a *vector*, like one of the following

<0.5 sphinges, 0.5 crocutes>,
<0.25 sphinges, 0.75 crocutes>,
<0.75sphinges, 0.25 crocutes>

and these would signify, respectively, that the document was equally about sphinges and crocutes, mostly about crocutes, or mostly about sphinges. So Salton is doing polytopical reduction, but his technique reduces the topics to a *topic vector*, or *subject vector*.

Salton goes further. The subject vector is essentially a signature or fingerprint for a document. This allows documents to be clustered together according to how similar their subject signatures or subject fingerprints are and that allows more discrimination in retrieval. Many information-seeking questions themselves can be represented by subject vectors. As a very simplified example, a searcher might ask one of

Please find documents about sphinges and crocutes, and roughly about those topics in equal proportion.

Please find documents which are mostly about crocutes with a little about sphinges.

Please find documents which are mostly about sphinges with a little about crocutes.

and those three requests themselves have subject fingerprints

<0.5 sphinges, 0.5 crocutes>,
<0.25 sphinges, 0.75 crocutes>,
<0.75sphinges, 0.25 crocutes>

Then the information retrieval task is merely that producing of the document cluster that has a subject signature that is most similar to the information request. Salton's approach has the potential to be much more discriminating in certain settings. Against this, polytopic reduction by logic has much richer powers of expression. Combining orthogonal concepts numerically in vectors cannot directly accommodate relations between the concepts. For example, in Reid's class hierarchy

Animal
Man
Frenchman
Parisian

the concepts are not orthogonal; there is no simple vector

<0.25 Parisian, 0.75 Man>

simply because all Parisians are 'Men'. And, in the cases we are interested in, such as Trees of Knowledge, there are always class hierarchies. Salton's theories have been developed to address these issues and often, as another development or divergence, they use terms or words rather than concepts (this divergence is a choice to work from the Symbol Vertex of the Triangle of Meaning rather than from the Concept Vertex). Actual empirical test might reveal which approaches work the best. For the present, it is enough to observe that there is a choice between either polytopics—as is the current practice in subject librarianship—or polytopic reduction to a single topic—as Ranganathan would favor—or polytopic reduction to a topic vector, as would be the practice with a certain approach to information retrieval.

# References

ANSI/NISO NISO (2005) ANSI/NISO Z39.19-2005: Guidelines for the construction, format, and management of monolingual controlled vocabularies. NISO Press, Bethesda

Baader F, Horrocks I, Sattler U (2007) Description logics. In: van Harmelen F, Lifschitz V, Porter B (eds) Handbook of knowledge representation. Elsevier, Amsterdam, pp 135–179

Baader F, McGuinness D, Nardi D (eds) (2003) The description logic handbook: theory, implementation, and applications. Cambridge University Press ebrary, Inc. Cambridge

Bates MJ, Maack MN (2009) Encyclopedia of library and information sciences, 3rd edn. CRC Press, Boca Raton

Bealer G (1982) Quality and concept. Oxford University Press, Oxford

Bealer G (1998) Intensional entities. In: Craig E (ed) Routledge encyclopedia of philosophy, vol 4. Routledge, London, pp 803–807

Blasius KH, Hedstuck U, Rollinger C-R (eds) (1989) Sorts and types in artificial intelligence. Lecture notes in AI, vol 418. Springer, Berlin

Bloomfield I (1935) Language. Allen and Unwin, London

Borko H (1977) Toward a theory of indexing. Inf Process Manage 13(6):355–365

Broughton V (2004) Essential classification. Neal-Schuman, New York

Broughton V, Hansson J, Hjørland B, López-Huertas MJ (2005) Knowledge organization. In: Kajberg L, Lørring L (eds) European curriculum reflections on library and information science education. Royal School of Library and Information Science, Copenhagen, pp 133–148

Buchanan B (1979) Theory of library classification. Clive Bingley, London

Chierchia G, McConnell-Ginet S (1990) Meaning and grammar: an introduction to semantics. The MIT Press, Cambridge

Cutter CA (1904) Rules for a dictionary catalog, 4th edn. U.S. Government Printing Office, Washington

Dickens C (1836) The posthumous papers of the pickwick club. 1943 edn. The Modern Library, New York

Enderton HB (2009) Second-order and higher-order logic. In: Zalta EN (ed) The stanford encyclopedia of philosophy (Spring 2009 edn)

Foskett AC (1977) Subject approach to information, 3rd edn. Clive Bingley, London

Frické M (2005) Software and Tutorials for instruction in Logic. http://SoftOption.Us. Accessed 29 Dec 2009

Guarino N, Welty C (2002) Identity and subsumption. In: Green R, Bean CA, Myaeng SH (eds) The semantics of relationships: an interdisciplinary perspective. Kluwer, Dordrecht, pp 111–126

Hjørland B (2006) Aspect or discipline versus entity or phenomena or "one place" classification. http://www.iva.dk/bh/lifeboat_ko/concepts/aspect_classification.htm. Accessed 10 Oct 2010

Hjørland B (2008) Lifeboat for knowledge organization. http://www.iva.dk/bh/lifeboat_ko/home.htm. Accessed 10 Oct 2010

Hovda P (2009) What is classical mereology? J Philos Logic 38:55–82

Kriesel G, Krivine JL (1971) Elements of mathematical logic. North-Holland, Amsterdam

Ladenson A (1953) Applications and limitations of subject headings: the social sciences. In: Tauber MF (ed) The subject analysis of library materials. Columbia University, New York

Manzano M (1993) Introduction to many-sorted logic. In: many-sorted logic and its applications. Wiley, New York, pp 3–86

Manzano M (1996) Extensions of first-order logic. Cambridge University Press, Cambridge

Mills J, Broughton V (1977) Bliss bibliographic classification. 2nd edn. Introduction and Auxiliary Schedules. Butterworths

NISO (2005) NISO Standards: Z39.19. http://www.niso.org/standards/resources/Z39-19.html. Accessed 10 Oct 2010

NLM US (2009) Using medical subject headings (MeSH®) in Cataloging. http://www.nlm.nih.gov/tsd/cataloging/trainingcourses/mesh/index.html. Accessed 10 Oct 2010

NLM US (2011) Use of medical subject headings for cataloging–2011. http://www.nlm.nih.gov/mesh/catpractices.html. Accessed 10 Oct 2010

Norvig P (1992) Paradigms of artificial intelligence programming: case studies in common lisp. Morgan Kaufmann, San Mateo

Oberschelp A (1990) Order-sorted predicate logic. In: Blasius KH, Hedstuck U, Rollinger C-R (eds) Sorts and types in artificial intelligence. Springer, Berlin

Parsons T (1970) Some problems concerning the logic of grammatical modifiers. Synthese 21:320–334

Pribbenow S (2002) Meronymic relationships: from classical mereology to complex part-whole relations. In: Green R, Bean CA, Myaeng SH (eds) The semantics of relationships: an interdisciplinary perspective. Kluwer Academic Publishers, Dordrecht, pp 34–50

Ranganathan SR (1937) Prolegomena to library classification. 3rd ed. 1967; 1st ed. 1937 edn. The Madras library association, Madras

Ranganathan SR (1951) Philosophy of library classification. Munksgaard, Copenhagen

Ranganathan SR (1960) Colon classification. Ranganathan series in library science, 4, 6 edn. Asia Pub. House, London

Ranganathan SR (1962) Elements of library classification, 3rd edn. Asia Publishing House, Bombay

Rogers FB (1960) Review of taube, mortimer. Studies in coordinate indexing. Bull Med Libr Assoc 42:380–384 (July 1954)

Salton G (1962) Manipulation of trees in information retrieval. Commun ACM 5(2):103–114

Salton G (1968) Automatic information organization and retrieval. McGraw Hill, New York

Salton G (1975) A theory of indexing. Regional conference series in applied mathematics, society for industrial and applied mathematics. Philadelphia

Simons P (1987) Parts. A study in ontology. Clarendon Press, Oxford

Smith B (2004) The logic of biological classification and the foundations of biomedical ontology. In: Westerståhl D (ed) Invited Papers from the 10th International Conference in Logic Methodology and Philosophy of Science, Oviedo, Spain, 2003. Elsevier North Holland

Sowa JF (2000) Knowledge representation: logical, philosophical, and computational foundations. Brooks/Cole, Pacific Grove

Thalheim B (2000) Entity-relationship modeling: foundations of database technology. Springer, New York

Tillett BB (2009) Definition of aggregates as works: tillett proposal. http://www.ifla.org/files/cataloguing/frbrrg/aggregates-as-works.pdf. Accessed 10 Oct 2010

Varzi A (2009) Mereology. http://plato.stanford.edu/archives/sum2009/entries/mereology/. Accessed 10 Oct 2010

Vickery BC (1975) Classification and indexing in science, 3rd edn. Butterworths, London

Vickery BC (2008) Faceted classification for the web. Axiomathes 18(2):145–160

Wang H (1952) Logic of many-sorted theories. J Symbolic Logic 17(2):105–116

Welty C, Guarino N (2001) Supporting ontological analysis of taxonomic relationships. Data Knowl Eng 39:51–74

Zeng ML (2005) Construction of controlled vocabularies, a primer (based on Z39.19). http://www.slis.kent.edu/~mzeng/Z3919/index.htm. Accessed 10 Oct 2010

# Chapter 5
# Classification

## 5.1 Introduction

We have already noted that we classify things into their kinds in part to condense our knowledge of those things. How the things are classified, the techniques and the results, is of relevance to information retrieval exactly because it is the IOs that contain a record of that knowledge and the Patron or User needs to be guided to the relevant parts. This leads to the idea of topics or subjects, and any of the kind-classification concepts can be subjects. But subjects are more general than plain-kind classifications. There are 'aspects', there is fiction, there are contradictory topics, and there are comparisons, influences, and so forth. This invites the use of a subject, topic, indexing, or topic language. This present chapter addresses plain kind classification: the next chapter is on topic annotation languages.

The three main 'analytic' relations for the purposes of kind classification are 'is a subtype of', 'is an instance of' and 'is a part of'. These are used in subtype-supertype hierarchies, in higher order properties, and in partitive hierarchies, respectively. These relations allow us to establish several common forms. There certainly are other relationships that can be used to establish indirect classifications; an obvious example is cladistics and evolutionary biology, which uses the 'ancestor of' or 'descended from' relation to establish links between species.

## 5.2 Aristotelian-Linnaean Classification

These are most commonly found in natural kind hierarchies. Schematically a fragment of such a classification might look like this (Fig. 5.1). This shows how some types are related to each other. In particular, for example, the fish-type is a subtype of the vertebrate-type, and so on. These classifications are, in a graph-theoretic sense, trees, which is to say they are acyclic and connected. So, in

M. Fricke, *Logic and the Organization of Information*,
DOI: 10.1007/978-1-4614-3088-9_5,
© Springer Science+Business Media New York 2012

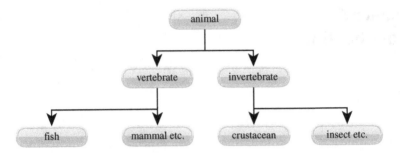

**Fig. 5.1** An Aristotelian-Linnaean classification

addition to the particular type relations f < v, m < v, v < a, etc. there are constraints on the whole structure which can easily be expressed in the logic (for example, that there is a path between any two types). The subtype relation imposed a partial order, not a total order (for example, above, fish is not a subtype of crustacean, nor is crustacean a subtype of fish. Aristotle himself would probably have required that each of the types be instantiated (Berg 1982); this is easy to impose if it is considered desirable (e.g. with formulas like $\exists x(\text{Animal}(x))$).

Additionally there is the notion of levels, which is just the distance of a type from the (animal) root: vertebrate is of level 1, fish of level 2, etc. These levels are higher order properties possessed by the types, thus if LevelOne(x) is the predicate to express level 1, then

LevelOne(vertebrate), and
LevelOne(invertebrate).

Usually these levels have particular names, or identifying predicates, of their own (e.g. Kingdom, Phylum, Family, Genus, and Species). Children of the same node are on the same level. But nodes on the same level are not necessarily children of the same node—they could be cousins or some other kind of relative. All that is required is that nodes on the same level have a common ancestor, which is the same distance from each of them (and all children have a common ancestor, the root is one).

True to their name, classification hierarchies are used for classifying, and the idea is that it is the leaves that are going to be the classification 'containers' or 'buckets'. They are going to provide an exclusive and exhaustive classification of everything within the classification's ambit. That means that every animal in the world at large belongs in exactly one of the leaf 'buckets' (and then, indirectly, they will inherit the types of the branch to which they belong). The displayed diagram is truly simplified. One view of biology is that there are 100 million species in the world; so there certainly are a large number of different animal species, displaying just four of the intermediate genera or families, as the diagram does, is just to be illustrate that what is to be classified goes with the leaves, not elsewhere. Often the classification process itself can be carried out top-down from the root to the leaves. There is 'narrowing' or differentiation going down the tree, and 'broadening' or generalizing going up the tree.

Navigation can be vertical, but it can also be horizontal via the levels (or Genus and Species etc.). This is useful. A librarian might ask a Patron 'What literary form are you interested in?' A car dealer might ask a customer 'What make of car are you interested in?' or 'What model of car can I show you?' This is to enter a hierarchy on a horizontal level; the technique is important for Information Architecture and website design.

The subtype-supertype relation used to establish these trees can be illustrated in many different domains. There are the biological and car manufacturing examples given earlier. An example from mathematics is that the geometrical shapes triangle, square, pentagon are all subtypes of the more general type of geometrical shape polyhedron. In geography (and with wines) the region Bordeaux is a subregion of France and so the type 'being from Bordeaux' is a subtype of 'being from France' (i.e. Bordeaux wine is a subtype of French wine). Then there are all the well-known shelf location classifications of traditional librarianship (Bliss, UDC, LCC, DCC, etc.).

Aristotelian classification hierarchies are usually taken to exemplify five properties. The classification should be:

exhaustive,
exclusive,
principled,
rich,
and narrowing.

*Exhaustive* requires that every classified item has some location in the classification (or in the classification 'schedule'). This is a base level constraint. If, for example, there is a classification schedule for wines, and a particular wine that has no place in the schedule, the task of classification simply has not been completed. Also if an item is an instance of a leaf node, it automatically is an instance of at least one type in each of the horizontal layers above that leaf. So the layers themselves are also exhaustive.

With an Aristotelian hierarchy it is the leaves that do the classifying, and, for each specific hierarchy, these leaves can be regarded as having predicates, or conditions, that represent them for example, Fish(x), Crustacean(x), and so on. To portray these leaf predicates in a general schema, let us call them $Leaf_1(x)$, $Leaf_2(x)$, ... [So, conceptually, we are introducing definitions, thus

$\forall x(Leaf_1(x) \equiv Fish(x))$
$\forall x(Leaf_2(x) \equiv Crustacean(x))$
...]

Then the *exhaustive* requirement is that everything has at least one of the leaf properties

$\forall x(Leaf_1(x) \lor Leaf_2(x) \lor Leaf_3(x) ...)$ [Exhaustive]

**Fig. 5.2** A division that does not use a single principle of division

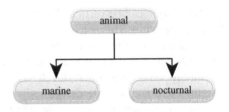

The *exclusive* requirement is that nothing has two or more leaf properties at the same time (e.g. nothing is both a fish and a crustacean): the leaves are 'pairwise disjoint'. There are various ways of depicting this. A simple way, suitable for our purposes, is just to say

$\sim \exists x(\text{Leaf}_1(x)\&\text{Leaf}_2(x))$ &
$\sim \exists x(\text{Leaf}_1(x)\&\text{Leaf}_3(x))$ &

...

$\sim \exists x(\text{Leaf}_2(x)\&\text{Leaf}_3(x))$ &

...

...

[Exclusive]

These first two requirements are sometimes called the **JEPD** (jointly exhaustive pairwise disjoint) property and it is possessed by Aristotelian classifications. [If JEPD holds for the leaves of a tree, it also holds for all the child nodes for any of the internal, non-leaf, parent nodes within the tree.]

The *principled* requirement concerns the 'sibling separator', or 'differentiating condition', or 'differentiae', which is used to separate children types. To be principled, each node should have just a single principle of subdivision which produces its children. Suppose, in the example, the first level separation had been to divide animals into marine animals and nocturnal animals, thus (Fig. 5.2): So that the division to marine animals is being made on the basis of where the animals live, and the division to nocturnal animals is being made on the basis of how they behave (cf. (Buchanan 1979)). This would *not* be using a *single* principle of division. There needs to be the same kind of separator along the children of a node. The division to marine and nocturnal could well have the JEPD property, but it would do so by luck or accident (in particular, the accident that none of the marine animals that we have ever met were also nocturnal). A classification which is not principled is suspect in that it might fail as we classify more items. Buchanan gives an example from the London Education Classification (Buchanan 1979) (Fig. 5.3). An 'educand' is a person being educated; and the classes 'teenager', 'adult', 'older person' are being produced on the basis of age: the class 'parent' arises on the basis of relationship and the class 'housewife' on the basis of occupation. The division is not principled. Actual educands in London in 1970, say, might, by the luck of it, fall into these classes in an exclusive and exhaustive way, but that would be a pure accident because it is quite possible for a housewife to be a parent (or an

**Fig. 5.3**  A fragment from the London Education Classification

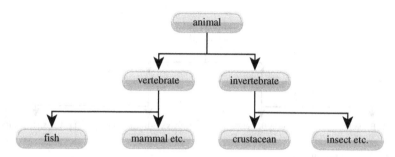

**Fig. 5.4**  The first of a pair of classifications

adult a parent, etc.). To generalize, the principled condition amounts to the following: for any node, there are conditions or predicates for each of its children, say

$Child_1(x)$,
$Child_2(x)$,
$Child_3(x)$,
…

and associated types

$c_1 = \{x: Child_1(x)\}$,
$c_2 = \{x: Child_2(x)\}$,
$c_3 = \{x: Child_3(x)\}$,
…

and those conditions or types have kinds. What needs to happen is that the kinds need to be the same for all the children of the parent in question, i.e.

$SameKind(c_1)\&SameKind(c_2)\& SameKind(c_3)$

So, for example, had educands been divided up in a principled way, perhaps by age, we would have that $\{x:Adult(x)\}$ is a by age kind of predicate, i.e.

$ByAge (\{x:Adult(x)\})$

And similarly for other children of the educand type.

   A classification is *rich* if it does not omit levels. The actual basic classification is done by the leaves. So, in that sense, the two classifications (Figs. 5.4, 5.5) and are the same in their capabilities for classification, in as much as they have the

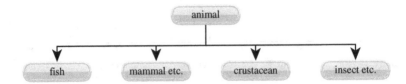

**Fig. 5.5** The second of a pair of classifications

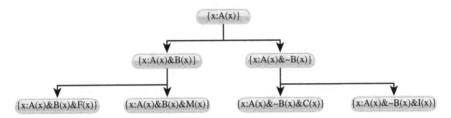

**Fig. 5.6** A tree built in stages

same leaves. However, a classification scheme also both contains knowledge or information about how the types relate to each other and has the ability to support inference. For example, the first scheme contains the information that all fish are vertebrates (and, in turn, in conjunction with the fact that Livingston is a fish, that knowledge supports the inference to Livingston is a vertebrate). The second scheme, by omitting a layer, omits information that the first scheme contains: it omits some relations between types. Generally, it is not easy to omit layers on other grounds, for example, on considerations relating to principled division. But, even when it is possible, it is not wise to do it because it leaves out information. Rich schemas contain their full quota of levels, their full quota of information.

Principled division and narrowing can be illustrated by imagining the example tree to be built in stages. That the root type are animals amounts to their possessing the property A(x) (i.e. x is an animal), then the example may be filled out (Fig. 5.6). For the next division to 'vertebrate' and 'invertebrate' a suitable predicate is needed that will divide up the animals *exclusively* and *exhaustively* between the two types so that every animal will end up being a vertebrate or a non-vertebrate and no animal will end up being both (i.e. JEPD). The property of having, or lacking, a backbone is one that will achieve this. And it is a *principled* differentiae. Of course, the use of a single predicate as the differentiae gives JEPD and principled division, but it also means that there can be only two 'species' at this level. Obviously this is insufficient in the general case. However, more than a single predicate can be used, for example, C(x) and D(x) could be used, and that would accommodate 4 species or subtypes, namely C(x)&D(x), C(x)&~D(x), ~C(x)&D(x), ~C(x)&~D(x). Generalization of this provides for 2, 4, 8, 16, etc. species; and other intermediate numbers can be accommodated by combining some of the possible categories together, for example $C(x)\&D(x)$, $C(x)\&\sim D(x)$, and $\sim C(x)$ (i.e. the combination $(\sim C(x)\&D(x)v\sim C(x)\&\sim D(x)))$ gives 3 species.

The last Aristotelian hierarchy property, *narrowing*, just means that starting at the root and coming down the appropriate branch refines and sharpens the classification of an item or items; narrowing almost always follows automatically—each type (other than the leaves) just has to have at least two subtypes. An individual child of a node is never going to have more instances than its parent—that is narrowing.

There is an analogy that can be used to illustrate the Classical Aristotelian Classification Hierarchy. Suppose there is a filing cabinet, containing manila folders and invoices (or bills and receipts), and the organization is as follows: first there are folders for years, say 2008, 2009, 2010, then within those folders there are further folders for the months of the years, January, February, through to December, and the receipts are placed within the relevant innermost month folders. Then, this is a hierarchy: it is exclusive and exhaustive, and the receipts are placed, by their dates, within the leaves only. The manila folders themselves are homogenous in what they contain, in the following sense: each folder contains either only other folders or only receipts, no folder contains a mixture of some other folders and some receipts.

There is a significant disanalogy here that we need to be mindful of. In an Aristotelian hierarchy, the links are based on the subtype relationship and this means that the leaves (and other nodes) are all subtypes of nodes higher up their respective branches. So, for example, if Shere Khan is a tiger, Shere Khan is also a vertebrate (an instance of type higher up the branch it belongs to), and he is also an animal. Now, if the two questions are asked 'How many animals are there?' and 'Is Shere Khan among them?' the answers will be 'Millions and millions' and 'Yes, Shere Khan is one of them'. In the filing cabinet and manila folders example, the links are based on the instantiation or membership relation and this means that each of the nodes are instances of their parents but they are *not* instances of their grandparents and nodes further up the respective branches. So, for example, a January 2009 invoice for a typewriter ribbon will physically be within the January 2009 folder, but it will not itself be *directly* within the 2009 folder; if the two questions are asked 'How many things are there within the 2009 folder? and 'Is the typewriter ribbon invoice one of them?' the answers will be '12 (namely the months' folders)' and 'No, the ribbon invoice is not one of those 12'. The difference between subtype and instance is not overly important when merely illustrating ideas of exclusive and exhaustive classification but, generally, it is not good to confuse the two.

Aristotelian classification is a worthy model: it is exemplary in its clarity, and it can do most everything that seems desirable. Other schemes are often not as good; indeed, many can be improved by being modified so as to approach the Aristotelian ideal.

## 5.3 Revisable Aristotelian

One aspect that is slightly curious about the Standard Aristotelian hierarchy is its static or set in stone nature. Think for one moment about the discovery of a new kind, or a new species, or the desire to have a new classification entry in the schedule. When a particular token or item is being classified, it is classified by being recognized as being an instance of one of the leaves of the tree (and it then is also an instance of all the supertypes up the branch its leaf belongs to). And the leaves are exclusive and exhaustive (everything goes in at least one leaf and nothing goes in more than one leaf). This does not just mean that each of the tokens you happen to have is allocated to exactly one leaf: it means that no matter what the tokens, old or new, each token belongs to one leaf. [Similarly, sibling internal nodes are collectively exclusive and exhaustive in their division of items that are instances of their parent.]

Yet this does not seem to fit well with some practical realities. Consider the Dewey Decimal Classification (DDC) as it was for Dewey, say around 1900. Any book that there was at that time could be classified by the scheme. And the scheme itself classified by subjects-within-disciplines. It was hierarchical in form and approximated an Aristotelian hierarchy (indeed, its distant ancestor was the Bacon Tree of Knowledge). The 1900 DDC was exclusive and exhaustive as to the IOs of 1900—every book had exactly one slot—but it was not exclusive and exhaustive in a pure logical sense. As time went by, new subjects arose—and new IOs that needed to be cataloged using those new subjects. For example, now, 2010, there are many books on Computer Science and 'Computer Science', among many other subjects, is a type or subject in modern DDC that was not there in 1900. The published DDC schedule is now at about its 22nd edition to accommodate the steady trickle or flood of new subjects.

There are two basic approaches: a global one, and a piecemeal one. With the global approach, the first entire Aristotelian classification is just discarded and replaced with a new Aristotelian classification. There is not a lot to be said about this option; the first classification is just deemed false or wrong or inadequate and abandoned for a new one. The piecemeal approach tries to retain much of the old classification by augmenting it with one or more leaves.

How can a new leaf be introduced? There is only one way: one of the existing leaves has to be divided into usually two or more types; so leaf A, say, gets divided into leaves B and C. This could be done 'vertically', increasing the depth of the A branch, or 'horizontally', removing A and giving A's siblings, or former siblings, B and C as new siblings.

In the 'vertical' case everything in the new B is also in the old A, so that B is a subtype of A (and, similarly, C is also a subtype of A). And A must be converted from a leaf node to being an internal node. Here is the growth pattern (Figs. 5.7, 5.8). The 'carnivore' node was formerly a leaf node, but after the growth it has become an internal node. (Conceptually this is not too difficult: we see it all the time with branching in real trees.)

**Fig. 5.7** Vertical growth, before

Before I

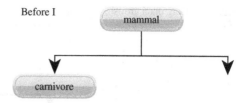

**Fig. 5.8** Vertical growth, after

After I

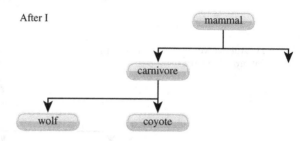

**Fig. 5.9** Horizontal growth, before

Before II

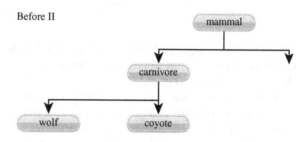

But often that is not what we want. Often we would like to do 'horizontal' growth that is growth along a level, adding a sibling. Suppose we have the above After I tree, and we know about the species 'wolf' and 'coyote'. We would like it to at least be possible for us to discover or identify a new species, say 'dingo'. We would like to be able to also grow a tree like this (Figs. 5.9, 5.10) and that is to add a new leaf on the same level, without that growth increasing the depth of the branches that are involved.

Consider the 'Before II' diagram here: if the leaf types 'wolf' and 'coyote' are an exclusive and exhaustive division of their parent 'carnivore', a new type 'dingo' simply cannot be added, leaving 'wolf' and 'coyote' unchanged, to create three leaves, all of which can contain instances, and yet which are collectively exclusive and exhaustive. The conclusion to be drawn is that the original 'wolf' and 'coyote', while exclusive (no carnivore is both), are *not* exhaustive (that is, there could be a carnivore which is neither). So really the 'Before' diagram should look like this (Fig. 5.11).

The leaves here are exclusive and exhaustive but the 'etc.' type is not itself a species, rather it is a catch all for those carnivores which are not wolves or coyotes. When we identify dingoes, and want to have them as a type, it is the 'etc.' leaf that

**Fig. 5.10** Horizontal growth, after          After II

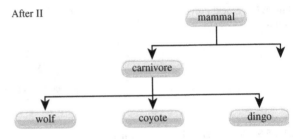

**Fig. 5.11** Alternative horizontal growth, before          Before III

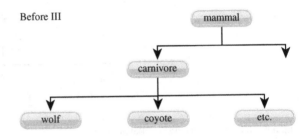

gets split into a 'dingo' leaf and a new 'etc.' leaf which is a new catch all for those carnivores which are not wolves or coyotes or dingoes. Thus, the 'After' diagram should look like this (Fig. 5.12).

Sometimes, as a matter of logic, sibling types are exclusive and exhaustive as they stand. We saw this in an earlier example: if the type 'vertebrate' is defined as those animals with backbones, and 'invertebrate' is defined as those animals without backbones, then the vertebrate-invertebrate classification of animals is exclusive and exhaustive. However, often, types along a level, in realistic classifications, will need an 'etc.' catch all type to get exhaustivity.

The differentiae, or sibling separating properties, are not, from a logical point of view, exhaustive.

In the setting of information resources and information retrieval, Jack Mills makes exactly this point as follows:

> The constituent species collectively must be coextensive with the extension of the genus. The obvious difficulty encountered here is that of our imperfect knowledge. This can be overcome in a technical sense by the process of dichotomy, in which one species is named and all the others are covered by its negative, e.g. the array (Buildings by material) could give just two classes, brick buildings and nonbrick buildings, and this would exhaust the array—no buildings would be missed. In practice, of course, all significant kinds of other materials would be enumerated with a possible residual class for "Others." (Mills 2004, p. 554)

Our filing cabinet analogy can be adapted to illustrate this. This time suppose it is looking after household receipts and its organization is as follows: first there are folders for years (say 2008, 2009, 2010) then within those folders there are further folders for the categories of invoices (say Food, Clothing, Utilities, and Auto). Now, presumably there will be some receipts that do not fit into any of these

After III

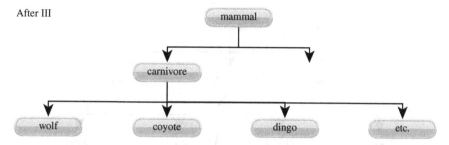

**Fig. 5.12** Alternative horizontal growth, after

categories. So each year will need to have one last folder in it, say Other. The receipts are placed within the relevant innermost category folders. This will constitute a hierarchy: it is exclusive and exhaustive, and the receipts are placed, by their nature, within the leaves only. The manila folders themselves are homogenous in what they contain, in the following sense: each folder contains either only other folders or only receipts, no folder contains a mixture of some other folders and some receipts. As time goes by, we might notice that our Other folder contains a large number of invoices that relate to Maintenance, and we might make the decision to insert a further category of inner folder, one for Maintenance. So we now have Food, Clothing, Utilities, Auto, Maintenance, and Other (we will still need an Other as a catch-all for unplaced invoices). The classification schedule has changed, while leaving the greater part of it intact.

There is a choice here with respect to these Other or 'etc.' categories. The 'etc.' types can be added explicitly to the tree or schedule. Or they can be omitted, or understood implicitly, in which case the strict classification is not exhaustive as it stands. Hence there is the notion of a revisable Aristotelian classification: an Aristotelian classification that is either not exhaustive or has Other categories that allow minor revisions to be made to it.

## 5.4 Librarian Aristotelian

A common pattern often used by librarians in shelving classification is similar to the Revisable Aristotelian Classification Hierarchy, but it is not exactly the same. The difference is, librarians use internal nodes, in addition to leaves, to catalog.

Here is a fragment of Dewey Decimal Classification (DDC), around 820 (Fig. 5.13). Some books are classified by the leaves (for example, Shakespeare's *Romeo and Juliet* is going to be Literature-English-Drama with classmark notation 822 (and it will gain some other decimal digits in a full classification), and others are classified by the internal nodes (for example, John Keats's *The Works of John Keats (complete Poetry and selected Prose)* will be Literature-English 820).

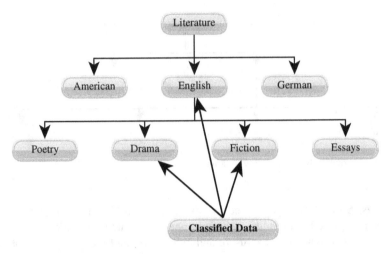

**Fig. 5.13** A fragment of the Dewey Decimal Classification around 820

**Fig. 5.14** A linearization of the Dewey Decimal Classification around 820

That there are works (e.g. works by Keats) that are instances of internal nodes, but yet not instances of any of that node's children, means that the sibling children are not exhaustive as to the contents of their parent. In this case, the *leaves* are not exhaustive: DDC does not have the JEPD property.

A different way of looking at this is to linearize the tree using a shelving traversal. Here is the result (omitting American and German literature for simplification and clarity) (Fig. 5.14). And here are the corresponding Dewey classification numbers (Fig. 5.15). When librarians go to catalog a book (a book in this range of books), they choose exactly one of these numbers for it. The assignation of numbers is 'exclusive and exhaustive'—every book receives exactly one number. In effect, then, this *primary* act of classification makes a decision as to which type the book instantiates, and for this act the types are 'exclusive and exhaustive'. However, many of the types bear subtype-supertype relations to other types—that is what is shown in the original classification tree—and in consequence of this if a book instantiates a subtype it automatically, and *secondarily*, instantiates the supertype. So, if a book is English Literature (820) it automatically is Literature (though it does not get a second class number). The subtype-supertype relations affect collocations in the shelving traversal—English Literature ends up close to other Literature as opposed to being close to, say, Mathematics.

This use of internal nodes, and its resulting linearization, is not without advantage for librarianship. The interior nodes are in some sense more general than the leaves, and the linearization places those more general books to the left of

**Fig. 5.15** Dewey Decimal Classification numbers around 820

the more specific ones. So the shelving does not merely collocate, it also goes from the general to the specific.

Our trusty filing cabinet analogy can be used to illustrate what is going on here and we can adapt it to look like a Dewey Classification. Once again we have manila folders, but instead of invoices we have catalog cards for the books, including a card for *Romeo and Juliet* and a card for Keats's *Works*. The (partial) folder organization is that the Literature folder contains the American, English, and German folders, and, in turn, the English folder contains Poetry, Drama, Fiction, and Essays folders within it. We place the Shakespeare catalog card within the Literature-English-Drama folder, nested deep within the structure, and the Keats card within the Literature folder, at the top level. The manila folders themselves are *not* now homogeneous in what they contain, they are *heterogeneous*, in the following sense: some folders contain a mixture of folders and cataloging cards, for example the Literature folder does so. We can, alternatively, linearize this into a filing cabinet. In which case there would be folders for Literature, etc. in a sequence. And no folder would contain another folder. Instead the folders would once again be homogeneous; each of them would contain only catalog cards.

We are very familiar with an arrangement like Librarian-Aristotelian Classifications in our ordinary work on personal computers. Often we will have Folders (or Directories) which contain, or can contain, both Documents (Images, Files, Podcasts, etc.) *and other Folders*; and all the Folders we use are like this. Every Document is in exactly one place, in that they all have their own unique paths from the root of the Folder tree structure.

The Librarian-Aristotelian Classification has disadvantages, ambiguities, or differences, when it comes to Searching for a Class or Category. In an ordinary Aristotelian Classification, any node (or the label of any node) can be used to launch a Search, and the process consists of following all the branches that go through that launch node down to their leaves, which is where the items are, and collecting together the items of the leaves. So, for example, with (Fig. 5.16). If the manager of car lot was asked to produce the Fords, she would retrieve the Explorers and the Focusses, if asked for the Chevrolets, she would reveal the Camaros and the Volts, and so on. But suppose this very same hierarchy were a Librarian Aristotelian Hierarchy and that the internal Ford node itself contains cars, *which were not further classified by the leaves* as Explorers or Focusses or anything else. Then the Search request 'Produce the Fords' becomes ambiguous: is it to be satisfied by the 'pure' Fords, or by the 'pure' Fords together with the Explorers and Focusses? To put this question back into the setting of the Dewey Classification. The two books used for illustration were Keats's *Works*, which is classified as (Literature->English) and Shakespeare's *Romeo and Juliet*, which is

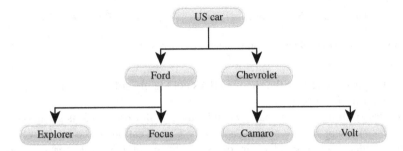

**Fig. 5.16** A classification of cars

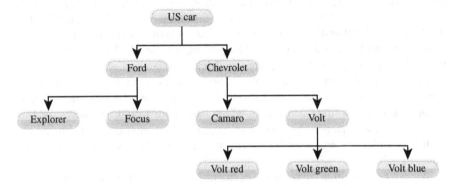

**Fig. 5.17** A classification of colored cars

classified as (Literature->English->Drama); should a Search for (Literature->English) return just Keats or both Keats and Shakespeare? It is unclear.

## 5.5  Polyhierarchies

There can be schemes of relationships among types where types can have more than one immediate supertype. (In object oriented programming this is 'multiple inheritance'.) Of course, once you have a polyhierarchy, the classification structure is not a tree (because it will have cycles). Also the notion of levels (e.g. Kingdom, Phylum, Family, Genus, Species etc.) is ill-defined or hard to define, because a type might have what amounts to different levels in the different hierarchies.

Here is an example. Say we wanted to classify colored cars. So we start with (Fig. 5.17).

[The drawing of red, green, and blue Explorers, Focusses, Camaros. etc. has been omitted for clarity.]

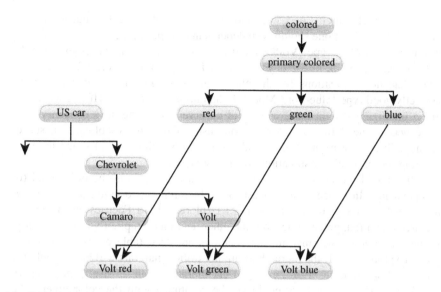

**Fig. 5.18**  A polyhierarchical classification of cars

The next step is to let the colored cars inherit their colors. Thus (Fig. 5.18). So, a Red Volt car is a Volt is a Chevrolet and is a US car; it is also a red item, it is a primary colored item and a colored item. A Red Volt has two separate parents that it inherits from. It inherits from Red Colored and it inherits from Volt. (And so too for the other colored cars, were we to draw them in.)

Only part of the classification has been drawn. Notice that, if it were all drawn, you would get red-green-blue links (or nodes) being repeated over and over under each of the models of car.

This polyhierarchy is not a tree. It has cycles (volt-redVolt-red-primary-green-greenVolt-volt is a cycle).

The logic of a polyhierarchy is merely that of conjoining the properties in the separate hierarchies. So, for example, a red Chevy Volt might be

{x:Red(x)&Volt(x)}

or, if we include the hierarchy information (that red is a primary color, that a Volt is a Chevrolet and a US Car) we get

{x:Red(x)&P(x)&C(x)&Volt(x)&D(x)&U(x)}

The types themselves in a polyhierarchy can have properties or be of kinds. For example, all the types in car hierarchy have the higher-order type 'being a car classification type', and all the types in the color hierarchy have the higher-order type 'being a color classification type' (and some types are in both these hierarchies and have both higher order types).

A true polyhierarchy needs its individual hierarchies to be independent or orthogonal. Types in one should be independent of types in the other. That there is in one hierarchy the type 'Volt' should have no implications whatsoever for the color hierarchy. Back in the days of Henry Ford, all Fords were black. That, in itself, had no implications for the classification scheme (it just meant that the perfectly good type 'blue-Ford-Model-T' had no instantiations). [If one wanted to affect intelligent insight here, one could observe that in the days of Henry Ford there was no need for car classifications using the primary colors, but, subsequently, 'literary warrant' (i.e. the advent of richly colored cars) suggested augmenting the original classifications with new types.]

Why should the component hierarchies in a polyhierarchy be orthogonal (or independent)? In conception, at least, these hierarchies are going to *postcoordinate*. That is to say, there will be Ford Explorers, Ford Focuses etc. from one hierarchy, and red, green, blue from the other; and then, implicitly (and explicitly, if there is literary warrant) all combinations are acceptable e.g. red Explorers, green Explorers etc. If the hierarchies are not orthogonal, this will be, or could be, violated. For example, if an envisaged car hierarchy had, of itself, the category 'red Explorer', that category could not be combined with the color green—the notion of a green red Explorer is a nonsense. This is because the hierarchies are not orthogonal. The orthogonality requirement points to something else. Each of the component hierarchies has differentiae, namely, the differentiation predicates that do the divisions down the levels. The types of one hierarchy must not be used as the differentiae in another (because that removes full postcoordinate combinations below). Fugmann alludes to exactly this when he writes

> a characteristic of a subdivision should be avoided which is in itself of the categorial kind [i.e. don't subdivide one category using another]. (Fugmann 1993, p. 137)

How do the important notions of exclusive, exhaustive, and JEPD apply to polyhierarchies? Well, there is nothing special about polyhierarchies in the following sense. If the classification is being done by the leaves, then the leaves collectively either are or are not JEPD is the standard way. And usually the leaves consist of all possible combinations of the component hierarchy's leaves, in which case, if the component hierarchies themselves have JEPD leaves, and the hierarchies are orthogonal, then the polyhierarchy will be JEPD.

## 5.6 Basic Synthetic Classification

An easier and better way of doing polyhierarchies is not to try to combine two (or more) hierarchies into one large graph. Instead, we can use two or more separate classification schemes simultaneously in parallel. A common example of this is where there is one classification scheme of, say, items, and then one or more 'Auxiliary Tables' (i.e. additional classification schemes) of Periods or Places. In such a case, the classification types are formed by synthesizing together a basic kind and a Period (and perhaps even a Place). So an antiques dealer may pull the type Chair from a classification scheme of furniture, the period nineteenth century from another, and French from a third, to make the synthesized type 'nineteenth century French Chair'.

Typically, with schemes that permit (basic) synthesis, the actual synthesis consists of the addition (meaning intersection) of the component types. This is easy to reproduce or portray with symbolic logic. For instance, the components

{x:NineteenthC(x)}
{x:French(x)}
{x:Chair(x)}

are synthesized by being logically ANDED together to yield

{x:NineteenthC(x)&French(x)&Chair(x)}

With some simple synthetic classifications, a natural datastructure to represent classified data is often a table or a relational database. For example, suppose the classification were a synthesis of Furniture [bed, chair, table ...], Places [England, France, Italy, ...] and Periods [sixteenth century, seventeenth century, ...]. Then each of the Antique dealer's items had as its synthetic classification a combination

| ID | Period | Place | Kind |
|----|--------|-------|------|
| 1 | 19thC | English | Chair |
| 2 | 19thC | French | Bed |
| 3 | 19thC | German | Chair |
| 4 | 19thC | English | Lamp |
| 5 | 19thC | English | Table |
| 6 | 19thC | German | Bed |
| 7 | 19thC | French | Chair |

of Furniture, Place and Period. The data could then go straight into a table (where the primary key and the ID name or identifier of the individual antiques are one and the same).

The different kinds, here Kind-of-furniture, Periods, and Places, would need to be orthogonal or independent (and the resulting database would be Third Normal Form [see (Date 1977) for explanations of 'primary key', 'Third Normal Form', and other database concepts)]. [There still will be a need to capture and represent any hierarchies, the semantics, in the synthetic classification e.g. should it have Europe as a Place that encompasses France, etc.] Logic would provide the type descriptions, e.g.

{x:NineteenthC(x)&French(x)&Chair(x)}

and usually, or possibly, also the information on hierarchies; and a relational database could hold the data values.

One question that arises with synthetic classification is how to linearize the synthesized results, should that be required. The antique dealer might want to arrange her wares in a particular way in her shop. And the librarian needs linearization for shelving, for bibliographies, catalogs, and lists of books. (Of course, as we have remarked, shelving is no longer the important problem that it was.) However, there are a variety of ways to do it, and typically what the linearizations will do is to collocate some items and scatter others. For example, if there is a synthesis of Kinds-of-furniture, Places. And Periods there will be linearizations that collocate Kinds-of-furniture (all the chairs together, for example) and scatter Places and Periods, and others which collocate Periods and scatter Places and Kinds. Much depends on what is desired. Typically the components of the synthesis will themselves individually have enumerations—so, for example, there are ordered or sorted lists of Kinds-of-furniture, of Places and of Periods. And the synthetic components are put together in a certain order, *citation order*; for example, Periods comes before Places, which, in turn, come before Kinds in a compound (or, indeed, Periods before Places). Producing a composite enumeration from this is easy to do. [We have seen it—and the phenomenon of scattering and distributed relatives—with tables, in Sect. 2.8.9]

## 5.7  Ersatz Facets

In conception, basic or simple faceted classification is an easier and better way of doing polyhierarchies (and can do more besides). It uses two or more classification schemes simultaneously in combination. Each of these schemes is a 'facet' or 'face'.

So, for example, a Car Dealership might use a faceted classification consisting of a Make-Model scheme and separately, simultaneously, in parallel, a Color scheme. So, any particular car for sale will have a Make-Model facet (or face) and a Color facet (or face) (Fig. 5.19). The data goes with the leaves, so the data is Explorer, Focus, etc. and also red, green, blue etc. The data might alternatively be depicted in a table. The rows would be the data, as usual. Then the values for the cars might be one column, and the colors a second column. Such a tabular representation might not be so clear on the hierarchies (for example, once a car is a Focus it also is a Ford and also a US car and there is no obvious depiction of this in a single row and column table). Also, often there are more than two facets—these would require more columns to depict.

What is attractive about relating facets to columns in relational databases is that facets are orthogonal (or independent), and that is exactly what is needed for helping to normalize the database (which itself it desirable).

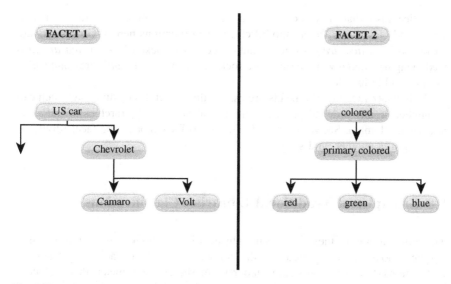

**Fig. 5.19**  A faceted classification of cars

From a logical point of view, the basic use of facets is similar to the use of a polyhierarchy: the properties are just conjoined. Faceting is synthesis. So to arrive at the red Volt type, the red property and the Volt property are conjoined:

$\{x{:}\mathrm{Red}(x)\&\mathrm{Volt}(x)\}$

The main difference from plain synthesis is that the synthesized faceted properties themselves explicitly have kinds. A Volt type is a Model-Of-Car kind, and a Red type is a Colored-Object kind, and the synthesis combines instances of the two different kinds.

An insightful theoretician is this area is Vanda Broughton (Broughton 2004, 2006), a central contributor to the Bliss II classification. In her publications she introduces faceted classification by means of an example involving physical socks. (She does this for pedagogical reasons.) We will use her example here. The socks are concrete items, each individually with five different attributes drawn from the 'facets' Color, Pattern, Material, Function, and Length—so there are black-striped-wool-work-ankle socks, white-striped-silk-work-knee socks etc. Each of the individual facets is (or could be) an Aristotelian exclusive and exhaustive hierarchical scheme, and the entire scheme synthesizes the five facets. This kind of arrangement is commonplace on the Web. Department stores, such as Amazon, Target, or Walmart; all display their wares essentially as a table or grid or database of orthogonal categories and provide navigation by means of hierarchical facets.

Orthogonal attributes can provide faceting, *ersatz* faceting, but, as we will see, it is not the style of faceting, or domain for faceting, envisaged by Otlet, Ranganathan, and the Classification Research Group (CRG) for subjects or topics.

Notice also that in orthogonal attribute ersatz faceting, the non-elemental compound classes are superimposed classes (no functions here!). Grey socks are socks (socks *which are also* grey), ankle socks are socks (socks *which are also* ankle length), and grey ankle socks are socks (socks *which are also* grey and *which are also* ankle length).

With ersatz faceting, the facets are essentially principles of division which can be applied in any order to produce similar, but different, hierarchies of the same underlying domain. So, with the socks (division) By Color is one facet (division) By Length is another, and so on.

## 5.8  Examples of Traditional Librarian Classifications

The principle aim of these is shelving physical items, 'books', in such a way that similar 'books' are collocated and the collocated groups are adjacent to similar collocations (to provide browsing support). The shelving aim means that each item can have only one location, position, or slot within the scheme.

As an intellectual goal, shelving is not the most exciting. As Shera writes,

> The Dewey *Decimal Classification*, in whatever edition, and the shelf of drab paper-bound volumes that are the classification of the Library of Congress, are not a gate though which the mind is led into the recorded world of the human adventure, they are only an address-book for the library stacks. (Shera 1965, p. 134)

Nevertheless, devising such schemes is challenging. Typically a mix of classification characteristics is used. The notion of *subject* is at the core of most classifications. What a book's subject is will determine where it is classified in the schedule, and where a book has been classified will, or should, reveal its subject. There is the (single) *subject* or *subject matter* of the book. And the subjects can be related to other subjects. (There will be further in depth discussion of that later under the separate topic of subject annotations.) In addition, there is also the form of both the content (for example, fiction or poetry) and the container (for example, encyclopaedia or anthology). And there are features of the authors (for example, their nationality or the period in which they write). Much might happen. For example, there certainly can be eighteenth century French authors writing about seventeenth century German literature (where those books should be shelved is, then, a question). [And actual shelving adds an additional layer in that usually there will be many books within each individual class—that is what collocation is aiming for—but these books themselves have to have a shelving order (for example, alphabetical by author, title, or similar).]

The label or name of the class, what we would call its type or intensional type, is often called its *classmark*. So, what these schemes have to do is to produce a schedule of classmarks.

Very likely the classmarks will be some synthetic combination of a subject matter together with entries from 'Auxiliary Tables' (which might contain Periods,

Places, Literary Form, etc.) This technique can be seen, to a greater or lesser degree (by design or by happenstance) in many traditional librarian schemes, such as Universal Decimal Classification (UDC), Bliss, Dewey Decimal Classification (DDC), Ranganathan's Colon Classification (CC) and even, mildly, in the Library of Congress Classification (LCC).

Synthetic schemes are often contrasted with *enumerative* or *enumerated* schemes which explicitly list all the classmarks, i.e. all the permitted combinations, in the schedule in advance of any actual classification of books. The Library of Congress Classification(LCC) is the standard example that is offered of an enumerative scheme: it is an enumerative schemes (with some synthetic elements). The labels come to the LCC cataloger pre-formed and the cataloger's task is to attach these ready-stamped labels to the books or IOs. This reduces the skill and initiative required of the cataloger, for the cataloger merely has to choose among alternatives as opposed to actually devising the labels. Of course, there is the occasional need for new classes, and some old classes may need revising in their terminology or some of the classes may just be no longer relevant. So an authoritative body meets regularly and revises LCC from one enumeration to another. Some of the individual compound types within an enumerated scheme can often be conceived of as synthesized types, for example, consisting of a period or a place put together with a subject, say a literary form subject like Poetry (and indeed, some of these enumerated schemes do allow genuine synthesis in small areas). Nevertheless, enumerated schemes are at heart pre-formed class or pre-formed label schemes.

*Synthetic* schemes are different in that they permit the cataloger both to construct the class or label and also then apply those created labels to IOs. A synthetic scheme gives the cataloger the building blocks (and acceptable ways of putting those blocks together) and the cataloger constructs classes (or class specifications) to meet needs.

One question that arises with synthetic classification is how to linearize the synthesized results, should that be required, for example, for shelving, for bibliographies, catalogs, and lists of books. As we have seen, there are a variety of ways to do it, and typically what the linearizations, and their supporting notation, will do is to collocate some compounds and scatter others. Much depends on what is desired. Typically the components of the synthesis will themselves individually have enumerations—so, for example, there is an ordered or sorted list of Places and a sorted list of Periods. And the synthetic components are put together in a certain order, *citation order*; for example, Places come before Periods in a compound (or, indeed, Periods before Places). Producing a composite enumeration from this is easy to do.

## 5.8.1 Dewey Decimal Classification

Librarians, real librarians, love the Dewey system, and they do so because it embodies some attractive features (features that were truly novel when they were first proposed). DDC is an enumerative scheme with some synthetic elements. Its great innovation lies with its Decimal Notation.

DDC, like most library classification hierarchies, is an ordered tree (not a plain or unordered tree, as most Aristotelian hierarchies are). And this is the locus of one of Dewey's great insights. The ordered tree is going to be linearized, using a shelving traversal, so that the books can be placed on shelves. The IOs are given a label (a classmark, a call number) using the favored notation. But if the underlying tree might get new nodes (i.e. new subjects) the existing applied notation for the linearization could be disturbed, forcing extensive revision. In fact, it would seem entirely possible that librarians might have to revise the classmarks on every book in their libraries. The prospect is daunting; call numbers are often written on the spines of books; and it might be that all those spines would need rewriting every time a new subject was added to the classification schedule. But Dewey realized that, in terms of order, between any two decimals, there is always a third one. So, for example, between the two decimals 0.34 and 0.35 there is the third decimal 0.341 (which is greater than the first one and lesser than the second). (In fact, there are infinitely many decimals between any two decimals, but we need not worry about that abundance.) And this means, as Dewey proposed, that if the books were given decimals as their classmarks, new subjects, and new classmarks, could be inserted anywhere in the schedule, and shelving, *without disturbing the existing numbers previously assigned to books*. This feature of a classification notation is known as *hospitality* (Foskett 1977, p. 178). The DDC Notation is hospitable thanks to Dewey's invention and choice of decimals for the notation.

This accommodation-by-insertion is always going to work, but it does not always have to work well. The First Edition Schedule for the Dewey system gave one page to the subject Logic and one page to the subject Engineering (and allocated ten 3 figure decimal numbers to each). Now, nearly a hundred years later, the current Schedule gives the same one page to Logic and yet 94 pages to Engineering (some of the Engineering decimal notations are now 10 digits long). What has happened here is that the originators thought that logic and engineering were both capable of similar growth as topics, but that conjecture was wrong. In tree terms, the classification tree has become very unbalanced.

The Dewey notation also allowed for relative shelf location. Many earlier systems, for example, the British Museum's, used absolute shelving. So, the shelves had slots, say A1, A2, A3, and those slot locations were allocated to the books that belonged to those slots. This has two problems. The library needs as much shelf length as there is total accumulated book length, even if half the books are not there (perhaps by virtue of being on loan to patrons). And, if a new book arrives which belongs in say A2 (thanks either to thematic or alphabetical considerations), all the other books, except A1 have to be re-allocated, not merely physically, but also by revising the statements of inventory record linking books to slots (and those reallocations could be 5 million books). The Dewey system does not bother with absolute slots on shelves. It shelves the books in their relative decimal order, and slides some along as books come and go. There is no need to change any notation on any books, or any other records.

The Dewey notation is also mildly *expressive* in as much as the decimals can identify paths or branches in the classification tree, for example

Insects has the call number 595.7
↓
Lepidoptera has the call number 595.78
↓
Butterflies has the call number 595.789

so the call number of the parent class or superclass can be obtained by dropping the last digit of the child's number. And there are many cases where the same (sub) notation is used across different branches. For example, the two digits 42 usually mean the country England; and so, whenever 42 appears within another number likely it will mean England. (The Universal Decimal Classification (UDC) system, based on Dewey, followed through on this.)

The DDC hierarchy is a relatively plain vanilla aspect-by-discipline hierarchy. So there is a Bacon style Tree of Knowledge, or Tree of Disciplines. And particular (atomic) topics, say, 'water' are classified by aspect, which will then scatter them across disciplines (which is why the Relative Index is needed to collect them up again).

The synthetic elements come from what essentially are Auxiliary Tables which cover form, period and place, and the like. For example, the two digits '03' on the end mean 'Encyclopedia'. So, if 123.456 was the classmark for a particular subject or topic, then 123.45603 would be an Encyclopedia on that very topic.

What is happening here is that the classification is being made impure. The classification purports to be by subject within a discipline, or one would think that it is, but form, period, place, language, etc. considerations are not usually subjects. However, all these classification are being done for retrieval, for the benefit of the Users and Patrons. And Users do occasionally want or need encyclopedias. To a degree, mixing in these Auxiliary Tables is a partial case of synthetic faceting.

A classification system of this type can be *broad*: meaning it has few, undiscriminating, coarse, classes or class numbers that have to span what might be slightly different subjects, or *narrow*: meaning that it has many classes and fine granulation. Professional librarians would probably say that DDC is a broad classification suitable for the public and public libraries. It is not best suited for research libraries. (Whether DDC is broad or narrow is not intrinsic to it. The number of subjects is largely in the control of a committee who can create them at will. Of course, the committee is mindful of the needs of the target User group, which, in this case, is the general public.)

## 5.8.2  Colon Classification

The Colon Classification (CC) was devised by Ranganathan starting in 1933, and it has had some acceptance and use in India. The CC scheme is both synthetic and faceted, and that makes it innovative and advanced. It has been

...one of the most influential classifications ever published, and the ideas incorporated in it have affected the whole of classification theory. (Foskett 1996, p. 315)

and

Until Ranganathan developed the theory of facet analysis, it was assumed that the way to build a classification was to take the most general topic and successively divide it into its parts. (Milstead 1984, p. 57)

And no less a person than Eugene Garfield (the main progenitor of citation indexing) has written

... Ranganathan is to library science what Einstein is to physics. (Garfield 1984, p. 46)

CC was intended to cover all of knowledge and to classify all kinds of IOs addressing all of that knowledge. Ranganathan was well aware that knowledge advanced and so the system also had to have the ability to accommodate new subjects. At the top level CC consisted of a tree of main classes (early versions had 42 main classes and that number increased as time went by). So, for example,

Literature
Linguistics
Philosophy
Religion
Psychology
Social Sciences
Education

were seven of the 42 main classes. Every class was a subclass of those 42. Thus far the system is very similar to many others, including DDC or LOC. The differences lie with what happens next. In a standard Aristotelian-Linnaean style of scheme, there would be further subdivisions, and yet further subdivisions, eventually ending with leaves. But CC does not do this. Instead it allows for the straight synthetic construction of subclasses of the main classes. Some background is needed to explain how that happens.

One of the main ideas of the system is the *Theory of Fundamental Categories*, which appears in the Fourth Edition of *Colon Classification*, 1952, and it is convenient to start the discussion at that point (see also (Ranganathan 1962)).

Ranganathan was inspired by the Meccano children's toy construction kit that he had seen in the Selfridges store in London (Ranganathan 1937; Meccano 2011). With Meccano, parts are bolted to other parts to produce elaborate constructions of bridges, cars, cranes, and other marvels. So too with classification, thought Ranganathan (Broughton 2007). There were atomic building blocks of concepts-or-classes, these were *isolates*. Isolates could be *special* isolates which are relative to their main classes or contexts; and, additionally, there were *common* isolates, which were available for use across classes. So, for example, Education is a main class, and Education has its own special isolates; and there were also common isolates such as those arising from dates or places. Effectively, isolates are modifiers that are used to construct the subclasses of, in this case, of Education. Atomic concepts-or-classes consisted of these isolates or atomic classes. Non-elemental basic classes consisted of constructions of the atoms. Each of the large number of basic classes of a classification was to be analyzed into its isolates, which were then synthesized back together again, to form the class, using the colon as a notational device. So, for example, a class might have the (schematic) notation

[Education] isolate 17: isolate 92: isolate 17

The Theory of Fundamental Categories suggested that these isolates could be partitioned into different categories. So, for example, a large number of isolates were periods or Times [T]; another large number were places or Space[S]. These Fundamental Categories were *facets*. And the values of the facets were called *foci*. The other three Fundamental Categories that were identified initially were Personality [P], Matter [M] and Energy [E].

Ranganathan's Fundamental Categories might be explained as follows

**Personality** distinguished the discipline, the objects of the study;
**Matter** is the material component of a subject;
**Energy** is any process (action, reaction, change, occurrent, growth, decay) component of a subject;
**Space** is the spatial location of a component of a subject.;
**Time** is the temporal location of a component of a subject.

So, for example, 'The decay of stone buildings in fifth century Rome', considered as a composite subject concept, would have buildings as its personality component, stone as its material concept, decay as its energy component, and space and time as specified. Notice also that the topic 'The decay of buildings' is also a perfectly good composite subject—it just does not use all of the facets in its definition.

So, at its most basic level, the simplest composite classes can be identified as though they were values in a 5 column table, where there are different tables for the different main classes. To shelve books, or to linearize the table, there is the need for a citation order and that was taken to be PMEST (personality-matter-energy-space-time), and that choice will collocate subjects and scatter places and times (and it orders from the 'Concrete' to the 'Abstract'). [There would also be the need to linearize the main classes, but that is not so important in as much as there was not an expectation that adjacent main classes should indicate contiguous or collocated subjects.]

From here on, it gets much more complicated, and there is a dizzying amount of detail. Single values of the categories often were not enough; for example, classes often had multiple 'Personalities'. In turn, the five PMEST categories themselves were not enough; for example, Matter was split into aspects (or different categories) of matter. Then few classes were basic; many more were composites out of the non-elemental—there were often subjects which consisted of comparisons of one thing on another, or influences of one thing on another. So many classes had several PMEST subclasses as components. In some cases, any class can be incorporated into another; as a sketched example, a subject like 'Teaching X' can have most any other subject substituted in for the placeholder X. In addition, at least some isolates could be in different Fundamental Categories in different contexts; for example, what we would call a form, say a Bibliography, can both be a true subject (which would make it a Personality isolate) and the form of another subject (which would make it a Matter isolate). This means that foci are isolates, but some isolates could be two different foci or be foci in two different categories. None of this detail is so-to-speak wrong or misguided; much of it goes with the territory. But the simple promise of faceted classification starts to fade. Finally the basic notational device of the colon is supplemented with periods, apostrophes, and parentheses.

In any thematic scheme there is the need for an index (or similar tool) to find where the classes are. With CC, some isolates appear under different main classes (for example, the concept University does), and some isolates can be foci of two different facets [for example, most any material (M) could itself be a subject or personality (P)]. So, index entry for a term could refer to multiple locations: some of these might amount to distributed relatives, others to disambiguated homographs.

How does a cataloger create a new class? There are new combinations of classes, of either isolates or non-elemental classes. Such combinations are new in the sense that, while the components may have been used elsewhere, the particular combination of those components had not. These could be new combinations of PMEST, or new combinations where one class is incorporated into another (e.g. 'Teaching X', 'School of Thought X'). There could be new isolates of Space or Time, which are simply new instances of places or periods that had no prior use. Of course, there might also be the need for absolutely brand new foci (or isolates), and even for absolutely brand new main classes. Effectively, neither of these are within the province of the working cataloger to create; it is for the ruling authority to create them with their publication of the schedules; and that is partially what the seven editions of *Colon Classification* were doing. So, apart from spaces and times, novelty for the working cataloger amounted to forming new combinations or syntheses out of the supplied building blocks.

## 5.9  Heterogeneous Classification Using Higher Order Types

In most standard classifications, all the nodes are types, and all the nodes are types of the *same* order, usually First Order. So all the nodes have as instances the same kinds of things as each other (tokens, animals, IOs, etc.).

It is possible, though, to set up hierarchies by instantiation, so that the tokens are instances of the leaves, and are thus the leaves are First Order Types; and the leaves themselves are *instances* of their parents, so that the parents are Second Order Types, and so on up the tree (thus the root might well be a Tenth Order Type). Not only is this possible, what it models is extremely common. The earlier Filing Cabinet, and Computer Directory Structure, examples are good illustrations of hierarchies by membership. With those, there are Folders and Items, and the

**Fig. 5.20** A tree depicting
instances of colors

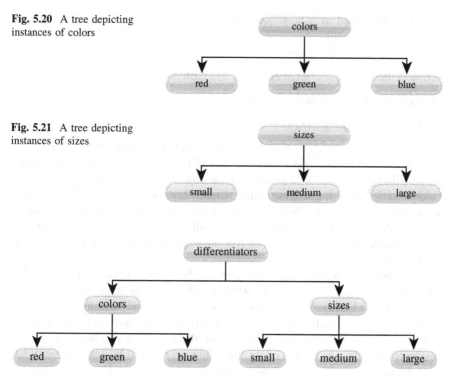

**Fig. 5.21** A tree depicting
instances of sizes

**Fig. 5.22** A tree of 'differentiators' of blocks

hierarchy is established by Items and Folders being within (i.e. being members of) other Folders. The Filing Cabinet itself could effectively be Tenth Order, meaning that it contains nine levels of nested Folders within it.

So, for example, there could be a predicate $Folder_6(x)$ that has the meaning 'x is in Folder number 6' and this could be used to make true or false statements like

$Folder_6(card_1)$ to mean 'Card1 is in Folder6'
$Folder_6(folder_5)$ to mean 'Folder5 is in Folder6'

And so on, to describe the hierarchy.

Trying to give a more abstract example of using Higher Order Types is a bit of a test for us and our understanding. But even children can do it. Ask a child for some colors and you might get (Fig. 5.20). We need to be careful with this diagram. The relationship between the red-type and the colors-type is *not* that of subtype to supertype (it is not the case that all red things are colors, a toy red fire engine is not a color); rather it is that the red-type itself has the (higher-order) type of being a color. This diagram is not a subtype-supertype classification; it is not a hierarchical classification. Rather it is a statement of instances or instantiation, but it is higher order instantiation. What this diagram is doing is taking what we have previously described as a horizontal level (for example, for Species). And then displaying it vertically.

In symbols, there are types

$r = \{x{:}Red(x)\},\ g = \{x{:}Green(x)\},\ y = \{x{:}Blue(x)\}$

and these types are instances of colors

Color(r), Color(g), Color(y)

To continue. Ask a child for some sizes and you might get (Fig. 5.21). And these two schemes can be combined. Suppose the child has a box of blocks to play with. Suppose these blocks come in different colors and different sizes. A child may well understand the following scheme to differentiate those blocks (Fig. 5.22). This tree is not using the subtype relation to connect nodes: it is ascending the type hierarchy. 'Colors' is a second order type that applies to types (and so too is 'sizes'). And 'differentiators' is a third order type that applies to the second order types 'colors' and 'sizes'.

A scheme like this might be used to provide 'horizontal access'. There could be a standard homogeneous subtype supertype classification (e.g. blocks->small-blocks medium-blocks large-blocks->red-small-blocks red-medium-blocks red-large-blocks green-small-blocks etc.) And this classification could be used to generate 'classification' and 'call' numbers to 'shelve' the blocks. But, overlaid on this, there could be a retrieval system that supported retrieval by color, retrieval by size, etc. i.e. horizontal or 'random' access. And the child, as User, may have an interest in different kinds of horizontal, or other direct, access (she might want to know who gave her the individual blocks, she might want to retrieve by donor).

# References

Berg J (1982) Aristotle's theory of definition. ATTI del Convegno Internazionale di Storia della Logica, San Gimignano, Bologna: CLUEB, 1983:19–30, 4–8 Dec 1982

Broughton V (2004) Essential classification. Neal-Schuman, New York

Broughton V (2006) The need for a faceted classification as the basis of all methods of information retrieval. Aslib Proc: New Inf Perspect 58(1/2):49–72

Broughton V (2007) Meccano, molecules, and the organization of knowledge: the continuing contribution of S. R. Ranganathan.. In: ISKO UK Open meeting, (proceedings) ISKO UK event Ranganathan revisited: facets for the future London, 5 Nov 2007

Buchanan B (1979) Theory of library classification. Clive Bingley, London

Date CJ (1977) An introduction to database systems, 2nd edn. Addison-Wesley, Reading, MA

Foskett AC (1977) Subject approach to information, 3rd edn. Clive Bingley, London

Foskett AC (1996) Subject approach to information, 5th edn. Facet Publishing, London

Fugmann R (1993) Subject analysis and indexing. Theoretical foundation and practical advice. Indeks Verlag, Frankfurt/Main

Garfield E (1984) A tribute to S.R. Ranganathan, the father of Indian library science. Part 2. In: Essays of an information scientist, vol 7. pp 45–49

Meccano (2011) Meccano Home Page. http://www.meccanouk.co.uk/. Accessed 10 Oct 2010

Mills J (2004) Faceted classification and logical division in information retrieval. Library Trends 52(3):541–570

Milstead JL (1984) Subject access systems: alternatives in design. Academic, Orlando

Ranganathan SR (1937) Prolegomena to library classification, 1st edn. The Madras Library Association, Madras (3rd edn 1967)

Ranganathan SR (1962) Facet analysis: fundamental categories. In: Chan LM, Richmond PA, Svenonius E (eds) Theory of subject analysis. Libraries Unlimited, Littleton CO, pp 88–93

Shera JH (1965) What lies ahead in classification. In: libraries and the organization of knowledge. Archon, Hamden, CT, pp 129–142

# Chapter 6
# Topic Annotation

## 6.1 Indexing Languages

We have a particular interest in topics or subjects and in annotations using those topics. Retrieval by subject is all important in librarianship (as Cutter and others emphasized), and, independently, the notion of subject is at the core of shelving classification schemes A collection of such topics is a (subject) indexing language. In addition, there are questions of what topics are permitted and what the links between them are i.e. what are the relations between the topics: what are the DAGs of topics.

Let us remind ourselves of the Triangle of Meaning (Fig. 6.1): In the last chapter, dealing with classification, the focus was with the referents or denotation—a museum is interested in which of its holdings are coins and which are sarcophagi. But with subject annotation the focus moves to the other two vertices of the Triangle. A subject indexing language can use the Symbol Vertex; in which case, it would typically use strings as its annotations and the ensemble of annotations would be called *subject headings*. Alternatively, although this seems rare in practice, it could use the Concept Vertex and then the annotations would be concepts or types and they could be called *subject concepts* or *topics*. We prefer the latter. With this alternative, the annotations are types or concepts—the IOs that are annotated do not fall under the concepts, they are not in the denotation of the concepts, rather the subject concepts identify their topics.

Each IO can be assigned more than one annotation (this is to recognize that IOs can be polytopical). The assigned topics on a specific individual IO are in the nature of a list of topics, and some systems, for example, MeSH (the Medical Subject Headings) put an emphasis on the order in the list; in particular, the first topic on an IO signifies its main topic or subject, and the others on the same IO are of subsidiary importance.

Systems of subject topics, headings, or concepts, can be enumerative or synthetic. An enumeration is a pre-formed and pre-defined finite list of annotations, whereas a synthetic scheme gives a recipe for producing annotations. As an example, the

M. Frické, *Logic and the Organization of Information*,
DOI: 10.1007/978-1-4614-3088-9_6,
© Springer Science+Business Media New York 2012

**Fig. 6.1** The triangle of
meaning

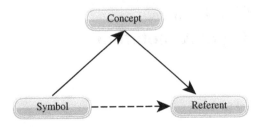

Library of Congress Subject Headings (LCSH) is largely an enumerative scheme (it
does have some synthetic elements). The present LCSH has about 320,000 headings
(and that core number is growing by virtue of an oversight committee which meets
regularly and makes revisions to the approved list). Synthetic schemes are different in
that they permit the cataloger both to construct the annotation or label and also then
apply those created labels to IOs. One marked difference between synthetic and
enumerative is the number of predefined possibilities that are required. In contrast
with LCSH's list of 300,000 or more subject entries, a synthetic scheme, with just
1,000 atomic terms can generate 1,000,000 two concept compounds straight off
(i.e. 1,000 × 1,000). Thus, synthetic schemes are more flexible, economical,
and powerful (and they treat the cataloger as an adult).

We already have an extensive infrastructure for discussing types, concepts, or
classes; for example, we observed that the class of tropical forests is a *superimposed* class. It is convenient to carry over that classification into classifying
headings, labels, topics, subjects, or tags. So, for example, the IO subject heading
'tropical forests' might be described as a superimposed subject heading. And this
is useful in allowing that annotation to be related to others, for example, to the
annotations 'tropical regions' and 'forests' (We should note that there is going to
be a semi-intentional (i.e. hard to avoid) looseness or ambiguity in the discussion.
Almost always what is being talked about here are the subjects i.e. the concepts,
and not what those concepts denote. Librarians, as librarians, are interested in
books, or IOs, about forests, not in forests themselves).

## 6.2  Canonical Identification of Topics: 'Notation'

Concepts, topics, or intensions need a canonical means of identification for the
purposes of discussion. We cannot talk about (or index) particular topics without
individual names for those topics.

Ranganathan discussed this under the heading of the 'Notational Plane'. He
wanted each topic to have a single notation that identified it so there would be a
1–1 correspondence between a topic and its notation. Further, since many topics
were synthesized compounds of other topics he wanted the notation for the
compounds to be, in some sense, a construction out of the notation for its constituents (nowadays this is called *expressive*). An analogy here is to chemistry; the

chemical notation for water, $H_2O$ is made out of the notation for hydrogen, H, and for oxygen, O, and it shows how the components fit together to make the compound. Other theorists of classification and classification systems, particularly synthetic ones, subscribe to similar ideas. In the Bliss classification system, the notation for compound classes usually shows the relations to the constituents. Interestingly enough, the theorists were also aware of the cross language capabilities of a notation—instead of having to translate the English phrases surrounding LCC, or Bliss, or DDC into French (or German, or Chinese) all that was needed was the classmark, the notation. For example, Broughton writes

> In principle, notation provides a language independent means of retrieval and exchange. (Broughton 2010a, p. 271)

As the reader will have concluded by now, we favor ordinary First Order Predicate Logic as the artificial language of topics. Topics are concepts, concepts are types, and types are intensional abstractions. Topics are just built in logic.

Complex or compound concepts are being constructed out of simple concepts. But there is no assumption here of a universal bedrock of atomic concepts (Spårck Jones 2007). The notion of atomicity or granularity is relative to an audience and the purpose at hand. What are atomic concepts for schoolchildren in a school library, for ordinary citizens in a public library, or for aircraft engineers in an aircraft construction facility, may well all be different. This is a matter of ontology—different ontologies usually will yield different atomic concepts. But then, with the atomic concepts in hand, the compounds can be constructed.

To a degree, librarians, and many of the rest of us, are familiar with some concept building, or something akin to concept building. When keywords are composed in a postcoordinated search entry using Boolean operations (for example, searching for 'academic library' using 'academic' Boolean-ANDED together with 'library'), in a sense concepts are being put together or composed together. But, first of all, such a composition is working at the level of expressions or signs, not at the level of concepts. And then Boolean operations themselves are limited as concept constructors. The abstractions in use here permit Boolean operations but they also permit quantifiers, types, higher order types, relations, etc. This is much more general than plain truth functional propositional Boolean operations.

Intensional abstractions provide transparency for structure. So types in large part reveal of their own subtypes and supertypes, and this, of itself, creates much of the topic graph or DAG.

## 6.3   Named Entities, 'Fido'-Fido

London, Napoleon, and Mount Everest, should certainly be able to be topics. An IO can be on the subject of Mount Everest. But there are some views of meaning that would not consider a name like 'Mount Everest' to have any connection with concepts or the Triangle of Meaning.

There is what is known as the 'Fido'-Fido theory of proper names. According to this theory, it is supposed that the name 'Fido' names the dog Fido directly. So there is no such thing as, and no need for, the Triangle of Meaning for names and named entities. The names connect with their referents directly: there is no need for concepts.

So, with the 'Fido'-Fido view there could be a subject heading 'Napoleon', and, of course, Napoleon himself, but there is no concept Napoleon and no subject-concept-annotation Napoleon. This theory also has other effects, principally, for us, that there can be no type hierarchies with the Napoleon concept in them such as

Animal
Man
Frenchman
Corsican
Napoleon [leaf]

because there is no Napoleon concept, there is only the named entity (person) Napoleon. Instead, the concept Corsican would have to be the leaf and Napoleon an instance of that type.

Animal
Man
Frenchman
Corsican [leaf]
Napoleon [instance]

But, actually, the 'Fido'-Fido theory does is not correct. An initial motivation for the Triangle of Meaning was that words might not refer; there might not be any moon for 'moon' to refer to, and there definitely are no unicorns for 'unicorn' to refer to. But names, proper names, seem exactly the same: 'Santa Claus' seems to be a perfectly good proper name of an individual named entity, but there is no Santa Claus for 'Santa Claus' to refer to.

In sum, we can, and will, use the Triangle of Meaning with named entities. There is the thing, a particular, Mount Everest, and the individual concept Mount Everest, and the former instantiates the latter. (There is also the heading 'Mount Everest'.)

But care is needed. Named entities are a special case. The Napoleon concept or type is a subtype of the Corsican type. But Napoleon himself is not a subtype of the Corsican type. He is an instance of the Corsican type (and an instance of the Napoleon type).

## 6.4  Classical Enumerated Subject Heading Lists

Librarians have been using alphabetical lists of subject headings certainly for a hundred years or more (Cutter's *Rules for a Dictionary Catalog* is about 1895). Some features of such lists are prominent. First, there is the choice of heading strings as the form of the annotation. This is the choice to use the Symbol Vertex of the Triangle of Meaning. It invites difficulties over synonyms and homographs. There are difficulties, and cataloging theorists have faced them. They introduce (or define) two notions: *uniform* headings and *unique* headings. Uniform headings occur when each subject has only one heading (i.e. there are no synonyms); and unique headings occur when each heading labels only one subject (i.e. there are no homographs). (There is something of a generalization going on here in the presentation. Synonyms and homographs are properties that apply largely to single words, but subject headings can be multiple word phrases. Nevertheless, a uniform and unique heading phrase is the precise analog of a phrase that is both without 'synonym' phrases and which is not a 'homograph' phrase.) Good subject heading lists need to have both uniform and unique headings. Often, some of these difficulties are mitigated by the incorporation of thesaurus support into the heading lists.

Second, the presentation of the heading lists is alphabetical. This is to favor erratic alphabetical collocations over trees or DAGs of topics (and hence Cutter's complaint about 'absurd proximity'). Alphabetical order requires consideration of filing order and citation order. That said, the computer has made many of these problems less serious than they were. For example, consider the topic of modern art and possible subject headings of 'Art, Modern' and 'Modern Art'. The principle of uniform headings would have required the choice of only one of these. What would have been chosen here depends on desired citation order, but then, in an alphabetical list, one would occur among the As and the other among the Ms. If there were 300,000 of so headings, it would be the easiest thing in the world for a User not to find the Modern Art heading. However, with a computer the story is entirely different because it is likely that what the software will do is to carry out a keyword search *within* the subject headings; so, for example, it will find the word 'modern' wherever it occurs in a heading (and possibly also 'art' where it occurs, or where the two words occur in combination). At a stroke the problem of the combination of alphabetical (filing) order and citation order is pretty well done away with. If a User looks up Library of Congress Subject Headings in a physical book or books, in the so-called Red Books, their task is many times more difficult than looking up the same LCSH Headings online (thanks to the device of keyword-in-heading search).

A heading list is to most intents and purposes just like a list of the keys for a back of the book index. And index terms usually are controlled and using such thesaurus devices of broader and narrow terms (i.e. subterms of terms) and preferred forms.

What is also usual is that an alphabetical list is a forest of short trees. There are many top-level entries, i.e. many trees. But while the roots of those trees might have some children (and those children further children) they do not have many distant descendants. A back of the book index might have headings, some sub-headings, and some sub-sub-headings, but it is almost unknown for a back of the book index to have sub-headings nested to a depth of, say, ten. Also the individual 'trees' really are going to be trees; there will be no multiple parents i.e. no multiple broader terms ascending in generality.

**Table 6.1** Results of a
search for 'War'

| Label | Identifier |
|---|---|
| War | sh85145114 |
| War (Philosophy) | sh85145144 |
| War—Economic aspects | sh85145116 |
| War—Mythology | sh85145122 |
| War—Quotations, maxims, etc. | sh85145125 |
| War—Religious aspects—Buddhism | sh85145129 |
| War—Religious aspects—Christianity | sh85145131 |
| War tax stamps | sh851451226 |

Thus, alphabetical lists of enumerated subject headings do have some characteristics (and some characteristic shortcomings).

### 6.4.1 An Example: Library of Congress Subject Headings (LCSH)

The most widely used and well-known collection of subject headings is the Library of Congress Subject Headings (LCSH). It has its origins with James C. M. Hanson around 1900. Supposedly it adopted a 'pragmatic' approach, as opposed to the theoretical approach of Cutter, Hanson's intellectual predecessor. However, it is influenced by the earlier work of Cutter, particularly with, for example, ideas of using common words and common-folk natural language word order. LCSH is a pre-coordinated, and largely enumerated, controlled vocabulary, alphabetical list of headings. As of 2011, there are 317,000 entries (but the synthetic elements allow that number to be increased at will). ((Broughton 2004, 2010b) are useful sources on LCSH.)

Typically, the headings are applied by human catalogers to books or IOs. A book can have up to about eight associated subject headings; although the average number of headings, through the items cataloged by the Library of Congress, is 1.5; so, in practice, books do not have many subject headings. (Catalogers use a 20% rule. If 20%, or more, of a book is on a topic, then a heading for that topic needs to be added to the heading list.)

As an example of subject headings, an online search for the keyword 'War' among the headings will return a fuller version of the following edited list (Table 6.1). The headings have the form

    Main heading
    Main heading-subdivision
    Main heading-subdivision-subdivision

So there are plain headings (for example, 'War'), and structured headings (for example 'War—Mythology').

**Table 6.2** The homograph
'Atlas'

| Label | Identifier |
|---|---|
| Atlas (Vertebra) | sh85009226 |
| Atlas (Missile) | sh85009225 |
| Atlas (Greek deity) | sh2002009664 |

Homographs are disambiguated by *qualifiers* in brackets (as in 'War' and 'War (Philosophy)'). A better example of homograph disambiguation is provided by 'Atlas' (Table 6.2). Where the topmost vertebra is disambiguated from a type of guided missile and a Greek god (and there is standard lead-> in-preferred-term support for synonyms).

There is only one heading per subject (i.e. *uniform* headings). For example, 'Butterflies' is a heading, but 'Rhopalocera' is not; however, a search for the latter will direct the User to the former. And the compound headings (and sub-headings) are usually pre-coordinated (for example, 'War tax stamps').

Some synthesis is permitted. For example, there are 'free floating' subdivisions such as 'Economic conditions' which essentially are patterns which can be used with certain named headings to form, say, 'London—Economic Conditions', 'Paris—Economic Conditions'.

Somewhat similarly, a cataloger can append subheadings like 'Dictionary' or 'Encyclopedia' to existing headings, for example, to 'Astronautics' to form 'Astronautics—Dictionary'. This latter practice is distinctly odd in that 'Astronautics—Dictionary' is not a subject or topic, it is a mixture of a subject ('Astronautics') and a form or form of presentation ('Dictionary'). A form is not a subject or topic, it is not what an IO is about; rather, it is what an IO *is*. It is worth drawing attention to these 'form headings', which might be characterized as being a useful inelegance. There are many 'forms' of literature: here are twenty or so of them (from a choice of about 600)

Abstracts
Almanacs
Atlases
Bibliography
Book reviews
Case studies
Catalogs
Dictionaries
Encyclopedias
Handbooks, manuals, etc.
Indexes
Inventories
Maps
Methods
Nomenclature
Outlines, syllabi, etc.
Quotations

**Table 6.3**  The entry for 'War memorials'

| |
|---|
| **War Memorials** |
| URI |
| <http://id.loc.gov/authorites/sh85145184#concept> |
| **Type** |
| Topical Term |
| **Alternate Labels** |
| >War monuments |
| **Broader Terms** |
| >Art and war |
| >Memorials |
| >Monuments |
| **Narrower Terms** |
| >Battlefield monuments |
| >Military trophies |
| **Related Terms** |
| >Military parks |
| >Soldiers' monuments |

Reviews
Software
Statistics
Tables of contents
Textbooks

What is important or useful about instances of these forms is that they are knowledgeable or insightful guides to other literature, to other IOs. When a User seeks IOs on Astronautics, likely that User will look for IOs with the subject heading 'Astronautics' and see what results. But there is another way: many Users, apart from experts, might do well to first find an Encyclopedia on Astronautics (which, after all, contains the distilled wisdom of many others) and to use that as a stepping-stone to what they want. LCSH enables and facilitates this retrieval practice by having form headings (including Astronautics—Encyclopedia).

Form headings are useful. But they are inelegant in as much as they are not subject headings yet they appear in subject heading lists. (Nowadays, with good computer support, forms of IOs could and would be kept separate from topics; they would be independently searchable fields or 'facets' for example, Faceted Application of Subject Terminology (FAST) does this (Chan and O'Neill 2010).)

At first glance, the LCSH is a forest of trees, which can have depth of up to three. The forest is generated from the headings and subheadings, and the headings and subheadings are short strings. So, for example, 'War—Religious Aspects' has as a broader subject 'War' and 'War—Religious Aspects—Buddhism' as one of its narrower subjects.

About 1986, thesaurus support was added but the implementation of the thesaurus is curious (which is not to say that the thesaurus itself might not be good and useful). What the thesaurus does is part expected, and part unexpected. Here is its entry for 'War memorials' (Table 6.3). We expect to see Broader and Narrower

Terms, which we do. But 'War memorials' is a top level heading, which means that it does not lie under any broader headings or subjects. It is a precoordinated phrase which, as it happens, does not have any associated subheadings. So, within the forest of headings this does not have any narrower subjects. But, yet, the thesaurus tells us that 'Battlefield monuments' and 'Military trophies' are Narrower Terms (in this context this means narrower subjects). 'War memorials' also has Broader Terms in the thesaurus, in fact three of them (i.e. multiple parents). This means that the thesaurus subject node structure is a DAG not a forest. We like this, but let us recognize that it is new and different. It is a layer on top. There is LCSH dating from about 1900, and LCSH-plus-thesaurus dating from about 1986.

There is another oddity here (that Mary Dykstra has drawn attention to, indeed fulminated against) (Dykstra 1988). Trees and standard thesaurus support would normally accompany atomic concepts or atomic terms. This is because there needs to be only one parent and only one broader term, going up the thesaurus tree. But many of the LCSH headings are actually compounds. For example, the LCSH heading 'Television and children' is a compound which, thinking freely about it, might have 'Mass media and children' and 'Television', 'Children' as parents (in fact, LCSH gives it 'Children' as its sole broader heading). Dyskstra's argument is that thesauri require atomic terms, and since many LCSH headings are lengthy phrases, which are compounds, LCSH headings cannot be proper traditional thesauri entries. This is correct, but we favor generalizing thesauri (as sketched in Sect. 2.14.2). A better analysis of a heading like 'Television and children' is available by first moving to the Concept Vertex to see just what kind of concept it is. Clearly it is not a superimposed, intersective, type. It is not

$$\{x:\text{Television}(x)\&\text{Children}(x)\}$$

It is not the topic about those things which are both televisions and children. Rather it is about, roughly, the interactions between television and children, covering the effects of television on children, the appearances of children on television, and more besides. In which case, the requisite topic is

$$\{x:x = \text{Interaction(children,television)}\}$$

When this is taken into a DAG of topics, logically speaking there can be broadening or narrowing on the interactions, the children, and the television. So, returning to actual string headings, 'media and children', 'television and young people', etc. might be broader headings and 'the effect of television on children', 'children appearing on television', etc. might be narrower headings. The actual LCSH suggestion of 'children' as a broader heading would not be correct as a logical link. However, links in topic DAGs can have a variety of origins, for example, from propaedias. It could be that a patron or student wishing to look at items tagged with 'television and children' would be helped by having those items tagged 'children' as being a broadening of the topic. Really, in this case, 'television and children' is just not a good choice as a heading. Patrons would be better served either by post coordinating on 'television' AND 'children' or string-in-string searching for ('television' AND 'children') among the other LCSH headings. In sum, Mary Dykstra's criticisms are exactly right, but it is possible develop LCSH in such a way as to answer the criticisms.

It is often said that LCSH has no theory and no principles behind its design and construction (see for example, (Chan 1986)). That it has no theory does not of itself mean that the result is bad. (LCSH used to have many eccentricities, it has fewer now. There are hundreds of publications on how poor LCSH is (Fischer 2005; Kirtland and Cochrane 1982; Shubert 1992; Berman 1971, 1993)).

## 6.5  Synthetic Annotations

Synthetic schemes provide building blocks and rules. For example, in an enumerated scheme a topic label might be 'red Ford Explorer', but a synthetic scheme needs to have some means of separating acceptable labels from unacceptable ones, e.g. are any or all of 'red Ford Explorer', 'Ford red Explorer', 'Explorer Ford red' proper labels? (It also needs a semantics for clarity on the inter-label relations.)

So, to be marginally more formal about the building block metaphor, what a synthetic annotation system should have is a vocabulary (the building blocks) and a grammar (the ways of constructing with the blocks). To produce synthetic labels, there would first be a need to state the vocabulary, say, as a simple example

Eighteenth Century [kind = Period],
Nineteenth Century [kind = Period],
French [kind = Place]
German [kind = Place]

And then a grammar to lay out the syntax of well formed topics, say

<a single vocabulary item of kind Period>|
<a single vocabulary item token of kind Place>|
<a single vocabulary item of kind Period><a single vocabulary item token of kind Place>

and that would permit the synthesis of well-formed topics like 'Nineteenth Century', 'Eighteenth Century French', but not topics like 'French Eighteenth Century' (which would be ill-formed under this grammar, because the period needs to come before the place).

A vocabulary and a grammar would yield the syntax for the type-labels in a synthetic scheme. There would be a need also for a semantics; that is, a specification of how the types relate to each other (as subtopics, supertopics, sibling topics, and the like).

A synthetic scheme may allow infinitely many types, or only a finite number of types, or, indeed, even a small number of types (the above example one permits 10 types only). In a sense, a synthetic scheme is a 'virtual' scheme—there is no special reason to write out, or enumerate, its classes as a whole. Each individual type is produced when it is needed for use, when there is a token or IO for it to be attached to.

Producing (basic) synthetic topics using symbolic logic is straightforward at an intellectual level. The starting point is a list of acceptable predicates, or conditions, for example

EighteenthC(x),
NineteenthC(x),
Fiction(x),
Drama(x),
French(x),
German(x)

[Of course, in a realistic case this list might run to thousands of conditions, but that does not affect the principles being explained.] And then each of the types, or intensional abstractions, the grammar, is formed by logical synthesis of these predicates to produce any well formed open sentence and its associated intensional abstraction, as examples

{x: EighteenthC(x)& Fiction(x)}.
{x: Drama(x)& German(x)}

This provides a formal grammar to determine the synthetic topics.

The synthesis in logic does not have to consist solely of ANDING components. Full Boolean operations are permitted to form the open sentence of the intensional abstract, and, indeed, further predicate logic operations that go beyond truth functional connectives. For example

{x:NineteenthC(x)&
~French(x)&
Drama(x)&
∃y(Dancing(y)&Allegorical(y)&Contains(x,y)}

would be a synthesized topic for 'Nineteenth century non-French Drama, with some allegorical dancing in it'.

As examples, here is a list of some non-elemental composite topics

Hibernating animals,
The hibernation of animals,
The fur of animals,
Comparing mammals and fish,
Statistics for biologists,
Statistics for chemists,
Chemistry for biologists,
The influence of man on grasslands

And, as an analysis: 'Hibernating animals' is a plain superimposed type. 'Comparisons' and 'Influences' are going to be topics which depend on (usually two) other types; so they might be constructed using functions, say

$\{x: x = comparison(man,fish)\}$
$\{x: x = influence(man,grasslands)\}$

or by relations, say

$\{x: Comparison(x,man,fish)\}$
$\{x: Influence(x,man,grasslands)\}$

'The hibernation of animals' and 'The fur of animals' are function types

$\{x: x = hibernationOf(animals)\}$
$\{x: x = furOf(animals)\}$

And 'Statistics for biologists' is

$\{x: x = forBiologists(statistics)\}$

In sum, generalized advanced synthesis, in particular logical synthesis centered on the construction of intensional abstractions, may take us a very long way with producing topics.

### 6.5.1 An Example of a Synthetic Subject Heading List

We are going to have to cheat a little here. Any controlled vocabulary thesaurus is, or can be, a subject heading list and there are hundreds, if not thousands, of thesauri (and there are international standards governing their construction). Basically, many fields of study, research areas, manufacturing and commercial enterprises, and so forth, produce thesauri to standardize the terms in their areas of concern. Many of these thesauri are synthetic. However, most of the synthetic ones are also faceted (and those are going to be discussed shortly). Synthetic schemes which are not faceted are rare. We can certainly fake one, though.

Prehistory is that subject matter studied by archaeologists, anthropologists, and others. It includes the Iron Age, the Bronze Age etc. One central interest here is the period or periods of study. Simple subject headings for these could be constructed from the pattern

xxx-yyy BCE
   where xxx and yyy are any natural numbers
   with xxx being larger than yyy

So

7,000-6,000 BCE
200,000-1,000 BCE and
100-10 BCE

are all subject headings. This imagined scheme is synthesized, non-faceted, and it has infinitely many headings.

## 6.6 Facets

One form of synthetic *topic* construction is the very important *faceted* construction of topics or *faceted* classification. And, maybe, as theoreticians have been telling us for sixty years, faceted classification is the only kind we need (Broughton 2006; Classification Research Group 1955). Faceted classification is typically considered to be a synthetic classification consisting of orthogonal facets which themselves are composed individually either of exclusive foci or of a hierarchy of foci. (Broughton 2004, 2006; Buchanan 1979; Ranganathan 1959, 1967; Wilson 2006; Gnoli 2008; Vickery 1960, 2008, 1966; La Barre 2006, 2010; Foskett 1996; Foskett 2003; Gardin 1965). All faceted classifications are (or should be) synthetic, but not all synthetic classifications are faceted (for example, a synthesis of a classification with itself is not faceted). Also there is what one might call real faceted classification (of subjects, concepts, types, or topics), as opposed to ersatz faceted classification (of things, or attributes of things). Ersatz faceted classification was discussed earlier in Sect. 5.6.

Faceted classification is widespread nowadays, in the small, so to speak. In the large, there are probably only two examples of traditional IO classification schemes which are faceted at their core: Ranganathan's Colon Classification (Ranganathan 1960) and the Bliss Classification of Mills, Broughton and the Classification Research Group (Mills and Broughton 1977). Both these schemes recognize that there are kinds of concepts. Categorizing concepts is also the approach of many others (Austin 1984; Foskett 1977; Lambe 2007; Morville and Rosenfeld 2006; Willetts 1975; Vickery 1960, 1966; Cheti and Paradisi 2008; Slavic 2008). The notion of a kind of concept or category of concept employs higher-order properties or higher-order types. It is a higher-order classification of types, not a first order classification of items or things.

### 6.6.1 Real Faceted Topics

Real faceted classification concerns subjects (or concepts or types or topics) not things (or attributes of things). Its origins are from puzzles concerning the nature of subject nodes in discipline-based Trees of Knowledge. So, for example, if we consider a Bacon style Tree of Knowledge, which is organized by discipline, there are branches (or part branches) for such disciplines as Physics, Chemistry, etc. [All the older main and traditional library classifications have this style.]

Then Paul Otlet and Henri La Fontaine, the founders of Universal Decimal Classification (UDC), and Ranganathan, the originator of Colon Classification (CC) noticed a few different features.

Almost all subject concepts (or types or nodes) were compound or composite concepts.

So there were, for example, 'concrete bridges', wooden bridges', 'history of bridges', 'electromagnetic radiation', 'infra-red radiation', 'radiation physics for engineers', 'children's literature', all of which are compound see also (Classification Research Group 1955). Then

> Many of the component concepts recurred in different compound concepts.

This was especially prominent with (historical) Periods, and (geographical) Places—for example, Eighteenth century, Nineteenth century, France, Britain. So, in effect, there is repetition and scattering of components among the composites (for example, the period 'eighteenth century' appears in different places in typical standard all-in-one schedules).

Finally

> The (atomic) component concepts themselves were in different categories. They were not as a whole homogeneous, they were heterogeneous. They could be grouped or partitioned into different kinds.

This suggests using a synthetic classification, using constructs with zero or components from the different categories or kinds of concepts.

That, essentially, is faceted classification—synthetic classification from different categories of elemental, or atomic, component concepts.

There are details. Instance concepts of a facet kind are sometimes called *foci*; and sometimes facets are described as being *arrays of foci*. What are to be the facets? As mentioned, Ranganathan wanted 5 facets, the CRG 13. This is a matter for the individual subject areas or disciplines. Most catalogers would be wary of taking on all of knowledge. Instead, they would restrict their interest to some disciplines or subdisciplines; then Facet Analysis (to be explained shortly) would indicate which facets were required. What is to be the structure of the individual facets? The standard view is that the facets be an exclusive and exhaustive array or an Aristotelian hierarchy, with a choice of no more than one focus from each facet (like the physical socks, which can, for example, be long or short but not both long and short) (Broughton 2006; Wilson 2006). We will discuss this requirement again, below.

What are the advantages of faceted classification? That there are composite subjects, composed across facets, simply seems to be the way most discipline based subjects have developed. Thus faceted classification makes a virtue out of this necessity, by allowing synthesis. This lets the classification be massively flexible in what it can accommodate. And it allows navigation of classified items to be refined and enlightened by the facets. The CRG group, in their 1955 paper, argue that the single most important relation to assist the information retriever with subject searches is that which connects a subject up a classification hierarchy to its parent and down a classification hierarchy to its children. However, if a subject like

> Eighteenth Century History

is located in a non-synthetic schedule, i.e. in a once-for-all enumerative schedule, its parents and children will have a considerable accidental quality to them. But if we can pull out

Eighteenth Century

on its own, and the entirely independent

History

on its own. And look at their parents and children in the different facets, the search can be much more focused.

## 6.6.2 Orthogonal Facets and Exclusive Foci?

Facets are going to be orthogonal or independent. This means that, when constructing a synthesized value, the choice of a focus from one facet has no repercussions whatsoever for combination with a focus from another facet. So, as a simple schematic for an example, if we have Periods and Subjects

Periods [Facet 1] = {eighteenth century, nineteenth century}
Subjects [Facet 2] = {History, Geography}

The choice of eighteenth century from Facet 1 neither compels, nor excludes, a particular choice from Facet 2—it can be combined with either History or Geography.

However, within a facet the foci are *not* typically assumed to be orthogonal or independent. In fact, they are assumed to be dependent. Choice of one focus precludes or affects choice of others. Broughton conceives of the foci as being an enumerated exclusive and exhaustive array, or an enumerated Aristotelian hierarchy, with a choice of no more than one focus from each facet (like a choice of attribute for each of the physical socks, in the Broughton pedagogical example) (Broughton 2006). And Anthony Foskett and Travis Wilson think the same (Wilson 2006; Foskett 1977) (See also (Vickery 2008).)

However, under one understanding of this, it does not seem to be desirable. It does not seem desirable for two separate reasons: first that the foci are enumerated, and second that they be 'exclusive'. The hierarchy for a facet should, perhaps, be Aristotelian or Librarian-Aristotelian, in order to give distinct labels for the foci. But shouldn't we permit synthesis of foci within a facet? Here is an example

Eighteenth Century History
Eighteenth Century Geography
Nineteenth Century History

are composite subjects synthesized from different facets. But presumably we would want also to have the ability to form subjects like

Eighteenth Century and Nineteenth Century History
Eighteenth Century History and Geography

and this requires synthesis within a facet (as well as the synthesis across facets). Neither Broughton nor Wilson would permit this because, for example, they hold that the choice of the focus eighteenth century specifically excludes the choice of nineteenth century.

Wilson offers an argument for his view. It first rests on his conception of facet analysis (which addresses mainly ersatz faceting rather than real faceting). Wilson suggests we start here with a 'tag soup', say

Eighteenth Century History and Geography, Eighteenth Century History, Nineteenth Century, Eighteenth Century Geography, Nineteenth Century History, Geography etc

And we discard the 'compounds', extracting only the 'atoms', and that leaves, say

Eighteenth Century, History, Geography, Nineteenth Century

These are still a 'soup'. There is not considered to be any order or structure here, yet. But suppose we wish to extract a structure, in particular a facet structure. One way we can do it is by asking 'Which atoms can be combined with which other atoms?' The ones that can be combined are independent, orthogonal, and belong in different facets. The ones that cannot be combined are dependent and belong as foci in the same facet. So, for example, if we said eighteenth century can be combined with Geography and, separately, with History, but it could not be combined with nineteenth century , and so on, that would generate for us the example Period and Subject facet classification we were using earlier. There is no compulsion to allow that particular kind of combination. We could allow eighteenth century to be combined with nineteenth century (and with History and with Geography), and so on, but that would generate a different faceted scheme, one with four facets each with one focus, namely

Facet 1 = {Eighteenth Century}
Facet 2 = {Nineteenth Century}
Facet 3 = {History}
Facet 4 = {Geography}

It is up to us what we do. However, the distinction between facets and foci is to be made on the basis of what is independent and what is dependent. And so foci, within a facet, have to be exclusive because they are defined to be exactly that.

Wilson's argument is certainly an argument, and he uses the view it embodies to generate faceted classifications by algorithm. And if the candidate labels were bare meaningless labels it would be a reasonable argument. If the atomic tag soup were

DF2, 27, Km + ,*,Wef

and we wanted to establish a faceted scheme of these, what Wilson suggests is presumably exactly right. But, in the realistic cases we encounter, the tags in the soup do have meanings, and they do have kinds, *independently of what can and cannot be combined*. For example, in the soup

Eighteenth Century, History, Geography, Nineteenth Century

two of the labels (or what they signify) are time periods. And we can use the kinds to do the facet analysis (which is exactly what Ranganathan and the CRG did). So Wilson's argument is not definitive. We can combine foci, if we think that desirable.

Anthony Foskett writes

> The foci within a particular facet should be *mutually exclusive*; that is, we cannot envisage a composite subject which consists of two foci from the same facet. We cannot have the seventeenth century 1800s, or German English, or copper aluminum, but we *can* have composite subjects consisting of combinations of foci from different facets: English novels, seventeenth century German literature, analysis of copper, heat treatment of aluminium. (Foskett 1977, p. 148)

This seems mistaken. An *entity*, a metal spoon, perhaps, made entirely of a single metal, cannot be both made entirely of copper and entirely of aluminum; but a subject (a subject matter, a concept, a type) presumably can encompass copper and aluminium—isn't *heat treatment of aluminium and copper* a subject? [There may just be some lack of clarity of expression here in the texts that are quoted. Foskett, and Broughton for that matter, will be well aware that the synthetic operations of UDC in effect permit the forming composites from foci within the same facet.]

The issue with Broughton concerns mainly the nomenclature 'exclusive'. Broughton is not entirely consistent on this (admittedly somewhat esoteric) point. She states

> An important thing to notice about the members of an array [i.e. the foci] is that they are all mutually exclusive classes (Broughton 2006, p. 54).

And

> ... because all the terms within a facet come into the same category ... the relationship between them will be those of a hierarchy... (Broughton 2006, p. 54, 2004, p. 270)

But if the terms are a hierarchy, for example {human, man, woman} they need not be mutually exclusive classes—man and human are not exclusive classes, one is a subtype of the other (a man is a human). (She might mean that they are exclusive in the shelving traversal Librarian-Aristotelian style of using internal nodes for classification.)

Broughton favors enumerative foci—fixed-in-stone hierarchical schemes for the foci—and synthesis between facets. But why not permit synthesis for everything?

A suggestion: talk of exclusive and exhaustive in the context of foci within a facets is mistaken or misleading because, with many realistic cases, the foci will be hierarchical and if they are hierarchical they are definitely not exclusive and exhaustive, when the foci or types are considered as a whole (cf. a man is a human). What is better is to say, or to deem, that there is at most a single value for a focus under a facet, for composite types. So, for example, for the facet Periods there might be the elemental foci [eighteenth century, Nineteenth century, Medieval, Ancient,...] and synthesized foci of these, such as [Medieval and eighteenth century, ...] but then when a value for a Period is composed with a value from another facet, e.g. Archery, at most exactly one value for a Period focus is used, for example Medieval and eighteenth century Archery.

### 6.6.3  Facet Analysis

Facet analysis is the process of producing a faceted classification for a discipline or area of study. In principle it should not be too demanding a task. The initial theory (or theories) for Facet Analysis, come from Ranganathan and the United Kingdom Classification Research Group (Broughton 2004; Classification Research Group 1955; Ranganathan 1937, 1967; Spiteri 1998; Gopinath 1992). There are some issues with the historical materials. Ranganathan, in these writings, though not elsewhere, is incoherent and obscurantist [please, read (Ranganathan 1937) and judge for yourself]. In addition, the Classification Research Group did not provide a single written authoritative body of theory published as a whole (Spiteri 1998). Furthermore, two of the three problems that these originators considered are irrelevant to pure classification and our interests. They looked at pure classification, the order of the facets in a compound, and the order of the foci within the facets. The latter two concerns (citation order and column sort order (filing order) within a table or database) are connected primarily with producing an overall linearization needed for a shelving traversal, and, to a lesser extent, with producing indexes and consistent and friendly interfaces for patrons. So, what is being explained here and now has its origins with Ranganathan and the Classification Research Group, though some tinkering has been done. [There are a number of relatively modern accounts of facet analysis; see, for example (Buchanan 1979; Soergel 1974; Broughton 2004; Aitchison et al. 2000; Mills 2004; Mills and Broughton 1977; La Barre 2004; Kwasnik 1992, 1999). And, nowadays, there is a wide literature on facet analysis. The Volume 18, Number 2, 2008 double issue of the journal *Axiomathes* is devoted to it. (Gnoli 2008) is a guide to the territory, and (Beghtol 2008) is useful on Sayers, Ranganathan and the CRG. (Ellis and Vasconcelos 2000) relates it to the Web.]

We can illustrate Facet Analysis using, and generalizing on, the examples that the CRG itself employs. The task starts by making a list of the terms or concepts that the discipline uses, paying particular attention to the atomic concepts. So, for example, a much abbreviated list for popular Chemistry might include

alcohol, liquid, volatility, solid, combustion, analysis, gas, boiling point, water

then categories are identified for these concepts. These might be

alcohol *(kind)*, liquid *(state)*, volatility *(property)*, solid *(state)*, combustion *(reaction)*, analysis *(operation performed on it)*, gas *(state)*, boiling point *(property)*, water *(kind)*,

And that generates the following (rudimentary and very incomplete) Facets and Foci

Kind: {alcohol, water}
State: {gas, liquid, solid}
Property: {boiling point, volatility}
Reaction: {combustion}
Operation: {analysis}

and that gives us such topics as: 'the combustion of alcohol', and 'the analysis of water'.

Of course, some attention needs to be paid here to syntax, grammar, and how foci for these facets are combined together. One way, using logic, would be to have suitable predicates, such as

Alcohol(?x) to mean '?x is alcohol'
Water(?x) to mean '?x is alcohol'
Etc.

And to combine these together in the ways illustrated earlier with Synthetic Annotations. The novelty with facets is that the component atomic concepts, the foci, themselves have kinds or are in categories. To express this novelty we need a second order classification of the foci. This is simulated in first order logic by forming the types and applying a predicate to those types; for example,

{x:Gas(x)}
{x:Water(x)}

might pick out the types gas and water i.e

gas = {x:Gas(x)}
water = {x:Water(x)}

and then

State(gas)
State(water)

could be used to assert that these foci were States see also (Gnoli 2006).

That is Facet Analysis. In the example, the foci are appropriate to Chemistry; they are not suitable for, say, English Literature. Most disciplines need their own facets and foci. Of course, while these particular facets may be adequate for simple popular Chemistry, we know already that we will need other facets elsewhere, for example, the facets of Period and Place. The CRG noted the categories of *organs* in biology, *uses* of crops in agriculture, *agents* which (or who) cause diseases, and so on.

A relatively complete list of CRG general categories, which would be shaped to meet the requirements of the individual disciplines, is

Thing
Kind
Part (organ, constituent)
Property
Material
Process (an action internal to the item)
Operation (an action performed on the item)
Patient (object of action, raw material)
Product (substance)
By-product
Agent
Space
Time
[Form]
[Genre]

(Form and Genre are, so to speak, afterthoughts. Many works in the humanities seemed to require them. They were not among the original CRG categories. They are an impurity. Form might include, for example, Dictionary and Encyclopedia. While it possible to have forms as components subjects or topics, for example, there could be a book about Physics Encyclopedias, likely a Physics Encyclopedia is about the subject Physics and, distinct from that, its form is that of an Encyclopedia. Forms should, or could, be facets in a general classification scheme, but they are not facets of *subjects* or *topics*.)

An important point to notice is that even from its origins, facet analysis permits non-superimposed types. For example, a simple faceted classification might have

Kind = (humans, dogs)
Processes = (birth, growth)

These foci may be synthesized to 'the birth of humans', 'the growth of dogs', etc. But a topic 'the birth of humans' is not a superimposed type. Roughly, the Kinds in this example come from predicates and the Processes come from functions and the faceted synthesis allows these to be combined.

From an intellectual and logical point of view, it is important to draw attention to this predicates-and-functions or predicates-and-relations feature of the classification. Prior to facet analysis and faceted classification, most classifications used monadic predicates or attributes, that is, the classification showed classes, subclasses and superclasses of individual things. But with Processes, Products etc. more than one 'thing' is involved: there is the item and there is the process it is involved in (or the product it produces). There are at least two 'things' related to each other. And to analyze these, relations or functions are required. This is a step beyond a standard Aristotelian classification hierarchy. It is an advance.

Within facet analysis, it is also possible to have sub-facets. These are merely the grouping of some facets together. Let us adapt an example from Buchanan concerning animals (Buchanan 1979). One (partial) way to facet animals or works on animals is to use the facets

By land form habitat
By ground cover habitat
By latitude habitat
By element habitat
By whether their effect is beneficial on man
By magnitude of effect on man

And then, if desired, these facets could be grouped, thus

By habitat (subfacet)
    By land form
    By ground cover
    By latitude
    By element
By effect on man (subfacet)
    By beneficiality
    By magnitude of effect

The difference made by the use of sub-facets is this. With citation order, the facets are the columns in the relevant table and the citation order is the order of the columns—change of citation order changes the order of the columns. If there are just facets then any citation order is permitted. However, if some of the columns represent sub-facets, citation orders should respect sub-faceting by keeping the columns together within their subfacets. So, for example, if A, B, C amount to one subfacet, and 1, 2, 3 another, citation orders like ABC123, ACB213, 321ABC are all fine, but C1B23A is not a permitted citation order because it is mixing facets across their sub-facet groups.

## 6.6.4 Faceting and Postcoordination

To a degree, facet analysis was also anticipated by Mortimer Taube and his ideas on postcoordination. In 1951, Taube was advocating bibliographic coordinates to identify topics. The idea here is that there are certain categories, within a subject area, which are independent of, or orthogonal to, each other and thus which can be combined together in a particular system to identify topics, much as coordinates on a map can be used to identify locations. So, for example, Taube writes

The other field in which we are experimenting with bibliographical coordinates has more dimensions, but is still relatively simple and presents few difficulties. We intend to organize the literature on nuclides by means of the following categories: elements, isotopes, properties, applications, reactions, radiations, and experimental techniques.... the mark of success will be that every important fact in the literature to be organized can be exhibited as a combination of items in one or more of the categories. (Taube 1951, p. 69)

Postcoordination and faceting are natural allies or counterparts. If the facets are orthogonal, which they are supposed to be, then they can be combined together, or synthesized, prior to indexing to produce any desired precoordinated subject headings or concept annotations. But, equally, they can be combined together after indexing, during retrieval or search, without loss of precision or recall. So, for example, if one facet is Place and another is Period, that invites postcoordination; indexing can be done for Place and, separately, for Period, and the searcher can combine Place and Period in the search.

### 6.6.5  Relationships and Further Synthesis

As has been noted, foci within a single facet for a particular scheme often bear relationships to each other that usually arise from a hierarchy that they are in. These inter-facet relationships are sometimes called 'semantic' relationships and they concern supertypes, subtypes, sibling types and the like. Often a User will be interested in navigating via these relationships (i.e. to look at broader or narrower or similar topics). This can be done merely by following the schedule depicting the hierarchy, either by hand or with support from a computer.

Although the facets are orthogonal, and thus any focus from one can be combined with any focus from another, often the fact that foci actually are combined and instantiated is of interest to a User or Patron. Relationships between facets, inter-facet relationships, 'syntactic' relationships, can be important for supporting navigation and retrieval. Say, for a particular discipline, perhaps one covering discoveries of some research laboratories, the faceted scheme has just two facets Causes and Effects (and that these are orthogonal, with appropriate foci). One useful form of search might be to find all the Effects (or documents relating to effects) when the cause is that of a sticking accelerator. The pattern here is identifying a focus within one facet and stepping over to another facet to find items of interest. It is hard to generalize here. Much depends on the details of the facets in use. But, to illustrate using some of the CRG categories, users interested in Processes are often also interested in Products and By-Products. So that would be another example of a useful navigation step from facet to facet.

It is also possible and desirable to generalize these linking relationships and consider that they might hold between complex concepts or topics which themselves are faceted. For example, consider the relationship of comparing or contrasting. There might be a perfectly good topic 'the comparison of rice farming in nineteenth century China with wheat farming in eighteenth century Britain'.

The immediate components of this topic, the 'rice farming in nineteenth century China' and 'wheat farming in eighteenth century Britain' are themselves faceted concepts. There is here the notion of construction using links or role indicators. Historically, such links as the following have been identified:

Environment,
Object of transitive action,
Subject of transitive action,
Agent,
Study region,
Part,
Action and Property,
Same and Opposite,
Cause and Effect,
Manner,
Entailment,
See, for example (Coates 1973, p. 392) or (Khoo and Na 2006)

In this context, there is a subtlety that needs to be acknowledged. Sometimes a relationship between topics itself forms a composite topic which belongs as an annotation on suitable IOs. At other times, a relationship between topics belongs as part of the link structure of the relevant DAG of topics. For example, consider the relationship part-whole, in particular in relationship to cars and their engines. It could be that there are IOs on the topic of 'diesel engines in family cars', in which case the part-whole gets embodied in the topic. But it could also be that there were IOs on 'diesel engines' and distinct IOs on 'family cars' but no IOs on 'diesel engines in family cars', and that, consequently, for the convenience of mechanics and interested readers, the Information Architect, or designer of the system, links the topic 'diesel engines' to the topic 'family cars' in the DAG of topics. The same phenomena or feature is paralleled in thesauri: a thesaurus might have an entry 'diesel engines in family cars' or, as a separate case, it might have entries for 'diesel engines' and 'family cars' and under one of these, say 'diesel engines' it will have some rubric like *Related Term (RT)* 'family cars' which connects the two entries.
Common linking relationships include

*Relations* between subjects: parallel, hierarchical, part–whole, opposition, comparison/
contrast, cause/effect, influence, main subject/instance, main subject/points of view, main
subject/purpose, theory/application

## 6.6.6  Appraising Faceted Classification

Faceting certainly has its advantages. There is an independence and encapsulation to the components. This means that new foci or new combinations of foci can be added without regard to what is already there. Experts working in one area are indifferent to the work of others in other areas. And there is a discipline to the construction mechanisms.

But there are disadvantages too. Some critics feel that there are issues with the relations between foci and, possibly, 'distances' between foci (or even between actual composite topics). A plain faceted classification itself does not put in any measures. So, for example, say there were three foci: France, Germany, and New Zealand. There is a question of which order these should be in for shelving or similar. Also, if a User seeks an IO on, say, France, which we will assume the collection does not have, should the system return, as 'second bests', IOs on Germany or IOs on New Zealand? And this point generalizes, would a User seeking 'Trade in eighteenth century France' like, as near misses, 'Trade in seventeenth France' as opposed to 'Trade in fifth century New Guinea'? Researchers who approach information retrieval by means of statistical analysis of texts, document subject fingerprints, and the like, will find faceted classification somewhat basic. The criticism here is not that faceted classification is wrong; rather, it is that faceted classification could be developed in certain useful ways.

Faceting also can make search more involved than it might be. The location of relatively simple composite topics via their facets is elegant and direct. But finding the old war horse

the manufacture of multi-wall kraft paper sacks for the packaging of cement

by means of facets may be clumsy. It may be quicker and more direct for the User to have that topic as a subject heading or string and to find it by means of a string-in-string search for the string 'kraft'.

### 6.6.7 An Example of Faceted Subject Headings: MeSH

MeSH, the Medical Subject Heading list, was devised by Frank Rogers from about 1953 onwards (Adams 1972; Coletti and Bleich 2001; Lipscomb 2000; Sewell 1964). Rogers was influenced by Mortimer Taube, who, in turn, had suggested coordinated indexes and postcoordination (Rogers 1960b). Of course, much development has been carried out on MeSH in the last fifty years or so. MeSH is a synthetic system, many of the actual subject headings can be created by synthesis. It is a faceted system, these synthetic elements used in the headings are often of different kinds, or faces, or facets. In addition, it is a post coordinate system, many IOs will carry multiple topics or headings and searches will invoke Boolean operations on topics (AND-ING, OR-ING, and NOT-ING topics) to increase precision and recall.

MeSH is a controlled vocabulary of about 25,000 words (and 160,000 'lead in' terms) (MeSH 2010). Each term or heading is, or represents, a single concept (i.e. it is uniform). Human beings then assign to each IO, anything up to about 10 subject terms in a list. (Also, the assigned terms are in two categories: primary/

main 'concepts' and secondary 'concepts'; so, within the assigned headings to an IO, there is a sense of some headings being more important than others.)

MeSH is a synthetic scheme, so it allows the construction of headings. A favored word here is *descriptor*. There are three kinds of descriptor: *main headings* (i.e. subjects or topics), *publication types* (such as Clinical Trials, Charts, and Newspaper Articles), and *geographics* (which deal with geographical regions such as Arizona or England).

In addition to the descriptors, there are *qualifiers* (i.e. subheadings). So, for example, 'Blood pressure' is a descriptor, and 'diagnosis' and 'standards' are two qualifiers, and so the cataloger is free to create the headings 'Blood pressure diagnosis' and 'Blood pressure standards' should the need arise. Not all combinations of qualifiers and descriptors are permitted. There are about 83 topical qualifiers, and typically an individual descriptor will be combinable with a subset of these.

Topical qualifiers produce new topics. But there are also: form and geographic descriptors (see (Rogers 1953).) Once again, it turns out that Users in retrieval of documents (in this case medical documents) are often interested in the *form*, or publication characteristics, of what they are searching for; for example, whether they are seeking Case Reports or, perhaps, Newspaper Articles. Also *geographic location* (and sometimes language) are often important; medical research studies often concern particular geographic regions. What MeSH does with these descriptors is slightly involved. Certainly Users can search and retrieve by, say, form or region. So, from a User's point of view the form or geographical region seems part of the heading. But, underneath the surface appearance, the form, language etc. will not be a part of the subject heading: they will be recorded separately in separate data fields (in, for example, the underlying MARC records). Thus, for example, form qualifiers do not really make new subjects. MeSH is careful. Obviously there can be clinical trials, reported in IOs, and IOs about clinical trials (just as there can be baseball films, which are films (about baseball), and books about baseball films, which are books (about baseball films)). Thus, MeSH has *Clinical Trials* as a publication type heading and *Clinical Trials as Topic* as a subject heading i.e. it makes the appropriate distinctions.

MeSH will handle compound or complex concepts in one of three different ways. To illustrate these let us conjure up an imaginary topic, say 'The effects of drugs on blood pressure'. MeSH sometimes precoordinates. If it did so in this case, there would need to be a single composite subject heading (or descriptor) like 'The effects of drugs on blood pressure' or 'Blood pressure, drug effects'. MeSH sometimes postcoordinates. If it did so in this case, there would need to be a subject heading (or descriptor) like 'drug effects' and another descriptor 'blood pressure' and any IO on 'The effects of drugs on blood pressure' would be assigned both headings. And, thirdly, MeSH sometimes uses its heading-qualifier constructor mechanism. If it did so in this case, there would need to be a subject heading (or descriptor) like 'Blood pressure' and a topic qualifier like 'Drug effects'. In fact, in MeSH, 'Blood pressure' is a heading, and 'Drug effects' is a qualifier that can be used with it, so the third technique would be the one that is used. An example of precoordination is 'Public Health Nursing', which is a heading in its own right; actually, 'Public Health' is a heading on its own, so too is 'Nursing', so it would be possible to postcoordinate by assigning both 'Public Health' and, separately, 'Nursing' to suitable IOs. However, with controlled vocabularies, precoordinated entries, if available, should always be preferred over postcoordinated versions (that strategy is guaranteed to avoid decreasing precision, without other costs). Postcoordination would be used with a topic like 'Alzheimer's disease, memory effects'; 'Alzheimer's disease' is a subject heading, 'Memory' is a subject heading; but there is no subject heading containing both of these topics, nor is either of the topics a qualifier; so the two headings would be used separately, yet together, to annotate suitable IOs and postcoordination would identify these IOs on retrieval.

MeSH main heading vocabulary is structured into a forest of 16 trees, referred to as the 'MeSH Tree Structure' (NLM 2011). These trees are deep and/or broad (to have 25,000 or so headings in 16 trees, they have to be).

A heading can apparently appear twice or more in a tree. For example, 'Influenza, Human' appears both in a branch headed by 'Virus Diseases' and in a branch headed by 'Respiratory Tract Diseases'. We discussed earlier, in Sect. 4.5, the desirability of topics having multiple parents, and of *cloning* topics. In MeSH, the headings do not really appear twice or more. A heading, say 'Influenza, Human' is a string together with a Descriptor ID, which is its identifier. The string 'Influenza, Human' appears twice, but those occurrences have different Descriptor IDs, so they are not the same descriptor, they are not the same heading. However, of course, a keyword, or string, search for 'Influenza, Human' among the trees will find both of them, and then the searcher can make an informed choice as to aspect or context. Within the trees, the searchers can work their way up or down branches to widen or narrow results.

MeSH is faceted in the direct way, and sense, that the headings and qualifiers are different types and can be composed and searched differently. It is also ersatz faceted in that the publication types, divide up, or partially divide up, the IOs. MeSH instructional literature informs us that MeSH data is recorded in its 'deconstructed' or 'faceted' form; that is to say topics, publication types, geographics, and language are recorded separately and are available for faceted access (NLM 2009).

## 6.7  Thesauri as Annotation Languages

Thesauri are annotation or indexing languages, and they certainly have wide suitability for topic annotation. Thesauri will be controlled vocabularies, and they will often have information on hierarchies, which, in turn, will allow for broadening and narrowing of topic. Their main drawback for use for topic tagging is that their entries represent only simple or unitary concepts so that the topics they can tag are only simple topics. That certainly is a good start, and it can be extended if post coordination is used to make compounds out of the simples. But likely this will still fall short of what is ideal in the general case.

## 6.7.1 WordNet

A good example of a hierarchical thesaurus is WordNet (Miller et al. 2010). WordNet is not quite a controlled vocabulary in the sense of having a strict one or two or three hundred controlled terms in it. Rather it admits as many natural language single words (or words for single concepts) as it can, then arranges them into synonym sets (*synsets*) and then links those synsets one to another by various semantical relations. The semantical relations set up hierarchies and other associations among synsets. The result is a thesaurus and classification scheme.

The semantic relations that are invoked depend on the type of word. For example, following Wikipedia (Wikipedia 2010), for **Nouns**

> *hypernyms*: $Y$ is a hypernym of $X$ if every $X$ is a (kind of) $Y$ (*canine* is a hypernym of *dog*)
> *hyponyms*: $Y$ is a hyponym of $X$ if every $Y$ is a (kind of) $X$ (*dog* is a hyponym of *canine*)
> *coordinate terms*: $Y$ is a coordinate term of $X$ if $X$ and $Y$ share a hypernym (*wolf* is a coordinate term of *dog*, and *dog* is a coordinate term of *wolf*)
> *holonym*: $Y$ is a holonym of $X$ if $X$ is a part of $Y$ (*building* is a holonym of *window*)
> *meronym*: $Y$ is a meronym of $X$ if $Y$ is a part of $X$ (*window* is a meronym of *building*)

In practice, WordNet runs together, or perhaps fails to distinguish, subtype of from instance of. To repeat the definition of hypernym,

> *hypernyms*: $Y$ is a hypernym of $X$ if every $X$ is a (kind of) $Y$ (*canine* is a hypernym of *dog*)

The English construction 'is a' marks 'instance of' so when we say 'Spot is a dog' we mean Spot is an instance of the type dog. Suppose a simple schematic type hierarchy can be represented by (Fig. 6.2). Then Spot is also a carnivore, and also a mammal, and the types carnivore and mammal are supertypes of dog. The type relationships are established by what is an instance of what. Notice that Spot himself does not appear anywhere in this diagram. The reason for this is that Spot is an *individual* not a type, and the diagram is a hierarchy of types. The notion of individual can be defined as an item *that cannot have instances* and then the diagram can be used to generate a hypernym hierarchy. The nodes now no longer represent types; the labels 'mammal', 'carnivore', 'dog' represent those words; and the directed links, the arrows, represent the hypernym-hyponym relationships; so that 'carnivore' is a hypernym of 'dog' and 'dog' a hyponym of 'carnivore'.

What would be expected, then, at this point, is that the hypernym-hyponym hierarchy would not have any individuals in it (Spot is not going to be there). It builds up a type hierarchy. But, as has been pointed out, for example, by (Gangemi et al. 2003; Martin 2003) in fact the actual WordNet has many case that violate this. For example, the hyponyms of 'Territorial Dominion' include Macao and Palestine, but these are individuals not types.

The English construction 'is a kind of' actually makes the problems worse. 'is a kind of' means exactly the same thing as 'is a' except that 'is a kind of' is typically employed with types and higher order types (or metaproperties). For example, 'dog is a Canid' and 'dog is a kind of Canid' mean exactly the same thing, but here 'dog' is a type not an individual and Canid is a second order type. We can say 'Spot is a dog' but it is unusual to say 'Spot is a kind of dog', unless we are being humorous (largely because Spot is an individual not a kind).

If the interest is to use logic and computers to make inferences among the types in a type hierarchy, these are bad mistakes to make. They are to mush together the 'vertical' and the 'horizontal'. To illustrate: there is the supertype of carnivorous mammals and subtypes of this include a group of about 36 species of Canines/canids which are (wolf, coyote, dingo, fox, dog etc.). So a fragment of the type hierarchy looks like this (Fig. 6.3). And this hierarchy supports inheritance inference vertically up the type hierarchy. Thus: if Fang is a wolf, Fang is also a carnivore and Fang is also a mammal. The species Canines/canids is a (part of a) horizontal level in this type hierarchy; in the fragment shown, it is the third level. So a more comprehensive diagram looks like this (Fig. 6.4). Where the arrows, with arrow heads, are connecting types to their immediate subtypes. And the presence of the types wolf, coyote, dingo, dog etc. within the higher order type rectangle labeled 'Canid' is depicting that those types are instances or members of the second order type or metatype 'Canid'. They are species. There should not be any inference from Fang's being a wolf to Fang being a Canid—Fang is not a Canid, only species are Canids.

There is a considerable difference between 'dog' and 'a dog': 'dog' is the name of a type; 'a dog' is an instance of that very type. Hence, 'dog' names a species, it is one of the canids; 'a dog' is not the name of a species, and 'a dog' is thus not a canid; dog (the species) is neither a carnivore nor a mammal, a dog is both a carnivore and a mammal. The distinctions here turn on the difference between instance and subtype (or, to phrase it in set theoretic terms, the difference between member and subset). WordNet's notions of 'hypernym' (and hyponym etc.) do not respect this distinction.

Hierarchies for words, say nouns, could certainly be produced using, for example, the hypernym relationship. But very likely these would be polyhier-archies or faceted schemes, with multiple inheritance because many nodes would have both supertypes and types they are members of—hypernym links would go to both. Dog is a subtype of Carnivore and a member of Canid—so if hypernym links are used Dog has two parents and thus the hierarchy is a polyhierarchy.

There are a couple of qualifying points to be made. In ordinary speech we effortlessly go back and forth between instance and subtype, fully understanding (or mostly fully understanding) what we are saying from the context. The explicit distinction between member and subset (or instance and subtype) arose with set theory, which, historically, is dated about 1870, with Cantor (Ferreirós 2008).

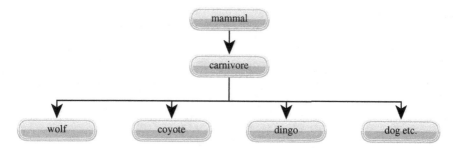

**Fig. 6.2** A schematic type hierarchy

Earlier than that instance and subtype were just run together with the notion of 'part of' or 'one of' or 'being one of'. So, insofar as WordNet is formulated to respect what we do and say, and that what we say goes back centuries, it probably uses the right distinctions. But, were this historical usage to be used in computers for making inferences, the distinctions mentioned above would need to be made carefully (and there have been projects to tidy up WordNet for use in inferencing (Martin 2003)).

## 6.7.2 Thesaurofacet and Classaurus

Thesaurofacet is a system designed by Jean Aitchison for use on engineering topics (Aitchison et al. 1969; Aitchison 1970). It is a combination of a faceted classification and a thesaurus, and the thesaurus part is built into the classification. Thesaurofacet was created for the English Electric Company, which was already using the *English Electric Faceted Classification for Engineering* (which had been produced by members of the Classification Research Group, those proselytes of faceted classification).

In practice, any thematic classification really is going to have two parts to it: the actual classification, or schedule, and an index to locate where the classes are in the graph of classes or schedule. We saw this with Dewey and his Relativ Index, and we saw it with Roget's Thesaurus and his Alphabetical Index. To bridge the two parts, the class nodes need names or locators for the index entries to refer to (and these node names can be used for shelving if that is the purpose of the system).

An information retrieval thesaurus is going to have information about synonyms, and also about broader and narrower terms. Ordinarily a thesaurus is thought of as an indexing language, so the location of information on broader and narrower terms appears to be in that index. But what constitutes a broader or narrower term is defined by the thematic classification or schedule. So information

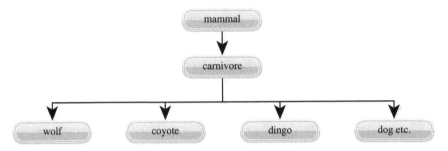

**Fig. 6.3** A fragment of a classification carnivorous mammals

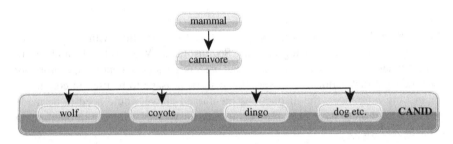

**Fig. 6.4** A fragment of a classification carnivorous mammals showing a species layer

on broader and narrower terms has its origin in the classification—the term for a parent of a node is a broader term than the term for the node (and similarly for narrower) (see also (Aitchison 1986)). Also, the schedule can have information in distant ancestors and descendants, and this is not easily represented in a thesaurus.

But information on synonyms, on preferred terms and lead-in terms, is definitely not directly in the schedule. And, independently, information about distributed relatives is not easily available from the schedule (that is why Dewey had a Relativ Index, to collect them up).

So, from an intellectual and theoretical point of view, what seems most elegant is to have an Index of synonyms and distributed relatives, which points to nodes in the schedule, and it is the schedule itself that informs on broader and narrower terms.

That, essentially, is what Thesaurofacet does (and it is also a faceted classification). Typically, the User looks up a term in the index and that will provide a reference to one or more nodes in the schedule, and then the structure of the schedule will reveal broader or narrower classes and broader and narrower terms.

A minor drawback or criticism is that no system should make regular tasks harder or slower for the User. If many Users were interested in broader or narrower terms, they should not have to do a double look-up, first in the index and then from the index to the schedule. Instead, at least some of the information in the schedule should be repeated in the index. That information would be redundant but useful.

One attractive feature of the Thesaurofacet arrangement is that it generalizes from elemental terms or concepts to compound ones. A standard thesaurus addresses simple concepts, but if the thesaurus information is in the schedule then all relevant concepts are covered. If 'the manufacture of multi-wall kraft paper sacks for the packaging of cement' is a subject or topic or class in the schedule, then the User will be able to find broader or narrower subjects than this one, and no ordinary thesaurus has that capability.

Classaurus (Bhattacharyya 1982; Biswas and Smith 1989; Devadason 1985) is a generalization of Thesaurofacet.

Classaurus is a vocabulary control tool that incorporates in itself features of both classification schemes as well as thesauri. Like any classification scheme, it displays hierarchical relationship among terms (broader, narrower, coordinate) in its schedules. Like a faceted classification scheme there are separate schedules for each of the "facets" or Elementary Categories (Fundamental Categories and NOT characteristics of division like "By Shape", "By Wave length" etc.) namely, Discipline, Entity, Property, and Action; with their Species/Parts and Special Modifiers for each. Also there are separate schedules for Common Modifiers like Form, Time, Place and Environment. Like any thesaurus each of the terms in the hierarchic schedules is enriched with synonyms, quasi-synonyms etc. Also, like a thesaurus, any term is permitted to appear in as many hierarchies as may be appropriate. Unlike a thesaurus, classaurus does not include other associatively related terms. (Devadason 1985, pp. 15–16)

Classaurus was aimed at subject headings, and it was intended to be a suite of software tools that would achieve desired aims. One central feature of it was its use of POPSI, one of its own devices, to generate 'rotated' or 'chained' index entries. POPSI is solution to a technical problem which is no longer so relevant to us. As mentioned in Sect. 2.8.4, there is an area of research, string indexing (Craven 1986), whose aim is to permute or rearrange compound terms or index keys into some desired format. PRECIS is a well known system to do this and POPSI is another one.

# References

Adams S (1972) The way of the innovator: notes toward a prehistory of MEDLARS. Bull Med Libr Assoc 60(4):7

Aitchison J (1970) The thesaurofacet: a multipurpose retrieval language tool. J Doc 26(3):187–203

Aitchison J (1986) A classification as a source for a thesaurus: the bibliographic classification of H. E. Bliss as a source of thesaurus terms and structure. J Doc 42(3):160–181

Aitchison J, Gilchrist A, Bawden D (2000) Thesaurus construction and use: a practical manual, 4th edn. Fitzroy Dearborn, Chicago

Aitchison J, Gomershall A, Ireland R (1969) Thesaurofacet: a thesaurus and faceted classification for engineering and related subjects. English Electric Co, Whetstone, Leicester

Austin D (1984) PRECIS: a manual of concept analysis and subject indexing, 2nd edn. The British Library, London

Beghtol C (2008) From the universe of knowledge to the universe of concepts: the structural revolution in classification for information retrieval. Axiomathes 18(2):131–144

Berman S (1971, 1993) Prejudices and antipathies: a tract on the lc subject heads concerning people. McFarland & Company Inc., Jefferson, North Carolina

Bhattacharyya G (1982) Classaurus: its fundamentals, design and use. In: Dahlberg I (ed) Universal classification: subject analysis and ordering systems: proceeding of the 4th international study conference on classification research, 6th annual conference of Gesellshaft für Klassifikation, Augsburg, 28 June–2 July 1982, vol 1. Indeks Verlag, Frankfurt, pp 139–148

Biswas SC, Smith F (1989) Classed thesauri in indexing and retrieval: a literature review and critical evaluation of online alphabetic classaurus. Libr Inf Sci Res 11(2):109–141

Broughton V (2004) Essential classification. Neal-Schuman, New York

Broughton V (2006) The need for a faceted classification as the basis of all methods of information retrieval. In: Aslib proceedings: new information perspectives, vol 58 (1/2), pp 49–72

Broughton V (2010a) Concepts and terms in the faceted classification: the case of UDC. Knowl Organiz 37:270–279

Broughton V (2010b) Essential library of congress subject headings. Facet Publishing, London

Buchanan B (1979) Theory of library classification. Clive Bingley, London

Chan LM (1986) Library of Congress Subject Headings: principles and application, 2nd edn. Libraries Unlimited, Colorado

Chan LM, O'Neill ET (2010) FAST: faceted application of subject terminology: principles and application. Libraries Unlimited, Colorado

Cheti A, Paradisi F (2008) Facet analysis in the development of a general controlled vocabulary. Axiomathes 18(2):223–241

Classification Research Group (1955) The need for a faceted classification as the basis of all methods for information retrieval. Libr Assoc Rec 57(7):262–268

Coates EJ (1973) Some properties of relationships in the structure of indexing languages. J Doc 29(4):390–404

Coletti MH, Bleich HL (2001) Medical subject headings used to search the biomedical literature. MeSH Searches 8:317–323

Craven TC (1986) String indexing. Academic Press, Orlando

Devadason FJ (1985) Online construction of alphabetic classaurus: a vocabulary control and indexing tool. Inf Process Manage 21(1):11–26

Dykstra M (1988) LC subject headings disguised as a thesaurus. Libr J 133(4):42–47

Ellis D, Vasconcelos A (2000) The relevance of facet analysis for world wide web subject organization and searching. J Internet Cataloging 2(3/4):97–114

Ferreirós J (2008) The early development of set theory. http://plato.stanford.edu/archives/fall2008/entries/settheory-early/. Accessed 10 Oct 2010

Fischer KS (2005) Critical views of LCSH, 1990–2001: the third bibliographic essay. Cataloging Classification Q 41(1):63–109

Foskett AC (1977) Subject approach to information, 3rd edn. Clive Bingley, London

Foskett AC (1996) Subject approach to information, 5th edn. Facet Publishing, London

Foskett DJ (2003) Facet analysis. In: Drake MA (ed) Encyclopedia of library and information science, 2nd edn. Marcel Dekker, New York, pp 1063–1067

Gangemi A, Guarino N, Masolo C, Oltramar A (2003) Sweetening WORDNET with DOLCE. AI Mag 24(3):13–24

Gardin J-C (1965) Free classifications and faceted classifications: their exploitation with computers. In: Atherton P (ed) Classification research: proceedings of the international conference elsinore 1964. Munksgaard, Copenhagen, pp 161–176

Gnoli C (2006) The meaning of facets in nondisciplinary classifications. In: Paper presented at the, proceedings of 9th ISKO conference. Vienna, pp 11–18

Gnoli C (2008) Facets: a fruitful notion in many domains. Axiomathes 18(2):127–130

Gopinath MA (1992) Ranganathan's theory of facet analysis and knowledge representation. DESIDOC Bull Inf Technol 12(5):16–20

Khoo CSG, Na JC (2006) Semantic relations in information science. Annu Rev Inf Sci Technol 40(1):157–228. doi:10.1002/aris.1440400112

Kirtland M, Cochrane P (1982) Critical views of LCSH—library of congress subject headings a bibliographic and bibliometric essay. Cataloging Classification Q 1(2):71–94

Kwasnik BH (1992) The legacy of facet analysis. In: Sharma RN (ed) SR Ranganathan and the west. Sterling, New Delhi, India, pp 98–111

Kwasnik BH (1999) The role of classification in knowledge representation and discovery. Library Trends 48(1):22–47

La Barre K (2004) Adventures in faceted classification: a brave new world or a world of confusion? Adv Knowl Organiz 9:79–84

La Barre K (2006) The use of faceted analytico-synthetic theory as revealed in the practice of website construction and design. Indiana University, Bloomington

La Barre K (2010) Facet analysis. In: Cronin B (ed) Annual review of information science and technology. Information Today, Inc, Medford, NJ, pp 243–286

Lambe P (2007) Organising knowledge: taxonomies, Knowledge and organisational effectiveness. Chandos Publishing, Oxford, England

Lipscomb C (2000) Medical subject headings (MeSH). Bull Med Libr Assoc 88(3):265–266

Martin PA (2003) Correction and extension of WordNet 1.7 for knowledge-based applications. In: Conceptual structures for knowledge creation and communication. vol lecture notes in computer science. Springer, Berlin/Heidelberg, pp 160–173

MeSH (2010) Medical subject headings–home page. http://www.nlm.nih.gov/mesh/. Accessed 27 March 2011

Miller GA, Fellbaum C, Tengi R, Langone H (2010) WordNet. http://wordnet.princeton.edu/. Accessed 10 Oct 2010

Mills J (2004) Faceted classification and logical division in information retrieval. Libr Trends 52(3):541–570

Mills J, Broughton V (1977) Bliss bibliographic classification. Introduction and auxiliary schedules, 2nd edn. Butterworths, London

Morville P, Rosenfeld L (2006) Information architecture for the world wide web. O'Reilly, Sebastopol, CA

NLM US (2009) Using medical subject headings (MeSH®) in cataloging. http://www.nlm.nih.gov/tsd/cataloging/trainingcourses/mesh/index.html. Accessed 10 Oct 2010

NLM US (2011) MeSH Tree Structures. http://www.nlm.nih.gov/mesh/trees.html. Accessed 10 Oct 2010

Ranganathan SR (1937) Prolegomena to library classification, 3rd edn 1967, 1st edn 1937. The Madras Library Association, Madras

Ranganathan SR (1959) Elements of library classification, 2nd edn. Association of Assistant Librarians, London

Ranganathan SR (1960) Colon classification. Ranganathan series in library science, 4, 6 edn. Asia Publishing House, London

Ranganathan SR (1967) Prolegomena to library classification. Available via http://worldcat.org. http://dlist.sir.arizona.edu. Accessed 10 Oct 2010

Rogers FB (1953) Applications and limitations of subject headings: the pure and applied sciences. In: Tauber MF (ed) The subject analysis of library materials. Columbia University, New York, pp 73–82

Rogers FB (1960) Review of Taube, mortimer. Studies in coordinate indexing. Bull Med Libr Assoc 42 (July 1954):380–384

Sewell W (1964) Medical subject headings in MEDLARS. Bull Med Libr Assoc 52(1):164–170. doi:PMCID:PMC198088

Shubert SB (1992) Critical views of LCSH–ten years later. Cataloging Classification Q 15(2):37–97

Slavic A (2008) Faceted classification: management and use. Axiomathes 18(2):257–271

Soergel D (1974) Indexing languages and thesauri: construction and maintenance. Melville, Los Angeles

Spårck Jones K (2007) Semantic primitives: the tip of the iceberg. In: Ahmad K, Brewster C, Stevenson M (ed) Words and intelligence II (electronic resource): essays in honor of Yorick Wilks. Springer, Dordrecht, pp 235–253

Spiteri L (1998) A simplified model for facet analysis: Ranganathan 101. Can J Libr Inf Sci 23:1–30

Taube M (1951) Functional approach to bibliographic organization: a critique and a proposal. In: Shera JH, Egan M (eds) Bibliographic organization: fifteenth annual conference of the graduate library school, 24–29 July 1950. University of Chicago Press, Chicago, pp 57–71

Vickery BC (1960) Faceted classification: a guide to construction and use of special schemes. Aslib, London

Vickery BC (1966) Faceted classification schemes. In: Artandi S (ed) Rutgers series on systems for the intellectual organization of information, vol 5. Graduate School of Library Science at Rutgers University, New Brunswick

Vickery BC (2008) Faceted classification for the web. Axiomathes 18(2):145–160

Wikipedia (2010) WordNet. http://en.wikipedia.org/wiki/WordNet. Accessed 10 Oct 2010

Willetts M (1975) An investigation of the nature of the relation between terms in thesauri. J Doc 31(3):158–184

Wilson T (2006) The strict faceted classification model. http://facetmap.com/pub/. Accessed 10 Oct 2010

# Chapter 7
# Indexing/Annotation

## 7.1 Introduction

> An indexer must be something of a prophet—envisioning the concepts likely to be sought by users of a document, expressing those concepts in terms likely to be sought by users, and providing cross-references from synonyms and alternative spellings as well as links to related terms to assist users in finding all the information that is relevant to their topics of interest. (Weinberg 2009)

Absolutely.

But a small generalization is needed. It is not always a *single* document or IO that needs to be indexed: sometimes, especially in the case of subject indexing, it is a *collection* of documents or IOs that are to be the individual recipients of indexing.

As noted in Sect. 2.13, a view adopted here is that back of the book indexing and subject annotation are essentially the same. This opinion is not new. It was certainly advocated in the 1950s by Frank Rogers and Mortimer Taube. Rogers wrote

> Much has been made of the presumed differences between headings used for cataloging and headings used for indexing; most of the difficulty lies in the ambiguity of the word "indexing". This has ordinarily thought of in terms of indexing a book. A book index is made up on an ad hoc basis; there is a brand new conceptual scheme evolved for every book indexed. It should be clear that the construction of continuing indexes in multiple periodicals is quite a different matter. We take the view that subject cataloging and periodical indexing, as exemplified in the Index Medicus and in the NLM [National Library of Medicine] Catalog, are identical processes in their major dimensions. A single list can and should be used for both purposes. This has two major virtues: simplicity for users, in requiring familiarity with only a single scheme; and economy to the Library in the development and maintenance of a single scheme (Rogers 1960a). (See also (Rogers 1960b).)

Indexing and subject annotation (which is sometimes called 'subject indexing' or even 'subject classification') are both just annotation. They are both concerned with concepts and the consideration of whether IOs address those concepts as topics.

M. Frické, *Logic and the Organization of Information*,
DOI: 10.1007/978-1-4614-3088-9_7,
© Springer Science+Business Media New York 2012

What is different about indexing a book and indexing a collection of books lies with the details of the indexing language that is used. Back-of-the-book indexes for an autobiography of Winston Churchill, a children's book of trains, or a reference book for Medieval Church Architecture would use topics of their own devising or from their own domains or topics or fields of interest. These topics may or may not have wider application beyond their original setting and use. We have already noted that many topic languages are imported into the wider classifications of librarianship from their home domains—that is the idea of parametric topic systems. And, as we will see, just how good indexes are, their retrieval effectiveness, depends on the goodness of their associated topic schemas. So, get the DAGs of topics right and all else follows.

An index is an association list between keys and values. Within the setting of information retrieval and IOs, there are two main kinds of indexes. There are indexes like plain Back-of-the-book Indexes. With these, the keys are strings, and the values are typically lists of IOs or references to IOs. So, for example, 'butterfly' might be a key in an index. What 'butterfly' means or signifies here is usually the word-type 'butterfly', or an approximation to that word type, and then the values in the index would just be the locations of the occurrences of tokens of 'butterfly' (or, perhaps, 'butterflies') in the relevant texts. This, to give it a rough label, is *string indexing*, and, conceptually, it works with the Symbol Vertex of the Triangle of Meaning. String indexing is often known as *derived indexing* (because it is derived from the text). It is pattern matching on the Verbal Plane. Then there are indexes like the more sophisticated Back-of-the-book Indexes, or like Subject Indexes, or (Dewey) Relative Indexes. These work with the Concept Vertex of the Triangle of Meaning, they involve *concept indexing*. Once again the keys are, or seem to be, strings, and once again the key 'butterfly' might occur. However, the string 'butterfly' does not now signify the word type 'butterfly' instead it is a label or notation for the concept butterfly and the values in the index are the locations of references to the concept butterfly in the relevant texts or class structures. The difference this makes is that the phenomenon of synonymy identifies or recognizes that concepts may have multiple labels, for example 'rhopalocera' also names the butterfly concept. Concepts themselves are abstract, but we have, or can have, names or references for them—and we can have an interest in indexes to tokens of those names or labels involving those names. To once again use the same standard example, a sophisticated Back-of-the-book Index with 'butterfly' as a preferred entry term will refer to a paragraph that uses the term 'rhopalocera' even though tokens of 'butterfly' are nowhere to be found. This second form of indexing is often known as *assigned* indexing.

Index keys often have structure. If they are plain terms, they might be tied into a thesaurus indicating broader or narrower terms. If they represent concepts, the concepts might be tied into a classification structure of broader and narrow topics. This means that the keys may have a form akin to heading->subheading, or topic->subtopic, and this will have semantic significance indicating structure. Structure can also be used to disambiguate homographs (as we saw with the alphabetical index in Roget's original thesaurus). In addition, structure can further be used to indicate related keys and entries, i.e. syndetic relations. [It is also possible, with an approach like Salton's, that the keys be weighted vectors of terms or vectors of labels for concepts.]

The language of the keys has significance. Michael Buckland and Christian Plaunt talk of the vocabularies of retrieval (Buckland 1999; Buckland and Plaunt 1994). We prefer the expression 'languages of retrieval'. An author writes a book using the language of the author; the book is indexed using the language of the indexer; and the index is accessed using the language of the searcher. There is room for much pliability here. The keys are to help the searcher, and so they should favor the language of the searcher. If the retriever is in some sense a layperson, natural language, ordinary everyday speech, might work best. But controlled keys are better technically. We see logic as underlying all this: it is the reserve currency. The language of the author, the language of the indexer, and the language of the searcher are all surface translations of the same foundational logic of types and concepts.

## 7.2  Evaluating Indexes

The purpose of an index is to help with finding, retrieving, and organizing [see also (Anderson 1985)] and indexes are good in so far as they promote high precision and high recall in combination, across targeted Users and targeted uses.

The goals of high precision and recall lead to further requirements on the indexing. Consider Reid's class hierarchy

    Animal
    Man
    Frenchman
    Parisian

and imagine the task is to index IOs in this kind of area using some or all of these labels as index keys. Suppose a particular document is about Parisians. (This cashes out as meaning: if a user of the index was trying to find an IO on Parisians that user would deem this particular IO relevant.) The IO might be labeled (or indexed) correctly with any of 'Animal', 'Man', 'Frenchman', or 'Parisian' (and we assume that if it is labeled with one of the labels lower in the hierarchy, it inherits the superclass labels). If the Parisian IO is not labeled 'Parisian' (but perhaps labeled 'Frenchman'), an index user following the key 'Parisian' will not find it and so the recall for that search will be less than it might be. So the indexing needs to be as specific as it can be: it needs to use keys that are the furthest down the classification tree. Now consider the list of keys or index entries themselves. Suppose there was no key for 'Parisian' and instead the most specific key was 'Frenchmen'—in which case, if the searcher wanted IOs about Parisians that searcher would be forced to use 'Frenchmen', but that label will presumably pull up IOs not just about Frenchmen from Paris, but also about Frenchmen from Marseilles, Frenchmen from Lyons, and so forth; and that decreases precision; inadequate keys, keys that are not specific enough, reduce precision. So, to maximize precision and recall, the available keys and their class hierarchy need to be as *detailed* as possible (relative to the interests of the User). Then, when those keys are attached to the IOs the indexes should use the narrowest, most *specific*, key.

There are more sophisticated ways of carrying out what essentially is the same process of analysis. When the concept or attribute or topic 'Parisian' is applied to IOs it partitions those IOs into the IOs that have the attribute and those that do not. It clusters the documents. If there are many attributes in use at once ('Parisian', 'Londoner', 'New Yorker' etc.), there are more clusters and those clusters are somewhat finer or more discriminating. When an index is used, or a search is made, the User is going to get back one of those clusters or a combination of them. And the returned combination will have a precision and recall according to the way that it contains relevant IOs. How well all this works depends on the clustering, the precision, and the recall across many retrievals. The Salton vector fingerprint achieves much the same. The fingerprints cluster the documents either into documents that have the same fingerprint or into documents whose fingerprints are sufficiently similar to be considered the same for retrieval purposes. There is room for adjustment here—both over what the fingerprints are and over the measures of similarity used to produce the clusters. But once there are clusters the analysis is the same (their value lies in how they support precision and recall).

There are at least three other desiderata that are often discussed: that the index keys should be (1) not-too-general, (2) not-too-specific, and (3) exhaustive. These three can be derived from considerations of precision and recall, but there is value in stating and explaining them independently.

There are other requirements that suggest themselves. The idea of indexing is to help search—it is to narrow the possibilities. Any key that refers to *all* the IOs does not do that, and so is not of help. Conversely, keys can be too specific. Of course, a key can refer to one page or one IO. But not too many keys should do this. There is often some slack between the Users conception of the world and what they want, and the indexers work and the resulting index. The Users often do not know what is relevant in advance of seeing the items (this lack is what browsing and berrypicking cater to). So, the argument can be made that index retrieval should often produce a small range of items for the User to choose among. In sum, the keys should not be too general or too specific (similarly, in a topic tree, the root might not be used—nor might many highly specific leaves).

Professional indexers themselves have a term of evaluation or description: *exhaustivity*. Exhaustivity is the number of keys, or index entries, and this would be a measure relative to the IO collection. So, for example, if the index is an index to a book of one hundred pages, and the index references, or locators, are to individual pages, then exhaustivity is a measure of how well the index entries cover the contents of those one hundred pages. [We would analyze this configuration slightly differently: we would regard each of the pages as being an IO in its own right, and then the indexing would range over a hundred IOs. This difference of analysis is unimportant.] Saying roughly what exhaustivity amounts to and whether it is present in particular cases is not too demanding a task; however, giving full detail is extremely difficult. What an index entry or key points to is a subset of the pages (or IOs) and with a hundred page book there are $(100 \times 100 =)$ 10,000 such subsets. Not only that, each page might address more than one topic and so each subset itself might be the proper reference for more than one topic. [For example, say crocutes appear on {2, 17, 29}, it could be that all and only pages that address crocutes also address the entirely different topic of sphinges so there should be an index entry indicating that sphinges also appear on the same subset {2, 17, 29}. The words 'sphinges' and 'crocutes' are neither synonyms nor homographs.] This pushes the number of possible index entries up to 100,000 or more, which is unusable if entries were to be provided in full in a printed text. At the other end of the spectrum, just one or ten index entries, would represent a very small proportion of what is possible and what might possibly be relevant to the needs of the reader. One controlling factor here is which keys Users actually use—or which keys they would use were those keys to be present. Furthermore, the use that is made of an index is typically not just one User on one occasion, rather it is many Users making many uses on many occasions. In electronic settings, a computer can certainly monitor index usage and remove unpopular entries. But it is hard to get an experimental and empirical connection to potential entries that are in fact not actually present, but which yet would be valuable were they to have been present. Once again, computers can help with this. For example, if the index is used by typing in the candidate key string, any time a User types in a key string which is not actually in the index that act can be regarded as a request for a new index entry and the request can be used as implicit feedback suggesting index revision. In sum, an index should be 'exhaustive' enough to meet Users needs, though quite what that amounts to is hard to say. However, if indexes can be revised in an ongoing basis then implicit feedback can help with exhaustivity and nowadays even 'print' books are becoming electronic e-books so index revision is definitely a live possibility.

## 7.3   How Good are Humans and Computers at Annotation?

The answer is: not very good.

Within the classical theory of research methods there are the two notions: *reliability* and *validity*. Reliability is where repetitions of the same measurement produce the same value. So, a bathroom scales which gives you the same 160lbs as you climb on it and off it—the same one morning at the same time—is reliable; a scale that weighs you as 160, then 157, then 163 is unreliable. Then if the instrument's reading is actually the correct value, the reading is valid. So, if the scale suggests 160lbs and you do indeed weigh 160lbs, the reading is valid. Any unreliable instrument is going to produce many invalid readings (and so is less than perfect). But a reliable instrument can also produce invalid readings; a bathroom scale that always weighs 3 lbs under has readings which are reliable but invalid; a scale which is broken and always suggests 160lbs as the weight, is also reliable but invalid.

Human indexers are unreliable (Golub 2006; Olson and Boll 2001; Chan 1989; Wolfram and Olson 2007; Cooper 1969). The often touted figure is 25%. That is to say, human indexers will only use the same term as each other, or the same term as themselves on a repeat assignment, 25% of the time. That is a very poor performance. However, there is more to be said here. If the indexers have first to produce the keys, to produce a classification and thesaurus, and then to assign the keys, unreliability is to be expected. In a way, it would be miraculous if all indexers choose the same synonym from a synonym set each time (why would they all independently choose 'butterflies', say?). What would make the difference here is whether the indexes are using a free vocabulary or a controlled one. Thus, if the keys are provided as a controlled vocabulary, complete with a topic graph and a thesaurus, we would see how good the human indexers are at assigning the keys. They are going to be better, but they still are not very good. If the humans are not reliable, many of their assignments are not going to be valid either.

Computer or software based indexing is going to be very reliable (in this technical sense of 'reliable'). Usually computer programs produce the same output from the same input. That means they are 100% reliable but this is an unimportant and unimpressive merit in this case. (Programs can be written to be non-deterministic and to produce varying outputs, but that is not the common way for most applications). What matters with computer indexing is whether the indexing is largely valid. Empirical evidence is hard to come by and interpret but the evidence (such as it is) is that for most cases of indexing it as valid as human indexing. Software indexing had other advantages: it is very quick, and it is 'tireless'. So, at least as a possibility, there could exhaustive or complete indexes to all texts that were available in electronic form.

> The bottom line is clear… automatic indexing works! And it appears to work just as well as human indexing, just differently. Automatic indexing is also considerably faster and cheaper than indexing based on human intellectual analysis. Automatic indexing can be applied to enormous collections of messages (such as the world-wide web) where the volume of texts and constant change, both in individual texts and in the composition of the collection as a whole, makes human indexing impractical, if not impossible (Anderson and Pérez-Carballo 2001a, p. 236).

It is hard to deny that Google, and other search engines, have effectively indexed the Web, and they have done a good job.

The one case that computer indexing has trouble with is the 'Holy Grail of Indexing', to be discussed shortly.

## 7.4  Are There Theories of Indexing? Can Indexing be Taught?

A leading authority, Bella Hass Weinberg, tells us there are no theories. She writes

> Indexing is not really a theory-based profession….

> Indexing is an art not a science Many intelligent people lack the ability to distill the essence of a document and to represent its main topics in a few words. Some people who have gone through formal training will never make good indexers, while others who are self-taught are excellent indexers, and have even won awards in the field. (Weinberg 2009, p. 2283)

Weinberg is not really talking about the act or activity of indexing in these passages, rather she is talking about people, the indexers, and the 'profession' of indexing. However, elsewhere she states

> The textbook of indexing authored by Lancaster records important principles, such as specificity, *and demonstrates that all so-called theories of indexing in fact are not.* (Weinberg 2009, p. 2284) emphasis added.

And another giant of indexing, Wellisch, writes

> Beginning indexers often ask whether there is a theory of indexing. If by this is meant a coherent system of propositions explaining the mental activities involved in transforming a text into its index, the only honest answer is that we do not have such a thing.... All we know is that indexing is a highly complex intellectual process involving the use of language in a specific and somewhat artificial way, and that it is also to a considerable extent a matter of intuition, the workings of which cannot be reduced to fixed rules.... In this respect, indexing is similar to other mental operations such as the recognition of faces and voices: we know that we can do it, but cannot describe in so many words how we do it, nor can we reduce it to a set of rules (Wellisch 1991, p. 218–219) (Anderson and Pérez-Carballo 2001a)

Other authorities add to this the assertion that indexing cannot be taught.

> I do not believe that indexing can be taught.... (Mulvany 1994, p. vii; Anderson and Pérez-Carballo 2001a)

This tends to be the view of practicing indexers. There certainly are some academics or researchers, for example, Harold Borko and Gerard Salton who hold the contrary position (Borko 1977; Salton 1975). (See also (Frohmann 1990; Quinn 1994). One of the Anderson and Pérez-Carballo articles has an extensive review of the literature on this topic.

There are three questions: whether we would like there to be theories of indexing, whether there are such theories, and whether indexing can be taught.

We certainly would like there to be theories. There is the need to index the deluge of IOs. Perhaps this task can be shared among many humans and also software. Theories facilitate this. Theories provide a rationale. Theories can be researched and articulated. They can be written down and disseminated. They can be distilled into practices and principles which themselves can be taught and learned. Where would we be if indexing were like painting *Les demoiselles d'Avignon*? Then only a gifted few could do it. Indexing could not be taught. And presumably the strategy for would-be indexers would be just to hang around, or apprentice themselves to, the titans of the profession, to gaze on great indexes, and to hope that some of the tacit and ineffable magic would rub off. [None of those strategies were needed by the creator of *Les demoiselles d'Avignon*.]

We would like theories– but are there any? There certainly are principles, such as specificity (and, to be fair, active indexers, like Weinberg and others, have educated us about these over and over again) and these principles can be tied into topic structures and the User's need for relevance (as has been done earlier). This provides a basis of theories of indexing. Now while a theory in empirical science offers understanding, explanation, and prediction, not all theories are theories in empirical science. Theories of indexing are going to offer shared knowledge and rationales. And there are such theories. We will see them in use with automatic indexing by computer. A hand-waving one can be offered here and now: indexing concerns the topics that should be assigned to IOs, and that is part a matter of the concepts that make up the content of the IOs, internal topics, and it is also a matter of how those internal topics relate into classification structures, external topics, etc. Indexes are relative to Users and the uses those Users make of the indexes. Thus, for example, if those Users were students, the requisite classification structures would be Bacon-d'Alembert Trees of Knowledge, Propaedias, or something similar. Who the Users are; what help they are expecting from the indexes; what the internal topics are; what the external topics are; are all questions for empirical research. So, there is empirical scope for theories of indexing which are directed at such questions.

When indexing authorities are skeptical about theories of indexing, they seem to have in mind that such theories should be in the nature of psychological, or socio-psychological, accounts connecting what indexers read to index with the indexing keys those indexers produce and assign (see the Wellisch quote above, (Anderson and Pérez-Carballo 2001a; Farrow 1995)). But these are not the kinds of theories that are required. Let us contrast the act of indexing with playing chess. Chess is primarily an intellectual activity (in fact, likely it is a more profound and demanding intellectual activity than indexing). The playing of chess can be carried out successfully or unsuccessfully (a player wins or loses) and chess players themselves can be of different levels of skill, which can be measured by their rankings. Not everyone can be good at chess, and to be really good the player probably has to have some innate ability or flair. But almost everyone can be taught to play. And there are theories related to the playing of chess. Such theories rarely have any connection with the psychology of the player. What the theories address are the problems that might be encountered in the course of play and what might be possible solutions to these problems. Chess can be taught and almost any chess player, even the very best, can improve his or her play by appropriate training involving study and application of the theories. Non-psychological chess-like theories are the ones needed for indexing. Indexing is more like playing chess than it is like recognizing faces (which was Wellisch's suggestion).

## 7.5  The Holy Grail of Indexing

The hardest task of indexing is indexing what it not there. Words refer to concepts, and it is the words that we read yet it is the concepts that we wish to index. Sometimes the concept is present but yet the preferred label is not. The simple examples of this are those with synonyms (car–automobile), (attorney–lawyer), (butterfly–rhopalocera), etc. And the simple examples are at least manageable, both by humans and by computers. They are manageable if what is being indexed, the key targets, are short, one or two or a few words, and there is thesaurus support. Basically if any of the terms in a synset is present, either 'attorney' or 'lawyer', say, then an index entry will be made using the headword, or preferred term, as the key, in this case 'attorney'. That process is not too difficult.

But indexing often requires summarization or abstraction. Consider a typical novel, say 300 pages, about 100,000 words. We may want to have the whole work, not parts of it, as an indexed value, as a referred to IO. In particular, we may want it to be one of the values of the key '[a tale of] unrequited love and betrayal'. So the 100,00 words of the novel have to be distilled down to the 4 words 'unrequited love and betrayal', and it could easily be that none of the words 'unrequited', 'love', and 'betrayal' occur anywhere in the text, the title, or in other materials associated with the novel. This task would trouble computers. Thesauri will not help. Thesauri do not do any summarization. And computers are better at *extracting* than they are at *abstracting*. It is worthwhile to explain this. Word processing programs (like Microsoft Word) often have a Summarize or Autosummarize feature or tool; this will take some text, perhaps a whole document, and 'summarize' it in a paragraph or even a sentence. But this summarization is extracting not abstracting. What the software does is to discard words and sentences that are actually there to produce a result. It will favor certain parts of the text, e.g. headings, the first or last sentences of paragraphs, and so on (Moens and Dumortier 2000). But everything in the result is there, as tokens, in the source. So indexing when the words of the key string are not present in an original poses problems. A human indexer could well succeed at this task. Especially so, if there were a controlled vocabulary for the key, and possibly even a limited choice among alternatives, or possibilities, for the key string. (These latter would also make the task slightly less impossible for a computer.) There is no guarantee that the human indexers would do better here, but likely they would do: the reason is that the indexing task requires that the text be understood and that is the locus of a human advantage over the computer. Weinberg, in her thesis, mentions that 10% is a figure for non-present entries.

> Brenner (1989, p. 66) has reported that a computer working with machine-readable abstracts and a thesaurus fails to assign 30% of the index terms assigned by humans. In my dissertation research (Weinberg 1981, p. 80), I found that approximately 10% of humanly assigned index terms do not occur in full text. This has been confirmed in subsequent studies which demonstrate that controlled vocabulary indexing enhances full text retrieval by 10% (Hersh and Hickam 1995). Alta Vista (1996), an Internet search engine, encourages authors of Web pages "to specify additional keywords to index" and to provide abstracts. (Weinberg 1996).

But thesauri are for small strings only—there is no summarization or abstraction process in a thesaurus, but indexing sometimes requires this.

## 7.6  Generalized Synonymy and Concept Indexing

Thus far we have talked about such access devices as the alphabetical list, alphabetical association list or alphabetical index, with words or strings as keys or entry points. But, in the setting of information in texts, there are two major problems with this, which we will label 'generalized synonymy' and 'generalized homography'.

Generalized synonymy is the ability we have to say the same thing in different ways—in fact, we can say the same thing in almost indefinitely many different ways. *We can paraphrase.* Here is a simple example from arithmetic. Consider the formula (4-2). Here are some expressions for it 'Four minus two', 'Four subtract two', 'Subtract two from four', 'Take away two from four', 'Four take away two', 'The difference between four and two', etc. This is a completely general phenomenon. We have the notion of synonymy: we see that as being word to word, or perhaps word to few words, equivalences. But, in fact, *generalized synonymy* is pervasive. All concepts have large numbers of expressions which can be used to identify them. As another simple illustration, 'the beautiful bride's wealthy father' is equivalent, more or less, to 'the wealthy father of the beautiful bride', 'the beautiful bride's father, who was wealthy', 'the wealthy father of the bride, who was beautiful' and so on. This is a problem because if you form an association list index from the basis of strings you would have to have every possible paraphrase string as a key in the index. It just would not work. A typical partial solution that most of us will be familiar with is to have certain atomic, or brief, keywords or keyword strings which are indexed and which can be compounded together using Boolean operations—postcoordination. So, within the system, we might have 'beautiful', 'bride', 'wealthy', and 'father' all indexed by themselves, and the system might have the ability to produce a value for 'beautiful AND bride AND wealthy AND father'. There is a school of thought, going back fifty years of more, that this is never going to work very well. There are two fatal flaws in it, as it has been described thus far. A Boolean literal string match from 'beautiful AND bride AND wealthy AND father' might retrieve permutations of 'the beautiful bride's wealthy father'; but generalized synonymy is more general than this; for example, 'the comely newlywed's affluent male parent' is a paraphrase of the original and it contains none of the indexed atomic search strings, so it will not be found. Also, Boolean operations are limited. Essentially they are propositional logic operations, whereas what we would like are operations sourced from predicate logic and even lambda calculus. We would like to be able to index or find 'philosophy of history' and have that as being something different from both 'history of philosophy' and 'philosophy and history'. Quite a few modern theorists think that a better response to generalized synonymy is to move from indexing words to indexing, or trying to index, concepts. This is the 'assigned' or concept indexing.

Generalize synonymy is the main intellectual reason to do concept indexing not expression indexing. As Fugmann puts it

General concepts and concept relations can be represented through what amounts to an infinity of different words in natural, colloquial language. Making the expression of a general concept predictable for adequate retrieval obviously requires interpretation, translation, and representation in a language different from its occurrence in the original text. (Fugmann 2004, p. 172)

Generalized synonymy suggests that Concept Plane indexing is what is required.

> In concept indexing, the indexer recognizes the concepts with which a document deals, rather than merely accepting the names he finds in the document. In practice, this means that he provides means for a client to find all works on a concept no matter what name the client uses for the concept, nor what name is used for the concept in the document; and that he distinguishes the different meanings of a homonym, so that the client is not led to irrelevant documents by the indexing system. (Buchanan 1979, pp. 12–13)

Assigned or concept indexing, favored, for example, by Foskett and Fugmann (Foskett 1977; Fugmann 1993, 2004) needs to be incisive on what it has to say about the concepts and the relationships between them. And, independently, librarianship needs to be a friend to the computer. That invites the use of symbolic logic; for it is logic that both embodies clarity and is semi-algorithmic.

We already have what we need for the description of concepts, namely: types or intensional abstractions.

## 7.7 Generalized Homography

Computers are weak with language and representing knowledge because of the 'tip of the iceberg' problem: that is, only a small proportion of what is required for understanding is actually there explicitly in the text or texts. We disambiguate using the context of the text or even the surrounding situation or circumstance.

There is a way of thinking about this. There is some text present that is associated with a conceptual unit: that text might be a fragment, a sentence, a paragraph, or an entire article or book. But the explicit text could be the tip of several *different* icebergs. We humans can sort this out, picking the intended iceberg, most of us, most of the time. So what is happening here is that the same explicit text might potentially identify different underlying concepts (from the different icebergs). Really, this is similar to homographs, where there is a one-to-many mapping from the words to the concepts. But it is generalized homography, it is not just single words that are mapped one to many rather it usually is text strings that map one-to-many to concepts. And it is we smart humans that can disambiguate them.

A text may have explicitly the words 'The fishermen went to the bank' and we humans can say whether this addresses the topic of retrieving cash or the topic of travel to the riverside. Computers would struggle with this task.

## 7.8 Automation

The deluge of digital IOs invites the use of computers and automation in classification (Slavic and Cordeiro 2004; Soergel 1974a; Srinivasan 1992). But, it seems, computers have their limits and some task seem to require humans. What is the appropriate balance here?

## 7.8.1  *Automatic Production of Schedules*

What are the possibilities for automation of the production of classification schemes, perhaps from the IOs themselves? This certainly is an active research area. See, for example, (Chen et al. 1995; Ingwersen and Wormell 1992; Soergel 1974b; Golub 2006; Chen 2003; Candan et al. 2008; Deerwester et al. 1990; Cimiano et al. 2003; Spårck Jones 1976; Ibekwe-SanJuan 2006). Generally the techniques here are something of an inversion to our approach. We look for conceptual classification schemes and use those to generate thesauri—top–down as it were. But many researchers in this area work bottom-up. They look at the documents or the IOs themselves, then the terms in those IOs are clustered by statistical techniques and related one cluster to another. And it is certainly possible to generate thesauri this way. The resulting thesauri can be used as ends in themselves, or they can be used for retrieval, or they can be put together in Self Organizing Maps (Kohonen 2001), graphs, or similar, or, finally, the thesauri can be used as stepping stones to conceptual classification.

But automating the production of classification schedules is not of first importance in the following sense. Classification schemes are typically produced once and used many times. In traditional librarianship there are the DDC, LCC, UDC, and other, schemes, and those same schemes are used on billions of IOs. The deluge of IOs does not force us to produce many schemes, it just forces us to classify exponentially many more IOs under the few schemes we have. It is true that schemes are revised: we noted earlier that 'computer science' as a subject was introduced into DDC. But the Dewey Classification is now only at its 22nd edition since about 1900. That does not suggest the need for fully automatic production without human intervention. There is time available here for the task.

Also, it is doubtful that automatic analysis of the IOs only could do what is required. Birger Hjørland writes

> Algorithms may indeed classify documents and may even produce hierarchies. What do traditional classifications contribute in addition to this? The fact is that traditional classification involves structures that cannot be produced by any empirical analysis of the documents (or of the users for that matter). A geographical structure, for example, places different regions in a structure that is *autonomous* in relation to the documents that are written about those regions. You cannot produce a geographical map of Spain by making, for example, bibliometrical maps of the literature about Spain. [Yet such autonomous structures as maps of Spain are often very useful for information retrieval about Spain] (Hjørland 2002, p. 452)

Exactly so: you are not going to produce a map of Spain by looking at words about Spain in IOs, and yet it is the map of Spain that is particularly helpful with a certain kind of information retrieval.

There may be value in automatic thesaurus construction. Small specialized document collections certainly lend themselves to it (a large collection like the IOs on the World Wide Web is another matter) and automation handles the issue of revision or updating very well. So if the document collection addresses an area or topics where the terminology is fluid or changing, automation may help.

In sum, almost certainly any production of a classification scheme is going to involve the use of computers, but it is not important that the computers produce the schemes *autonomously* and *without* human assistance.

## 7.8.2 Automatic Annotation

Much indexing or annotation can be done by computer, as Anderson and Pérez-Carballo and others have assured us (Anderson and Pérez-Carballo 2001b; Spårck Jones 1971, 1974a, b). But the hard generalized synonymy and generalized homography cases cannot. They need humans, and skilled humans at that. The conclusion to be drawn is: use computers for the vast bulk of (routine) cases, use a human indexer for the hard cases. A computer can index technical reports, but a human will do much better with a standard published book, like, for example, *A History of Philosophy*. (See also (Albrechtsen 1993; Bates 1998).)

## 7.8.3 Automatic Clustering

There are approaches to IO retrieval that do not use, or simply bypass, schedules and annotation. For example, there is Salton's term/concept vectors or fingerprints (Salton 1968). Another recent example is Latent Semantic Analysis or Latent Semantic Indexing (Deerwester et al. 1990; Koll 1979; Dumais 1995; Telcordia 2011). Some of these at least assert the ability to find terms that are not there.

> As a result, terms that did not actually appear in a document may still end up close to the document, if that is consistent with the major patterns of association in the data. (Deerwester et al. 1990, p. 1)

The ideas here are these: there are terms and documents, and there are terms which actually do appear in the documents. These can be used to associate, or cluster, documents with each other. Then each document cluster associates terms with its component documents, and, in particular, there may be an association between a specific term and a document even though that term does not appear in the document. So: there may be hundreds of documents, from a collection of thousands, that contain 'car' and 'automobile' (and many other terms). The clustering on the terms as a whole may group the 'car–automobile' documents together and, in particular, 'car' may get associated with a document that does not contain it as a token.

Whether, and how well, this works is presumably a matter of empirical test. But the position here is one of skepticism toward it. It will not work if the tokens (e.g. 'car') are not there at all—in any of the documents—or if their occurrences are rare. And Hjørland's Map-of-Spain argument seems a core rebuttal.

# References

Albrechtsen H (1993) Subject analysis and indexing: from automated indexing to domain analysis. Indexer 18(4):219–224

Anderson JD (1985) Indexing systems: extensions of the mind's organizing power. In: Ruben BD (ed) Information and behaviour. Transaction Books, New Brunswick, pp 287–323

Anderson JD, Pérez-Carballo J (2001a) The nature of indexing how humans and machines analyze messages and texts for retrieval Part I Research, and the nature of human indexing. Inf Process Manage 37(2):231–254

Anderson JD, Pérez-Carballo J (2001b) b The nature of indexing: how humans and machines analyze messages and texts for retrieval Part II Machine indexing, and the allocation of human versus machine effort. Inf Process Manage 37(2):255–277

Bates MJ (1998) Indexing and access for digital libraries and the Internet: human, database, and domain factors. J Am Soc Inf Sci 49:1185–1205

Borko H (1977) Toward a theory of indexing. Inf Process Manage 13(6):355–365

Brenner EH (1989) Vocabulary control. In: Weinberg BH (ed.) Indexing: the state of our knowledge and the state of our ignorance: Proceedings of the 20th Annual Meeting of the American Society of Indexers, 1988. Medford, NJ, pp. 62–67. (Learned Information)

Buchanan B (1979) Theory of library classification. Clive Bingley, London

Buckland M (1999) Vocabulary as a central concept in library and information science. In: Aparac T, Saracevic T, Ingwersen P, Vakkari P (eds) Digital libraries: interdisciplinary concepts, challenges, and opportunities. Proceedings of the third international conference on conceptions of library and information science, CoLIS3, Dubrovnik, Croatia, 23–26 May 1999. Lokve, Zagreb, Croatia, pp 3–12

Buckland M, Plaunt C (1994) On the construction of selection systems. Library Hi Tech 12(4):15–28

Candan KS, Di Caro L, Sapino ML (2008) Creating tag hierarchies for effective navigation in social media. In: ACM workshop on search in social media, Napa Valley, CA. ACM, pp 75–82

Chan LM (1989) Inter-indexer consistency in subject cataloging. Inf Technol Libraries 8(4):349–357

Chen C (2003) Mapping scientific frontiers: the quest for knowledge visualization. Springer, Berlin

Chen H, Yim T, Fye D, Schatz B (1995) Automatic thesaurus generation for an electronic community system. J Am Soc Inf Sci 46(3):175–193. doi:10.1002/(sici)1097-4571(199504)46:3<175::aid-asi3>3.0.co;2-u

Cimiano P, Staab S, Tane J (2003) Automatic acquisition of taxonomies from text: FCA meets NLP. In: ECML/PKDD workshop on adaptive text extraction and mining, 2003

Cooper WS (1969) Is interindexer consistency a hobgoblin? Am Documentation 20(3):268–278

Deerwester S, Dumais ST, Furnas GW, Landauer TK, Harshman R (1990) Indexing by latent semantic analysis. J Am Soc Inf Sci 41(6):391–407

Dumais ST (1995) Using LSI for information filtering: TREC-3 experiments. In: Harman D (ed) The third text REtrieval conference (TREC3). National Institute of Standards and Technology Special Publication

Farrow J (1995) All in the mind: concept analysis in indexing. Indexer 19(4):243–247

Foskett AC (1977) Subject approach to information, 3rd edn. Clive Bingley, London

Frohmann B (1990) Rules of indexing: a critique of mentalism in information retrieval theory. J Documentation 46:94

Fugmann R (1993) Subject analysis and indexing. Theoretical foundation and practical advice. Indeks Verlag, Frankfurt/Main

Fugmann R (2004) Learning the lessons of the past. In: Rayward WB, Bowden ME (eds) The history and heritage of scientific and technical information systems: proceedings of the 2002 conference, Chemical Heritage Foundation. Information Today, Medford, NJ, pp 168–181

Golub K (2006) Automated subject classification of textual web documents. J Documentation 62(3):350–371

Hersh WR, Hickam D (1995) Information retrieval in medicine: the SAPHIRE experience. J Am Soc Inf Sci 46:743–747. (Letter by S.M. Humphrey. (1996). JASIS, 47:407–408)

Hjørland B (2002) The methodology of constructing classification schemes: a discussion of the state-of-art. In: López-Huertas MJ (ed) Challenges in Knowledge Representation and Organization for the 21th Century. Integration of Knowledge across Boundaries, Granada, Spain, Ergon Verlag, Wu rzburg. Proceedings of the seventh international ISKO conference, pp 450–456

Ibekwe-SanJuan F (2006) Constructing and maintaining knowledge organization tools: a symbolic approach. J Documentation 62(2):229–250

Ingwersen P, Wormell I (1992) Ranganathan in the perspective of advanced information retrieval. Libri 42(3):184–201

Kohonen T (2001) Self-organizing maps, 3rd edn. Springer-Verlag, Berlin

Koll MB (1979) WEIRD: An approach to concept-based information retrieval. ACM SIGIR Forum, XIII 32–50

Moens M-F, Dumortier J (2000) Use of a text grammar for generating highlight abstracts of magazine articles. J Documentation 56(5):520–539

Mulvany NC (1994) Indexing books. University of Chicago Press, Chicago

Olson HA, Boll JJ (2001) Subject analysis in online catalogs, 2nd edn. Libraries Unlimited, Englewood

Quinn BA (1994) Recent theoretical approaches in classification and indexing. Knowl Organiz 21(3):140–147

Rogers FB (1960a) Medical subject headings. Preface and introduction. In. U.S. Department of Health, Education, and Welfare, Washington D.C., pp i–xix

Rogers FB (1960b) Review of Taube, Mortimer. Studies in coordinate indexing. Bull Med Libr Assoc 42:380–384 (July 1954)

Salton G (1968) Automatic information organization and retrieval. McGraw Hill, NY

Salton G (1975) A theory of indexing. Regional conference series in applied mathematics, society for industrial and applied mathematics. Philadelphia, PA

Slavic A, Cordeiro MI (2004) Core requirements for automation of analytico-synthetic classifications. Adv Knowledge Organiz 9:187–192

Soergel D (1974a) Automatic and semi-automatic methods as an aid in the construction of indexing languages and thesauri. Int Classification 1(1):34–39

Soergel D (1974b) Indexing languages and thesauri: construction and maintenance. Melville, Los Angeles

Spårck Jones K (1971) Automatic keyword classification. Butterworths, London

Spårck Jones K (1974a) Automatic indexing. J Documentation 30(4):393–432

Spårck Jones K (1974b) Automatic indexing 1974 computer laboratory. University of Cambridge, Cambridge

Spårck Jones K (1976) Automatic classification. In: Maltby A (ed) Classification in the 1970s: a second look. Bingley, London, pp 209–225

Srinivasan P (1992) Thesaurus construction. In: Frakes WBaB-Y R (ed) Information retrieval: data structures and algorithms. Prentice Hall, Upper Saddle River New Jersey, pp 161–218

Telcordia T (2011) Telcordia Latent Semantic Indexing (LSI) Demo Machine. http://lsi.research.telcordia.com/. Accessed 10 Oct 2010

Weinberg BH (1981) Word frequency and automatic indexing (dissertation). Columbia University, New York

Weinberg BH (1996) Compexity In Indexing Systems - Abandonment And Failure: Implications For Organizing The Internet. http://www.asis.org/annual-96/ElectronicProceedings/weinberg.html. Accessed 12 Oct 2010

Weinberg BH (2009) Indexing: history and theory. Encyclopedia of library and information sciences, 3rd edn. pp 2277–2290

Wellisch HH (1991) Indexing from A to Z. H.W.Wilson Co

Wolfram D, Olson HA (2007) A method for comparing large scale inter-indexer consistency using IR modeling. In: Canadian association for information science proceedings

# Chapter 8
# Distributed Libraries, Information and Databases

## 8.1 Introduction

Nowadays, the Users of IOs are often distant from the owners, managers, or providers of those IOs. Classical Librarianship has the solution to the basic physical 'document' case of this. When libraries started to provide Union Catalogs—which would both publish details of their collection to others and inform their own patrons about the holdings of other libraries—they ensured that there was consistency, and accuracy, of document or container descriptions. The same infrastructure supports libraries lending to each other, namely Inter Library Loan. And the syntax and semantics of container descriptions, is the difference between success and failure with distributed documents. So reasonable consistency and accuracy of metadata, coupled with harvesting and publication of that metadata should prove sufficient. Of course, there are issues with producing consistent and accurate metadata, principally that the important parts of it, such as subject annotation, require human catalogers, but humans are swamped by the deluge of IOs.

Retrieving distant information or distributed data—in abstract content form as opposed the physical document form—is a harder problem. The central difficulty is coming to terms with the semantics or meaning of what the remote sources are saying. Barry Smith uses the example of business cards (Smith 2009a). A businessman has printed, say, 100 cards carrying such information as his name, phone number, the company he works for etc. and he gives them to people he meets so the hundred cards end up widely distributed. So there are 100 of his 'documents', each containing (actually the same) information. But, of course, the businessman is not alone. Pretty well all business people have business cards and give them out. And there is no standard format—and no standard meaning—to the contents of business cards. The syntax and semantics of business cards is a confusion. Imagine simulating this by computer, and in particular attempting to retrieve information about, say, the business person Jane Jones's phone number. Software would have to hope that some 'business card' somewhere had the name or title 'Jane Jones' on it and also a phone

M. Frické, *Logic and the Organization of Information*,
DOI: 10.1007/978-1-4614-3088-9_8,
© Springer Science+Business Media New York 2012

number field, which it would then return. But the syntax is problematical, is the field that carries Jane Jones's name called the *name* field or is it called the *title* field or is it called something else? What is the format of her name. Might it be 'Jane Jones'? might it be 'J. Jones'?, might it be 'Dr. J. Jones'? And similar considerations apply to the other fields, such as the phone number field. There are also problems, in fact larger problems, with the semantics. Say the card does have field labeled the 'title' field. What does the value for this field mean? The card itself (say, each of the individual 100 of them) has a name or title, the person the card describes has a name or title, the company the person described works for has a name or title. What does the 'title' field mean? Extracting information is near impossible.

So, here is the contrast. Imagine every business card ever produced had its own unique barcode stamped on it, for example, a barcoded URI. And consider the problem of retrieving a particular business card i.e. the card with a sought-for barcode. That problem—essentially physical document retrieval—is close to Inter Library Loan and likely it can be solved by traditional techniques. But the data problem is different. That problem is, for example, to find Dr Janet Jones's phone number from the business cards. And to do that, the various parties have to know what the individual business cards mean. That is a problem of *information representation* or *knowledge representation*.

To a degree, the syntax and data structures of remote data can be managed. There are also modern digital systems and formats, such as Extensible Markup Language XML (which has the ability to describe the syntax of the data that it is used to convey, usually in electronic files). But none of these techniques or systems address the contents of the IO 'documents'; they do not address the semantics, i.e. the information that the IOs contain. There is a worry about *information silos*. Certain institutions, especially research and experimental institutions can generate and hold vast amounts of data or information. And it can be relatively easy to get that uninterpreted information—in the sense of being able to download electronic 0s and 1s over a network. However, knowing what that information is, and what it signifies, is a different issue altogether. The information might be within a silo, unavailable to the world. There is the need for cooperation and standards.

The publisher or producer can help by providing the semantics—and often this is a matter of 'ontology' or conceptual scheme. The publisher can, in effect, say: we approach our fragment of the world as though it had the following structure, and within that ontology here is some information. That is the hope of the Semantic Web and the Linked Data movement. Those initiatives are mostly an application of symbolic logic.

## 8.2 Metadata (Metacrap?)

Viable metadata systems are central to managing distributed information. The metadata both provides information about 'flat' data fields of interest concerning an IO, such as author, title, and the like, but also it can provide information about structure—both of the IO and of its data fields (NISO 2004). (Metadata is also used for digital rights management and for archiving management, topics which are not addressed in this book.) Any reasonable metadata scheme is going to have control of names of the keys and of its basic semantics.

A standard modern example is the Dublin Core, devised in Dublin, Ohio, about 1995 (DCMI 2011). The initial goal with this was to define some simple rules and metadata elements so that ordinary folk, who were not professional catalogers, could describe their own Web pages and digital creations.

The present (simple) Dublin Core Metadata Element Set has 15 metadata fields. They are

1. Title
2. Creator
3. Subject
4. Description
5. Publisher
6. Contributor
7. Date
8. Type
9. Format
10. Identifier
11. Source
12. Language
13. Relation
14. Coverage
15. Rights

And the many schemes and projects which use Dublin Core try to ensure standards, in particular a consistent semantics ('domain specific agreements'). There are conferences and initiatives attempting to agree what, for example, the Title field, and the other fields, should mean.

In 2001, Cory Doctorow published the challenging and provocative 'Metacrap: Putting the torch to seven straw-men of the meta-utopia' (Doctorow 2001) which is a critique of the idea that metadata initiatives for the Internet and Web can lead to the utopia of widespread interoperable data and systems. It will be worthwhile evaluating his arguments. The salient ones are that people lie, people are lazy, people are stupid, and that people are fallible and inaccurate in any metadata assignments that they make. (The somewhat in-your-face terminology is Doctorow's own.) [Clifford Lynch made much the same points, in a more sober way, in his (Lynch 2001).]

People lie in as much as they sometimes deliberately create false metadata for various purposes, usually commercial gain. An example (not from Doctorow) is that there is a private seller in the Furniture section of the Tucson Craigslist who writes in every one of their For Sale entries

keewords: danish modern mid century midcentury copenhagen potterybarn italian ikea

Let us not worry about their misspelling of 'keywords', but what this does is it ensures that anyone who searches for, say, 'danish' is directed to their advert, whether or not what they are selling is, in fact, Danish furniture. So, it is deliberate 'lying' for potential commercial gain. This is commonplace, usually on a much grander scale than this example. It is what so-called Search Engine Optimization (SEO) companies offer as a commercial service.

This point, though, does not apply to traditional libraries. No library would label *Tables of Moon Phases* 1800-2199 as having the subject matter 'Harry Potter adventure' or 'racy romance novel' merely to attract readers to it. And nor would separate Biodiversity silos lie to manipulate traffic. In the cases of interest to the present book, no one is going to be 'lying'.

People are lazy in as much as they will not bother to set important metadata fields—or at least set them into useful values. For example, many of us initially save word processing document by their default title, which might be 'Untitled.doc'. And once there are many 'Untitled.docs' in the world meaningful cooperation and retrieval gets a whole lot more difficult. This point is surely right. However, many metadata fields can be set close to automatically, and many of the setters, especially professional and institutional ones, are not lazy.

How are the values of typical metadata fields to be set, in the general case of IOs? There is an algorithmic spectrum. Many can be set automatically on a computer, by its Operating System or the running Applications. For example, whenever a User creates a document in a word processor, the computer and the word processor between them produce something like a couple of hundred metadata pairs connected with the document (such as file creation date, file type, owner application, and so on). But much metadata cannot be managed trivially in this way. Determining such metadata as the subject matter of an IO is semi-algorithmic: human catalogers can do it, machines may be able to do some of it in whole or in part—research continues on this. At the other end of the spectrum, there are non algorithmic kinds, such as a user-defined metadata field for files that the User found interesting for some particular purpose. There are problems with these, as Doctorow observes: people are lazy (and stupid).

What single individuals do, in the privacy of their own homes so-to-speak, is rather different to what would be best practice with institutions, publishers, or commercial bodies. For example, archives are not going to store many documents under the title of 'Untitled.doc'. The parties concerned are motivated to be assiduous: they know the value of metadata, and wish to ensure that it is comprehensive and correct.

People are stupid. They cannot spell or do punctuation and grammar. This means that controlled vocabularies are likely not a possibility, and the free vocabularies people use are rather too free and inconsistent. Two points here. Once again this concerns small time private users and does not apply to 'serious professionals'. And also, there are some counter moves that can be made. For example, a system might not require correct spelling from a User, instead the User would make a menu choice from a menu of correctly spelled alternatives.

The final criticisms are that that people's judgments are fallible and not very reliable, so it is unlikely that their judgments would capture much objective truth in metadata assignments. Again this is a consideration about casual single users. Fallibility is universal, of course. But many of the assignments of professionals are reliable and valid. If the Library of Congress determines that the title of a particular book is 'Hamlet' we can take that as the objective truth. Of course, sometimes professionals do less well than they might. Geoffrey Nunberg tells us that Google's Book Search metadata are a

> train wreck: a mishmash wrapped in a muddle wrapped in a mess (Nunberg 2009).

So, the conclusions to be drawn from Doctorow are: be careful when money and commerce are concerned; and ordinary Joe and Jane Public, left to their own devices, are not going to be much help with metadata.

Neither of these conclusions affect well motivated professionals.

## 8.3 Functional Requirements for Bibliographic Records

Functional Requirements for Bibliographic Records (FRBR) is an international initiative to provide a record substrate for IOs which is adequate for modern needs (Denton 2007; Maxwell 2008; IFLA 1997; Taylor 2007a, b). Its architects were smart enough to design the system in terms of the functions it needed to perform, and to leave the implementation details to different communities of adopters. (Otherwise, there would have been much resistance from vested interests and owners of legacy systems.) It uses the Entity-Relationship (ER) modeling which is standard in database design (Martin 1982).

FRBR is something of a work in progress, but the main settled core parts of it date from 1998.

> [FRBR is] a new model of the bibliographic universe. That universe includes everything that libraries, bookstores, museums, and other similar entities might collect. It also includes all persons, bodies, or families that might interact with those collections in any way—as authors, as owners, as producers. It also includes all concepts that might be needed to describe other entities in the bibliographic universe. The model shows us ways these entities all interact with each other and ways users of libraries and other providers of bibliographic information interact with databases to obtain what they need. (Maxwell 2008, pp. 1, 2)

### 8.3.1 Group I Entities

From a certain point of view, FRBR, or FRBR Group I Entities, can be seen as a very natural generalization of traditional library cataloging practice. With Panizzi, in the nineteenth century, the library ontology contained three kinds of things: *works*, *editions*, and physical *copies*. This centuries old ontology is tied to books.

Yet it is clear that many IOs, or, more generally, 'artistic creations', never appear as books—there are musical symphonies, operas, films, performed plays, and so on. So there needs to be a category to catch this 'medium of expression' of a work. FRBR just calls it *expression*. At this point, conceptually, the ontology contains four kinds of things: *works, expressions, editions*, and *copies*. FRBR then uses a slightly different terminology, preferring to use the word 'manifestation' for 'edition' and the word 'item' for 'copy'.

Thus, FRBR uses four definitions (*work, expression, manifestation, item*) to identify the primary bibliographic entities. What is FRBR trying to do?

Consider Shakespeare's Hamlet. There is the play. There is the play on stage, in text, on film. There are particular productions on stage, particular versions in text, and particular film versions. There are performances of productions on stage, items in text, and particular strips of celluloid or pieces of plastic. There are critics writing about the play, writing about productions of the play, writing about per-formances of productions of the play. There are characters in the play, there are actors portraying those characters in productions and performances, on stage and on film. The actor Kenneth Branagh has portrayed Hamlet on stage, in several productions, and he has portrayed Hamlet in a film. Branagh has also directed a film version of Hamlet. And so on. The question is: how to slice and dice this. There is no unique definitive answer. We will want to have some kind of type-token distinction, but beyond that it is a question of what is best for the Users. The driving principle is: what is best for the patrons? FRBR answers as follows: let's have works (Hamlet), expressions (Hamlet in text, Hamlet on stage, Hamlet on film), manifestations (publications or editions of Hamlet in text, productions of Hamlet on stage, etc.) and items (actual physical books, performances of a pro-duction of Hamlet on stage). It seems a reasonable proposal.

FRBR defines a *work*

> The first entity defined in the model is *work*: a distinct intellectual or artistic creation.
> (IFLA 1997, p. 17)

Shakespeare's *Hamlet* is a work, and so too are Beethoven's 9th and the Beatles *All you need is love*. These are plain abstract objects. Works exist as common-alities of content. A token book *Hamlet,* one of the film versions of *Hamlet,* and a stage performance of *Hamlet* have a commonality of content, namely *Hamlet*; that commonality of content is the work *Hamlet*. Works are typically identified by their title and author, but there may be other ways (some works might not have either an author or a title, or that information may be unknown). Distinguishing one work from another might be difficult. When Beethoven was writing the 9th, no doubt there were many preliminary versions with some different notes, re-arranged sections, etc. Just what constitutes the 9th itself, and what constitutes an early or draft version is impossible to say definitively. It is a matter for decision. And the decision will be motivated by the interests of the patrons; that is, the eventual patrons that wish to retrieve or use items that have direct or indirect reference to the work. If scholars, listeners, the 'culture' etc. wish to regard some intellectual or artistic creations as being distinct, those creations are distinct.

FRBR defines an *expression*

> The second entity defined in the model is *expression*: the intellectual or artistic realization of a *work* in the form of alpha-numeric, musical, or choreographic notation, sound, image, object, movement, etc., or any combination of such forms. (IFLA 1997, p. 19)

Expressions also are plain abstract objects. Expressions are, though, related to works. They are related by the 'realization' relation. They are 'forms' of a work. So, Henry Gray's *Anatomy of the human body* could be realized in the form of text, it could also be realized in the form of a musical. All the forms, qua abstract objects, exist. But some of them (e.g. Gray as a musical) may never participate in a chain of being that ends with a concrete item (and we will be getting to that) so there would be lesser interest in those. This set-up depends on notions of 'realization' and 'form'. And these notions are important because, eventually, we are going to want to count, and that will depend on whether two forms are the same realizations of the same work or are different realizations of the same work, etc. We do have good pre-theoretical ideas as to what forms are and what realization is. And the FRBR gives an abundance of examples to clarify intuition and decision.

Then there are *manifestations*.

> The third entity defined in the model is *manifestation*: the physical embodiment of an *expression* of a *work*.
> The entity defined as *manifestation* encompasses a wide range of materials, including manuscripts, books, periodicals, maps, posters, sound recordings, films, video recordings, CD-ROMs, multimedia kits, etc. As an entity, *manifestation* represents all the physical objects that bear the same characteristics, in respect to both intellectual content and physical form. (IFLA 1997, p. 21)

There is a slight muddle or unfortunate phrasing here. If, as in the first sentence, a manifestation was 'the physical embodiment of an expression of a work', it would be a concrete object existing in space and time (that is what a physical embodiment is). If, on the other hand, as in the third sentence 'As an entity, manifestation represents all the physical objects that bear the same characteristics', manifestation would just be a type (pretty well a Peirce-type, which is a notion that has been explained at length earlier). It would be another abstract object. The second meaning is what is intended here. The first sentence would have been better had it been written, with the plural 'embodiments', 'The third entity defined in the model is *manifestation*: the physical embodiments of an *expression* of a *work*.' Manifestations are also abstract objects. (Many of the actual IFLA authors say otherwise. They say that manifestations are physical. For example, Barbara Tillett does so on page 22 of (Tillett 2001). This is a slip or a mistake. Manifestations are the types, and types are not physical.)

Finally, there are *items*.

> The fourth entity defined in the model is *item*: a single exemplar of a *manifestation*.
> The entity defined as *item* is a concrete entity. It is in many instances a single physical object (e.g., a copy of a one-volume monograph, a single audio cassette, etc.). There are instances, however, where the entity defined as *item* comprises more than one physical object (e.g., a monograph issued as two separately bound volumes, a recording issued on three separate compact discs, etc.). (IFLA 1997, p. 21)

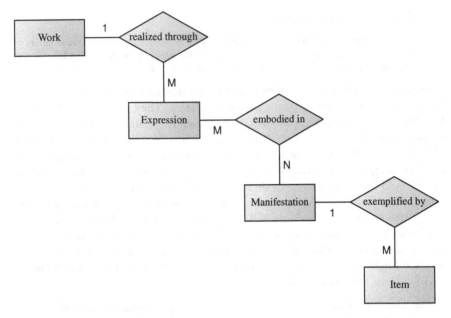

**Fig. 8.1** An E-R diagram of Group I entities

Items are concrete objects that instantiate or exemplify manifestations. They are the tokens.

Sometimes a single item can be more than one physical object, in the mereological sense of parts and wholes. A racing car with a wheel in the crowd is somewhat spread. Part of it is in the crowd, the other parts of it are on the track. Similarly, one bibliographical item may consist of two volumes, one volume (one part) in one library, and another volume (another part) perhaps in a completely different library.

So, *items* are physical objects; items *exemplify* (or are instances of, or are in the extension of or denotation of) *manifestations*; *manifestations* are abstract objects which embody *expressions*; and *expressions* are abstract objects which realize *works*. (Fig. 8.1). See (IFLA 1997, p. 14)

The Ms and Ns, as labels here, are a convention from Entity-Relationship modeling. What they say, for example, is that a work can be realized in multiple expressions, but, going the other way, any expression is the expression of exactly one work. (And similarly for the other connections in the diagram.)

There are a number of attributes or properties that Group I entities might have. Conceptually, these are just key-value pairs i.e. just plain vanilla metadata. To give an illustration, works can have 12 attributes

The logical attributes of a *work* defined for this study are the following:
title of the *work*
form of *work*
date of the *work*
other distinguishing characteristic
intended termination
intended audience
context for the *work*
medium of performance (musical work)
numeric designation (musical work)
key (musical work)
coordinates (cartographic work)
equinox (cartographic work)
(IFLA 1997, p. 33)

Somewhat similarly, expressions can have 25 attributes, manifestations can have 38 attributes. and items can have 9 attributes. For each of the 84 attributes here there are definitions or descriptions of what they are and criteria for their application or use. These are available from the original source documents. Suffice it to say, there is intended to be enough standardized metadata in the records to support the desired bibliographical tasks and manipulations.

## 8.3.2  Group II Entities

The entities in the second group ... represent those responsible for the intellectual or artistic content, the physical production and dissemination, or the custodianship of the entities in the first group. The entities in the second group include *person* (an individual) and *corporate body* (an organization or group of individuals and/or organizations). (IFLA 1997, p. 14)

The Group II entities include *Person* and *Corporate Body* and these entities may bear interesting relationships to Group I entities. A relationship is just a two-place or dyadic predicate and here are the central ones:

x is created by y
x is realized by y
x is produced by y
x is owned by y

Works are *created* by people or corporate bodies. Expressions are *realized* by people or corporate bodies. Manifestations are *produced* by people or corporate bodies. Items are *owned* by people or corporate bodies (Fig. 8.2). See (IFLA 1997, p. 15)

Group II entities also might have attributes. There are 9 such attributes including 'name of person' and 'name of corporate body'.

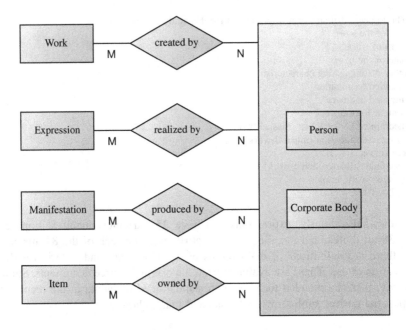

**Fig. 8.2**  An E-R diagram of Group II entities

### 8.3.3  Group III Entities

> The entities in the third group ... serve as the subjects of *works*. The group includes
> *concept* (an abstract notion or idea), *object* (a material thing), *event* (an action or occur-
> rence), and *place* (a location).

So, we have *concepts*, *objects*, *events*, and *places* as the subject matter or
subject classification of works (the Group I entity).

Concepts, objects, events, and places can be the subjects of works. But also,
works can have as their subject matter other works. When Toynbee writes the
*History of the World*, and Trevor-Roper writes *Arnold Toynbee's Millenium,* the
subject matter of Trevor-Roper's article is not history, it is Toynbee's work.
Following this line of thought, works can have as their subjects any combination of
works, expressions, manifestations, items, persons, and corporate bodies
(Fig. 8.3). See (IFLA 1997, p. 16)

Each of the Group III entities might have one attribute ('term for the concept',
'term for the object', 'term for the event', 'term for the place') so what we have
here is (presumably controlled) vocabulary terms as identifiers of the subjects in
the subject classification.

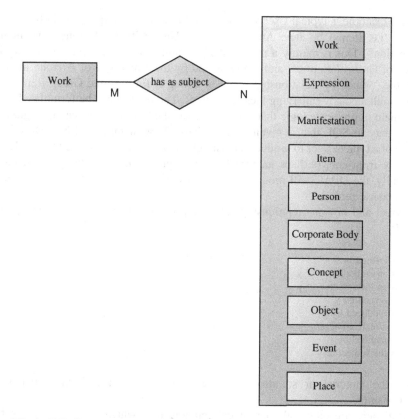

**Fig. 8.3**  An E-R diagram of Group III entities

FRBR seems somewhat awkward over subjects compared with what is advocated in this text. We would just use concepts as subjects for everything—including using 'Fido'-Fido reasoning for objects.

## 8.3.4 Relationships and Queries

As noted earlier, 'relationships' are the foundations of bibliography and bibliographical information retrieval.

The FRBR report itself states

In the context of the model, relationships serve as the vehicle for depicting the link between one entity and another, and thus as the means of assisting the user to "navigate" the universe that is represented in a bibliography, catalogue, or bibliographic database. Typically the user will formulate a search query using one or more attributes of the entity for which he or she is searching, and it is through the attribute that the user finds the entity sought. The relationships reflected in the bibliographic record provide additional information that assists the user in making connections between the entity found and other entities that are related to that entity. (IFLA 1997, p. 55)

So, for example, a typical User 'catalog-style' information request might be 'What books (i.e. items) by Jane Austen does the University of Arizona have in its collection?' This is merely a matter of items authored by Jane Austen (i.e. attributes of Group I Entities) and items owned by the University of Arizona library (i.e. the 'owned by' relationship between Group II Entities and Group I entities) and simultaneously satisfying these two goals. The request can be formulated as a statement in predicate logic that needs to be satisfied. In turn, this can be regarded as a query in SQL that is given to a database. Now, it may well be beyond the range of a typical User to produce such a SQL query so there will need to be a User friendly front-end, perhaps an OPAC (online public access catalog). But, conceptually, the OPAC will produce a piece of logic that will act as a specification for database retrieval.

Direct and obvious relationships involving the seven primary relationships in FRBR,

x is created by y
x is an embodiment of y
x is an instantiation of y
x is owned by y
x is produced by y
x is a realization of y
x is realized by y
x is the subject of y

(plus the hundred or so attributes) are what we might call direct database relationships.

But there are other bibliographical relationships, which may or may not be amenable to FRBR treatment. Barbara Tillett, in her foundational works on Bibliographic relationships (Tillett 1991b, 1987, 1991a, 1995, 2001), introduces a taxonomy of 7 kinds of bibliographic relationships

Equivalence
Derivative
Descriptive
Whole-part
Accompanying
Sequential
Shared-characteristic

Some brief examples of each category are:- Equivalence covers copies; derivative are revisions, modifications, translations; descriptive are reviews and annotations (where the second IO refers to the first IO); whole-part amounts to composites and aggregrates; accompanying are IOs which are accompanied by maps, videos, indexes, supplements; sequential covers serials and journal runs; shared-characteristic is not really a relationship; it is classing; it is the forming of a class from an attribute or characteristic (such as subject matter or form); of course, two or more IOs can be in the same class, in which case they would 'share' the characteristic in question. Tillett's taxonomy is widely accepted as the basis of modern theory (Bean and Green 2001; Green 2008; Tillett 2001; Green et al. 2002). And, indeed, FRBR can do justice to most of the requirements of relationships under this taxonomy (Barbara Tillett was one of the consultants to the IFLA study group which produced FRBR). There are many interesting details here, but they would take us too far afield. However, for our purposes it is useful to look at equivalence relationships, for equivalence is needed for counting.

## 8.3.5 Counting FRBR Group I Entities

The counting proceeds as follows. The items themselves can be counted just as ordinary physical objects (subject to the proviso that some of the objects may consist of parts, possibly disparate). Items which exemplify the same manifestation are separate copies. [This is to use the word 'copy' in the sense that it occurs in, for example, 'The main library has three copies of the Gray text'.] The separate copies are equivalent to each other.

Manifestations are abstract objects. Might two manifestations be equivalent? Might two manifestations be 'copies' of each other? Maxwell points out that work could be published in an identical edition by two separate publishers in two separate markets. Further, closely similar, but textually different, editions can be published, perhaps in different markets (exemplified in the case of an English spelling version and an American spelling version of the same edition of a Harry Potter book). A pragmatic decision is required here: it is a matter of what the User wants (noting, of course, that there are different Users and they may well want different things). If two manifestations are deemed to be equivalent (say English spelling and American spelling), there are, of course, two of them, but they are embodiments of the *same* expression (not different expressions). They are copies of each other, even though the items instantiating them might have different spelling and text. Thus far, then, we can have items and copies of items, and manifestations and copies of manifestations.

What about expressions? Expressions realize works in forms (as text, film etc.). Might two different expressions be equivalent? It does not seem so, although, again, this may be a matter of decision.

Manifestations are abstract objects and, in one way, they are indefinitely many of them. However our, focus of interest is only with manifestations that have been instantiated at least once. So, if Gray the text (in a particular edition, by a particular publisher, etc.) has been instantiated i.e. there is, or has been, an item that exemplifies it, whereas Gray the musical (by a particular choral ensemble on particular occasion, etc.) has never been instantiated i.e. there has never been such a performance, we tend to be focused on the first but not the second. So, when we are counting manifestations, we tend to count not manifestations *simpliciter* but rather manifestations that have been instantiated. So here are typical questions 'How many instantiated text form manifestations are there of Gray? 'How many instantiated manifestations are there of Gray, in any form whatsoever? Expressions are similar. We typically want to count only those expressions that have been embodied in manifestations which are, in turn, instantiated. Similarly for works: if a work is never realized in any expression that has at least one manifestation that has an instance, we do not have an interest in that work. When counting works, we count 'instantiated' works (instantiated remotely via the various intermediaries).

### 8.3.6 FRBR Tasks

FRBR has an interest in basic information retrieval, to processes similar to searching, browsing, and berrypicking. It defines four generic user tasks: finding, identifying, selecting, and obtaining (IFLA 1997, pp. 8, 79)). The first three tasks work under the assumption that the User wants something, and has search criteria, though perhaps not well specified search criteria; and then there is a successive approximation process in which the system produces some candidate items (or descriptions thereof) and the User settles on what is actually required. The fourth task is obtaining the item or items, possibly from remote repositories or sources.

There are uses of the data which are slightly different to these elementary uses. The stored data actually is a vast amount of metadata. And there will be Users who are interested solely in the metadata and not in obtaining any items. For example, an English scholar might want to know how many editions of *Paradise Lost* were published before 1800. A FRBR database can answer this, and there is no post-answer *obtaining* required.

### 8.3.7 Appraising FRBR

It is probably a little early in its history to be appraising FRBR. It certainly seems to be a very reasonable attempt at an intellectually demanding task. One critical remark can be made about it. There is not much in it about electronic digital resources. The fact of it is, FRBR appears biased toward print.

> FRBR is somewhat print oriented. (Maxwell 2008, p. 5)

This is unsurprising in as much as FRBR makes its appearance in 1997, which is before the digital really began to bite. But it is unfortunate now and will be more so in the future.

### 8.3.8 What About the Digital?

The most obvious differences in capabilities between electronic or digital resources and paper documents concern copying and transmission. Essentially, it is trivial to copy a digital resource and easy to transmit it from one place to another.

Everything that takes place, though, takes place in the physical realm. So it is at the level of items or tokens. Within a single computer a file may reside in memory, either permanent or temporary memory, and that file then can be used to produce various signal, and computational, processes that end with a rendering or display on one or more monitors. It is similar if the file is printed, and similar if the file is an image or is music. There are a number of physical processes taking place here, but they are all physical processes. And we can give a fairly good account of them if we need to. There is Shannon's Theory of Communication, Signaling, and Coding. There are various properties of the physical storage, transmission, and computational devices and media. It is possible, and even common, to assemble the source 'file'—the original that is to be copied—at the moment of need. For example, a word processing document may apparently have images in it (it may really have images in it, or it may have images which reside elsewhere and exist only as pointers or links in the document). These links allow for assembly at time of need. It is similar with many web pages; they do not exist as complete web pages at the source until they are requested by a User.

There is complexity here, but not mystery and bafflement. In principle, we know, or can know, exactly what is going on.

Copying has been available for a very long time. Recording, transmitting, and reproducing are of the essence of recorded IOs. 'Copying' is central. Hand-written copies of texts have existed for thousands of years, so have copies of images, forgeries, reproductions, and the like. And many modern copying technologies, such as cameras and photographs, photo-copiers, tape-recorders, video-recorders, etc., have been present for long enough to be very familiar.

However, digital copying has special qualities of its own. The copy is a perfect copy, there is no degradation in copying. This usually will mean that there is not a lot a point in distinguishing between the original and a copy. Copying is a very quick process. True, copying large files can take some time but to all practical intents and purposes copying is pretty well instantaneous. Copying is cheap. There are little or no labor costs. There is just the cost of the media used for the copy (and often that media can be re-used for other purposes or other copies). And digital files can be readily transmitted over networks or the Internet.

Producing items by digital copying has features of its own. With print media, there can be a manifestation of, say, *Pride and Prejudice*, and, additionally, many items which are instances of that manifestation. The manifestation itself is abstract, a type, and the items are copies in that they all instantiate the same manifestation. These copies would not ordinarily have been produced by 'copying'. (A photocopy of a *Pride and Prejudice* item is different to a plain instance of a particular manifestation.) Similarly, a performance of Beethoven's 9th is not produced by having an existing performance of Beethoven's 9th and copying it. Digital copies work in a different way. There is a starting item, which is an original, a source, an archetype, a master, or a pattern. This original is itself physical. It is an item or a token. Then a second token, or more tokens, are made which are copies of the original. The copies can themselves be originals to further copies, and so on. Of course, a digital copy need not be that similar, as a physical item, to that which it is a copy of. The digital resources are means to an end, to produce a display on screen, or a piece of music, or a video. Digital files may have the same capabilities, for producing the same music or video, without themselves being especially similar—storage in different media would be examples of this. And many copies are transient: when a document from permanent memory is rendered on a monitor, the processing would usually be done on a copy of the file from memory—a copy which disappears when the computer is shutdown.

The modern highly active field of Digital Rights Management (DRM) is to protect the rights of intellectual property owners specifically in regard to access to IOs. Typically, DRM would pay attention to those devices (computers, tablets, music players, etc.) that a file can be rendered or played from—and the Users (who can do the looking, listening, or accessing) through 'copying' (and whether there can be print outs, back-up copies, and the like). DRM has had to make a study of digital copying.

The present book is largely about access and retrieval. It is not about restricting access. In so far as FRBR can be quickly connected with the digital, the required modifications seem to be something like these. The higher level concept of work and expression can remain much as they are. Manifestation might need to be slightly different. As it was, a manifestation is a type identified without reference to its instances; for example, a print run of a particular edition, a specific concert series with a time and location, a run of performances of a play. But any digital object can be copied. And the copy is of the same manifestation type as the original. So some manifestations, collections of item instances, can be produced by prototype-and-copy techniques. Some manifestations are digital copies, or copies of copies, of a 'golden' master. In turn, items may now be of a little less importance. Items used to be the actual physical copies that a library or repository housed, and they were important in that if no copies were present physically the User would not have access. But with a digital resources, all that the User requires is access to a golden master, which, while it might be subject to DRM, at least it is not subject to being issued to other Patrons. Obviously, our musings here, related to this topic, are only scratching the surface. (See also (CNRI 2011; IDF 2011; Paskin 2010; Bainbridge et al. 2001; Buchanan 2006).)

## 8.4 Knowledge Representation

Knowledge representation has not been a main concern of this book. Knowledge is expressed in statements, which are connected with true of false assertions, propositions, sentences and logical formulas. Whereas the central topic for most of this book is concepts, and they are just components of statements (they are the nouns or noun phrases in sentences or the logical terms as components in logical formulas). However, on the wider horizon, as far as knowledge representation is concerned, Leibniz was right. Knowledge can be represented in logic or as logic: there is a whole domain of study, a discipline, that is witness to this (Sowa 2000; Brachman and Levesque 2004; Cycorp 2011). And we can reason to this conclusion in a different way. Knowledge is represented in natural language, and those parts of natural language most amenable to computation and algorithm are representable in logic. So knowledge-in-logic can be a focus.

But there certainly are problems and issues especially with sharing knowledge and with distributed information. Within logic, the extra logical components, that is, those pieces other than the pure logical symbols, can be of two kinds: interpreted and uninterpreted. Consider the two formulas

A(a)
Author(austen)

/*where, in the second formula, the predicate 'Author(?x) is a symbolization of the property of being an author and the term 'austen' is a symbolization naming Jane Austen */

These are both well formed formulas and they both apply a predicate to a term. The first one applies the predicate 'A(?x)' to the term 'a'; quite what either the predicate or the term mean is left open. Their meaning is *uninterpreted*. The second one applies the predicate 'Author(?x)' to the term 'austen'; but, thanks to the conventions of symbolization, which were freely chosen by the creators of the system, the predicate names a property and the term names a person; the meanings of the predicate and the term are *interpreted*: the symbols are interpreted symbols. (The first formula, 'A(a)' also could be interpreted; it is not debarred from that; it would just need suitable conventions of symbolization.)

So far so good. But a remote, and different system, might assert in logic that

Writer(jane)

is an item of information. We will assume that the symbols in this formula are interpreted symbols. But what is the remote system saying? Is it saying the same thing as the first system? Or something different? We can assume that the two systems can communicate with each other and rapidly sort out the syntax (in a sense, the separate controlled vocabularies). The problem comes with translation and with what the symbols mean outside of logic, for example, do 'Author(?x)' and 'Writer(?x)' both denote the same property of being an author.

There are techniques for addressing this—the Semantic Web has some, as we will see.

A statement like

Author(austen)

is, from a logical point of view, as simple as it gets. It is asserting an atomic fact or piece of data.

Knowledge is more than a collection of atomic facts (Frické 2009). And so, the general case of knowledge representation, and distributed information, is much more elaborate than addressing distributed data.

## 8.5  The Semantic Web

> The Semantic Web is about two things. It is about common formats for integration and combination of data drawn from diverse sources, whereas the original Web mainly concentrated on the interchange of documents. It is also about language for recording how the data relates to real world objects. That allows a person, or a machine, to start off in one database, and then move through an unending set of databases which are connected not by wires but by being about the same thing (W3C 2011).

It is a series of technologies and initiatives which use the Resource Description Framework (RDF) (Allemang and Hendler 2008; Horrocks 2008).

### 8.5.1  Resource Description Framework and Triples

Resource Description Framework (RDF) is a (very restricted) fragment of logic (RDF 2004). It sees everything as being *triples*. So, for example, it conceives of all statements as being triples:

    subject->predicate->object

Then what we have to do here is to cast or frame or translate any true/false indicative statement into a triple. Here are a few

    John likes Mary
    is
    John[subject] likes[predicate] Mary[object]
    Mary is liked by John
    is
    John [subject] likes[predicate] Mary[object]
    'Pride and prejudice' is a novel
    is
    'Pride and prejudice'[subject] is a[predicate] novel[object]
    Jane Austen is the author of 'Pride and prejudice'
    is
    Jane Austen[subject] is the author of[predicate] 'Pride and prejudice'[object]

Notice here that there is no distinction between triples of data and triples of metadata, RDF accommodates both. That John likes Mary is 'data' and that Jane Austen is the author of 'Pride and prejudice' is 'metadata'.

We already are familiar with two ways of depicting RDF triples. They can be seen as atomic relational statements from First Order Logic, in which case 'John likes Mary' could be symbolized

    Likes(john, mary)

And they can also be seen as directed links in a labeled graph, in which case 'John likes Mary' could be (Fig. 8.4). Another favorite use for triples lies with the

**Fig. 8.4** A labeled graph showing that John likes Mary

| Name | Transport | Wheels |
|---|---|---|
| **Jane** | **Bicycle** | **2** |
| **Sue** | **Tricycle** | **3** |
| **Tom** | **Bicycle** | **2** |
| **Dick** | **Unicycle** | **1** |
| **Harriet** | **Bicycle** | **2** |

description of a database. A (relational) database is just a table or collection of tables, for example
The data here, for each individual item, lies with each row. For the hand-waving explanation here we will call the items or entities ent1, ent2, etc., and data about those items, row1, row2, etc. So, row1 has the information that the ent1 has name Jane, has transport Bicycle, and she rides on 2 Wheels. That information can be expressed as triples in logic as follows:

```
Name(ent1, Jane)
Transport(ent1, Bicycle)
Wheels(ent1, 2)
```

Or as triples, in a directed graph, as (Fig. 8.5). And similarly for the other rows in the table.

The technique here is to regard the row as the subject, the column as the predicate, and the cell contents as the object. The cell in question, of course, is the one corresponding to the intersection of the relevant row and the relevant column. Usually there will be many different tables that are in use, in which case each table itself would need to be identified or named to establish the cell-to-triple correspondence.

This way, every database may be regarded as a collection of triples or a *triple store*. And, conversely, triple stores can be converted into databases.

Notice that the order of the triples within a triple store is a matter of complete indifference. The three logical statements

```
Name(ent1, Jane)
Transport(ent1, Bicycle)
Wheels(ent1, 2)
```

supplied, stored, or presented, in that order, have exactly the same logical force as the same three statements presented in a different order, say

**Fig. 8.5**  A labeled graph
showing a row in a database

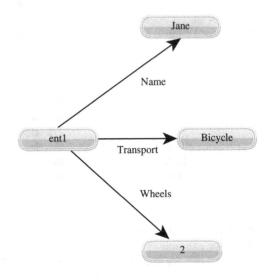

Wheels(ent1, 2)
Name(ent1, Jane)
Transport(ent1, Bicycle)

(and, similarly for the labeled directed graph created by the three links).

## 8.5.2 Namespace Control and Combining Distributed Data

RDF triples will likely be distributed. That is to say, some triples will be in one place, perhaps in one database or triple store, while other triples, germane to the *same* subject or subject matter, will be somewhere else, perhaps in another database. So, for example,

Likes(john, mary)

might be in one database and

Likes(john, alice)

in another database. A pre-requisite to combining these two, into the information that John likes both Mary and Alice, is that there is control over the names. For example, Johns are often called 'Jack' and if the triple in the second database had been recorded as

Likes(jack, alice)

combining the triples starts to get a whole lot harder, especially if there are other men called Jack and other triples involving these other Jacks.

Classical librarians have exactly the answer to this: controlled vocabularies, authorized forms for names, and so on—essentially no synonyms or homographs for names (see also (Harper and Tillett 2007)). For the Web, this is slightly more than strictly is necessary: synonyms (or aliases) are fine, but there should be no homographs. And a solution to this is Uniform Resource Identifiers (URIs) (Berners-Lee et al. 2001). There are an abundance of these, enough for each of them to name only one thing (i.e., no homographs, no Mates and Honeys). There is a consideration. The Web consists of web pages and the like, i.e., electronic documents, and, in the first instance, URLs and URIs name web resources. But John is a real human being; he is nothing to do with the web; he would live, breathe, and walk around even if there was no Internet. However, there are plenty of URIs, enough, in fact, to label things outside the web as well as within the web. So, with

Likes(john, alice)

URIs would be used in RDF for John, for Alice, and, for that matter, for the 'Likes' relation or predicate. And this means that the separate databases must co-operate or communicate on syntactic and semantic conventions. They need to arrange to use the same, or synonym, URIs for the same things.

This is a solution to the earlier problem of getting interpreted symbols to mean the same things, or to be able to inter-translate them. With

Author(austen)
Writer(jane)

all parties can use URIs for both the terms and the predicate: then it is a matter of whether the relevant URIs identify the same things. This is not easy to ascertain, but it is a step forward.

Then, with namespace control in place, combining distributed databases, or separate triple stores, is essentially trivial. They are just added together. So if one triple store has

Likes(john, mary)

and another

Likes(john, alice)

Then the first triple can be added to the second store, or the second triple to the first, or both triples to some new triple store, or whatever is desired. Needless to say, getting the initial proper namespace control is not easy.

With database theory, there is concern with certain properties of the databases, in particular whether they were in normal form, maybe 3rd Normal Form (Date 1977). This gives them 'consistency' and certain desirable properties for updating (such as a lack of redundancy in the data). Basic triple stores just ignore those considerations. So a triple store might have

PhoneNumber(john,123)

and another

PhoneNumber(john,456)

Then it is a bit of a question as to what John's phone number is (and how to update it if that is required). Advocates of the Semantic Web and triple stores answer 'some people (i.e. some triple stores) say John's phone number is 123, other people (i.e. other triple stores) say it is 456'. And this is supposed to be a virtue, because all of this technical machinery is aimed at the Web and it is patently clear that anyone can say anything they like on the Web.

The take-home point for us is that triple stores are non-normalized: they are not in any kind of normal form. Anything goes.


### 8.5.3  The Open World Assumption

RDF does not have negation, and that makes it difficult to say certain things. For example, that John likes Mary can be represented by

Likes(john, mary)

and that triple can be placed in a triple store; then if the question 'Does John like Mary?' is asked of that triple store, the relevant triple will be found and the answer 'Yes' returned. However, suppose that John does not like Mary i.e., in logic

~Likes(john, mary)

but *RDF does not have negation*; this cannot be represented as a triple and so it cannot be placed in a triple store. What to do? Presumably the affirmative triple Likes(john, mary) will not be in the relevant triple store, and so the question 'Does John like Mary?' will not be answered 'Yes'. At this point there is a choice.

It is a choice between what researchers in Artificial Intelligence call the *Open World Assumption* versus the *Closed World Assumption*. Many areas of Artificial Intelligence, for example with the Prolog programming language and many systems that it implements, the assumption is made that *any true/false statement or 'fact' that is not known to be true is thereby deemed to be false*. So, for example, if a database or triple store does not assert, or contain, the triple

Likes(john, mary)

it may be assumed, as a fact, that John does *not* like Mary. This assumption, in its general form, is known as the *Closed World Assumption*. It amounts to saying that everything not asserted to be true, is false. Considered in a general way, the Closed World Assumption is absurd. Each of us, individually, would be prudent to say something like 'what I don't know is a lot', but that does not mean that everything that each individual does not know is false. However, the Closed World

Assumption has its uses. Consider programming some computer software for chess; the Queen is on one square of the 64 square board; and the state of the game will record which square the Queen is on—there is no point or need to list the other 63 squares that the Queen is not on. In effect, this is a Closed World Assumption, if the software does not assert positively that the Queen is on the Rook1 square then the Queen is not there. The Closed World Assumption is suitable for chess games largely because of their small circumscribed nature. But small and circumscribed is exactly what the Web is not (and, as mentioned earlier, there are triple stores with tens of billions of triples in them).

So, RDF triple store implementations would typically adopt the *Open World Assumption* (and this amounts to saying that anything that is not known to be true is not known to be true). So if

Likes(john, mary)

is in the triple store, and the question is 'Does John like Mary?' the answer will be, or should be, 'Yes'. If

Likes(john, mary)

is *not* in the triple store, and the question is 'Does John like Mary?' the answer will be, or should be, 'We don't know'.

That still leaves the problem and how to record the fact, were it a fact, that John does not like Mary. One thought is to have a second predicate, say 'Not-Likes(?x,?y)' and then record the triple

NotLikes(john, mary)

Unfortunately this does not help, or it helps only to a limited degree. For now a problematic question is 'Does John not like Mary?' which can be answered Yes if the triple is there, but again there is no way of representing the denial of it, so if the triple is not there the conclusion needs to be 'We don't know whether John does not like Mary'.

In sum, the Open World Assumption in conjunction with the fact that RDF has no representation of negation means that the Semantic Web RDF combination is very limited in what it can say.

### 8.5.4 rdf:type and rdfs:subClassOf

Recall that in earlier discussions of type or class hierarchies it was important to distinguish 'instance of' from 'subclass or subtype of'. For example,

Toulouse-Lautrec is an instance of Parisian.
Toulouse-Lautrec is an instance of Frenchman.

The type Parisian is a subclass/subtype of the type Frenchman
The type Parisian is NOT is an instance of the type Frenchman

RDF does have some built-in or reserved predicates and one of these is 'rdf-type'. This is used to say that subject of the triple is an instance of the object of the triple and this can be used as a stepping-stone to establish type hierarchies of a kind familiar to us. We are not in this text using actual RDF syntax, but in our portrayal of the syntax, the triples

    RdfType(toulouseLautrec,parisian)
    RdfType(toulouseLautrec,frenchman)

say

    Toulouse-Lautrec is an instance of Parisian.
    Toulouse-Lautrec is an instance of Frenchman.

For type hierarchies, in addition to the 'instance of' relation there is the need for the 'is subclass of' relation to indicate that a particular type or class is a subtype of another. There is an extension language to RDF, RDF Schema language (RDFS) which provides the 'is subclass of' relation through its predefined *rdfs:subClassOf* relation. So, in our syntax.

    RdfsSubClassOf(parisian,frenchman)

says that Parisian is a subtype of Frenchman.

## 8.5.5 *Appending and Inferring*

As mentioned earlier, triple stores can be augmented or combined merely by adding the triples together. But as soon as there is class hierarchy information, triple stores can be extended in another way: by inference. (This is merely to exploit the Reid information compression of Sect. 2.1.)

Say a triple store has in it the two triples

    RdfType(toulouseLautrec,parisian)
    RdfsSubClassOf(parisian,frenchman)

These say that Toulouse Lautrec is a Parisian, and All Parisians are Frenchmen. This, of course, means that Toulouse Lautrec is a Frenchman. That fact is implicit in the other two statements or triples; it is a logical consequence of them; and it can be drawn out by logical inference. It is also a triple, namely

    RdfType(toulouseLautrec,parisian)

This means that a logical inference engine, or theorem prover, could take the initial triple store

RdfType(toulouseLautrec,parisian)
RdfsSubClassOf(parisian,frenchman)

and extend it to

RdfType(toulouseLautrec,parisian)
RdfsSubClassOf(parisian,frenchman)
RdfType(toulouseLautrec,frenchman)

The initial two triples might be in the same triple store, or they might be in different triple stores. The inferencing could be done pre-emptively at the moment of combination, or it could be done just-in-time when a query is asked. The latter possibility is the following: the triple store has in it

RdfType(toulouseLautrec,parisian)
RdfsSubClassOf(parisian,frenchman)

and no inferencing is done with those, the system sits quiescent. Then a User comes and asks 'Is Toulouse Lautrec a Frenchman?', at that point the relevant reasoning is done to produce the answer 'Yes'. [Pre-emptive inferencing is better in that there is plenty of time to do it; however, it may produce billions of triples that are never used and clog everything up. Just-in-time is better in that no resources are wasted. However, it may not be possible to do the reasoning fast enough; Users will not want to wait a month for an answer.]

The inferencing here is very limited, from a logical point of view, in what it can do. For example, ordinarily we might want to reason from the fact that the painter Constable was not a Frenchman, together with the premise that All Parisians are Frenchman, to reach the conclusion that Constable was not a Parisian. That we cannot do (because RDF/RDFS does not have negation). And there are many other styles of inference that cannot be done.

## 8.6  Semantic Web Ontologies

The problem with distributed information lies with the meaning of the statements, i.e. the semantics. There are many subtleties of meaning which, essentially, can spoil cooperation. Imagine, for example, online banking. It certainly will have use for the notion of a 'transaction'. But what exactly is a 'transaction'? Is it a thing (a continuant), or is it a process (an occurrent)? And if, say, it is an occurrent, what continuants does it depend on? What really matters here is that the different banks, or different banking systems, either agree on what a transaction is, or can understand each other's different conceptions. This suggests having some background ontology or ontologies to give context to the postulated entities; it suggests the need for classification structures.

There used to be a lack of awareness of quite how difficult combining disparate sources might be. In 2005, Andrew Updegrove records Tim Berners-Lee as saying

> The vast bulk of data to be on the Semantic Web is already sitting in databases—and files in proprietary data formats. Downloaded bank statements, weather and stock quote information, human resource information, geospatial data, maps, and so on...all that is needed to write an adapter to convert a particular format into RDF and all the content in that format is available (Updegrove 2005)

Sir Tim Berners-Lee, who, of course, devised the Web, certainly knows what he is talking about. But in this case, combining two triples like Transaction(bill,fred) and Transaction(fred,jim), from *different* databases seems to need more than an 'adapter'. And ontologies seem to be the current prophylactic of choice! (See (McGuinness 2003))

There is a second reason for invoking ontologies. Plain facts, or plain data, are relatively uninteresting. As Reid observed knowing the general is superior to knowing the particular. Knowing that the tiger Shere Khan (lurking around our village) is dangerous has its value, but knowing that a tiger, a tiger in general, is dangerous is better (it cautions us about the tigers of other villages). Classification, essentially the compression of general knowledge, is what is required. To do this on the Web, or with distributed knowledge, 'ontologies' are what is needed. We might note that here are different uses of the terminological labels. Ontology here equals 'meaning classification scheme' (and then 'inventory' would mean those items classified in the schemes). So, the word 'ontology' in this context amounts to either natural kind taxonomies or structured gerrymanders.

There are initiatives to provide general ontologies for the Web. WonderWeb is an example. WonderWeb is a project of a number of researchers who individually are both expert in Description Logics and in the needs of the Semantic Web. Its aim is to provide general logical structures, or tools, suitable for libraries of ontologies (Masolo et al. 2001). It gives detailed formal expression to a number of the ideas explained earlier, such as tokens and types, parts and wholes, continuants and occurrents, and Aristotle's Ontological Square. It covers several different approaches: DOLCE (Descriptive Ontology for Linguistic and Cognitive Engineering). BFO (Basic Formal Ontology), SUMO (Suggested Upper Merged Ontology).

Much symbolic logic is used.

## 8.6.1 Web Ontology Language

OWL, the Web Ontology Language, brings the power of Description Logics, or even First Order Logic, to the Web. It was adopted in 2003.

There are some qualifications on the desirability of bringing First Order Logic to the Web, and these mostly concern trade-offs between computability and expressibility. Full First Order Logic can express or say most everything that we would want to—certainly in the areas of classification and information retrieval.

However, as was proved by Godel in his well known theorems, First Order Logic is not decidable. What this means in this context is that if you want to use a computer to help you with the relevant reasoning, there will be parts of the reasoning that the computer cannot do. We do want to use computers for reasoning, to help with the inferring from triples stores, to flesh out the classification schemes, and even to test whether the classification schemes are consistent. A possible move here is to decide not to use full First Order Logic, but instead to use a subset of it, in particular a decidable subset that computers can master. In sum, there are choices lying between full expressivity with limited computer support and limited expressivity with full computer support.

This shows itself with OWL. There are different flavors or versions or species of OWL. There is OWL-Lite, OWL-DL, and OWL-Full and these differ in what they can say and what computer support they can receive.

As a rough characterization, OWL consists of individuals, classes, and (binary) relations. The individuals and classes allow the construction of classification hierarchies similar to the ones in this book. The relations are of three kinds. There are relations between individuals (so, if Jane Austen is an individual and Cassandra Austen is an individual, then the relationship SiblingOf(?x,?y) can be used to say that Jane and Cassandra were siblings). There are relations between individuals and datatypes (so, if Jane Austen is an individual and 1775 is a date, then the datatype relationship BornOn(?x,?y) can be used to say that Jane Austen was born in 1775). Annotation relations are annotations, i.e., in a sense, the attachment of metadata, but they are more general than the other relations in that classes (as well as individuals) can be annotated.

OWL has negation, but it does not have second order properties or meta-properties i.e. classes cannot be instances of or members of other classes. However, annotations can be used to fake metaproperties, to a degree. So, for example, if there were a class of Poetry (books), a class of Drama (books), and a class of Fiction (books), we could not put those classes as *instances* of another class, say, Literary Form. However we could annotate each of those three classes as being 'Literary Form' and that would achieve much the same result.

OWL certainly is a very reasonable attempt to provide web-based ontological support for information representation or knowledge representation. However, our central interest has been with topics, topic annotation, and DAGs of topics: it is not so clear that OWL is exactly what is required for that.

## 8.7 Simple Knowledge Organization System

Simple Knowledge Organization System (SKOS) is an initiative to develop specifications and standards within the Semantic Web for such information retrieval artifacts as classification schemes, subject headings, thesauri, and taxonomies (W3C 2010; Miles et al. 2005). That is to say, it addresses many of the problems and concerns of this book, but it is going to use as its base resource RDF triples (not first order logic in general). RDF triples are to ensure its suitability for distributed resources and applications.

SKOS has concepts which are identified by URIs. Concepts can be 'broader' or 'narrower' than other concepts, or, indeed, 'associated' with other concepts. This allows for the construction of a graph of concepts. Concepts can have multiple parents, and they can have multiple children. SKOS itself does not rule out cycles (in basic SKOS, concept A might be broader then concept B, and concept B broader than concept A). This is slightly different to our DAGs of topics, which do not allow concepts to be ancestors of themselves. What the relations 'broader', 'narrower', and 'associated with' actual mean is left open at the core level. A concept A might be narrower than B by being a subtype or subclass of B, by being an instance of B, by being a 'part of' B, and in other ways. SKOS is a framework for designers to use: what happens is their choice. If any indexing is carried out using SKOS, that indexing would be based on concepts (i.e. it would be assigned or concept indexing).

The core of SKOS works with the Concept Vertex of the Triangle of Meaning, but SKOS then adds to this Symbol Vertex support.

Concepts can have labels (strings) including preferred labels and alternative labels. In effect, this is like generalized Roget-style synsets with a headword, or preferred term, which are associated with the concepts. That technique allows us to bridge from a graph of topics to a thesaurus of terms.

There is much to admire here. In a way, it is exactly the approach favored in this book. The two main differences are: SKOS uses RDF, which, while suitable for the Web and distributed resources, is somewhat limited when compared with full First Order Logic.

And, second, the approach of this book is to construct synthetic types of arbitrary complexity (cf. Ranganathan's heritage). Then logic, together with the form of the types, reveals much about their interrelations. But, by contrast, SKOS leaves concepts as black boxes. So, for example, in SKOS there can be a concept for Forests and a concept for Tropical Forests and, effectively, both of these are black boxes: SKOS is completely unaware of any relation between the two. But if Forests and Tropical Forests are symbolized as intensional abstractions we know straight away that Tropical Forests are a subtype of Forests. In sum, there is hope that logic and automatic reasoning will be able to build a good part of the concept graph automatically. In SKOS, that is all done by hand. And, because SKOS concepts are atomic black boxes, there is no simple notion of the faceting of compound concepts, and thus no immediate support for faceted search. So, for example, the concept 'nineteenth century France' would be a SKOS black box; it may have the concept 'nineteenth century' as a parent and it may have 'France' as another parent, and thus it may be possible to narrow to 'nineteenth century France' from 'nineteenth century' or from 'France', but that would be pure good fortune. It seems far better, at a theoretical level, to allow 'nineteenth century France' to be a synthesized compound concept (then much else would come automatically).

SKOS, like much else in the Semantic Web, is also primarily logic—in truth, SKOS is RDF and RDF is logic.

## 8.8 Topic Maps

There is a modern initiative—Topic Maps ISO/IEC 13250 (Standardization 2002; Pepper 2001)—which has some connections with our DAGs of topics.

With Topic Maps there are Topics, Occurrences, and Associations. Topics can be 'anything', they are just topics. In effect, the theory of Topic Maps sees Topics themselves as being unanalyzed black box concepts. The topics are black box in the sense that if Forest is a topic and Temperate Forest is a topic, there is no awareness of, or mechanism for detecting, the fact that these two topics are connected. Each individual topic can have multiple names. This namespace control addresses the problem of synonyms.

Occurrences are those IOs in which a Topic occurs. There is an association list between Topics and Occurrences. This is what we would call a 'subject index'— Topics are the keys and Occurrences are the values.

Associations are relationships between topics. So, for example, considering operas for one moment—Puccini is a topic, Tosca is a topic, and Rome is a topic. Then, that Puccini *wrote* Tosca is an association between topics, and that Tosca *takes place in* Rome is another association between topics (Pepper 2001). So, if the Topics are nodes in the map or a graph, then associations are labeled directed links i.e. relations in First Order Logic, or triples in RDF. This part of Topic Maps is knowledge representation (related to other knowledge representation techniques in Artificial Intelligence, such as semantic networks). (Of course, the topic Puccini did not write the topic Tosca, rather it was the composer Puccini who wrote the opera Tosca—but let us not worry about that.)

The theory of Topic Maps is a kind of combination of subject indexing and semantic network knowledge representation, and it succeeds or fails in so far as it meets its design objectives (which are giving some infrastructure support to the Semantic Web). Our DAGs of topics are quite different. The DAGs of topics do not directly represent knowledge (none will say that Puccini wrote Tosca). Their main purpose is to allow a User to navigate from node to node to broaden or narrow a topic. And essential to establishing this DAG structure is the fact that the nodes have a detailed internal structure (which we have analyzed by intensional abstractions).

## References

Allemang D, Hendler J (2008) Semantic web for the working ontologist: effective modeling in RDFS and OWL. Morgan Kaufman, Burlington

Bainbridge D, Buchanan G, McPherson J, Jones S, Mahoui A, Witten IH (2001) Greenstone: A platform for distributed digital library applications. In: In ECDL'01: Proceedings. 5th European Conference on Digital Libraries, London, UK, Springer, pp 137–148

Bean CA, Green R (2001) Relationships in the organization of knowledge. Kluwer Academic Publishers, Dordrecht

Berners-Lee T, Hendler J, Lasilla O (2001) The semantic web. Sci Am 284(5):34–43

Brachman RJ, Levesque HJ (2004) Knowledge representation and reasoning. Elsevier, Amsterdam

Buchanan G (2006) FRBR: Enriching and Integrating Digital Libraries. In: JCDL'06, 11–15 June, 2006, Chapel Hill, North Carolina. pp 260–269

CNRI (2011) Handle System. http://www.handle.net/. Accessed 10 Oct 2010

Cycorp (2011) CYC Home Page. http://www.cyc.com. Accessed 10 Oct 2010

Date CJ (1977) An introduction to database systems, 2nd edn. Addison-Wesley, Reading

DCMI (2011) Dublin core metadata initiative. http://dublincore.org. Accessed 9 July 2011

Denton W (2007) FRBR and the history of cataloging. In: Taylor AG (ed) Understanding FRBR: what it is and how it will affect our retrieval. Westport, CT

Doctorow C (2001) Metacrap: Putting the torch to seven straw-men of the meta-utopia. http://www.well.com/~doctorow/metacrap.htm. Accessed 10 Oct 2010

Frické M (2009) The knowledge pyramid: a critique of the DIKW hierarchy. J Inf Sci 35:131–142

Green R (2008) Relationships in knowledge organization. Knowl Organiz 35(2/3):150–159

Green R, Bean CA, Myaeng SH (eds) (2002) The semantics of relationships: an interdisciplinary perspective. Kluwer Academic Publishers, Dordrecht

Harper CA, Tillett BB (2007) Library of Congress controlled vocabularies and their application to the Semantic Web. Cataloging Classification Q 43(3/4):47–68

Horrocks I (2008) Ontologies and the semantic web. Commun ACM 51(12):58–67

IDF (2011) The DOI System. http://www.doi.org. Accessed 10 Oct 2010

IFLA (1997) Functional requirements for bibliographic records: Final report. Saur. http://www.ifla.org/files/cataloguing/frbr/frbr_2008.pdf

Lynch CA (2001) When documents deceive: trust and provenance as new factors for information retrieval in a tangled web. J Am Soc Inf Sci Technol 52(1):12–17

Martin J (1982) Strategic data-planning methodologies. Prentice-Hall, Englewood Cliffs

Masolo C, Borgo S, Gangemi A, Guarino N, Oltramari A (2001) WonderWeb Deliverable D18. http://wonderweb.semanticweb.org/deliverables/documents/D18.pdf

Maxwell RL (2008) FRBR: A guide for the perplexed. Am Library Assoc, Chicago

McGuinness DL (2003) Ontologies come of age. In: Fensel D, Hendler Ji, Lieberman H, Wahlster W (eds) Spinning the semantic web: bringing the world wide web to its full potential. MIT Press, MA

Miles A, Mathews B, Wilson M, Dan B (2005) SKOS Core: Simple Knowledge Organisation for the Web. In: In: Proceedings of the International Conference on Dublin Core and Metadata Applications, Madrid, Spain, 12–15 Sept 2005. pp 5–13. Retrieved 15 April 2006, from: http://www.slais.ubc.ca/PEOPLE/faculty/tennis-p/dcpapers/paper01.pdf

NISO (2004) Understanding metadata. NISO Press. http://www.niso.org/publications/press/ UnderstandingMetadata.pdf. Accessed 10 Oct 2010

Nunberg G (2009) Google's book search: A disaster for scholars. http://chronicle.com/article/ Googles-Book-Search-A/48245. Accessed 10 Oct 2010

Paskin N (2010) Digital Object Identifier (DOI®) System. In: Encyclopedia of library and information sciences, vol 1. 3rd edn, pp 1586–1592

Pepper S (2001) The TAO of topic maps: finding the way in the age of infoglut. http://www.ontopia.net/topicmaps/materials/tao.html. Accessed 17 May 2011

RDF WG (2004) Resource Description Framework (RDF). http://www.w3.org/RDF/. Accessed 10 Oct 2010

Smith B (2009a) An introduction to ontology: from Aristotle to the universal core. http://ontology.buffalo.edu/smith/IntroOntology_Course.html. Accessed 10 Oct 2010

Sowa JF (2000) Knowledge representation: logical, philosophical, and computational foundations. Brooks/Cole, Pacific Grove

Standardization IOf (2002) ISO/IEC 13250 Topic Maps (Second Edition). ISO. http://www.topicmapslab.de/standards/TM20. Accessed 10 Oct 2010

Taylor AG (ed) (2007a) FRBR: What it is and how it will affect our retrieval tools. Libraries Unlimited

Taylor AG (2007b) An introduction to functional requirements for bibliographic records. In: Taylor AG (ed) FRBR: What it is and how it will affect our retrieval tools. Libraries Unlimited

Tillett BB (1987) Bibliographic relationships: Toward a conceptual structure of bibliographic information used in cataloging. University of California, LA

Tillett BB (1991a) A summary of the treatment of bibliographic relationships in cataloging rules. Library Res Tech Serv 35(4):393–405

Tillett BB (1991b) A taxonomy of bibliographic relationships. Library Res Tech Serv 35(2):150–158

Tillett BB (1995) Theoretical and practical foundations. Int Cataloguing Bibliographic Control 24:43–44

Tillett BB (2001) Bibliographic relationships. In: Bean CA, Green R (eds) Relationships in the organization of knowledge. Kluwer Academic, Dordrecht, pp 19–35

Updegrove A (2005) The semantic web: An interview with Tim Berners-Lee. Consortium Standards Bulletin 5(6)

W3C (2010) Introduction to SKOS. http://www.w3.org/2004/02/skos/intro. Accessed 10 Oct 2010

W3C (2011) W3C Semantic Web Actitivity. http://www.w3.org/2001/sw/. Accessed 16 May 2011

# Chapter 9
# Logic and the Organization of Information

## 9.1 Symbolization

Symbolization, or formalization, carries with it some characteristic advantages: clarity, reasoning, and friendliness to algorithms. Proper symbolization of any domain of assertions or knowledge will make transparent exactly what is and what is not being claimed. Logic informs on inference. It can determine which assertions follow from which others. This means that it can organize or structure a domain of knowledge—both as to the explicit assertions that are known and are to hand—and also as to implicit new knowledge that lies awaiting discovery. And logic is the ideal intermediary for programming computers. There are a range of programming languages, from assembly languages through to ADA, C++, and other esoterica. In one sense, all these programming languages can do the same things, but they do so with greater or lesser clarity for the programmers and with respect to the underlying domains of application. But logic is an ideal intermediary, either as a means of specifying what algorithms should do or as a declarative programming language in its own right.

If librarianship is to be brought to computers, then symbolization and logic will be invaluable allies.

## 9.2 Concepts

Librarianship is information organization for retrieval. Central to this are concepts. Classification is the organization of concepts. Assigned indexing should be indexing by concepts.

In turn, the ideal 'notation' for concepts is logic. It can identify the concepts and their inter-relations.

M. Frické, *Logic and the Organization of Information*,
DOI: 10.1007/978-1-4614-3088-9_9,
© Springer Science+Business Media New York 2012

As an illustration of where current librarianship could be helped, here is a passage from Aida Slavic and Maria Ines Cordeiro writing on 'Core requirements for automation of analytico-synthetic classifications'.

> Since the 1980s, several authors have pointed out a lack of sufficiently detailed component representation in complex notations, thus not allowing retrieval and management at the level of each component. In fact, it has often been emphasised that providing facet indicators (i.e. symbols to identify facets to which the concepts belong) is paramount for automation of the classification and for IR (Goedert 1991; Pollitt and Tinker 2000; Goedert 1991; Pollitt and Tinker 2000). It has been said that classifications such as UDC and Colon Classification (CC) have many advantages, because they have declared syntax marks upon which to base tools for automated functions (Buxton 1990; Gopinath and Prasad 1994; Madalli and Prasad 2002; Buxton 1990; Gopinath and Prasad 1994; Madalli Prasad 2002). However, in spite of these advantages, data structures adopted for automation do not make use of such syntax marks, rather treating classification notations as simple *text strings*. This is the case, for example, of the data structures provided for classification data in MARC bibliographic formats, to mention the most relevant domain where classifications have been used. (Slavic and Cordeiro 2004)

First, what does the passage mean? Slavic and Coreiro are talking about notations for compound concepts and the desirability of automatic retrieval of those concepts by means of their components. So, for example, there might be the concepts 'wooden bridges', 'wooden towers', 'concrete bridges', 'concrete towers' and it should be possible to retrieve these, or IOs indexed or classified by them, by means of their components such as 'wooden' or 'concrete'. Those components likely will be faceted (e.g. 'wooden' and 'concrete' might be in the category of Materials, and 'bridges' and 'towers' in the category Structures). Now, say Slavic and Cordeiro, those components do have a notation and syntax marks within such systems as UDC or Ranganathan's Colon Classification. But programmers writing algorithms ignore that notation and work using text strings. (And text strings are a problem, as Slavic and Cordeiro assume the reader knows, because of issues of postcoordination: for example, UDC and CC will easily distinguish a 'blind Venetian' from a 'Venetian blind' but string-in-string search for the component token 'blind' likely will not.) UDC and CC use numbers and put those numbers together to form composites; and the Dewey Decimal Classification (DDC) does the same—to an extent. But composition of numbers and letters does not work very well, and Slavic and Cordeiro would like it to work better. There is a solution: use symbolic logic.

There are historical echoes here. Leibniz's *Characteristica Universalis*, from the 1660s, wanted to use numbers and their factors as a notation for concepts and their components (so the concept with notation 6 (i.e. $3 \times 2$) might be composed of the concept with notation 3 and the concept with notation 2). Modern logic replaced these arithmetic notation systems (as it should do for librarian notation of concepts).

## 9.3  Indexing and Search

The higher form of indexing is assigned indexing. And that will involve concepts and their indexing should use logic. The actual assigning of index concepts to IOs will probably need to be done by humans.

Search is a counterpart to indexing. There are many kinds of searches and much of the routine kinds can be done as database retrievals or string-in-string pattern matches on text or metadata. But the most important and challenging kind of search involves subjects or topics i.e. concepts and logic.

Many, or even most, of the concepts for indexing are going to be compounds. So, from a logical point of view, they will be synthesized from components, often faceted components, as and when needed. Synthesis goes along with postcoordination. This suggests that many of the searches for multiterm strings will be postcoordinate searches. To date, attempts with postcoordination have been restricted to Boolean constructions and they have characteristic shortcomings. For example, a search for 'school AND library' will return IOs associated with school libraries as well as those associated with library schools and this suggests some noise and lack of precision (Srinivasan 1992, p. 163). But First Order Logic goes beyond Boolean constructions and it will be able to read, parse, and postcoordinate 'large library school' as being different from 'large school library'.

## 9.4  Synonyms and Homographs

Synonyms and homographs—and generalized synonymy and generalized homography—are problems for librarianship and information retrieval. For example, consider the popular keyword-in-text search; the presence of synonyms lowers recall (a search for 'butterflies' will not find those IOs that use only 'rhopalocera'); the presence of homographs lowers precision (a search for 'bank' will find IOs addressing the wrong, or unintended, kind of bank). A solution is to invoke the Triangle of Meaning and to do all the important operations using the Concept Vertex. In turn, working with the Concept Vertex is best done using symbolic logic.

Symbolized formulas are the scaffolding or reserve currency or universal translation language lying in the background.

For the basic cases, this might proceed as follows. Synonyms are collected into synsets. But the label or identifier for each synset is not a headword or preferred term, rather it is a concept which in turn is a logical formula. Much of the back and forth between tokens in indexed text, and the like, and keys in indexes, can be done by machine. Managing preferred terms, and 'lead-in' terms, which would occur in controlled vocabularies, would be done via the concepts. Homographs, where the relationship between word and concept is one-to-many, would likely need humans to disambiguate the more difficult cases.

Generalized synonyms and generalized homonyms would also likely need humans for correct identification and rendering in logic. That does not necessarily mean that the human indexers have to be expert in logic. The various indexed concepts can be used to produce canonical strings (in any natural language such as English, French or German) and then the task for the human indexer is to identify paraphrases of the canonical strings.

Using underlying concepts to produce string representations of themselves is flexible and powerful. There was the classical problem of *string indexing*, which was to control the syntax of the key entries in indexes (for example, whether a key should be 'Modern Art' or 'Art, Modern' and similarly for more demanding cases of nouns, verbs, adjectives, active and passive voice, abstract and concrete, general and particular, and so on). But it is relatively easy to generate from a logical formula a representation in any string syntax and vocabulary that is considered desirable (i.e. for different audiences, children and adults, and different natural languages).

## 9.5  Classification and Annotation

Classification structures, such as Aristotelian-Linnaean, are easily described in logic. And annotations for topics should, once again, be concepts and so Directed Acyclic Graphs (DAGs) of topics can be described as DAGs of intensional abstractions.

## 9.6  Information Navigation

Many of the retrieval patterns, such as searching, browsing, and berrypicking, and their generalizations involve following trails of 'bibliographical relationships'.

For example, as mentioned earlier, the CRG group, in their 1955 paper, argue that the single most important relation to assist the information retriever with subject searches is that which connects a subject up a classification hierarchy to its parent and down a classification hierarchy to its children. This is traveling a DAG of topics.

Many of these bibliographical relationships, in so far as they can be computed and assembled into paths, involved logic either as database retrievals or topic DAG manipulations.

Elaine Svenonius tells us of the need for what she calls 'subject languages' for *collocation*, of IOs on the same topics, and for *navigation*, around the bibliographical universe (Svenonius 2000). The suggestion of the present text is that assigned indexing by concept provides collocation, and DAGs of concepts provide the navigation.

## 9.7 Distributed IOs and Information

With present practices with respect to distributed information, not so much of an argument needs to be made. The Semantic Web, foundational ontologies, OWL, SKOS, RDF, inferencing in triples stores, and the like, are all just logic.

## 9.8 What Logic Cannot do for Organization

There is one area, and it is getting to become a very large area, in which logic offers nothing.

The area is citation analysis and generalizations thereof (Garfield 1955). The value of citation and linking has steadily become more apparent. It inserts humans into the connections between IOs. Humans cite, or link, for a number of reasons (Smith 1991; Garfield 1997), and there often seems to be no underlying rationale. However, there is useful indeed vital information to be gleaned from the generalizations. Much of Bates's berrypicking involves following citation networks, following the incites and outcites. Most of the modern search engines on the Web interpret a link, a html hyperlink, as a vote and use weighted votes to rank relevance when returning search results. Thesauri can be built using mainly citation analysis (Schneider and Borlund 2004). Indeed links can even apparently partially solve the problem of the Holy Grail of Indexing.

Thus: a web link has a source text, and an IO that is linked to; and that source text might not appear at all in the linked-to IO. This is the mechanism for so-called Google bombing. In 2001, Adam Mathes discovered that the text 'internet rockstar' was indexed by Google to the web site for Ben Brown even though that text key did not appear on the Brown site (Mathes 2001). What happened behind the scenes was that thousands of fans used the key 'internet rockstar' to link to that site and Google read this collective information and made the appropriate inferences. (Hence 'bombing' is artificially manipulating this process.) Effectively, the fans are human indexers (which we want) using a free vocabulary (which we do not want) but the end result across collective linking is reasonable, indeed pretty good. Also, the use of a free vocabulary tends to connect all interested parties viz. the linkers and the searchers.

Link and citation analysis involves statistics and inference across collective human behavior. It requires empirical study: observing, collecting data, and experimenting. Logic, which is essentially non-empirical, and a priori, has nothing to say about this.

# References

Buxton AB (1990) Computer searching of UDC numbers. J Documentation 46(3):193–217

Garfield E (1955) Citation indexes for science. Science 122:108–111

Garfield E (1997) Validation of citation analysis. J Am Soc Inf Sci 48(10):962–964

Goedert W (1991) Facet classification in online retrieval. Int Classification 18(2):95–108

Gopinath MA, Prasad ARD (1994) A knowledge representation model for analytico-synthetic classification. In: The third international ISKO conference, Copenhagen, Denmark. Frankfurt am Main; Indeks Verlag, pp 320–327

Madalli DP, Prasad ARD (2002) VYASA: a knowledge representation system for automatic maintenance of analytico-synthetic scheme. In: The seventh international ISKO conference, Granada, Spain. Wurzburg, Ergon, pp 288–294

Mathes A (2001) Google bombing. http://uber.nu/2001/04/06/. Accessed 10 Oct 2010

Pollitt AS, Tinker AJ (2000) Enhanced view-based searching through the decomposition of Dewey Decimal Classification Codes. In: Sixth international ISKO conference, Toronto, Canada. Wurzburg, Ergon, pp 288–294

Schneider JW, Borlund P (2004) Introduction to bibliometrics for construction and maintenance of thesauri: methodical considerations. J Documentation 60(5):524–549

Slavic A, Cordeiro MI (2004) Core requirements for automation of analytico-synthetic classifications. Adv Knowl Organiz 9:187–192

Smith LC (1991) Citation analysis. Library Trends 30(1):83–106

Srinivasan P (1992) Thesaurus construction. In: Frakes WBaB-Y R (ed) Information retrieval: data structures and algorithms. Prentice Hall, Upper Saddle River New Jersey, pp 161–218

Svenonius E (2000) The intellectual foundations of information organization. MIT Press, Cambridge

# Appendix A
# Extended First Order Predicate Calculus

## A.1 Propositional Logic

We start with propositional logic. Indicative English sentences are either true or false. For example, 'Jane Austen is an author' is an indicative sentence (which happens to be true). Such sentences express *propositions*. Not all pieces of English express propositions. For example, the question 'Is Jane Austen an author?' is neither true nor false (although reasonable long form answers to it will be either true or false); again, the exclamation 'Jane Austen, what an author!' is not either true or false.

Propositions can be atomic or compound. 'Jane Austen is an author'.' expresses an atomic proposition; whereas 'Jane Austen is an author and 'Emily Bronte is an athlete' expresses a compound proposition composed of two atomic propositions (one false one and one true one).

Symbols are used to stand for propositions. In the systems used here, the capital letters 'A–Z' to stand for *atomic* propositions—a capital letter is used as a shorthand or code for a proposition. You decide which letter you want to stand for each particular atomic proposition; then having formed a convention or Dictionary, you stick to it throughout the context. For example, you may decide to let 'A' stand for the proposition expressed by 'Jane Austen is an author' in which case when you are trying to symbolize, every time you meet 'Jane Austen is an author' you symbolize it by 'A' (and, if you are trying to translate back from symbols, every time you meet 'A' you translate it back to 'Jane Austen is an author').

Not all propositions are atomic propositions. Consider the proposition asserted by 'It is not the case that Emily Bronte is an athlete'. This is a true proposition, yet it is not an atomic one. It is made up of the atomic proposition 'Emily Bronte is an athlete' (which is false) and negation (expressed by 'It is not the case that...'), and the resulting compound proposition, which is the negation of a false proposition, is true.

M. Frické, *Logic and the Organization of Information*,
DOI: 10.1007/978-1-4614-3088-9,
© Springer Science+Business Media New York 2012

There are several types of compound proposition.

Negation is one. To symbolize negation, the symbol ' $\sim$ ' is used to express the 'It is not the case that ...' and then the remaining simpler proposition is symbolized in the standard way. For example, to symbolize 'It is not the case that Jane Austen is an author.' first the 'It is not the case that ... ' is symbolized to get' $\sim$ (JANE AUSTEN IS AN AUTHOR)' and then the 'Jane Austen is an author' is symbolized (which is A, under the conventions in use) to get $\sim$(A) as the final symbolization.

Notice that some brackets appeared around the A—brackets or parentheses are used to avoid ambiguity. (They are actually not needed in this particular case, for there is no ambiguity.)

Conjunction is another type of compound proposition. The proposition asserted by 'Jane Austen is an author and Blackwell is a publisher' is a compound proposition composed of the two atomic propositions 'Jane Austen is an author' and 'Blackwell is a publisher'. To symbolize conjunction, the symbol '&' is used to express the '...and ...' and then the remaining two simpler propositions are symbolized in the standard way. With the example, the result is (A&B).

The symbols ' $\sim$ ' and '&' are examples of logical connectives. Each compound proposition has a main connective which links up its immediate components. For example, the main connective of (A& $\sim$(B)) is '&', and it connects up A and $\sim$(B); and in turn the compound formula $\sim$(B) has ' $\sim$ ' as its main connective. Atomic propositions do not have main connectives (they are atomic and have no parts that need connecting up).

If you can tell whether an English sentence expresses a compound proposition and can recognize what that proposition's main connective is, then you have the skills to symbolize any proposition. (All you do is use your skills on the sentence as a whole, perhaps dividing it up into a main connective, and some parts; then use your skills on the parts; and keep doing this until there are no parts left).

Equally, if you can recognize the main connective in a logical formula—and can translate it into English—you should be able to translate any symbolic formula back to English by repeated use of a similar 'divide-and-conquer' tactic.

There are a few more types of compound proposition.

Disjunction is one. The proposition asserted by 'Jane Austen is an author or Blackwell is a publisher.' is a compound proposition composed of the two atomic propositions 'Jane Austen is an author' and 'Blackwell is a publisher'. To symbolize disjunction, the symbol '∨' is used to express the 'or' and then the remaining two simpler propositions are symbolized in the standard way. With the example, the result is (A ∨ B).

Conditional is another. The proposition asserted by 'If Jane Austen is an author, then Blackwell is a publisher.' is a compound proposition composed of the two atomic propositions 'Jane Austen is an author' and 'Blackwell is a publisher'. To symbolize a conditional, the symbol '→' is used to express the 'If ...then ...'. It is placed between the two propositions, and then the remaining two simpler propositions are symbolized in the standard way. With the example, the result is (A→B).

And biconditional is the final connective. The proposition asserted by 'Jane Austen is an author if, and only if, Blackwell is a publisher.' is a compound proposition composed of the two atomic propositions 'Jane Austen is an author' and 'Blackwell is a publisher'. To symbolize a biconditional, the symbol ' $\equiv$ ' is used to express the ' ...if and only if ...', and then the remaining two simpler propositions are symbolized in the standard way. With the example, the result is $(A \equiv B)$.

The symbols '$\vee$', '$\rightarrow$' and '$\equiv$' are examples of logical connectives.

In English there is usually more than one way to say the same thing. For example, the sentences 'Jane Austen is an author or Charlotte Bronte is an author.' and 'Either Jane Austen or Charlotte Bronte are authors.' assert the same compound proposition—the new word 'either' at the beginning of the second sentence does not alter the underlying logical structure, nor does the way the nouns are laid out. Both these sentences should be symbolized by a formula like $(A \vee C)$.

One symbolic formula can represent the logical structure of a proposition asserted by several different English sentences (this is one reason why we symbolize).

Of course, when we translate a symbolization back into English we might not get exactly the same English sentence that we started with—but we will get an English sentence which accurately depicts the underlying logical structure of the starting sentence. For example, 'Either Jane Austen or Charlotte Bronte are authors.' should be symbolized $(A \vee C)$, and if $(A \vee C)$ is translated back into English we might get 'Jane Austen is an author or Charlotte Bronte is an author.' which is not what we started with (the 'either' is missing etc.) but the retranslation conveys the entire logical force of the original.

Some further remarks on the more difficult cases. From the point of view of logic:-

'Neither A nor B' amounts to 'It is not the case that either A or B'.
'A if B' amounts to 'If B then A'. For example, 'The bomb explodes if the red button is pushed' amounts to 'If the red button is pushed the bomb explodes'.
'A only if B' amounts to 'If A then B'. For example, 'Plants flourish only if there is sunlight' amounts to 'If plants flourish there is sunlight'.
'A unless B' amounts to 'A or B'. For example, 'Plants flourish unless there is no sunlight' amounts to 'Plants flourish or there is no sunlight'.

A suggestion regarding how to solve translation problems: If you do not recognize the English as an example of a standard form, try to paraphrase it into a standard form. For example, 'Taxes are unpopular, but revenue is needed' is not in a form that has been mentioned here, but paraphrasing it to 'Taxes are unpopular and revenue is needed' takes it to a form that we know and which has the same logical structure as the original.

In review:-

There is the idea of setting up a code or convention or dictionary between atomic propositions and capital letters (or strings starting with upper case letters).

There are compound propositions, each of which has a main connective which connects its components.

There are five propositional logical connectives:

  '∼' which translates back to 'it is not the case that...'
  '&' which translates back to '... and ...'
  '∨' which translates back to '... or ...'
  '→' which translates back to 'if... then ...'
  '≡' which translates back to '... if and only if ...'

## A.2 Predicate Logic

While propositional logic is very useful and certainly can take us a long way, it is not rich enough and discriminating enough in the general case.

The problem is that it sees separate atomic propositions as being independent unanalyzable wholes. Let us, for example, see how propositional logic would analyze the follow two propositions

Jane Austen is an author.
Jane Austen is an English author.

The first is a true or false atomic proposition (there are no 'nots', 'ands' etc. in it), and it would need to be symbolized by, say, 'A'. The second also is a true or false atomic proposition (there are no 'nots', 'ands' etc. in it), *but it is not the same proposition as the first one*, so it would need to be symbolized by a different letter, say, 'E'. Now the problems start to arise. In propositional logic, it is assumed that the propositions can all be true or false independently of each other, so we should be able to have (A true with E true), (A true with E false), (A false with E true), and (A false with E false). But, for example, were it true that Jane Austen is an English author it would also be true that Jane Austen is an author; so you cannot have the first sentence true with the second false. The reason is: these two propositions are not independent of each other. A finer level of analysis is needed, and that is what predicate logic brings.

In predicate logic, atomic propositions are analyzed at a finer level. A proposition like 'Jane Austen is an author' is not just something which is true or is false; rather it is something with a structure: there is an entity (or individual or 'thing'), Jane Austen, which has the property of being an author.

To symbolize at predicate logic level, entities like Jane Austen are symbolized by constant terms which, in the system used here, start with a lower case letter from all but the end of the alphabet, i.e. from 'a' to 'v'. Entities can be symbolized with just one letter, so 'a' would be fine for 'Jane Austen'. But clarity is all important; and, to help with that, the syntax in use here permits terms to consist of any mix of upper and lower case letters, provided the first one is lower case 'a–v'. So 'janeAusten' is also a perfectly good term. Properties are symbolized by starting with an upper case letter, then following that with zero or more upper and lower case letters. (So A 'would be fine for '..is an author', and so too would 'Is AnAuthor'.) Predicates, and the individuals to which they apply, are put together by writing the property first followed, in parentheses, by the individual it applies to. The result, using the conventions mentioned here, is

Jane Austen is an author

could be symbolized by

A(a)

Or by

Author(janeAusten)

In predicate logic, many different styles of expression in English get cast into the same 'property-is-had-by-entity' form. For example,

Jane Austen is English. (i.e. adjective)
Jane Austen writes. (i.e. verb)
Jane Austen is an author. (i.e. noun)

might be symbolized

E(a),
W(a), and
A(a), respectively.

[There can be some subtleties with English verbs, adjectives, etc., but there is no need for us to consider them right now.]

Earlier, with Aristotle, we talked of Socrates's being a man as identifying a kind for Socrates, and of Socrates's having a beard as ascribing an accidental property to Socrates. With predicate logic, at this level of analysis, these two styles are not distinguished. So

Man (socrates)
Bearded (socrates)

would symbolize the two propositions.

The propositional logical connectives, introduced earlier are used to extend the basic predicate symbolization; for example,

Jane Austen is English and Jane Austen writes
might be symbolized

(E(a) & W(a))

Another innovation in predicate logic is its use of variables and quantifiers. In Predicate Logic there are two new logical connectives, the *Universal Quantifier* $\forall$x and the *Existential Quantifier* $\exists$x. These are used for symbolizing certain

English constructions. The Universal Quantifier ∀x is read in English 'For all x,' or 'Whatever x you choose,'. The x here is a variable; that is, it is a term and so is like a name but unlike a constant term, a for example, it does not name a specific object in particular. In the system here, the lower case letters a–v are *constant terms*. The lower case letters at the end of the alphabet, 'w', 'x', 'y', 'z', are *variables*. The variable that is associated with a particular quantifier in a formula is often called—surprise—'the variable of quantification'.

When a Universal Quantifier, with its variable of quantification appear, they are followed by a formula known as the *scope*. Let us put the scope in brackets for the time being. The following is an example of a Universally Quantified formula

∀x(T(x))

and it is read as 'Whatever x you chose, x is T. So, for example, if you wished to symbolize

Everything is text.

you would first re-cast this as

Whatever x you chose, x is text.

and then, using the convention Text = is text, symbolize this to

∀x(Text(x))

The Existential Quantifier ∃x is read in English 'There is an x such that...'. The x here is a variable and when an Existential Quantifier appears it is followed by a formula known as its *scope*. The following is an example of an Existentially Quantified formula

∃y(Text(y))

and it is read in 'There is a y such that y is Text'. So, for example, if you wished to symbolize

Something is text.

you would first re-cast this as

There is a y such that y is text.

and then, using the convention T = is text, symbolize this to

∃y(Text(y))

The symbols a, b ,c...l are the constant terms (used for depicting Jane Austens and Bill Browns and suchlike) and the lower case letters m...z are the variable terms. Usually it will not matter which variable you use—'There is a y such that y is text' and 'There is an x such that x text' mean one and the same thing.

It is good practice or style to use parentheses to show the scope, as examples ∀x(T(x)), ∀x(T(x)∨G(x)), and ∀x(T(x)→G(x)). But if the parentheses are omitted we need to remember that the quantifiers have 'high precedence' and so bind tightly to whatever is immediately following them (only negation has higher precedence). So, as examples,

$\forall x T(x)$ means $\forall x (T(x))$

$\forall x \sim T(x)$ means $\forall x (\sim T(x))$

$\forall x T(x) \lor G(x)$ means $\forall x (T(x)) \lor G(x)$ (i.e. the scope of the quantifier does not run the full remaining length of this formula)

$\forall x T(x) \rightarrow G(x)$ means $\forall x (T(x)) \rightarrow G(x)$ (i.e. the scope of the quantifier does not run the full remaining length of this formula)

and similarly for the existential quantifier e.g.

$\exists x (T(x) \& G(x))$ of course means $\exists x (T(x) \& G(x))$

but $\exists x T(x) \& G(x)$ means $\exists x (T(x)) \& G(x)$ (the scope is not the rest of the formula, and the main connective of the whole formula is the &)

Any occurrences of a variable of quantification within the scope of that quantification are *bound* occurrences. And any occurrences of a variable which are not bound are *free* occurrences. For example, in

$\exists x (T(x) \& G(y))$

the occurrence of x in the scope is bound, the occurrence of y, also in the scope of the x quantifier, is free; and in

$T(z) \& \forall z \sim T(z)$

the first occurrence of z is free, but the occurrence of z within the scope of the universal quantifier is bound.

Thus far only 'monadic' (or one place) predicates have been used as illustrations. But there are plenty enough 'diadic' or two place predicates (usually called relations). For example, in

Jane Austen wrote Pride and Prejudice

The 'predicate' is '...wrote...'. There are two, so-to-speak, gaps here: its form is '?x wrote ?y' and so, using Wrote(?x,?y) to indicate the symbolization of this predicate, the whole statement could be

Wrote(a,p)

So, with dyadic predicates, the terms are written, in order, within the brackets, and they are separated by commas. There can also be predicates of 'arity' higher than 2, for example 'x gave y to z' and these are accommodated by a simple generalization, e.g. Gave (bill, toy, jimmy).

To review:-

Predicate logic extends propositional logic.

A start can be made in predicate logic by taking apart 'atomic' propositions and by re-phrasing what they have to say in an 'entity-has-property' way.

The constant terms a, b, c...v are used to denote entities, the predicates A, B, C...Z are used to denote properties that these entities have, and these are put together by writing the predicate first followed by the term, for example G(b).

This technique of symbolization often may be used with English nouns, with English verbs, or with English adjectives (for example, with 'George is a runner', with 'George runs', and with 'George is running').

The propositional logical connectives can be used to extend the basic symbolization; for example, 'George runs and George is happy' might be symbolized R(g)&H(g).

There are two new logical connectives, the *Universal Quantifier* ∀x (read in English 'Whatever x you choose...') and the *Existential Quantifier* ∃x (read in English 'There is an x such that...'). These are used for symbolizing certain English constructions. There are the variables 'w', 'x', 'y', 'z', and constants a–v. There is the scope of the quantifier, and the notions of free and bound occurrences of variables.

There are polyadic predicates (relations) in addition to monadic ones.

[There is a minor point to be made, which most everybody can ignore. The tip-toeing around with ?xs and ?ys comes from the following problem. Sometimes we want to talk about just the predicates or the predicate part of a formula. So, for example, we might want to identify the predicate part of

Wrote(austen,pride)

What notation might we use to do this? Logicians would often just write

Wrote(x,y)

to do it. Most of the time this is fine as a rough and ready notation. But the trouble with it is: x and y are terms in our system, actually they are variables. So

Wrote(x,y)

is a proper formula and if we ask what is the predicate in that formula the answer

Wrote(x,y)

is wrong—the whole thing is not a part of itself. To avoid this, on those rare occasions when we need to be careful, we can use the notation Wrote(?x,?y) to identify the predicate, and say that the predicate gets applied to a couple of terms to produce a formula in the system. If Wrote(?x,?y) is applied to austen and pride, the formula

Wrote(austen,pride)

results. If Wrote(?x,?y) is applied to x and y, the formula

Wrote(x,y)
is the result.]

## A.3 Symbolization Templates

It can take some time to master the art of symbolization. But here are some templates that can be used as shortcuts to advance our skills to a reasonable level.

As explained in Sect. 2.4, in English, and most other natural language, there are less elaborate and more elaborate names for things—these are the nouns or noun phrases; there is 'construction material'—verbs, adjectives, etc—and there are the resulting true or false statements that can be built from the components.

The simplest nouns are proper nouns, or proper names, such as 'Jane Austen', and a plain term like 'austen' would be used to symbolize a proper noun. Then basic constructions, using predicates or relations, are used to symbolize plain ascriptions of a sort noun, or plain uses of verbs and adjectives. So

Jane Austen is a writer.
Jane Austen is English.
Jane Austen edits.

could be

Writer(austen)
English(austen)
Edits(austen)

Then there are common nouns such as 'writer' which are usually employed in combination with *determiners* such as 'a', 'an', 'some', 'all' 'every', 'the', etc. Thus

A writer...
An author...
Some writers...
All writers...
No writers...

These will usually involve quantifiers. 'A', 'An', or 'Some' would be read as 'There is at least one ...' so

'A writer is in the editorial team' could be $\exists x(Writer(x)\&Editorial(x))$ and the $\exists x(Writer(x))...$ fragment of that says 'There is at least one x, such that x is a writer ...'

More examples will be given shortly in a table.

Then *modifiers* can be used to convert basic noun phrases into more elaborate forms. Modifiers include adjectives, relative clauses, prepositional phrases, and so on. Modifiers are mostly symbolized by conjoining a predicate, or relation, in the appropriate location. So

'A busy writer...' and 'A writer who is busy...', which grammatically are an adjective-noun combination and a relative clause, could be

∃x(Writer(x)&Busy(x))…

A prepositional phrase 'A writer in a library…' is a slightly more complicated case. Typically, to say something like 'The King is in London', the symbolization would use a relation 'In(?x,?y)' and the result would be 'In(king,london)' where 'london' is the symbolic term for the proper noun 'London'. So

'A writer in the British Museum library…'

would have symbolization fragment

∃x(Writer(x)&In(x,bMusLib))…

Of course, it could be that the noun phrase for the library is not a proper noun, but instead is itself formed from a common noun and a determiner. So two quantifiers will be involved. For example.

'A writer in a library…'

would have symbolization fragment

∃x(Writer(x)&∃y(Library(y)&In(x,y))…

i.e. 'There is an x, which is a writer, and there is a y, which is a library, and x is in y…'

As noted in Sect. 4.2.2, modifiers can have special subtleties of their own.

Let us set out typical symbolizations in a table. The 1997 Functional Requirements for Bibliographic Records (FRBR), which was explained earlier, has a number of 'entities', 'attributes', and 'relations' these include

Entities: Work, Expression, Manifestation, Item
Attributes: title (of the work)
Relations: x is created by y

We will use these—and similar one and two-place predicates—to provide illustrations of logical symbolizations. The resulting formulas make true or false statements about the FRBR world i.e. about the FRBR *ontology*.

## Using the Universal Quantifier (but not relations) (Table A.1)

**Table A.1** Universal quantifier without relations

| | |
|---|---|
| 'Everything is text' we understand as meaning 'Whatever thing you may choose, it is text' and this becomes | $\forall x T(x)$ |
| Similarly 'Nothing is text' is read as 'Whatever thing you may choose, it is not going text' and this becomes | $\forall x \sim T(x)$ |
| 'Manifestation are expressions' is read 'Whatever x you may choose, if it is a manifestation, then it is an expression' which is | $\forall x(M(x) \rightarrow E(x))$ |
| Everything is either textual or pictorial. | $\forall x(T(x) \vee P(x))$ |
| Nothing is both textual and pictorial. | $\forall x \sim (T(x) \& P(x))$ |
| All and only expressions are works. | $\forall x(E(x) \equiv W(x))$ |
| All texts are works. | |
| Texts are all works | |
| A text is a work. | |
| To be a text is to be a work. | |
| Every (any, each) text is a work. | $\forall x(T(x) \rightarrow W(x))$ |
| If anything's (thing's) a text, it's a work | |
| Only works are texts. | |
| None but works are texts. | |
| No texts are works. | $\forall x(T(x) \rightarrow \sim W(x))$ |
| No texts are unavailable. | $\forall x(T(x) \rightarrow \sim U(x))$ (*if you use 'unavailable' as a predicate in its own right; if you use 'available' as the predicate you would get*) |
| | $\forall x(T(x) \rightarrow A(x))$ |
| Old texts are all available. | $\forall x((T(x) \& O(x)) \rightarrow A(x))$ |
| Texts and DVDs are all available. | $\forall x((T(x) \vee D(x)) \rightarrow A(x))$ (*note the 'or' *) |
| Texts are available if they are not on reserve. | $\forall x(T(x) \rightarrow (\sim R(x) \rightarrow A(x)))$ |

## Universal Quantifier, with relations (Table A.2)

**Table A.2** Universal quantifier with relations

| | |
|---|---|
| Jane Austen created everything. | $\forall x C(a,x)$ |
| Everything is text created by Jane Austen. | $\forall x(T(x) \& C(a,x))$ |
| The main library acquires everything created by Jane Austen. | $\forall x(C(a,x) \rightarrow A(m,x))$ |
| Nothing that the main library acquired was under copyright. | $\forall x(A(m,x) \rightarrow \sim C(x))$ |

### Existential Quantifier, no relations (Table A.3)

**Table A.3** Existential quantifier without relations

| | |
|---|---|
| 'Something is on the shelf' is understood as 'There is at least one thing, x, such that x is on the shelf'. | $\exists xO(x)$ |
| 'Some books are on the shelf' is understood as 'There is at least one thing, x, such that x is a book and x is on the shelf'. | $\exists x(B(x)\&O(x))$ |
| Some books are not on the shelf. | $\exists x(B(x)\&\sim O(x))$ |
| Something is a text. | $\exists xT(x)$ |
| There are texts. | |
| There is a text. | |
| Texts exist. | |
| Some books are on the shelf, if they are in English. | $\exists x(B(x)\&(E(x)\rightarrow O(x)))$ |
| Some long texts are neither readable nor copyrighted. | $\exists x((T(x)\&L(x))\&\sim(R(x)\vee C(x)))$ |

### Existential Quantifier, with relations (Table A.4)

**Table A.4** Existential quantifier with relations

| | |
|---|---|
| Jane Austen did not create something. | $\exists x\sim C(a,x)$ |
| Somebody created something. | $\exists x\exists y(P(x)\&C(x,y))$ or $\exists x(P(x)\&\exists y(C(x,y)))$ |

### Both Quantifiers, with relations (Table A.5)

**Table A.5** Both quantifiers with relations

| | |
|---|---|
| 'Everything has a creator' becomes 'Whatever thing you may choose, something (or other) is the creator of it'. | $\forall x\exists yC(y,x)$ |
| 'Something is the creator of everything' becomes 'There is a something (the same thing) such that whatever thing you may choose, that something is the creator of it'. | $\exists y\forall xC(y,x)$ |
| Everything is the creator of everything. | $\forall y\forall xC(y,x)$ |

[The core of this is from Leblanc and Wisdom (1972, p. 117 and f.)]

## A.4 Functions, Functional Terms, and Identity

The word 'term' in logic means 'name' and thus far we have met two kinds of terms: constants (or proper names), and variables.

These are not the only names there are. In English consider 'the author of *Pride and Prejudice*'; now, this is not a statement—it does not say something true or false—rather it is a construction which names an individual. It takes *Pride and Prejudice* and what we might call the 'author of' function and uses the two of those to name an individual. Similarly in mathematics, the expression $7 + 2$ does not assert something true or false, rather it is a construction which names a number (which also happens to have the name 9).

The logic we are using, First Order Logic, can accommodate these more elaborate terms, and it does so by means of 'functional terms'. For example, author(prideAndPrejudice), g(b), f(x), g(a,c), h(g(c),b) ... are all functional terms.

To symbolize, say, 'The author of *Pride and Prejudice* is generous' we choose, perhaps, authorOf(?x) to represent the 'author of ?x' function, prideAndPrejudice to represent *Pride and Prejudice*, and Generous(?x) to represent the predicate '?x is generous' and the requisite symbolization is:

Generous(authorOf(prideAndPrejudice))

Somewhat analogously to free and bound occurrences of variables in formulas, if a function term contains a variable it is an *open term*, if it does not contain a variable it is a *closed term*.

Identities are true or false statements of identity between terms, so

a=b
b=7

are identities.

Functional terms often appear in identities. For example, 'Allison's brother's wife's sister is her very best friend' might be symbolized

s(w(b(a)))=f(a)

where a=Allison, b(x)= is the brother of x, s(x)= is the sister of x, w(x)= is the wife of x, f(x)= is the very best friend of x.

Identities can be components of other more complex formulas. For example

$\sim$ (b=f(a))
$\sim \exists$x(b=f(x))

might symbolize 'Bert is not Allison's best friend' and 'Bert is no one's best friend' respectively.

Functional terms have an 'arity', which is the number of arguments they apply to. With predicates you can have one place predicates like F(x), and two place predicates, or relations, like T(x,y) (and three place...). So too with functional terms. The 'author of' function is of arity one—it expects one term as an argument. In mathematics there are plenty of functions of higher arity. For example, the plus function usually expects two arguments, so 'plus x y' might be represented p(x,y).

There is another small issue that comes up here. The way we write functional terms is to write the function first, followed by the arguments. In mathematics itself, a fair few functions are 'infix', that is to say they are written between their arguments instead of before them—mathematicians generally write $(1 + 2)$ not $+(1,2)$. We will meet this only rarely, but it is good to be aware of it as a possibility.

## A.5 Lambda Calculus

We have some remarkable skills in the way we conceptualize the world and can talk about it. And these skills seem universal in that they are common across all cultures and natural languages. First of all we can produce arbitrarily many statements or sentences. No matter what the culture or language, a native speaker has some vocabulary and some internalized grammar rules. Then he or she can say indefinitely many different things. No natural language has, say, just 30 sentences in it, and is such that once a native speaker has learned those 30 sentences he can say them, but having said them he is done and there is nothing else for him to say; rather, always, he can say, indefinitely many different sentences—he can make as many statements as he wishes limited only by his energy and lifespan. This ability seems to come from the fact that we can take parts or well-formed wholes of our sentence output and then plug those back in as input to our grammar to generate more output. Another language related ability that is universal is our skill with functions and function application (indeed, as we will see, it can be argued that the second skill underlies the first).

Consider the statement that Allison's brother's wife's sister is her very best friend. There is barely a person on Earth who does not understand what this means. True the assertion is expressed in English and many may not be familiar with this language. But English here is just a notation or syntax. The same assertion can be made in probably all natural languages, and what everyone understands is that which is asserted not the notation of assertion. Most everyone also knows full well what it is for the assertion to be true and for the assertion to be known to be true.

The example is interesting because it illustrates instantiation of the use and understanding of high-level concepts, which seem to be universal. These include partial functions, function application or composition, constructions, types, and the distinction between a construction and that which the construction constructs. Being an only brother, wife, only sister, etc. are all partial functions. Functions are rules, or procedures, which carry one thing to another, and partial functions are a sub-class of functions, namely functions which are not defined everywhere. Being an only brother, wife, only sister, etc. are partial functions (some people have only brothers, other people have no brothers or more than one brother, so the function is not defined everywhere). These partial functions also have 'types'—they are defined on humans (or, perhaps, animals) and definitely not on cars or tables or trees. Trying to talk about the only brother of a car makes no sense. So 'only brother' is a partial function available for application to the type humans. This function can be applied to humans; in particular it can be applied to Allison;

suppose Allison does indeed have an only brother, Fred, in which case the application of the only brother (partial) function to Allison yields the value Fred. We can see that the value of the function, Fred, is also a human and so, to be more explicit on the type of the only brother function, it has type (Human⟹Human); similarly the 'only dog' function, if we were interested in that, would have type (Human⟹Dog). Once we get Fred we can apply the (only) wife function to get someone else, perhaps Greer. So we take the output of one function, the brother of function, and use that output as input to another function, the wife of function. This use of the output of one function as input to another is known as (function) 'composition': the component functions are 'composed'. There is a useful term of art here to cover these whole phenomena—'construction'. This is a notion highlighted by Tichy (1986). It means 'way of arriving at, usually by means of functions and function abstractions, compositions and applications', so the expression 'Allison brother's wife's sister' refers to a construction. Further, suppose that all the various partial functions are properly defined, with suitable uniqueness for the arguments, so that the construction via the (only) brother function etc. picks someone, say Flora, and, supposing the assertion to be true, the other construction, via the very best friend partial function, also constructs Flora; we are all very well aware that the two constructions and that which they construct, Flora, are three different things. [Many of us would also realize, with reflection, that there is universal widespread systematic ambiguity between constructions and that which they construct. But that is another story, not entered into here.] So,

Allison brother's wife's sister is a construction, and Flora is what it constructs.
[Allison's] very best friend is a construction, and Flora is what it constructs.

And what Allison's brother's wife's sister is her very best friend is telling us is that the two different constructions construct the same thing (and notice, as an aside, that it is not telling us that Flora is Flora).

That there are these universal abilities and understandings with respect to functions is certainly in need of explanation. None is offered here. Even a Mongolian yak herder knows exactly what it is for Allison's brother's wife's sister to be her very best friend. In a way, it is amazing. We need in this text to take advantage of these skills we all have, and to have some means for describing them. Earlier we used them to talk of classification, and of putting concepts together to make composite concepts for indexing and search. There is a view nowadays, pretty well the standard view, that our core language skills and core concept building skills are all a matter of these functions and function applications. This view really comes, once again, from the nineteenth century German philosopher Frege. whose main work was *Begriffsschrift* ('concept writing')

If the task of philosophy is to break the domination of words over the human mind [...], then my concept notation, being developed for these purposes, can be a useful instrument for philosophers [...] I believe the cause of logic has been advanced already by the invention of this concept notation." (Preface to the *Begriffsschrift*) and Frege's main theoretical tools were functions and function applications (Heim and Kratzer 1998; Tichy 1988).

The logic that we have thus far, First Order Predicate Logic with Functional Terms and Identity, does have functions in it. But it is not really strong on its handling of functions, in particular, it is weak on creating new functions and on being clear on the distinction between a function application and the value of that application. Here is how it would make that statement about Allison

s(w(b(a)))=f(a)

in this, the function letters, for example, 's(x)' pick out some 'external' function, here 'is the sister of'. But, we might already have in our symbolization the predicate 'S(x,y)' with the meaning 'x is the sister of y', we should be able to construct a function from this simply—and easily—and that we cannot do. We would like to be able to create functions from functions and predicates, and we would like to be able to 'compose' functions (for example, in elementary geometry multiplying by the number $\pi$ (pi) is a function, squaring a number is a function, and the area of a circle is $\pi r^2$, which is one function composed with another). These also we cannot do easily in plain Predicate Logic. Also the notation 'f(a)', on the right of the identity, denotes, or has the value of, say Flora. But what, in our logic, represents the function 'best friend of'? f(a) does not really do it (because that is Flora)), f(x) does not do it either (that, really, is an open term i.e. a term with a free variable in it, in this case x).

What would help here is Lambda Calculus.


## A.5.1 Plain Lambda Calculus


Lambda Calculus was devised by Alonzo Church in 1941. It is very simple (based on elementary textual substitution), and it is very powerful. It can both express most everything that one would wish to about functions and their applications: it can also serve as a means of, or as a model of, computing the values of those functions, where that is appropriate. Hence it can serve as a programming language. The modern functional programming languages, and their constructs, Haskell, ML, and, to a lesser extent, LISP are, as it is commonly said, just Lambda Calculus dressed up with syntactic sugar. Lambda Calculus is also a foundational theory in linguistics, philosophy, and computer science, three disciplines vital for librarianship.

We need to meet lambda calculus. One relatively gentle way of introducing it is by means of the standard Find/Replace operation of word processors. When a word processing program is given the instruction 'Find 'colour' and Replace with 'color'' it will run through the selected text finding all occurrences of the word 'colour' and replacing those with the word 'color' (thus Americanizing the spelling of one word in the text). So-called 'Lambda application evaluation' is an analog of this. Let us develop some terminology and syntax to describe the Find and Replace.

Let us call the 'selected text' the *scope* and enclose it in rounded parentheses. So if the selected text were 'colour + shape + colour' the scope would be

(colour + shape + colour)
> the contents of the brackets is the, or a, scope

We need to identify what it is that is going to be replaced (i.e. the Find part). We do that by regarding it as a variable, putting it in front of the bracketed scope, and marking it with the Greek letter lambda '$\lambda$'. The result of this is called an *abstraction* or a *lambda abstraction*. Thus

$\lambda$ colour(colour + shape + colour)
> this is an abstraction or lambda abstraction. The colour token
> immediately after the lambda is a variable. And the other two colour
> tokens within the scope are occurrences of that variable

So, a lambda abstraction has the form $\lambda$ <variable> (<scope>). Finally, we need to identify what is going to do the replacing (in this case, the American spelling 'color'). We do that by placing that in square brackets after the lambda abstraction, and the whole expression is known as an *application*. The content of the square brackets is the *argument*. Thus

$\lambda$ colour(colour + shape + colour)[color]
> this is an application and color is the argument.

And this application evaluates (or reduces) to

color + shape + color

(that is what the result of the Find and Replace operation is). Here is a further example,

$\lambda$ shape(colour + shape + colour)[color]

evaluates to

colour + color + colour

because this time it is 'shape' that we are replacing (notice the different variable with the lambda). These lambda expressions can be nested one within another (effectively that is doing one replacement (say 'colors' for 'colours') and then doing another replacement on the result (say 'organize' for 'organise'). So

$\lambda$ organize ($\lambda$ colours(organise colours)[colors]) [organize]

can be reduced to

$\lambda$ colours(organize colours)[colors]

and then to

organize colors

Find and Replace operations on text are typically done on paragraphs, pages, or even entire books. Lambda scopes usually are nothing like the length of this. Usually they will be a few symbols, maybe half a dozen symbols, only. But nevertheless lambda application evaluation and Find and Replace are essentially the same.

We need to go beyond the hand waving introduction to lambda calculus and be a little more formal on what is permitted and what is not (especially within the scope).

For lambda calculus, there are three kinds of lambda expressions:

variables,
applications, and
functions [these are sometimes called
        'abstractions' or 'lambda abstractions'.]

For us, a lambda variable is going to be exactly the same as our variables of Predicate logic i.e. any string of letters which starts with a lower case letter from the end of the alphabet [w,x,y,z]. So, three lambda expressions, which are variables, are

x,
variable, and
zVar.

An application consists of an opening lambda expression, a left square bracket, another lambda expression, and then a closing right square bracket. So their form is <expression> [< expression>], these are understood as the application of a function to an argument, so it might help to think of these as <function-expression> [<argument-expression>] Three lambda expressions which are applications are

x[y],
xFunction[yArgument], and
z[w]

Conceptually, applications are the application of a function to an argument, just as, in trigonometry, 'cos[30]' is the application of the cosine function to the value 30, in the Lambda Calculus, 'x[y]' is the application of the function 'a' to the argument 'b'.

A function (also known as an abstraction or a lambda abstraction or an anonymous function) consists of the Greek letter lambda followed by a variable followed by an opening left bracket, followed by another lambda expression, and finished by a closing right bracket. That is, they have the form $\lambda$<variable>(<expression>). Often it is convenient to identify or label the right hand expression, the contents of the bracket, as being the 'scope' of the abstraction. The variable itself, that goes with the lambda, is the 'binding' variable. [We are familiar with these notions from plain predicate logic, where there is talk of the 'scope' of quantifiers and the 'variable of quantification'.] Three lambda expressions which are abstractions, or *anonymous* functions, are

$\lambda$x(y),
$\lambda$x(y[z]), and
$\lambda$w($\lambda$x(x))

Here are some examples of more complex expressions and an analysis of what they are:

x
xHello[xCruel][xWorld]
$\lambda$x(x[y])
$\lambda$x(ay)
$\lambda$x($\lambda$y(x[y]))[z]

'x' is a variable. 'xHello[xCruel][xWorld]' is an application which contains within itself another application, it is an application of the variable 'xHello' to the variable 'xCruel' and then an application of that to the variable 'xWorld'. '$\lambda$a(a[b])' is an abstraction whose scope is the application of the variable 'a' to the variable 'b'. '$\lambda$a(ab)' is an abstraction, but it is an oddity: 'a' is a variable, and 'ab' (notice no space) is an entirely different variable which just happens to start with lower case 'a'; so the variable of the abstraction does not occur at all in the scope of the abstraction (that is unusual and also not much use). '$\lambda$x($\lambda$y(x[y]))[z]' is an application whose function has a scope which itself is a function and the scope of that second function is an application.

The main manipulation that can be done with lambda expressions is done on those expressions which are applications, and the manipulation is that of evaluating the application. The mechanism here is very simple textual substitution. Here is an example: the application

$\lambda$variable(variable)[theArgument]

is evaluated, like any other application of an abstraction function, by taking the scope of the abstraction and substituting the argument in for all (free) occurrences of the variable in the scope. In this case the result is

theArgument

[In the general case, there are some technical details that can arise at this point concerning 'naming conflicts'. In this setting, we can circumvent these. A wise precaution, with complicated formulas, is to use novel or new variables as binding variables for lambda abstractions that occur in it. When need be, we will be doing that.]

As mentioned earlier, a familiar analog of lambda application evaluation is the standard Find/Replace operation of word processors. Lambda application evaluation is exactly like this. It runs through the scope of the lambda abstraction and replaces all the free occurrences of the binding variable with the argument and returns the changed contents of the scope as the result.

Here is a step by step evaluation (or reduction) of nested lambda applications. The example formula is

λx(λy(y)[x])[z]

We start by spotting a suitable application, with a lambda, its scope, and an argument. The outer one will do

so now, in the expression
    λx            (λy(y)[x])       [z]
the **λx** is the variable
the **(λy(y)[x])** is the scope. And
the **[z]** is the argument

Then, the argument is substituted for occurrences of the binding variable in the scope to yield

λy(y)[z]

This itself is an application and it reduces in a similar way to

z

With this example, the reduction was done on the outer reduction first. In fact, the order does not matter. [It is a theorem of formal lambda calculus that if the reductions can be carried through, the result if the same no matter what the reduction order.]

## A.5.2 Convenient Generalizations Within Lambda Calculus

There are some steps that can be taken to allow Lambda Calculus to be useful for us. First, constants can be introduced as expressions. These could include the numbers 0, 1, 2 etc, truth values (True or False or, as they are sometimes called, 'top' or 'bottom'), and proper names of individuals of interest. As mentioned, to distinguish variables from constants, we will insist that variables start with lower case letters from the end of the alphabet (i.e. w, x, y, z), just as they do in our predicate logic.

That leads to expressions like

λx(x)[henry][1]

and that is the application of a function to the constant henry and then the application of what results to the number 1 i.e. its value is

henry[1]

Quite what this expression is, or what the significance of it is, is an open question—but there may be contexts in which it is useful.

Another expansion is to allow in already known or predefined functions from outside. For example, the 'successor' function is a well-known function, it adds 1 to a natural number (thus taking 3 to 4, 117 to 118 etc.). These predefined functions come in syntactically in the function position in an application, and they have the semantics, or evaluation properties, that they bring with them. We will name them in the language using constants, so 'successor' needs to start with a lower case letter not from the end of the alphabet (it does). Then, for example,

successor[1]

is now a well-defined lambda expression, and also we know how to evaluate it (by adding 1 to its argument. So successor[1] evaluates to

2

And, as a further example,

$\lambda x(x)$ [successor] [1]

also evaluates to 2, by a two step evaluation. It is also possible to bring in parts of ordinary predicate logic. But we will approach this in a different way.

## A.5.3  Combining Lambda Calculus and Predicate Logic

In predicate logic, there are two kinds of expressions. There are terms, which are names for things; and there are formulas, well formed formulas, which signify true or false statements or propositions or assertions. For example, a, b, x, y, f(a), g(a,h(b)) are all terms, and $\forall x(T(x) \rightarrow W(x))$, A&B, and $\exists y \forall x C(y,x)$ are all formulas. And there is some 'construction material', that allows terms to be assembled and built into formulas (that mortar is composed mainly of predicates and various logical connectives and operations). [There is a parallel here with the world view of Sect. 2.3.]

We are going to add lambda expressions as a third ingredient to the terms and formulas that are already there. But we want to do that in a way that makes sense, and that we can understand.

In predicate calculus, quantified formulas are very similar to lambda expressions. With, for example,

$\forall y(T(y) \rightarrow W(y))$, and
$\exists x(A(x) \& B(x))$

there is a Greek symbol, followed by a variable, followed by the scope of the quantification in which there are usually scattered occurrences of the variable. In predicate logic, there are inference rules, which allow the transformation of formulas to make valid or truth preserving inferences. For example, there is the rule of Universal Instantiation which permits the formal counterpart of the inferences such as that from 'All texts are works' to the conclusion 'If *Pride and Prejudice* is a text, then *Pride and Prejudice* is a work'. If this inference is done formally, the premise might be

$\forall y(T(y) \rightarrow W(y))$

and the conclusion is

$T(p) \rightarrow W(p)$

and what Universal Instantiation does is to take the scope of the universally quantified formula and to substitute in a term for free occurrences of the binding variable throughout the scope. So $\forall y(T(y) \rightarrow W(y))$ is Universally Instantiated to $T(p) \rightarrow W(p)$. In this case, the scope of the Universally Quantified formula is

$T(y) \rightarrow W(y)$

And a formula of this kind is often called an *open sentence*: it has free occurrences of a variable (in this case occurrences of y). $T(y) \rightarrow W(y)$ is a perfectly good well formed formula (what is marginally difficult about it is that it has the variable y in it, and until we know what y stands for, we do not really know whether the formula is true or false).

The lambda abstractions we have been using thus far are quite like quantified formulas in syntactic form

$\lambda x(x)$

and when they are applied to an argument they reduce or evaluate in something of a similar way.

$\lambda x(x)[b]$

evaluates to

b

Now we need to take care. First, a lambda evaluation is not—and is not intended to be—a truth preserving valid inference (like plain Universal Instantiation). Rather it is a textual substitution. An analog here is macros in computer programming. Many programming systems, for example, LISP, C, and PHP have 'macros' (or preprocessors). In fact, even some common and widely used word processors and spreadsheet programs, such as Microsoft Word and Microsoft Excel, have macros. And what macros typically do is to permit the transformation of input text prior to execution of that text as a command or program. A lambda evaluation within our predicate logic is like a macro (at its most basic, it is a form of Find and Replace). The second issue is that a quantified expression like $\forall y(T(y) \rightarrow W(y))$ is a well formed formula, which is true or false, it is not a term. But lambda abstractions (and lambda applications) themselves seem to be more like terms. The ones that we have met thus far do not seem to be true or false.

In fact, if set up correctly, a lambda abstraction can either be like a predicate logic function or like a predicate logic predicate. And then, when it is applied, the application will produce either a term or a formula. So lambdas, or lambda applications, can be 'builders' for terms or formulas. And lambda expressions can do all this in a very general and flexible way.

There already are function symbols in our predicate logic. We can have, for example, 'alice' to mean *Alice in Wonderland* and 'authorOf(...)' to mean the function 'author of ...' and 'Tall(...)' to mean the predicate '... is tall' and then construct 'Tall(authorOf(alice))' to mean 'the author of *Alice in Wonderland* is tall'. Let us dissect this formula

Tall(authorOf(alice))

The 'alice' we know about: it is a term (actually signifying *Alice in Wonderland*). And the 'authorOf(alice)' we also know about: it too is a term, it is the result of applying the 'author of' function to 'alice' (and this result actually signifies Lewis Carroll, but the logic does not tell us that). We do not have any notation for the 'author of' function or constructor itself, but if we were to invent some here and now it would need to be something like 'authorOf(...)' or 'authorOf(?x)'. The function itself has to have a 'gap' in it—that is where 'alice' is going to get placed in to make the composite term—and to show the gap we can either use ellipsis '...' or give it a name different in style from the ones we already use, say '?x'. [We will come back to the Tall part of the formula shortly.]

This quick and casual piece of symbolism 'authorOf(...)' or 'authorOf(?x)' can have a proper representation in the formal logic, and a lambda abstraction is exactly the device to do it; one such abstraction is

$\lambda$x(authorOf(x))

That is an actual name of the 'author Of' function. Then, when this function (or lambda abstraction) is applied to a term, 'alice', and reduced, 'authorOf(alice)' is the result

$\lambda$x(authorOf(x))[alice] reduces to
authorOf(alice)

So, in effect, the lambdas give us a clearer and better way of doing functions.

Originally within predicate logic we did not have names for the actual functions themselves (as opposed to the application of functions to arguments), but lambda calculus provides names or a means of describing the functions.

One point to notice about this is that, in this kind of use, the scope of the lambda abstraction i.e. the 'authorOf(x)' in '$\lambda$x(authorOf(x))' is a *term*. In fact, it is what is called an *open term* because it has a free occurrence of a variable in it (in this case, the free variable 'x').

It is often useful to have some kind of mental diagram or visualization of what is going on here. When a lambda abstraction is applied to a Term the result is a Term, so the lambda abstraction itself is a function from terms to terms. We can diagram this as follows. The abstraction is

Term $\Longrightarrow$ Term

and applications apply this to a term, to yield a term

(Term $\Longrightarrow$ Term) applied to Term yields Term

All of this reasoning can be mimicked or paralleled for predicates. Consider a symbolized formula for 'Arthur is tall', say

Tall(arthur)

There is here the formula 'Tall(arthur)' and the term 'arthur' and there is some predicate construction material that allows us to build one into the other. We do not have any notation for the predicate itself, but if we were to invent some here and now if would need to be something like 'Tall(...)' or 'Tall(?x)'. The predicate itself has to have a 'gap' in it; that is where 'arthur' is going to get place in to make the formula; and to show the gap we use '...' or '?x'.

What would happen if we allowed open sentences to be inserted as the scope of lambda abstractions? Let us start with a simple example. 'Tall(y)' is an open sentence which says 'y is tall'. If we put this into a lambda abstraction we would get

$\lambda$y(Tall(y))

(quite what this is we are not sure about at present, but any lambda abstraction is supposed to be a function). Suppose this abstraction is then made into part of an application by being applied to a term, say 'albert', thus

$\lambda$y(Tall(y))[albert]

and then we follow our absolutely standard lambda evaluation of textual substitution of the argument for the variable throughout the scope, we get

Tall(albert)

which is a perfectly good well formed formula (which says that Albert is tall).

The result here is a Formula, and the application that was used to produce it had as its argument a Term. This means that the lambda abstraction is a function which carries a term to a formula. We can diagram this

Term $\Longrightarrow$ Formula

And applications apply this to a term, to yield a Formula

(Term $\Longrightarrow$ Formula) applied to Term yields Formula

We are going to adopt and use this extension.

We need to be careful with this since lambdas have a dual use. Sometimes lambda applications yields terms (which go with predicates, identity statements, etc.) and sometimes lambda applications yield formulas (which go with truth functional connectives like ands ors equivalences etc.). It all depends on what is in the scope of the lambda.

$\lambda y(Tall(y))[albert]$ & $\lambda y(Tall(y))[bill]$

is a perfectly good formula which says that Albert and Bill are tall

$\lambda y(successor[y])[1]$ & $\lambda y(successor[y])[2]$

is nonsense, it tries to say '1 & 2' and that is gobbledygook.

$\lambda y(successor[y])[1] = \lambda y(successor[y])[2]$

is good, it says 2=3 which is a good statement, but a false one

$\lambda y(T(y))[albert] = \lambda y(T(y))[bill]$

is nonsense, it attempts to say that (Albert is tall = Bert is tall) and that does not mean anything.

The formula that this discussion started with, namely

Tall(authorOf(alice))

can be written in the alternative form

$\lambda y(Tall\ (y))[\lambda x(authorOf(x))[alice]]$

and there are occasions when it is useful to do that.

A plain lambda abstraction itself, over an open sentence, is just considered to be a property, for example,

$\lambda y(Tall\ (y))$

is the property of being tall.

# References

Heim I, Kratzer A (1998) Semantics in generative grammar. Blackwell, Oxford
Leblanc H, Wisdom WA (1972) Deductive logic. Allyn and Bacon, Boston
Tichy P (1986) Constructions. Philos Sci 53:514–534
Tichy P (1988) The foundations of Frege's logic. de Gruyter, Berlin

# Index

M. Frické, *Logic and the Organization of Information*,
DOI: 10.1007/978-1-4614-3088-9,
© Springer Science+Business Media New York 2012